IMPACT OF MECHANIZATION ON SMALL FISHERMEN

Centre for Management in Agriculture Monograph Series No. 114

IMPACT OF MECHANIZATION ON SMALL FISHERMEN
Analysis and Village Studies

U.K. SRIVASTAVA
M. DHARMA REDDY
B. SUBRAHMANYAM
V.K. GUPTA

INDIAN INSTITUTE OF MANAGEMENT,
AHMEDABAD

CONCEPT PUBLISHING COMPANY, NEW DELHI

First Published 1986

Published by

Naurang Rai
Concept Publishing Company
H-13, Bali Nagar
NEW DELHI-110015 (India)

Printed in India by

Lohia Composing Agency
at Sunil Printers
1067, Ajay Palace, Naraina
NEW DELHI-110028

Foreword

THE Centre for Management in Agriculture at this Institute is engaged in research on problems of management in the agricultural sector. Problem-oriented research programmes cover the following broad areas : (i) planning and implementation of programmes in the agriculture/rural sector, (ii) production, marketing and processing of agricultural commodities, (iii) input supply systems, (iv) agricultural finance, (v) management of social change in rural areas, (vi) agricultural development administration, and (vii) rural development.

The Centre has been involved in major programmes of research in fisheries since 1979, although some work began as far back as 1973 when a few faculty members of the Centre offered a training programme in India in the management of fisheries in collaboration with FAO. Subsequently, two such training programmes were offered in Sri Lanka (1975) and Malaysia (1976).

In 1979, the Centre undertook a study on Management of Marine Fishing Industry in Gujarat. With the completion of this study, another major study on Marine Fish Marketing in India was undertaken during 1979-81, and the report was brought out in six volumes covering all the maritime States and Union Territories. In 1980, another major study was undertaken on All-India Inland Fish Marketing. This report was completed in 1983 and published in 1984 in eight volumes.

Both these studies were subjected to comprehensive discussions at two national seminars. The proceedings of these seminars were printed and widely disseminated. Subsequently, the Institute faculty completed a Systems Study on Marine Foods Industry in India in collaboration with the Visvesvaraya Industrial Research and Development Centre, Bombay. As continuation of the work in fisheries, the present study on "Impact of Mechanization on Small Fishermen" was conducted.

The study is unique in the sense that, for the first time, fishing villages and impact of mechanization have been studied in depth. The study provides insights into the problems of small fishermen in the process of technological changes.

It is hoped the study will be useful not only to administrators involved in the development of fisheries, but also various bodies and research institutes engaged in the field. Coming as it does in the wake of the Seventh Five Year Plan, it is hoped that the study will also be found timely.

Chairman
Centre for Management in Agriculture
Indian Institute of Management
Ahmedabad

RANJIT GUPTA

May 1985

Acknowledgements

THIS study was carried out as part of the work done every year by the Centre for Management in Agriculture (CMA), Indian Institute of Management, Ahmedabad, for the Ministry of Agriculture, Government of India. We are grateful to the Ministry for the opportunity to conduct this study.

The team would like to express thanks and gratitude to Shri H.L. Chawla, Economic and Statistical Adviser; Dr. P.V. Dehadri, Fisheries Development Commissioner; and Dr. V.D. Singh, Deputy Commissioner (Fisheries), Ministry of Agriculture, for very useful discussions.

We have received support and encouragement from Dr. I.G. Patel, former Director, and Dr. N.R. Sheth, the present Director of the Indian Institute of Management in Agriculture, and Prof. Ranjit Gupta, Chairman, Centre for Management in Agriculture, Ahmedabad, and Prof. C. Gopinath, former Chairman, CMA.

We would like to express our gratitude to Shri Vijay Ranchan, IAS, former Commissioner of Fisheries, Mr. A Luke, the present Commissioner of Fisheries, Government of Gujarat, who gave us great support, and a large number of their colleagues for sharing secondary data and also finding time for discussions with the team. We are thankful for similar support and encouragement from the Director of Fisheries, Government of Karnataka. We would also like to express our gratitude to Mr. M. Jayaraj, and his colleagues in this regard.

A large number of people have helped us in data collection and field work. We would like to place our appreciation on record to Ms. G. N. Kulkarni, Thothya Naik, H. N. S. Rao, Sudarshan Choudhary, Atul Shah and Bhaskar Bhatt.

We owe a deep debt of gratitude to Ms. Rajeshwari Mehta

and Mr. G. Ramachandran Nair for their constant support at various stages of report writing.

We wish to make a special note of thanks to Mr. G. Krishnan who handled the major burden of typing the successive drafts of the bulky manuscript and also to Ms. P. Mahadevan, M. Kaliappan, T. M. Durairajan, P. G. Muralidharan and P. V. R. Nair of CMA Programmes Office for completing the task of stencilling this report in record time.

U.K. SRIVASTAVA
M. DHARMA REDDY
B. SUBRAHMANYAM
V.K. GUPTA

Contents

List of Tables

List of Figures

1

Technology and Development of Marine Fisheries

INTRODUCTION

FISHERY is regarded as a powerful income and employment generator as it stimulates the growth of a number of subsidiary industries.[1] This is also an exchange earner besides providing balanced protein food to all classes of people. The evaluation of the impact of mechanization on fisheries is, therefore, of fundamental importance for resource allocation and employment policy, and the development of fisheries as an organized industry in the Indian economy.

In addition, there are other reasons that make it particularly important to study the problem of the impacts of mechanization on fisheries. First, mechanization of fishing craft of late has resulted in the conflict of interest between traditional fishermen and mechanized boat owners and has complicated the fishing rights in the marine fisheries sector, the non-wage mode of employment and a substantial use of wage labour co-exists and this makes resource allocation difficult. Further, technological differences in labour cost need special attention, particularly in view of what looks like the emergence of modern capitalist fishermen.

There have been variations in the type of mechanization.[2] While the mechanization has progressed quite rapidly in the rural economy of some of the states, it has raised questions in regard to the choice of technology in mechanization, with reference to employment planning and income distribution. Mechanization also raises questions about its impact on the type of fish production and fluctuations in output. There are also questions in regard to the changes in the quality of life of small fishermen.

MECHANIZATION IN INDIAN MARINE FISHERIES

Since fisheries is basically a biological process, a pertinent beginning would be to distinguish between mechanical and biological technology. The former makes non-human power (generally mechanical) available in the boat or in actual fishing. Biological technology, on the other hand, improves the growth of fish by means of culturing and supply of improved fish seed for culturing.

Innovations in the field of mechanical technology are said to be "embodied" in machines and equipment of various kinds. The mechanical technology is intended for the modernization of the industry. Modernization has been accomplished by introducing power driven fishing craft or by motorization on the traditional craft. Modernization of the fishing craft in all the states has been undertaken to enable fishermen to go deeper into the sea and fish for a longer time. This has resulted in increased productivity and consequently increased incomes.

Usually, the term mechanized craft is used to refer to craft of any size with any range of power. Mechanized craft broadly can be classified into outboard motor (OBM) boats and in-board engine (IBE) boats. Different types of gears (nets, hooks and lines) are provided and operated from both OBM and IBE boats. The type of gear operated from the boat is the key factor in determining the nature of fishing and the species of fish to be harvested. Trawler, purse-seiner, long liner, etc., are names given to particular types of IBE boats and basically indicate the type of fishing technique and gear operated. OBM boats are called motorized boats irrespective of the type of the gear.

A clear understanding of the fishery resource base is essential for social science research in fisheries in general and evaluate the impact of mechanization in particular. Therefore, a brief summary[3] of the resource base and its characteristics is presented here before undertaking any analysis of mechanization of fishing craft.

The ocean contains many species of fishes. So far over

25,000 species of marine fishes and shell fishes have been identified. The different species of marine fishes require different environmental and oceanographic conditions. Over 90 per cent of the marine fishery resources are concentrated in about 10 per cent water above the continental shelf area. Further, as indicated by Kurien,[4] generally in the ocean there is much greater stock of smaller fish than larger fish. He adds that small fish have the tendency to live in waters closer to the shore while large fish tend to move away from the shore. The marine fisheries stock grows fast in temperate waters and regions of turbulence.

A recent study by Kurien and Mathew[5] enumerates three important characteristics in relation to the mechanization of the fishing craft. They are:

(i) There are wide regional variations in the species—mix of the marine resource of the country, which lies in a tropical region.

(ii) The nutritive value of all species of fish/crustaceans are almost the same but the market demand for different species varies and consequently results in varying prices for different species. For example, oil sardines fetch a very low price (Re. 1 per kg.) while prawns, usually called "pink gold", command a very high price (up to Rs. 90 per kg.).

(iii) The marine fishery resource is a "common property" and is accessible to all. However, the cost of production (catching) varies directly with the distance of the fishing ground from the shore. Therefore, all boat owners, irrespective of the level of technology of their boats, tend to fish as close to the shore as possible.

In addition to the economic/ecological consequences of the above characteristics, there are dimensions such as living habits of different marine fishery species which are relevant for a comprehensive understanding of the technological impact on fisheries and fishermen.

The fish move in shoals of different sizes. Migration of fish during the life-cycle makes the comprehensive understanding of fishery resources very difficult. Further, different types of fish live at different depth levels. Depending upon the living habits, fish are classified into three broad categories: demarsal, midwater and pelagic.[6]

Resource factor in technological change

The impact of technological changes in general and mechanization in particular may not be the same on fishermen. The impact of technological changes depends on the level of control over resources and markets, the economic and social background of the beneficiaries and the traditional fishermen, and the nature of technological change in terms of labour displacement/absorption.[7]

Various new types of mechanized craft have been introduced through Government policy initiatives with a view to harvesting resources which were so far beyond the reach of traditional craft. It may be correct to state that the Government never intended to replace the traditional craft. However, instead of going into deep sea, most mechanized boats have started fishing in shallow waters for various reasons and thus compete with the traditional craft. This conflict for fishing activities is very much significant in the case of trawlers and purse-seiners. In a way deep-sea fishing for exploiting the resources beyond the reach of the traditional fishermen has not yet developed in India.

Trends in the number of mechanized boats

In 1961 there were only about 2,160 mechanized boats in operation. By 1972 the number had increased to around 12,600 and by 1979 it was well over 16,100. The sharp upward trend has accelerated further since then, and the latest estimates (1980) have indicated that the total mechanized boats in operation in Indian marine fisheries number well over 19,000.

The progress of mechanized boats in different maritime states is presented in Table 1.1. The programme of mechanization of fishing craft developed in most of the states after the Second Five-Year Plan. The total number of mechanized boats introduced during the Third Five-Year Plan was more than the existing total stock of mechanized craft in all the states. The trend in the number of mechanized boats introduced during the various Plans has decelerated after the Fourth Five-Year Plan in almost all states.

TABLE 1.1

Statewise mechanized boats introduced during various Five-Year Plans, India

State	Number of mechanized boats introduced in the state								
	By the end of Second Plan	During Third Plan	1966-67	1967-68	1968-69	During Fourth Plan	During Fifth Plan	Total	Target for Sixth Five Year Plan
1. West Bengal	4	9	—	—	—	4	107	124	422
2. Orissa	—	37	3	12	4	68	237	498	886
3. Andhra Pradesh	66	193	21	26	30	115	67	518	820
4. Tamil Nadu	82	477	154	170	200	917	500	2500	1190
5. Kerala	138	822	216	250	174	322	47	1969	3000
6. Karnataka	48	226	100	135	115	763	328	1715	1701
7. Maharashtra	1302	528	224	120	67	404	620	3265	1235
8. Gujarat	413	888	—	189	—	453	1006	2949	2328

Note: Pondicherry and Goa are not included.

Source: The information up to the annual plans is obtained from Anonymous, *Evaluation of the Programme of Mechanization of Fishing Boats* (New Delhi; Programme Evaluation Organization, Planning Commission, Government of India), 1971, p. 5.

Statewise and typewise distribution of mechanized craft in the country are presented in Table 1.2. Statewise distribution of mechanized craft in the country indicates that most of the craft are operating on the west coast. Maharashtra accounts for the maximum (4,718) and is followed by Gujarat, Kerala, Tamil Nadu, Karnataka and Goa with 3,413, 3.038, 2,757, 2,004 and 908 craft respectively. Typewise distribution of the craft indicates that trawlers account for a large share ranging from 100 per cent in Andhra Pradesh to over 35 per cent in Gujarat of the total craft in almost all the states. Gillnetters are second largest type of mechanized craft in the country. The maximum number (1,547) of gillnetters are in Gujarat[8], followed by West Bengal, Kerala, Goa and Tamil Nadu with 740, 362, 274 and 143 craft respectively. Purse-seiners are a recent phenomenon and are confined to Karnataka and Goa, to some extent, to Kerala. Purse-seiners account for 2.25 per cent of the mechanized craft in the country. Dolenetters or bagnetters are in operation only in Gujarat and Maharashtra.

The number of mechanized craft in each state may not be indicative of the intensity of mechanization there. To rank the states according to the intensity of mechanization we have used two indexes: number of mechanized boats per kilometre of the coastline and per square kilometre of the continental shelf area. The level of intensity of mechanization as measured by the above two indicators in each state is presented in Table 1.3. The intensity of mechanization as measured by the number of mechanized boats per km. of coastline was in the range of 0.6 boat in Andhra Pradesh to 8.25 boats in Goa. It is clear from Table 1.3 that the level of mechanization is consistently very high in the states on the west coast. The number of mechanized boats per 1,000 sq. km. of shelf area was as high as 90 boats in Goa while it was only 0 62 boat in the Andamans. The average number of mechanized boats per 1,000 sq. km. of continental shelf area was just over 39.50 boats for the states on the east coast and 51.10 boats for the states on the west coast. Thus, we find that the states on the west coast are more intensively mechanized.

Slightly over 34 per cent of the total mechanized boats in the country are owned by non-fishermen and the rest by traditional fishermen. Mechanized boats owned by non-fishermen ranged

TABLE 1.2

Statewise and typewise distribution of mechanized boats in operation, India (1980)

State	Trawlers	Gillnetters	Purse-seiners	Dolnetters	Others	Total
1. West Bengal	—	740(100.0)	—	—	—	740(100.0)
2. Orissa	350(74.63)	119(25.37)	—	—	—	469(100.0)
3. Andhra Pradesh	580(100.0)	—	—	—	—	580(100.0)
4. Tamil Nadu	2614(94.81)	143(5.19)	—	—	—	2757(100.0)
5. Pondicherry	160(98.16)	3(1.84)	—	—	—	163(100.0)
6. Kerala	2630(86.57)	362(11.92)	37(1.22)	—	9(0.29)	3038(100.0)
7. Karnataka	1553(77.49)	28(1.40)	325(16.22)	—	98(4.89)	2004(100.0)
8. Goa	494(54.40)	274(30.18)	66(7.27)	—	74(8.15)	908(100.0)
9. Maharashtra*		—	No break-up	—		4718
10. Gujarat	1209(35.42)	1547(45.33)	—	650(19.04)	7(0.21)	3413
11. Andamans*		—	No break-up	—		10
12. Lakshadweep*		—	No break-up	—		213
Total		—	No break-up	—		19013

Note: 1. (—) indicates nil.
2. Figures in parentheses are percentages to row total.

Source: 1. For all the states except for Maharashtra, Andamans and Lakshadweep, in *Marine Information Service* No. 30 (Cochin: Central Marine Fisheries Research Institute, 1981, p. 21).
2. *Data presented here relate to 1977, obtained from *Indian Fisheries 1947-77* (Cochin: Marine Products Export Development Authority, 1977).

TABLE 1.3

Statewise length of coastline, continental shelf area and the intensity of mechanization, India (1980)

State	Length of coastline (km.)	Number of mechanized craft per km. of coastline	Area of continental shelf (sq. km.)	Number of mechanized craft per '000 sq. km. of shelf area
1. West Bengal and Orissa	1080	1.12	46490	26.01
2. Andhra Pradesh	970	0.60	31040	18.69
3. Tamil Nadu and Pondicherry	960	3.04	41420	70.50
4. Kerala	600	5.06	35940	84.53
5. Karnataka	270	7.42	25470	78.68
6. Goa	110	8.25	9980	90.98
7. Maharashtra	600	7.86	104760	45.04
8. Gujarat	1500	2.27	99370	34.34
9. Andamans	—	—	16060	0.62
10. Lakshadweep	—	—	4340	49.08
Total	6090	—	414870	—

Note: (—) indicates not available.
Source: "All India Census of Marine Fishermen Craft and Gear, 1980", op. cit.

from 4.72 per cent in Tamil Nadu to 77.40 per cent in Orissa. A closer look indicates that ownership by non-traditional fishermen is uniformly high in states having a long history of mechanization of fishing craft while it is very low in states where mechanization is recent except in Orissa (Table 1.4). This might have occurred mainly because of the super-normal profits[9] (because of large unexploited resources) in the early stages of mechanized and the consequent rush for mechanization craft by well-to-do non-fishermen and traditional fishermen.

Mechanization of fishing craft in Gujarat and Karnataka

Mechanization of craft in Gujarat and Karnataka deserves a closer look since the process in these states is distinct. In

TABLE 1.4

Statewise distribution of mechanized boats according to the ownership pattern, India (1980)

State	Number of mechanized boats owned by		Total
	Traditional fishermen	Non-fisherman community	
1. West Bengal	310 (41 89)	430 (58.11)	740 (100.0)
2. Orissa	106 (22.60)	363 (77.40)	469 (100.0)
3. Andhra Pradesh	456 (78.62)	124 (21.38)	580 (100.0)
4. Tamil Nadu	2627 (95.28)	130 (4.72)	2757 (100.0)
5. Pondicherry	176(100.00)	—	176** (100.0)
6. Kerala	983 (32.36)	2055 (67.64)	3038 (100.0)
7. Karnataka	1078 (53.79)	926 (46.21)	2004 (100.0)
8. Goa	659 (72.58)	249 (27.42)	908 (100.0)
9. Gujarat	2894 (84.79)	519 (15.21)	3413 (100.0)
Total*	9289 (65.97)	4729 (34.03)	14081 (100.0)

Note: 1. Figures in parentheses are percentages in total.

2. * Excluding the number of boats in Maharashtra, Andamans, and Lakshadweep for which the data was not available.

3. ** Including Mahim and Yanam.

Source: "All India Census of Marine Fishermen, Craft and Gear: 1980" op. cit.

Gujarat modernization of fishing craft has been quite smooth. It began with motorization of traditional craft and progressed to introduction of trawlers. The process, as has been indicated by John Kurien and Sebastain Mathew[10], has created a healthy and complementary relationship between the traditional and modern sectors. In Karnataka direct induction of trawlers and purse-seiners subsequently has been quite rapid and is accompanied by the occasional resistance to mechanization of fishing craft by the traditional sector.

Gujarat: Mechanization of fishing craft in Gujarat began with the introduction of 3 h.p. OBM in Jaleswar[11] in 1953, while the first ever IBE was fitted to a dugout canoe in the Veraval region in 1956. Later, mechanized boats fitted with 12.20 h.p. engines were promoted by the Department of Fisheries through liberal loans and subsidy on the cost of the boat. It was only in 1962 that the first set of three trawler-cum-gillnetters were introduced by the Department of Fisheries, on an exploratory basis. The operations of these vessels were found to be quite encouraging and the demand for trawlers (IBE boats) increased considerably. The number of mechanized boats of both types added during the period 1951 to 1980 with financial aid[12] from the state government is presented in Table 1.5. The induction of OBM boats was quite intensive during the period 1961-66 with an average rate of addition of 97.6 boats a year. In the case of IBE boats an average rate of induction of 272.5 boats per annum was experienced between 1974 and 1980. The relatively high rate of induction of IBE boats during 1974-80 is mainly because of the commencement of the World Bank-aided fishery project in the state. Excluding the period 1974-1980, the rate of addition of mechanized boats to the fishing fleet was the highest during 1961-66 for both types of boats. This perhaps could be the period during which most of the non-traditional fishermen might have entered the then highly remunerative mechanized fishing sector, particularly the IBE boats sector.

TABLE 1.5

Number of different types of mechanized boats added to the fishing fleet with financial aid from the State Government, Gujarat (1951-80)

Period	Number of mechanized boats added during the stated period of type					
	OBM		IBE		Total	
	Total	Per year	Total	Per year	Total	Per year
1951-61	295	29.5	116	11.6	411	41.1
1961-66	488	97.6	403	80.6	891	178.2
1966-69	2	0.7	187	62.3	189	63.0
1969-74	109	21.8	344	68.8	453	90.6
1974-80	153	25.5	1635	272.5	1788	298.0
Total	1047	—	2685	—	3732	—

Source: Planning Division of the Commissionerate of Fisheries, Government of Gujarat, Ahmedabad.

Districtwise distribution of different types of mechanized

boats owned by the fishermen is presented in Table 1.6. Junagarh accounts for over 61.54 per cent of the mechanized

TABLE 1.6

Districtwise distribution of mechanized boats according to type owned by fishermen community, Gujarat (1980)

District	Number of boats in stated district owned by fishermen of					Total mechanized boats in the district
	Trawlers	Gill-netters	Dol-netters	Others	Total	
1. Valsad	348 (24.68)	285 (23.27)	99 (41.08)	18 (100.0)	750 (25.92)	905 (26.97)
2. Surat	—	3 (0.25)	—	—	3 (0.10)	5 (0.16)
3. Bharuch	—	—	—	—	—	2 (0.06)
4. Kheda	—	—	—	—	—	—
5. Bhavnagar	—	1 (0.08)	—	—	1 (0.03)	—
6. Amreli	117 (8.30)	93 (7.59)	51 (21.16)	—	261 (9.02)	312 (9.30)
7. Junagarh	900 (63.83)	790 (64.49)	91 (37.76)	—	1781 (61.54)	2039 (60.77)
8. Jamnagar	28 (1.99)	51 (4.16)	—	—	79 (2.73)	85 (2.53)
9. Rajkot	—	—	—	—	—	—
10. Kutch	17 (1.20)	2 (0.16)	—	—	19 (0.66)	7 (0.21)
Total	1410 (100.00)	1225 (100.00)	241 (100.00)	18 (100.00)	2894 (100.00)	3355 (100.00)

Note: 1. (—) indicates nil.

2. Figures in parentheses are percentages to column total.

3. The total number of mechanized boats in the state as indicated in the last column may not tally with the total given in Table 1.3 since the two sets of data are from two different sources.

Source: "All India Census of Marine Fishermen, Craft and Gear: 1980", *op. cit.* Aggregate data in the last column is obtained from *Status Paper on the Fisheries of Gujarat, op. cit.*, p. 62.

boats owned by traditional fishermen. Junagarh is followed by Valsad, Amreli, Jamnagar and others with a number of mechanized boats owned by traditional fishermen as 750 (25.92 per cent), 261 (9.02 per cent), 79 (2.73 per cent), and 23 (0.79 per cent) respectively. In absolute terms the incidence of ownership of the mechanized boats by the non-fishermen community is maximum in Junagarh with 255 boats (12.65 per cent of the total boats in the district) and is followed by Valsad with 155 boats or 16.32 per cent of the total in the district. Further, about 48.72 per cent of the total mechanized boats owned by fishermen are trawlers, and OBM boats account for about 24.71 per cent of the total mechanized boats in the state. The intensity of mechanization as measured by the number of mechanized boats per kilometre, of coastline is the highest in Junagarh with over 12.75 boats per kilometre of coastline, followed by Valsad with over 10 boats per kilometre.

Karnataka: The mechanization programme in the state started in the year 1957-58. Initially, mechanized boats were given to groups of trained[13] fishermen on a loan-and-subsidy basis. Starting with two small mechanized boats in 1956-57, the state had over 1500 coastal trawlers by 1977. The number of mechanized boats has increased to 2004 by 1980.

Mechanization of fishing craft in the state started with the induction of coastal water trawlers to catch prawns and shrimps. Till 1975-76, by and large, only trawlers were promoted. The mechanization programme of the state took a new turn with the introduction of two purse-seine units by the government on a demonstration basis during 1975-76. The promotion of purse-seining fishery was backed up by various incentives such as subsidy, arrangement for the easy availability of the institutional finance and training facilities. The state incentives alongwith the successful operations of the demonstration vessels have contributed to a large extent to the development of the purse-seine industry. Currently (1982) there are over 325 purse-seine boats in Karnataka. The number of purse-seine units in the state has increased very rapidly between 1977 and 1979.

It is pertinent to note that the rapid expansion of purse-seine boats is accompanied by a rapid decline in the use of the rampani boats, the traditional mode of production.[14] About

160 rampanis were operating in Karnataka in 1976 but this number declined to 35 in 1979 and 20 in 1981. Even these are not operated. The complete replacement of rampanis by purse-seiners has resulted in a total shift from the traditional sector to the modern sector. Another important aspect is the total routing of a community mode of production, which had evolved around the rampanis, and has been replaced by a system of organization with the traditional fishermen reduced to wage labourers.[15]

Typewise and districtwise distribution of mechanized boats along with the total number of boats is presented in Table 1.7. Over 80 per cent of the boats owned by fishermen were trawlers. Purse-seiners account for about 16 per cent of the mechanized boats. Of the total 325 purse-seiners in the state

TABLE 1.7

Districtwise and typewise distribution of mechanized boats owned by fishermen community and total boats, Karnataka (1980)

Type of boat	Number of boats of stated category owned by fishermen of			Total No. of boats of the state
	South Kanara	North Kanara	Total	
1. Trawlers*	519 (80.22)	356 (82.60)	875 (81.17)	1553 (77.49)
2. Purse-seiners	110 (17.00)	63 (15.62)	173 (16.05)	325 (16.22)
3. Gillnetters	16 (2.47)	7 (1.62)	23 (2.13)	28 (1.40)
4. Others	2 (0.31)	5 (0.16)	7 (0.65)	98 (4.98)
Total	647 (100.00)	431 (100.00)	1078 (100.00)	2004 (100.00)

Note: 1. *Including carrier boats.

2. Figures in parentheses are percentages to column total.

Source: "All India Census of Marine Fishermen, Craft and Gear: 1980", *op. cit.*

only 173 are owned by the persons from the fishermen community; the rest are owned by non-fishermen community individuals. About 41.92 per cent of trawlers are owned by non-fishermen. Despite the planned promotion of purse-seine fishing, only 53.23 per cent of the purse-seiners are owned by traditional fishermen while over 56.34 per cent of the trawlers are owned by the traditional fishermen. The larger incidence of the ownership of purse-seiners by individuals from other than the fishermen community may be mainly because of the larger returns on investment on purse-seiners in the initial stages coupled with their better economic conditions which enable them to avail finance from formal financial institutions.

OBJECTIVES OF THE STUDY

As indicated earlier, the programme of mechanization of fishing craft was initiated by the Government of India during the First Five-Year Plan mainly with an objective to increase the fish production in terms of quantity and quality on scientific lines.[16] It was also envisaged to improve the socio-economic conditions of small fishermen. Indian fishery has experienced intensive fisheries technology. Such technological changes have influenced both forward and backward linkages in the industry.

A brief review of the existing literature[17] on the impact of mechanization of fishing craft on small fishermen can be summarized as follows:

1. Excessive preoccupation of the mechanized boats in catching prawns in shallow waters, may be in view of their own limitations, has created dissatisfaction and a feeling of powerlessness among small fishermen. In some cases it has resulted in violent demonstrations.
2. Genuine small fishermen have not been able to reap the benefits of the mechanization programme. The bulk of the surplus seems to have accrued to the private entrepreneurs, many of whom may be at best members of the fishing community but seldom active fishermen.
3. As a result of mechanization of fishing craft, there is a decline or stagnation in total landings of the traditional fishing craft in almost all the states. Further, this

trend has resulted in shortages of locally consumed fish and a rapid increase in the prices of fish.

Studies on the impact of mechanization on small fishermen have concentrated on analysing the trends in total landings of fish due to mechanization and usually are based on data obtained from official agencies involved in the implementation of the mechanization programme. The current study has been undertaken to fill many gaps in the field on the basis of information obtained from actual village situations. The objectives of the study are:

1. Study the trends in production of marine fish in the country and the impact of mechanization on marine fish production.
2. Understand the factors affecting the mechanization of fishing craft.
3. Understand the current socio-economic status of small fishermen and assess the changes taking place due to mechanization.
4. Study the benefits accruing to small fishermen from various programmes of mechanization and their impact on distribution gains.
5. Evaluate the changes in the utilization pattern or end use of fish production due to mechanization and their consequent impact on the product market.
6. Identify the problem areas in the development of small fishermen.

METHODOLOGY AND DATA

This study is based on both primary and published data. Primary data have been obtained through a four-stage stratified sampling with states as the first stage units, district as the second stage units, villages as the third stage units, and fishermen as the ultimate sampling units.

Selecting the states

The first-stage sampling involved identification of states. It was intended to include two maritime states in the sample, taking the intensity of mechanization[18] into consideration, with a view to including highly mechanized states in the sample. In addition, it was felt necessary to include the states with different types of mechanized boats in operation. Thus, two maritime states, namely, Gujarat and Karnataka, were selected at the first stage.[19] The contrasting pattern of mechanization of fishing craft in both states was another reason for their selection.

Selecting the districts

Identification of one or two districts in each of the selected states was the next step. Junagarh in Gujarat and South Kanara in Karnataka were selected at the second stage using the intensity of mechanization as the criterion. However, owing to physical constraints village samples could not be drawn from Junagarh district. Therefore, Bharuch district was included in the sample.

Selecting the villages

Three fishing villages were to be selected from the selected districts. While selecting them, care was taken to include villages with different levels of mechanization in the sample.

Villages in the selected districts were ranked according to the ratio of mechanized to non-mechanized boats after taking into account the horse power of the motor/engine of the mechanized boat. After ranking the villages according to the mechanization, six to seven villages were identified for further sampling. While identifying the villages, it was felt necessary to include villages with different levels of mechanization and eliminate villages with large populations owing to difficulties involved an in-depth understanding. Therefore, villages with a population of over 2000 and urban places were excluded from the sample. Thus, the sample included one set of villages with the lowest level of mechanization or with no mechanized boats and two sets of experimental villages with medium to high level of mechanization. Physical verification was done before final selection. Since we could not find a control village from Junagarh district, it was decided to include one from Bharuch district. The villages thus selected for an in-depth study in Gujarat were: (1) Chorwad Bander with the highest level of mechanization, (2) Hirakot with medium level of mechanization, and (3) Bhadbhut, a non-mechanized village. Incidentally, it so happened that the village with highest level of mechanized boats has a combination of trawlers, OBM boats, and non-mechanized boats while the medium mechanized village has only OBM boats (or intermediate type of mechanized boats) and non-mechanized boats and the lowest mechanized village has only non-mechanized boats.

We have deviated slightly from this methodology for selecting the villages from Karnataka in view of the paucity of villagewise data.[20]

A list of villages falling under the three categories of levels of mechanization was, therefore, developed based upon discussions with the officials of the Deputy Director of Fisheries, Mangalore. Physical verification of over 12 villages in the district was undertaken based upon the above list with a view to finally selecting three villages. The villages were (1) Kadekar, a highly mechanized village, (2) Bokkapatna Bengre, a medium mechanized village, and (3) Idya, a low mechanized fishing village.

Selecting the sample respondents and data collection techniques

For collecting data four methods were developed. These are enumeration of households, observation of operations, discussions—both individual and group—and interviews through structured questionnaires. This combination of methods enabled us to obtain reliable data and gain a deeper understanding of the different study areas and the village communities.

In the first phase, enumeration of the fishermen households was undertaken in all the selected villages using a structured enumeration schedule. The information recorded in these schedules related to the socio-economic characteristics of households, assets position, occupation, consumption and expenditure pattern of fishermen households.

The second phase of the data collection was through observations and discussions method with a view to understanding the life-style of the fishermen. During this phase, information was also collected about infrastructure and organizations at the village level for the development of fisheries and fishermen. The investigations in this phase were based on a set of guidelines.

The third phase of the data collection for the study was undertaken through a structured questionnaire which was administered to a sample respondent. The objective of this phase was to investigate in depth the impact of mechanization. The sample selection of various respondents is indicated.

The details of the total number of households, number of households enumerated and the sample sizes planned and actual are presented in Table 1.8. The selection of households from the total households has been done on the basis of occupational pattern. The stratification of the households was undertaken on the basis of the occupations of the households in the village. The household enumeration data were used as the basis for stratifying the households. The sample allocation to various strata is based on the method of probability proportion to the population size. The details of sample sizes drawn from different villages according to the occupation of the selected households along with the sample sizes planned is presented in Table 1.9.

ORGANIZATION OF THE STUDY

The contents of the report are presented in two parts. The first part deals mainly with the analysis of macro data and the inter-village comparisons to evaluate the impact of mechanization on small fishermen and fishing villages. The second part presents case studies of selected villages.

The first part of the report contains four chapters including the current chapter. The present chapter is mainly intended to analyse the trends in mechanization of fishing craft and the regional variations in the mechanization. In addition, the rationale, objectives and methodology of the study are also indicated in this chapter. The second chapter, whose analysis is mainly based on the secondary data, has been devoted to evaluation of the macro impact of the mechanization in Indian marine fisheries. Based on the case studies of different villages, various conclusions have been drawn regarding the impact of mechanization in Indian marine fisheries. A summary of the

TABLE 1.8

Number of total and sample households in the selected villages

Name of village	Total No. of households	No. of households enumerated	Sample size Planned	Sample size Actual
1. Chorwad	108 (100.00)	107 (99.07)	43 (39.81)	39 (36.11)
2. Hirakot	195 (100.00)	173 (88.72)	49 (25.13)	45 (23.08)
3. Bhadbhut	170 (100.00)	155 (91.18)	47 (27.65)	41 (24.12)
4. Kadekar	103 (100.00)	103 (100.00)	41 (39.81)	38 (36. 6)
5. B. Bengre	80 (100.00)	79 (98.75)	39 (48.75)	37 (46.25)
6. Idya	99 (100.00)	99 (100.00)	33 (33.33)	30 (30.30)
Total	755	716	252	230

Note: Figures in parentheses indicate the per cent of sample households in total households.

TABLE 1.9

Distribution of sample size according to main occupation in selected villages

Occupation	Villages of Gujarat: Hira-kot	Chor-wad	Bhad-bhut	Villages of Karnataka: Kadekar	B. Bengre	Idya
1. Partner in Tr (MB)	—	—	—	3 (3)	3 (2)	0 (0)
2. Partner in Ps. (MB)	14(15)	15(15)*	0 (0)	7 (7)	2 (2)	6 } (10)
3. Partner in Tr+Ps. (MB)	0(0)	2(5)**	0 (0)	2 (2)	1 (1)	4 }
4. MB+NMB	2(1)	1(0)	0 (0)	3 (3)	0 (0)	0 (0)
5. MB+NMB+Crew	0(0)	0(0)	0 (0)	5 (5)	0 (0)	0 (0)
6. NMB	4(4)	10(10)	29 (25)	3 (3)	15 (15)	0 (2)
7. NMB+Crew	1(1)	0(0)	3 (5)	5 (5)	12 (0)	1 (0)

TABLE 1.9 (*Contd.*)

8. Crew	20(20)	10(10)	7 (15)	10 (10)	3 (14)	5 (6)
9. Rampani	0(0)	0(0)	0 (0)	0 (1)	0 (0)	8 } (12)
10. NMB+Rampani	0(0)	0(0)	0 (0)	0 (0)	0 (0)	6 }
11. Fish Retail Marketing	0(3)	0(1)	0 (2)	0 (2)	0 (3)	0 (2)
12. Fish Merchant	0(0)	0(0)	0 (0)	0 (0)	0 (1)	0 (1)
13. MB+Retail Merchant	2(1)	1(0)	0 (0)	0 (0)	0 (0)	0 (0)
14. Business	2(2)	0(0)	0 (0)	0 (0)	0 (0)	0 (0)
15. NMB+Retail Fish Merchant	0(0)	0(0)	2 (0)	0 (0)	0 (0)	0 (0)
16. MB+Crew Member	0(2)	0(0)	0 (0)	0 (0)	0 (0)	0 (0)
Total	45(49)	39(43)	41 (47)	38 (41)	37 (39)	30 (33)

Note: 1. Figures in parentheses indicate the planned sample size.

2. *Indicates number of OBM owners.

3. **Indicates number of trawler owners.

various conclusions drawn on the basis of the case studies, a comparison of the villages of different levels of mechanization of fishing craft is presented in the third chapter. The recommendations for the rapid growth of the marine fishing industry through the technological developments form the subject matter of the fourth chapter.

The second part of the report contains case studies of six marine fishing villages in Gujarat and Karnataka. The case studies include three villages from each state with varying degrees of mechanization of fishing craft. In order to make the case studies, comparable, the contents of each of the case studies have been divided into five sections. The first section of the case study of each village gives the location of the fishing village alongwith the details of general and fishery-related infrastructure facilities in the village. The second section contains the socio-ethnographic profile of the fishermen and the fishing community. The third section of each of the case studies is devoted to analysing the impact of mechanization of fishing craft on the production systems. The impact of mechanization of fishing craft on various input and output markets of the villages has been the subject matter of the fourth section. The fifth section of each of the case studies includes the study of the village economy and balances.

REFERENCES

1. Despite considerable industrialization, about two per cent of the Indian national income at market prices and about 954,000 fishermen are accounted by this sector. See Srivastava, U.K., Reddy, M.D., and Gupta, V.K., *Management of Marine Fishing Industry* (New Delhi: Oxford & IBH, 1982), p. 3.
2. The production process in marine fisheries mainly consists of two major activities: sailing to the fishing ground and back to the shore, and the actual catching of fish. Mechanization can broadly be divided into two categories. In the first category of mechanization, sailing to fishing grounds and back is only mechanized, while in the second type both are mechanized. Usually, the first type of mechanization is referred to as mechanization of fishing craft and the other is known as mechanization of fishing.
3. In fact, the study of the resource base appears to fall in the domain of biologists. The interested reader can refer to George, M.J., *et al.*, "A case of overfishing: depletion of shrimp resources along Neendakara Coast, Kerala", *Marine Fisheries Information Services,* No. 18 (Cochin: Central Marine Fisheries Research Institute, 1980); George, P.C., *et. al.*, "Fishery Resources of the Indian Economy Zone", *Souvenir* issued on the occasion of Silver Jubilee Celebrations (Cochin: Integrated Fisheries Projects, 1971); and *Proceedings oj the Symposium on Living Resources of the Seas Around India* (Cochin: Central Marine Fisheries Research Institute, 1973).
4. See Kurien, John, "Entry of Big Business into Fishing: Its impact on the fish economy", *Economic and Political Weekly*, 13 (36), October 1978, pp. 1557-1965.
5. See Kurien, J. and Sebastain Mathew, *Technological Changes in Fishing* : *Its Impact on Fishermen* (Trivandrum: Centre for Development Studies, 1982), pp. 12-13.
6. For details of the species included in each category see Gupta, V.K., *et al., Marine Fish Marketing in India,* Vol. III, *Supplies* (Ahmedabad: Indian Institute of Management, 1983).
7. Vandana Shiva and Bandyopadhyaya, J., "Political Economy of Technological Polarization", *Economic and Political Weekly*, XVII (45), November 6, 1982, p. 1829.
8. When OBM boats using gill nets are excluded from the total number of gillnetters in Gujarat, the state gets pushed down to the second place. Further details about the composition of the mechanized craft in Gujarat and Karnataka are discussed in the next section.
9. The expansion of the fishing industry in general and mechanized

craft in particular follows a near cyclical pattern. In this regard it has been pointed out by Kurien that in the initial stages supernormal profits (because of large unexploited resources) encourage rapid expansion of the industry (particularly the mechanized sector) until profits are totally competed away (when the optimal exploitation levels are reached) and consequently lead to losses (when resources have been beyond revival). See John Kurien, "Entry of Big Business into Fishing: Its Impact on the Fish Economy", *Economic and Political Weekly*, 13 (36), 1978, pp. 1557-1665.

10. Op. cit.
11. Then the state of Saurashtra received some low horse power OBMs and IBEs under the Technical Co-operative Mission (TCM) aid of the USA. For details see *A Status Paper on the Fisheries of Gujarat* (Ahmedabad: Commissionerate of Fisheries, Government of Gujarat 1981), pp. 20-22.
12. Financial aid was mainly in the form of subsidy and loans at lower rates of interest. However, the Government has stopped the subsidy and granting of loans from 1979 and 1974 respectively. Instead of subsidy, the Government is now granting interest-free loans equivalent to the subsidy and the lending for construction of boats is mainly through the State Financial Corporation and commercial banks.
13. Training centres for fishermen were started simultaneously with the programmes of mechanization.
14. Rampani is a shore seine of exceptionally large size and consists of 150 to 200 pieces laced together. The operation of the net requires about 80 to 100 persons. The net is used for catching the shoals of fish which come close to the shore. See George, "Fishing Gears of Karnataka", CIFT *Bulletin* (Cochin: Central Institute of Fisheries Technology, 1982).
15. In a bid to retain the community ownership of rampanis in the modern sector of purse-seine industry, the state government has encouraged owning of purse-seine boats by traditional rampani groups.
16. The process of mechanization of fishing craft in the country was initiated with the launching of the Indo-Norwegian Project (INP) in 1952. The main objective of the project was to modernize the traditional fishing craft. In the process, however, instead of modernization of traditional craft, induction of trawlers has become the primary activity of the project in particular and of the mechanization programme in general.
17. For example, see Kurien, J., *Towards an Understanding of the Fish Economy of Kerala State*, W.P. No. 68 (Trivandrum: Centre for Development Studies, 1978); Kurien, J., and Mathew, S., *Technological Changes in Fishing: Its Impact on Fishermen*, (Trivandrum : Centre for Development Studies, 1982); Devaraj, J., *Keel Handling of Traditional Fishermen: The Impact of Purse-seiner Operations on*

the Fish Economy of Dakshana Kanada District in Karnataka, ICSSR/ FRC Study (Trivandrum: Programme for Community Organization, 1980); Bhushan, B., Technological Change in Fishing in Kerala: 1953-1977, M. Phil Dissertation (Trivandrum: Centre for Development Studies, 1979), and Srivastava, U.K., Reddy, M.D., and Gupta, V.K., *Management of Marine Fishing Industry*, op. cit.

18. Intensity of mechanization has been defined as the number of mechanized boats per km. of coastline.
19. It should be noted that Gujarat is not a very highly mechanized state when we consider the aggregate number of mechanized boats and the total length of coastline. However, when we consider the regional distribution of mechanized boats the intensity of mechanization in the state works out to be very high, since most of its mechanized boats operate in a single zone with a coastline of less than 20 per cent of the coastline of the state.
20. Villagewise information for the villages in the selected districts of Gujarat has been obtained from the Commissionerate of Fisheries, Government of Gujarat. In the case of Karnataka no such information was available with the Directorate of Fisheries, Government of Karnataka. The Central Marine Fisheries Research Institute, Cochin, was not willing to part with the data, though it had them.

2

Impact of Mechanization: A Macro Analysis

IN RECENT years there has been a marked increase in the use of mechanized (both OBM and IBE) boats in Indian marine fisheries particularly in the states on the west coast. In the context of the rapid progress of mechanized fishing, the question really is whether the role of mechanization of fishing, craft is merely to provide a manmade source of energy to replace human energy or does it have a wider technological significance, in that, it directly and indirectly transforms the entire production economy of the fishermen. There has not been any evidence to support either of the above arguments. In order, therefore, to understand the impact of mechanization on the production system and the economy of the fishermen and fishing villages, we have followed two approaches, viz. an analysis based upon macro evidence and the study based upon the analysis of the in-depth village studies conducted by us. The analysis of the impact of mechanization on the basis of macro evidence is presented in this chapter, while the micro analysis based upon our village studies is reserved for the following chapter.

MECHANIZATION OF FISHING CRAFT AND GROWTH IN FISH PRODUCTION

The effect of mechanization on production of marine fish can be assessed either by estimating the increase in output attributable to mechanized craft in a given period or by studying the trends in production during the pre- and post-mechanization periods. The former method, however, is beset with problems of relevant data and methods of estimation. The latter is more manageable, although it would provide only a rough approximation on output. In view of data problems we will mainly use the latter method for estimating the growth of fish production due to mechanization of fishing craft.

For analysing the growth in output of marine fish the entire period (1956-81), for which the comparable data on marine fish production is available, has been divided into two periods, viz. pre-mechanization (1956-69) and post-mechanization (1970-81) periods.[1] The statewise growth rates[2] of effort, fish output and catch per unit effort during pre-mechanization, post-mechanization and the entire period are presented in Table 2.1. Despite the mechanization of small shrimp trawlers after the mid-sixties the growth rate of fish production has decelerated during the post-mechanization period as compared to pre-mechanization period in most of the states except West Bengal, Orissa, Maharashtra and Gujarat. However, the growth rate for the country has increased marginally from 1.58 per cent during the pre-mechanization period to 2.32 per cent during the post-mechanization period. West Bengal, Orissa, Maharashtra and Gujarat experienced accelerated growth rates

During the pre-mechanized period (1956-69), the fishing effort (labour input) declined at the rate of 4.6 per cent per annum. If all the inputs were so decreased that productivity in terms of catch per unit effort remained constant, the fish production would decrease at the same rate as fishing effort. Since the overall actual production increased at a rate of 1.58 per cent per annum, the entire increase in production can be attributed to the increase in the productivity (in terms of catch per unit effort). The total fishing effort during the post-mechanization period (1970-81) increased at the rate of 4.58 per cent per annum. Since the actual fish production has increased at the rate of 2.32 per cent per annum during this (1970-81) period, increase in productivity per unit effort accounted for over 400 per cent of the fish production. However, there was a marked deceleration in the growth rate of productivity.

In the case of Karnataka the fishing effort seemed to have decreased at the rate of 5.51 per cent per annum during the

TABLE 2.1

Statewise growth rates of effort, fish output and catch per unit effort, India (1956-1981)

States	Effort			Output			Catch per unit effort		
	1956-69	1970-79	1956-79	1956-69	1970-81	1956-81	1956-69	1970-79	1956-79
1. West Bengal and Orissa	4.61	—33.13	7.91	9.24	10.40	9.42	6.94	1.61	3.07
2. Andhra Pradesh	—3.65	3.21	—1.19	6.82	2.07	4.79	10.76	—0.65	6.31
3. Tamil Nadu and Pondicherry	—4.27	5.19	—0.32	3.04	3.63	4.03	7.64	—0.57	4.52
4. Kerala	—5.88	—3.45	—0.08	3.55	—3.13	1.82	9.99	3.26	2.61
5. Karnataka	—5.51	11.18	1.60	3.82	3.37	4.86	9.50	—1.08	2.81
6. Maharashtra	—7.09	4.47	—0.56	—2.64	3.13	2.97	4.73	0.31	3.58
7. Gujarat	—4.60	0.51	—0.30	—2.20	10.47	3.46	2.51	5.29	3.21
All India*	—4.60	4.58	—0.01	1.58	2.32	3.31	6.61	—1.43	3.23

Note: *Excluding Andamans, Lakshadweep and Goa.
Source: Central Marine Fisheries Research Institute, Cochin.

pre-mechanization period. Since the actual growth rate of fish output during the same period is 3.82 per cent per annum, the entire increase in output could be attributed to the increase in productivity. During the post-mechanization period the fishing effort has increased at the rate of 11.18 per cent per annum. Since the actual growth rate of fish output during the same period is less than 3.37 per cent per annum, the entire increase in production can be attributed to the increase in the effort. In fact, the productivity per unit effort during this period has decreased at a rate of 1.08 per cent per annum during the post-mechanization period.

In the case of Gujarat the fishing effort has decreased at the rate of 4.60 per cent per annum during the pre-mechanization period and resulted in the decrease of total output at a rate of 2.20 per cent. The marginal recovery in the decrease in the output during the pre-mechanization period was due to the increase in productivity. During the post-mechanization period fish production has increased at the rate of 10.47 per cent per annum mainly because of the increase in productivity. Productivity per unit of fishing effort during the post-mechanization period is characterized by marked acceleration, which may be mainly because of mechanization.

The states showing a higher growth rate of fish production during the post-mechanization period are the ones where the level of mechanization is low. It may be true that higher profitability associated with the use of mechanized boats for fishing may have induced many to invest more in them. But fishery being a renewable resources, it imposes a limitation on the level of catch However, this crowding of mechanized boats in a limited area (up to 25 fathoms in the continental shelf area) thus may have resulted in the deceleration of fish production.

Specieswise growth rates of production during 1956-81 and during the pre- and post-mechanization periods are presented in Table 2.2. Species such as harpodon neherous, sciaenids, prawns, pomfrets, etc., are characterized by a marked acceleration during the post-mechanized period, while species such as oil sardines, other sardines, leiagnathus, etc., are characterized by either deceleration or negative growth. Most of the species which are characterized by accelerated growth rates during the post-mechanization period usually are demersal species while

TABLE 2.2

Specieswise growth rates of output, India (1956-81)

Species	Growth rates during		
	1956-69	1970-81	1956-81
1. Elasmobranches	3.17	2.84	3.96
2. Catfishes	–0.02	–0.37	5.00
3. Oil Sardines	15.12	–1.03	3.15
4. Other Sardines	2.14	0.21	4.20
5. Harpodon neherous	–2.17	6.97	0.42
6. Sciaenids	–1.62	8.12	6.32
7. Ribbonfish	0.70	4.79	4.16
8. Carangids	–0.23	–0.11	0.91
9. Leiognathur	10.20	3.93	6.02
10. Pomfret	4.07	9.89	3.92
11. Mackerel	0.33	8.03	1.10
12. Seer fish	1.84	4.99	5.20
13. Penacid Prawns	–2.68	1.68	5.36
14. Non-Penacid Prawns	–5.18	0.79	2.12
Others	2.41	6.24	5.32
Total	1.56	2.32	3.31

Source: Central Marine Fisheries Institute, Cochin.

species characterized by deceleration or a negative growth rate are the pelatics. The observed trend is mainly because of the large-scale introduction of demersal trawlers for shrimps during the early post-mechanization period and the consequent decrease in the number of non-mechanized units particularly involved in catching pelagic fish.

Specieswise growth rates of fish production in Gujarat and Karnataka are presented in Tables 2.3 and 2.4. The trend behaviour of different species in Gujarat during the post- and pre-mechanization periods is more or less similar to that of all India. However, the growth rates of most of the demersal species particularly crustaceans and sciaenids have increased at a very rapid rate during the post-mechanization period in Gujarat, as compared to those for the country during the same period. In the case of Karnataka the pelagic species have

TABLE 2.3

Specieswise growth rates of output, Gujarat (1956-81)

Species	Growth rates of output of state variety during		
	1956-69	1970-81	1956-81
1. Elasmobranches	5.92	7.73	7.18
2. Catfishes	5.45	9.63	6.40
3. Eels	—21.00	16.79	7.94
4. Polynomids	—26.50	—7.38	0.66
5. Harpode neherous	0.84	—0.99	—3.66
6. Sciaenids	—8.85	22.27	12.90
7. Ribbon fish	—0.10	26.62	11.60
8. Carangids	13.06	13.87	9.77
9. Pomfrets	4.63	7.57	2.41
10. Seer fish	6.70	10.93	20.16
11. Hilsa	1.07	9.89	5.69
12. Crustaceans	—15.98	19.61	1.03
Others	2.94	13.09	10.70
Total	2.09	8.12	2.44

Source: Central Marine Fisheries Research Institute, Cochin.

TABLE 2.4

Specieswise growth rates of output, Karnataka (1956-81)

Species	Growth rates of stated variety during		
	1956-69	1970-81	1956-81
1. Elasmobranches	—5.42	3.62	2.04
2. Catfishes	—2.32	8.08	5.58
3. Oil Sardines	34.61	11.29	12.73
4. Other Sardines	11.93	15.27	5.22
5. Sciaenids	—7.69	5.22	1.20
6. Carangids	7.59	12.08	6.41
7. Leiognathus	5.18	7.73	7.42

TABLE 2.4 (*Contd.*)

8. Pomfret	15.07	—4.86	5.22
9. Mackerel	—8.39	—4.36	1.60
10. Seer fish	−10.51	0.20	5.34
11. Crustaceans	10.39	0.18	11.27
Others	3.64	7.07	8.11
Total	3.90	3.42	4.72

Source: Central Marine Fisheries Research Institute, Cochin.

grown at a faster rate during the post-mechanization period as compared to the country during the same period. This may be mainly because of the type of mechanized boats inducted, and their consequent impact on the production system. For example, in Gujarat the mechanization is characterized by the induction of shrimp trawlers, which are solely involved in catching shrimps and other demersal fishes and, therefore, the landings of demersal species grew at a faster rate during the post-mechanization period. Similarly, large-scale introduction of purse-seiners, which by and large replaced the traditional rampanis, have contributed to the accelerated growth of pelagic species during the post-mechanization period in Karnataka.

Contribution of the mechanization of fishing craft

Ideally, the contribution of mechanization of fishing craft to the growth of fish production in the country should be obtained through the production function analysis, where the traditional and modern factors of production are identified and introduced explicitly as input variables.[3] However, such an analysis is ruled out owing to non-availability of data. Therefore, we adopt an alternative that can provide an approximation to contribution of mechanization of fishing craft to the growth of output.[4] In this procedure, we compare the output between successive peaks in the production of output to get an idea of the extent of growth in output after adjusting for ecological effects.[5]

Table 2.5 gives the output and specieswise composition in peak years in India during 1961-1981. From a comparison of three post-mechanization peak years of fish production (1961, 1964 and 1968), it appears that fish output in the country would have grown by about 3.5 to 4 per cent per annum in the absence of mechanization of fishing craft.[6] Between 1968—the

TABLE 2.5

Fish output and species composition in peak years (1961-1981)

(*in '000 tonnes*)

Year	Gap (years)	Elasmo-branches	Catfish	Sardines	Bombay Duck	Sciae-nids	Pomfret	Mackerel	Crusta-ceans	Total landings
1961	—	33.55	10.93	187.64	93.84	29.92	16.49	34.49	64.81	674.91
1964	3	34.89	22.73	314.73	81.34	25.20	19.58	23.86	99.46	854.29
		(1.33)	(35.99)	(22.58)	(—4.44)	(—5.26)	(6.25)	(—10.27)	(17.82)	(8.86)
1968	4	31.03	23.75	343.19	82.40	26.14	27.80	20.79	103.52	871.33
		(—2.55)	(1.12)	(2.26)	(0.33)	(0.93)	(10.50)	(—3.22)	(1.02)	(0.50)
1973	4	44.92	52.64	252.71	64.35	87.68	22.05	79.42	215.98	1220.24
		(11.19)	(30.41)	(—5.59)	(—5.48)	(58.86)	(—5.17)	(70.50)	(27.16)	(10.01)
1975	2	65.23	68.69	271.36	99.61	114.54	24.99	45.95	243.64	1422.69
		(22.61)	(15.25)	(3.69)	(27.40)	(15.31)	(6.67)	(—21.07)	(6.40)	(9.30)
1978	3	61.62	39.23	220.92	125.48	96.38	41.43	85.23	195.37	1403.61
		(—1.84)	(—14.30)	(—6.20)	(8.66)	(—5.28)	(21.93)	(28.49)	(—6 60)	(—0.45)

TABLE 2.5 (*Contd.*)

Between 1961 and 1968	7	(—1.07)	(16.76)	(11.84)	(—1.74)	(—1.80)	(9.80)	(—5.67)	(8.53)	(4.16)
Between 1968 and 1981	13	(0.52)	(11.54)	(—1.35)	(5.17)	(16.64)	(6.65)	(10.31)	(6.45)	(4.48)

Notes: 1. Figures in parentheses indicate the annual per cent differences over the preceding peak.

2. The negative sign for the annual per cent difference over the preceding peak indicates decrease in landings.

Source: Central Marine Fisheries Research Institute, Cochin.

base year—and 1981 fish output has increased at a rate of about 4.5 per cent per annum. If it is assumed that fish production would have grown at the rate of 3.5 per cent per annum, without the mechanization, the contribution of mechanization of the fishing craft works out to 1 per cent (4.5-3.5) per annum, i.e. about 23 per cent of output growth. Thus, the contribution of the mechanization of fishing craft amounts to over 122,000 tonnes of the fish production out of an increase of 532,000 tonnes between 1968 and 1981. If the pre-mechanization period growth rate of fish production is assumed to be 4 per cent, the contribution of mechanization works out to be about 60,000 tonnes. Further, modernization has resulted in an increase in the production of a few of the species and a decrease in the case of others.

A comparison of two pre-mechanization peak outputs in 1963 and 1968 in Gujarat reveals that fish production in the state decreased at the rate of 3 per cent per annum, while it increased at the rate of 12 per cent per annum during the post-mechanization period. Thus, the contribution of mechanization in the state accounts for the entire increase of about 14,792,000 tonnes (Table 2.6). In the case of Karnataka, the comparison of the pre- and post-mechanization peaks indicates that the contribution of mechanization is quite negligible at aggregate level. However, specieswise analysis indicates that mechanization has contributed to the growth of landings of mackerel, elasmobranches and leognathus, but has caused a decrease in the output of sardines and catfishes (Table 2.7).

MECHANIZATION OF FISHING CRAFT AND FLUCTUATIONS IN FISH PRODUCTION

Mechanization can be expected to increase the duration of fishing, mainly by reducing the steaming time to reach the fishing grounds and back to the shore, and by increasing the number of fishing days during the season. The increase in the number of fishing days could be due to the ability of mechanized craft to fish in moderately rough weather conditions. These two factors may contribute to even out the fish production between monsoon and non-monsoon seasons of the year. Further, the catching of certain varieties of fish such as sardines, mackerel, catfish, etc., with shore-seiners during the

TABLE 2.6

Fish output and species composition in Gujarat (1961-1981)

(in '000 tonnes)

Year	Gap (years)	Elasmo-branches	Bombay Duck	Sciaenids	Pomfret	Seer fish	Crusta-ceans	Total landings
1963	—	6.53	65.89	2.47	7.27	0.59	3.66	102.04
1968	5	3.32	54.68	1.50	5.78	0.89	3.72	86.59
		(−9.83)	(−3.40)	(−7.85)	(−4.10)	(−10.17)	(0.33)	(−3.03)
1970	2	5.76	43.62	3.99	7.98	1.04	3.60	89.03
		(36.75)	(−10.11)	(83.0)	(19.03)	(8.43)	(−1.61)	(1.41)
1978	8	11.51	53.87	33.97	15.14	3.73	11.96	201.93
		(12.48)	(2.94)	(93.92)	(11.22)	(32.33)	(29.02)	(15.85)
1981	3	13.43	54.11	35.24	19.17	5.54	36.06	234.51
		(5.56)	(0.15)	(1.25)	(8.87)	(16.18)	(67.17)	(5.38)

Between 1961 and 1968	7	(6.98)	(—2.49)	(1.71)	(—0.77)	(13.97)	(2.27)	(—0.76)
Between 1968 and 1981	13	(23.42)	(—0.08)	(173.03)	(17.82)	(40.19)	(66.87)	(12.44)

Note: 1. Figures in parentheses indicate the annual percentage change over the preceding peak.
2. The negative sign for the annual percentage change over the preceding peak indicates the decrease in total landings.

Source: Central Marine Fisheries Research Institute, Cochin.

TABLE 2.7

Fish output and its species composition in peak years, Karnataka (1962-1981)

(in '000 tonnes)

Year	Gap (years)	Landings in the stated year of						
		Elasmo-branches	Catfish	Sardines	Leiagna-thus	Mackerel	Crusta-ceans	Total landings
1962		1.75	0.48	14.34	3.75	11.45	2.87	45.13
1964	2	0.86	0.60	85.85	0.42	7.26	1.36	104.22
		(—25.43)	(12.50)	(249.33)	(—44.4)	(—18.30)	(—26.31)	(65.47)
1968	4	1.54	4.47	54.98	1.46	5.74	5.44	87.82
		(19.77)	(161.25)	(—8.99)	(61.90)	(—5.20)	(75.00)	(—3.93)
1970	2	1.42	9.22	35.85	1.33	44.74	7.53	103.72
		(—3.90)	(53.13)	(—17.40)	(—3.77)	(339.72)	(19.21)	(9.05)
1973	3	1.69	2.37	16.66	2.66	35.47	9.17	91.48
		(6.34)	(—24.76)	(—17.84)	(33.33)	(—6.91)	(7.26)	(—3.93)
1978	5	2.05	2.83	49.28	4.24	50.70	9.22	152.86
		(4.26)	(3.88)	(39.16)	(11.88)	(8.59)	(0.11)	(13.42)

1981	3	4.07	7.50	70.94	1.64	19.77	13.49	153.39
		(32.84)	(55.01)	(14.65)	(—20.44)	(—20.34)	(15.44)	(0.12)
Between 1962 and 1968	6	(2.00)	(138.54)	(47.23)	(—10.18)	(—8.31)	(14.92)	(15.77)
Between 1968 and 1981	13	(12.64)	(5.21)	(2.23)	(0.95)	(18.80)	(11.38)	(5.74)

Note: 1. Figures in parentheses are annual per cent difference over the preceding peak.

2. The negative sign for the annual per cent change over the preceding year indicates decrease in total landings.

Source: Central Marine Fisheries Research Institute, Cochin.

early monsoon season when these species migrate closer to the shore contributes to the increased seasonal variations in fish production, while the introduction of purse-seiners which catch the same species throughout the year on the high seas can help even out the fish production between various seasons. Further, mechanization can also help reduce the annual variations in total landings.

For analysing the role of mechanization of fishing craft in reducing the fluctuations in fish production over the years, we have computed the share of monsoon landings in total landings. The share of monsoon fish landings in total landings of different states during four triannum periods between 1956 and 1978 is presented in Table 2.8. The share of monsoon landings at all India level has decreased from 19.25 per cent during 1956-58 to 15.22 per cent during 1970-72. Subsequently, the share of monsoon landings has increased to 21.76 per cent during 1976-78. However, the share of monsoon landings in total landings has increased at different rates between 1956-58

TABLE 2.8

Share of monsoon fish landings (1956-78)

State	Share (%)			
	1956-58	1966-68	1970-72	1976-78
1. West Bengal and Orissa	8.21	7.06	17.03	15.00
2. Andhra Pradesh	16.88	20.87	19.97	25.43
3. Tamil Nadu and Pondicherry	43.22	25.32	28.45	32.91
4. Kerala	29.01	27.13	21.89	31.48
5. Karnataka	9.65	7.65	6.57	52.58
6. Maharashtra	6.48	6.26	8.31	11.90
7. Gujarat	5.39	6.26	4.73	8.50
India	19.28	18.82	15.22	21.96

Note: 1. Data for 1978 not available so the landings from 1975 to 1977 are used for the calculation.

2. The share of three successive monsoon landings in the total of three annual landings has been worked out to even out annual fluctuations.

Source: Central Marine Fisheries Research Institute, Cochin.

and 1976-78 in Kerala, Karnataka, Maharashtra and Gujarat. Thus, we can infer that mechanization has helped reduce the seasonal variations.

Table 2.9 shows the statewise coefficients of variation for fishing efforts, fish catches and catch per unit effort during the pre- and post-mechanization periods. An analysis indicates that its fluctuations are high during the post-mechanization period as compared to the pre-mechanization period in the case of all maritime states except Maharashtra. In the case of Maharashtra the coefficient of variation during the post-mechanization period indicates that the fluctuations are less in amplitude as compared to the pre-mechanization period. The large fluctuations during the post-mechanization period are mainly because of underutilization of mechanized craft during the bad years for fishing, which in turn is mainly because of high operational coasts.[7] In view of the selective fishing, particularly during fish famine years, productivity in terms of catch per unit effort during the post-mechanized period is characterized by less fluctuations as compared to that of pre-mechanization period in all states except Gujarat. Also the fluctuations in output during the post-mechanization period are less as compared to those during the pre-mechanization period in all states except Gujarat.

MECHANIZATION OF FISHING CRAFT: THE CONTRIBUTING FACTORS

We will now discuss the context in which mechanization of fishing craft is taken place in India. First, mechanization may be taking place when human labour for fishing operations becomes costlier and fishermen desire to lessen the drudgery and hardness of work. Secondly, it may be taking place to expand the scope of fishery in terms of species and area and depth of operation. It may be even argued that mechanization is pursued with an objective to enhance the scope of fishing while it may be taking the form in which it is replacing the traditional form of production.

It may be counter-argued that how the cost of human labour as a source of energy can increase relative to that of the mechanical source when unemployment and underemployment is growing in the economy and when growth in the per capita income is negligible? Hanumantha Rao indicated that the

TABLE 2.9

Statewise coefficients of variation

State	Fishing effort			Fish catch			Catch per unit effort		
	1956-69	1970-81	1956-81	1956-69	1970-81	1956-81	1956-69	1970-81	1956-81
1. West Bengal and Orissa	43.50	51.03	63.60	58.98	44.75	74.32	46.63	23.45	37.44
2. Andhra Pradesh	24.16	36.82	21.57	29.11	26.29	40.32	44.65	27.50	46.38
3. Tamil Nadu	21.21	30.71	19.45	17.07	14.32	31.48	32.32	8.91	31.05
4. Kerala	41.65	25.92	34.27	24.47	17.31	24.12	38.48	27.49	33.51
5. Karnataka	35.06	80.83	34.65	43.39	22.73	41.96	63.33	25.52	49.95
6. Maharashtra	48.63	19.67	39.04	27.26	15.52	32.76	29.85	18.56	31.30
7. Gujarat	25.83	39.40	28.43	21.12	34.13	41.17	24.61	37.91	39.12
All India	24.50	34.71	20.77	13.89	11.00	27.29	28.39	12.18	25.72

Source: Central Marine Fisheries Research Institute, Cochin.

incentive for farm mechanization is provided by the rise in the prices of agricultural commodities as a result of rapid growth of population.[8] The same argument can be extended to the mechanization of fishing craft in the country.

Institutional credit and mechanization of fishing craft

Availability of institutional credit on liberal terms and a large amount of subsidy to the extent of one-third of the capital cost have encouraged modernization of fishing craft at a rapid rate. The rich from the fishermen and other communities were more inclined in view of high profitability of mechanized fishing.

The data on loans advanced by the Government of Gujarat to fishermen to acquire mechanized boats (till the end of 1972-73) indicate that over 85 per cent of the mechanized boats (excluding OBM boats) were bought with loans.[9] Interest on these loans was around 11 per cent and was much lower than the rate of interest charged on similar long-term loans by institutional agencies for other purposes. Thus, it implies that availability of institutional credit on liberal terms assisted in a rapid growth of mechanization of fishing craft. This, however, does not imply that high profitability of mechanization did not contribute to the rapid expansion.

Relative prices and wages in fisheries and modern inputs

The wholesale price index of fish has increased sevenfold in the course of less than a decade. Population pressure accompanied by the slow growth of domestic supplies of fish is one of the major factors for this steep increase. As the prices of fish rise the money value of wages paid in kind or in terms of share of total catch value also rises in the same proportion. Thus, the price indexes of fish can be a close approximation of the trend of wage rates of the crew in fisheries.

Table 2.10 gives the wholesale price indexes of fish and fuel prices. The fish price index has increased from 384.9 in 1971-72 (with 1961-62=100) to 2906.1 in 1981-82. In the same period the fuel price index increased from 172.1 to 691.7, a nearly four-fold increase. Although the fuel price has increased rapidly during the last decade, the fish prices have increased much faster. The price rise in the case of fish has been particularly

TABLE 2.10

Wholesale price indexes of fish and fuel oil

(1981-82=100)

Year	Fish	Fuel, power, etc.
1971-72	384.9	172.1
1972-73	484.7	180.7
1973-74	757.1	215.1
1974-75	1021.3	316.4
1975-76	1271.3	354.7
1976-77	1397.4	373.4
1977-78	1599.0	379.1
1978-79	1851.4	395.9
1979-80	2082.3	458.1
1980-81	2240.3	573.3
1981-82	2906.1	691.7

Source: Office of the Economic Adviser, Ministry of Industry, New Delhi.

steep after the fuel price increase during the past few years. Thus, the wholesale price index of wages in marine fisheries also increased at a very rapid rate as compared to fuel prices. In other words, the ever-increasing wage pattern at a very rapid rate may have motivated the boat owners to replace human source by mechanized source of energy.

REFERENCES

1. Mechanization is a continuous process and therefore a demarcation in the pre- and post-mechanization periods is very difficult. While the process of mechanization of fishing craft in the country started as early as 1950, it picked up very rapidly only after the Second Five-Year Plan. Only by the end of three annual plans (i.e. by about 1969) the number of mechanized boats increased to a position where their contribution in fish catch became significant. Therefore, we have taken 1969 as the cut-off year.
2. These growth rates have been obtained by fitting the regression equation $\log_e Y = a + bt$ (where Y=output, or effort or catch per

unit effort, a=constant, antilog$_e$ b= $\left(\frac{1+r}{100}\right)$ for r=growth rate and t=time) to the relevant series published by the Central Marine Fisheries Research Institute, Cochin.

3. A similar view has been expressed by C.H.H. Rao in his study of contribution of technological change to growth of output in Indian agriculture. He added that a production function analysis was ruled out at that time because of the non-availability of the relevant data and method of estimation. See C.H.H. Rao, *Technological Change and Distribution of Gains in Indian Agriculture* (Delhi: MacMillan, 1975), p. 6.
4. The method used is the one followed by Rao, Ibid.
5. Here we have assumed that ecological conditions influence marine fish production and the peak output in a given period is considered best in terms of ecology of the sea.
6. There are reasons to believe that even without the mechanization of fishing craft, the growth of fish output would have been maintained at about 3.5 per cent per annum. The availability of fishery resources within the reach of non-mechanized fishing craft owners would not have imposed any ceiling on the growth of fish landings, as the mechanized boats in the country also fished in the same areas. Further, the increasing prices of fish would have induced more fishermen to take up fishing.
7. During the bad years for fishing, the decision of fishermen operating the mechanized boats depends on their anticipation of catch quantity in a trip. The fishermen do not go fishing, if they expect that the returns may not be sufficient to cover their operating costs. In such situations the observation of off-season for fishing is somewhat earlier as compared to normal fishing year. See Srivastava, Reddy, and Gupta, op. cit., p. 129.
8. See Rao, op. cit., p. 35.
9. Evidence available from the Gujarat State Financial Corporation (GSFC) suggests that in recent years (from 1974-78) also the share of mechanized boats purchased through the loans from GSFC accounts for over 80 per cent of the boats inducted during the period under consideration. See Srivastava, Reddy, and Gupta, op. cit., p. 70.

3

Impact of Mechanization: Evidence from Village Studies

INTRODUCTION

As EXPLAINED in the previous chapter, the process of mechanization of Gujarat and Karnataka has been quite different. In Gujarat, mechanization began with motorization of traditional craft in 1953 followed by the introduction of trawlers. In Karnataka, mechanization started with the introduction of trawlers during 1957-58, followed by purse-seiners. Very little effort was made to motorize the non-mechanized craft in Karnataka since they were assumed[1] to be unsuitable for motorization. Contrary to this assumption, some of the enterprising fishermen of Karnataka successfully motorized their traditional craft during the early 80s.

The major objective of this chapter is to present the highlights of the village studies from Gujarat and Karnataka in a comparative framework. They cover the analysis of a large number of socio-economic variables and the changes that have occurred due to mechanization in the selected villages. Ideally, we should have assessed the changes due to mechanization by comparing the situation during the pre-mechnization period with that during the post-mechanization period in the same villages. In some cases there was a reasonably good data available to assess the changes due to mechanization and this has been presented in the respective village studies (Chapters 5 to 10). Since we did not have comparative historical data, some of the changes due to mechanization were assessed by comparing the situation in the control/low mechanized village with that in the medium and high medium and high mechanized villages.

Of the three sample villages in Gujarat, only Chorwad—a highly mechanized village--had trawlers, outboard motor

(OBM) boats and non-mechanized boats. The medium mechanized Hirakot village had only OBM and non-mechanized boats while in Bhadbhut—a control village—all the fishing craft were non-mechanized. There were 169 fishing craft in Chorwad and Hirakot villages of which 134 (76 per cent) were mechanized/motorized craft and the rest were non-mechanized. All the 119 fishing craft in Bhadbhut were non-mechanized. Only 5 of 134 mechanized craft in Chorwad and Hirakot were trawlers and all were in Chorwad.

In Karnataka all the three sample villages had purse-seiners and trawlers in addition to non-mechanized boats. Kadekar—a highly mechanized village—had 7.2 purse-seiners, 9.1 trawlers[2] and 40 non-mechanized boats while the control village of Idya had only 2 mechanized craft and 9 non-mechanized craft. The three villages put together owned about 120 craft of which 22.3 were mechanized. The mechanized craft in the villages consisted of 9 purse-seiners and 13 trawlers. All the purse-seiners and trawlers were operating on partnership basis and often some partners lived in villages not covered by the study (Table 3.1).

MECHANIZATION AND CHANGES IN SOCIO-ECONOMIC CHARACTERISTICS OF FISHERMEN

Changes in demographic characteristics

The various demographic characteristics analysed in this section include the family size and structure, rate of literacy and migration pattern. Average family size of different types of households in the selected villages of Gujarat and Karnataka is presented in Table 3.2. It is interesting to note that mechanized boat households had larger families as compared to crew and other households in both the states. On an average the size of a family amongst mechanized boat households was larger than the average of all the households together in both the states. Such a difference was more marked in the case of Gujarat as comparad to Karnataka. In Gujarat the average size of a family amongst the mechanized boat owners was 8.15 while it was 6.44 in the case of non-mechanized boat owners. In Karnataka the average family size was 7.9 for mechanized boat owners and 7.5 for non-mechanized boat owners. Further, it was also observed that the average family size of non-mechanized boat owners was

TABLE 3.1

Distribution of different types of boats present in different villages, Gujarat and Karnataka

Type of boat	Gujarat				Karnataka			
	Chorwad	Hirakot	Bhadbhut	Total	Kadekar	Bengre	Idya	Total
1. NMB (less than 25 ft.)	20	10	10	40	40	48	8	96
2. NMB (more than 25 ft.)	2	3	109	114	—	1	1	2
3. OBM (less than 25 ft.)	35	4	—	39	—	—	—	—
4. OBM (more than 25 ft.)	24	66	—	90	—	—	—	—
5. Rampani	—	—	—	—	—	—	1	1
6. Purse-seiner	—	—	—	—	13 (7.2)	3 (1)	2 (1)	18 (9.2)
7. Trawler	5	—	—	5	11 (9.1)	6 (3)	1 (1)	18 (13.1)
Total	86	83	119	288	64 (56.3)	58 (53.0)	13 (11)	135 (120.3)

Note: 1. (—) indicates nil.

2. Figures in parentheses in the case of Karnataka villages indicate the effective number of craft after discounting for the partner from other villages.

Source: Based on the data given in case studies (Chapters 5 to 10).

TABLE 3.2

Average family size of different types of households in selected villages of Gujarat and Karnataka

State/ Village	Average family size of				
	MB households	NMB households	Crew households	Other households	Of all households
Gujarat	8.15	6.44	5.82	5.05	6.70
(a) Chorwad	7.14	4.23	6.42	—	7.00
(b) Hirakot	8.97	6.00	6.07	5.21	6.96
(c) Bhadbhut	—	6.84	4.85	2.00	6.20
Karnataka	7.90	7.49	6.73	6.38	7.13
(a) Kadekar	8.82	8.80	6.78	8.00	7.92
(b) B. Bengre	6.30	6.00	6.05	5.37	6.24
(c) Idya	7.72	7.10	7.88	6.44	7.01

Note: (—) indicates nil.

Source: Compiled on the basis of information in the respective case studies (Chapters 5 to 10).

larger as compared to crew member households in Gujarat and Karnataka. There were 112 mechanized boat-owning households in Gujarat villages and 62 in Karnataka villages. In Gujarat 47 (41.96 per cent) had a family size of 10 and above while in Karnataka 21 (33.87 per cent) households belonged to the same category.

It was also observed that the large percentage of motor boat (MB) owner households had a joint family structure as compared to non-mechanized boat owners and crew member households. The majority of the crew member households had a nuclear family structure. Both features might have been dictated by the economic necessities in terms of supply of skilled and labour required for large fishing vessels. This aspect will be elaborated later while analysing labour market situation in the selected villages.

In general the literacy rate was higher in all Karnataka villages as compared to Gujarat villages, but no relationship was observed between level of mechanization and literacy levels amongst the selected villages. In fact, both in Gujarat and Karnataka control/low mechanized villages had a higher percentage of educated as compared to mechanized villages (Table 3.3). However, the comparison of the level of education across the different classes of households indicated that the rate of literacy was higher amongst the mechanized boat owner households compared to non-mechanized boat owners and crew member households.

For understanding the extent of long-term migration we elicited information regarding the birth place of all heads of households in the selected villages. The distribution is presented in Table 3.4. An overwhelming majority (72 in the case of Gujarat villages and 80.8 in the case of Karnataka villages) of the heads had their place of birth in the same village. Thus, it could be observed that the mechanization process did not attract entrepreneurs from other villages/states. Only in Hirakot, about half of the heads came from locations outside Gujarat. In all other selected villages inter-state migration of fishermen was found to be completely absent. However, it was observed that fishermen, particularly mechanized boat owners, moved around and sought temporary landing facilities in other villages in Gujarat. This might be done so as to reach better fishing grounds during different periods of the season.

In Karnataka short-term migration as described now was found to be completely absent amongst mechanized and non-mechanized boat owners. This aspect might be related to the nature of mechanization. For instance, it is easier to move around the coast in OBM boats with a crew of three persons per boat, who may be family members, as compared to trawlers and purse-seiners which require relatively a larger crew. In fact the trawler owners in Chorwad village did not seek temporary shifts in landing places, perhaps because of this reason. Also the capacity of trawlers and purse-seiners to stay on the high seas is considerably higher than OBMs and non-mechanized boats.

Occupational pattern of households

The majority of households were dependent on fishing and allied activities. The distribution of households is presented in Table 3.5. At an aggregate level there were 435 households in

TABLE 3.3

Population distribution according to level of education of different villages, Gujarat and Karnataka

Education level	Gujarat				Karnataka			
	Chorwad	Hirakot	Bhadbhut	Total	Kadekar	Bengre	Idya	Total
1. Illiterate	663	1082	727	2472	420	244	301	965
	(84.9)	(89.9)	(75.6)	(83.9)	(51.9)	(49.5)	(41.7)	(47.7)
2. Read-write	2	—	1	3	—	1	—	1
3. Primary	116	105	134	355	65	63	29	157
4. Middle	—	1	12	13	77	41	70	188
5. Higher Secondary	—	16	81	97	169	136	244	549
6. Graduation (—AB)	—	—	7	7	79	8	77	164
7. Number of educated	118	122	235	475	390	249	420	1059
	(15.1)	(10.1)	(24.4)	(16.1)	(48.2)	(50.5)	(58.3)	(52.3)
Total	781	1204	962	2947	810	493	721	2024
	(100)	(100)	(100)	(100)	(100)	(100)	(100)	(100)

Note: 1. (—) indicates nil.
2. Figures in parentheses are percentages to column total.

Source: Based on data given in the case studies (Chapters 5 to 10).

TABLE 3.4

Distribution of households based on birthplace location of the household head of different villages, Gujarat and Karnataka

Location of the birth place	Gujarat				Karnataka			
	Chorwad	Hirakot	Bhadbhut	Total	Kadekar	Bengre	Idya	Total
1. Same village	86 (80.4)	73 (42.2)	154 (99.4)	313 (72.0)	98 (95.1)	34 (43.0)	95 (96.0)	227 (80 8)
2. Outside the village	20 (18.7)	18 (10.4)	—	38 (8.7)	4 (3.9)	45 (57.0)	4 (4.0)	53 (18.9)
3. Outside the district	1 (0.9)	2 (1.2)	1 (0.6)	4 (0.9)	1 (1.0)	—	—	1 (0.3)
4. Outside the state	—	80 (46.2)	—	80 (18.4)	—	—	—	—
Total	107 (100)	173 (100)	155 (100)	435 (100)	103 (100)	79 (100)	99 (100)	281 (100)

Note: 1. (—) indicates nil.
2. Figures in parentheses are percentages to column total.

Source: Based on data given in the case studies (Chapters 5 to 10).

TABLE 3.5

Distribution of households and population according to occupational pattern of different villages, Gujarat and Karnataka

Type of household	Gujarat							
	Chorwad		Hirakot		Bhadbhut		Total	
	No. of households	Total population	No. of households	Total population	No. of households	Total population	No. of households	Total population
1. MB	50 (47.73)	402 (51.47)	62 (35.84)	550 (45.68)	—	—	112 (25.75)	952 (32.30)
2. NMB	17 (15.89)	122 (15.62)	11 (6.36)	66 (5.48)	107 (69.03)	732 (76.09)	135 (31.03)	920 (31.22)
3. Crew	40 (37.38)	257 (32.91)	81 (46.82)	489 (40.62)	47 (30.32)	228 (23.70)	168 (38.62)	974 (33.05)
4. Others	—	—	19 (10.93)	99 (8.22)	1 (0.65)	2 (0.21)	20 (4.60)	101 (3.43)
Total	107 (100)	781 (100)	173 (100)	1204 (100)	155 (100)	962 (100)	435 (100)	2947 (100)

TABLE 3.5 (*Contd.*)

	Karnataka							
	Kadekar		Bengre		Idya		Total	
	No. of households	Total population	No. of households	Total population	No. of households	Total population	No. of households	Total population
1. MB	23	200	6	38	33	249	62	487
	(22.33)	(24.69)	(7.60)	(7.71)	(33.33)	(34.54)	(22.06)	(24.06)
2. NMB	30	264	39	260	10	71	79	595
	(29.13)	(32.59)	(49.37)	(52.74)	(10.10)	(9.85)	(28.11)	(29.40)
3. Crew	42	282	18	109	9	74	69	465
	(40.70)	(34.82)	(22.78)	(22.11)	(9.09)	(10.26)	(24.56)	(22.97)
4. Others	8	64	16	86	47	327	71	477
	(7.76)	(7.90)	(20.25)	(17.44)	(47.48)	(45.35)	(25.27)	(23.57)
Total	103	810	79	493	99	721	281	2024
	(100)	(100)	(100)	(100)	(100)	(100)	(100)	(100)

Note: 1. (—) indicates nil.

2. Figures in parentheses are percentages to column total.

Source: Based on data given in the case studies (Chapters 5 to 10).

the sample villages of Gujarat from which 415 (95.40 per cent) were involved in fishing and allied activities, while in Karnataka there were 281 households in three selected villages of which only 210 (74.73 per cent) were involved in fishing and allied activities. The population dependent on fishing and allied activities accounted for 96.97 per cent in Gujarat villages while only 76.43 per cent accounted for in Karnataka villages. Further, there was no relationship between the level of mechanization and the number of non-fishing households. The number of non-fishing households decreased with increased level of mechanization.

Of the households dependent on fishing and allied activities in Gujarat villages, 247 (59.52 per cent) were owning boats and gear; and in Karnataka 141 households (67.14 per cent) were dependent on fishing and allied activities. In the case of Gujarat about 69 per cent of the households in Bhadbhut were owning fishing boats and gear. In the highly mechanized village of Chorwad 37 per cent of the households and in the medium-mechanized village of Hirakot 57.8 per cent of total households did not possess boats and gear. Further, the share of households without any fishing boats and gear was 40.7 per cent in Kadekar, 22.78 per cent in Bengre and 9.09 per cent in Idya. At an aggregate level such households accounted for 24.56 per cent of total households in the selected villages of Karnataka. Despite the promotion of partnership as a basis of ownership of boats, the proportion of boat-owning households was quite low in the Karnataka villages as compared to the Gujarat villages. The difference in the nature of mechanization in the two states might be responsible for the difference in the pattern of boat ownership.

Of the 247 boat-owning households, 112 households (45 per cent) owned mechanized/motorized boats in the selected villages of Gujarat. In Karnataka villages 62 of the 141 boat-owning households (443 per cent) owned or had partnership in mechanized boats. Of the 112 mechanized boat-owing households in Gujarat villages 50 were from Chorwad and the rest from Hirakot. In the case of Karnataka villages the distribution of mechanized-boat owning households was as follows: Kadekar 26, Bengre 6, Idya 33. The non-mechanized boat-owning households in Gujarat were maximum in Bhadbhut with 107 and was followed by Chorwad and Hirakot with 17 and 11 households respectively. There were 79 households owning non-mechanized craft in all the three selected villages of Karnataka of which 30 were from Kadekar, 39 from Bengre and 10 from Idya. In brief, while the spread of mechanization amongst the boat-owning households was similar between the two states, the distribution of mechanized boats was slightly more concentrated in Gujarat.

Distribution of fishing assets

Fishing boats and gear were the main form of fishing assets owned by the fishermen of the selected villages. It was observed that 288 fishing craft with necessary gear were owned by 247 households in the Gujarat villages while 120 fishing craft along with necessary fishing gear were owned by 141 households in the Karnataka villages. This clearly indicates the ownership of more than one boat alongwith necessary gear by households in Gujarat. In the case of Karnataka villages the number of boat-owning households was more than the number of fishing boats and gear in the villages due to partnership basis of owning mechanized craft.

For understanding the distribution inequality of fishing assets we have computed the Gini ratio[3] for the value of fishing assets.[4] The values of the Gini ratio are presented in Table 3.6.

TABLE 3.6

Gini ratios of fishing assets distribution in different sample villages, Gujarat and Karnataka

State/Village	Gini ratio
I. *Gujarat*	
Chorwad	0.6025
Hirakot	0.5648
Bhadbhut	0.3277
II. *Karnataka*	
Kadekar	0.8265
Bengre	0.8122
Idya	0.6151

Source: Compiled from the respective village studies (Chapters 5 to 10).

In general the inequality in owning of fishing assets was less in all the villages of Gujarat. Inequality of the ownership of fishing assets increased with the level of mechanization in the village. Inequality was the highest in Chorwad and Kadekar, two highly mechanized villages. The reasons for lesser inequality in the ownership of assets in the case of Gujarat villages as compared to the corresponding villages in Karnataka may again perhaps be the type of mechanization.

Ownership and distribution of other assets

Other assets of the households included the house, household articles, land and livestock. Fishermen in the villages of both states owned very few of such assets.

The distribution of households according to the value of owned house alongwith the share of mechanized boat owners is presented in Table 3.7. Most of the fishermen owned houses in the two states. In Gujarat about 56 per cent houses fell in the value category of Rs. 5,000 and above of which 29.29 per cent were owned by mechanized boat owners. Similarly, only 15.97 per cent of households owned houses valued at over Rs. 10,000 and the share of mechanized boat owners in this category was 32.25 per cent. Thus, on an aggregate basis, it may appear that valuewise ownership of houses was not associated with the mechanization process. This is confirmed when we look at different villages separately. In the highly mechanized village of Chorwad, 45.83 per cent of the total households owned houses in the value range of Rs 5,000 and above. The share of mechanized boat owners in this was 59.08 per cent. In Hirakot 47.92 per cent owned houses valued above Rs. 5,000 and the share of mechanized boat owners was 58.1 per cent. In the non-mechanized village of Bhadbhut 70 per cent owned houses valued at more than Rs. 5,000 and all were owned by non-mechanized boat owners and crew members.

In Karnataka at an aggregate level 57.67 per cent owned houses valued at over Rs. 5,000 and the share of mechanized boat owners was 37.03 per cent. Similarly 27.91 per cent owned houses worth Rs. 10,000 and above. The share of mechanized boat owners in this category was 46.6 per cent. It may be noted that in this respect Karnataka was quite different from Gujarat. Not only a greater percentage of houses fell in the category of

TABLE 3.7

Distribution of households according to the value of owned houses with percentage share of MB owners of different villages, Gujarat and Karnataka

Type	Gujarat								Karnataka							
	Chorwad		Hirakot		Bhadbhut		Total		Kadekar		Bengre		Idya		Total	
	Total	% share of MB owner	Total	% share of MB owner	Total	% share of MB owner	Total	% share of MB owner	Total	% share of MB owner	Total	% share of MB owner	Total	% share of MB owner	Total	% share of MB owner
Rented house	11	18.18	29	6.90	7	—	47	8.51	6	—	53	11.32	7	—	66	9.09
Owned:																
Less than 1000	3	—	9	11.11	—	—	12	8.33	33	9.09	12	—	3	66.67	48	10.41
1001-3000	25	32.00	23	26.09	12	—	60	23.33	10	10.00	6	—	3	33.33	19	10.52
3001-5000	24	58.33	45	31.11	32	—	101	27.72	11	18.18	4	—	9	11.11	23	13.04
5001-10000	26	53.84	59	54.39	70	—	155	29.03	24	20.83	2	—	38	34.22	64	28.01
10001 and above	18	66.66	10	80.00	34	—	62	32.25	19	63.16	2	—	39	41.01	60	46.66
Sub-total of owned houses	96	50.00	144	41.67	148	—	388	27.83	97	23 71	26	—	92	35.86	215	26.04
Total houses	107	46.72	173	35.84	155	—	435	25.74	103	22.33	79	7.59	99	33.33	281	22.06

Note: (—) indicates nil.
Source: Based on data given in the case studies (Chapters 5 to 10).

Rs. 10,000 and above, but the share of mechanized boat owners was also considerably higher in both categories.

The distribution of households according to the value of owned household articles was estimated and is given in Table 3.8. It was noticed that more than 40 per cent of the total households in all the villages owned such assets valued at less than Rs. 500. Further, it was noticed in most villages that only mechanized boat owners owned TV sets and other luxury items. The mechanized boat owners thus accounted for a much larger share in the value of other household assets. On the whole, it appeared that mechanized boat owners possessed assets of a much higher value than the non-mechanized boat owners and crew members in both the states. The only exception to it is the village Bhadbhut in Gujarat which is a non-mechanized village. The explanation for this exception to the general rule might be in the higher value estuarine fisheries undertaken in the village compared to marine fisheries in other villages.

Technology of gear and their distribution

In terms of changes in gear technology, it was observed that the early motorization of traditional craft in Gujarat did not bring about any drastic changes in the use of gill nets. Introduction of trawlers necessitated introduction of new types of nets, viz. trawl nets. In the case of Karnataka also the introduction of trawlers induced the use of trawl nets in addition to the gill nets, cast nets, rampani and kairampani nets used by traditional boat owners. Later, the introduction of purse-seiners brought about the use of purse-seine nets in the selected villages replacing the rampani nets. The distribution of different types of gear owned by different villages of Gujarat and Karnataka is presented in Table 3.9. Gill nets are only the type of nets which are operated from both mechanized and non-mechanized craft. Ownership of multiple type of nets was relatively high in the case of non-mechanized boats of Karnataka villages as compared to the Gujarat villages. Though the cast nets were owned both by the Karnataka and Gujarat fishermen, fishing with cast nets was predominant in Karnataka villages only. Further, hook and line, long line and encircling net fishing was unique for non-mechanized craft of Karnataka while stake net and drag net fishing was unique in Bhadbhut. The gear technology of

TABLE 3.8

Distribution of households according to the value of owned household articles of different villages, Gujarat and Karnataka

Frequency interval (Rs.)	Gujarat				Karnataka			
	Chorwad	Hirakot	Bhadbhut	Total	Kadekar	Bengre	Idya	Total
Up to 500	52 (48.50)	86 (49.71)	63 (40.64)	201 (46.20)	56 (50.4)	53 (67.0)	34 (34.3)	143 (50.9)
501-1000	21 (19.63)	28 (16.18)	34 (21.93)	83 (19.08)	12 (11.7)	11 (13.9)	16 (16.2)	39 (13.9)
1001-1500	7 (6.54)	15 (8.67)	16 (10.32)	38 (8.73)	7 (6.8)	7 (8.9)	6 (6.1)	20 (7.1)
1501-2000	4 (3.74)	9 (5.20)	13 (8.38)	26 (5.98)	7 (6.8)	3 (3.8)	9 (9.1)	19 (6.8)
2001-2500	5 (4.67)	11 (6.36)	10 (6.45)	26 (5.98)	4 (3.9)	—	6 (6.1)	10 (3.5)
2501-3000	4 (3.74)	1 (0.58)	4 (2.58)	9 (2.07)	2 (1.9)	1 (1.3)	2 (2.0)	5 (1.8)
3001-3500	1 (0.94)	5 (2.89)	4 (2.58)	10 (2.30)	5 (2.9)	—	4 (4.0)	7 (2.5)

3501-4000	1 (0.93)	2 (1.16)	—	3 (0.69)	2 (1.9)	1 (1.3)	10 (10.1)	13 (4.7)
4001-4500	1 (0.93)	3 (1.73)	2 (1.29)	6 (1.38)	2 (1.9)	1 (1.3)	4 (4.0)	7 (2.5)
4501-5000	1 (0.94)	3 (1.73)	—	4 (0.92)	3 (2.9)	—	2 (2.0)	5 (1.8)
5001-5500	2 (1.87)	—	1 (0.65)	3 (0.69)	4 (3.9)	2 (2.5)	6 (6.1)	10 (3.5)
5501-6000	—	—	2 (1.29)	2 (0.46)	—	—	—	—
6001-6500	3 (2.80)	1 (0.58)	1 (0.65)	5 (1.15)	—	—	—	—
6501-7000	—	3 (1.73)	1 (0.65)	4 (0.92)	—	—	—	—
7001-7500	1 (0.93)	2 (1.16)	2 (1.29)	5 (1.15)	—	—	—	—
7501-8000	—	1 (0.58)	—	1 (0.23)	—	—	—	—
8001-8500	1 (0.93)	—	—	1 (0.23)	—	—	—	—

TABLE 3.8 (*Contd.*)

8501-9000	—	1 (0.58)	—	1 (0.23)	—	—	—	—
9001-9500	—	—	—	—	—	—	—	—
9501-10000	1 (0.94)	—	1 (0.65)	2 (0.46)	—	—	—	—
10001 and above	2 (1.87)	2 (1.16)	1 (0.65)	5 (1.15)	—	—	—	—
Total	107 (100)	173 (100)	155 (100)	435 (100)	103 (100)	79 (100)	99 (100)	281 (100)

Note: 1. (—) indicates nil.
2. Figures in parentheses are percentages to column total.

Source: Based on data given in the case studies (Chapters 5 to 10).

TABLE 3.9

Distribution of different types of gear owned households* in different villages, Gujarat and Karnataka

Type of gear	Gujarat				Karnataka			
	Chorwad	Hirakot	Bhadbhut	Total	Kadekar	Bengre	Idya	Total
1. Gill nets	81	76	140	287	24	10	8	42
2. Cast nets	3	4	4	11	47	22	13	82
3. Shore-seine nets	—	—	—	—	1	—	1	2
4. Rampani nets	—	—	—	—	—	1	1	2
5. Trawler nets	5	—	—	5	11	6	1	18
6. Purse-seine nets	—	—	—	—	13	3	2	18
7. Encircling nets	—	—	—	—	—	4	—	4
8. Hookline nets	—	—	—	—	—	9	—	9
9. Longline nets	—	—	—	—	—	11	—	11
10. Stake nets	—	—	72	72	—	—	—	—
11. Drag nets	—	—	3	3	—	—	—	—

Note: 1. *Gill nets having different mesh sizes are present in the same households so the total number in the same village is differing in Tables 3.3, 3.4, and 3.5.

2. (—) indicates nil.

Source : Based on data given in the case studies (Chapters 5 to 10).

Karnataka villages with special reference to non-mechanized craft seems to be far more diversified as compared to that of Gujarat villages. The observed pattern of catch composition in Karnataka with a high share of small pelagic fishes during the post-mechanization period might be owing to a considerable fall in the number of non-mechanized craft having diversified gear technologies.

A comparison of mesh sizes of gill nets possessed by different types of boats indicated that gill nets used by mechanized boats in Gujarat have larger mesh sizes as compared to those with non-mechanized boats. While mechanized boats hardly used gill nets in Karnataka, non-mechanized boats using gill nets had a mesh size of up to 2 inches, which was much smaller than the mesh size used by similar boats in Gujarat (Table 3.10). It may thus be noted that the Gujarat fishermen did not attempt to catch very small size of fish for reasons of market considerations while in Karnataka, fishermen caught even the smallest fish as there was a market for it.

It was observed that the length of the gill nets used by non-mechanized boats in Gujarat was much smaller than the ones used by the mechanized boats in Gujarat. In the case of Karnataka villages, however, all the gill nets were less than 1,000 feet in length and were used by only non-mechanized boats. In Gujarat while OBM boats and mechanized gillnetters used nets ranging from 5,000 to 10,000 feet in length, the non-mechanized boats used lengths of 2,500 feet which is more than twice in length used in Karnataka (Table 3.11).

Further, two important changes took place in the area of subsidiary industries after motorization/mechanization. First, motorized craft began to use synthetic yarn in place of cotton yarn, resulting in closure of village industry producing cotton yarn, and providing subsidiary employment particularly to the womenfolk and non-seaworthy menfolk. Second, switch over to synthetic yarn resulted in the complete dependence of boat owners and other families engaged in net repairing upon the fish merchant for supply of synthetic yarn which also required large credit. It must be noted that synthetic nets are relatively very capital intensive. This dependence led to transactions often unfavourable to fishermen. This process is getting reinforced by the increasing tendency to replace manually mended nets by machine mended nets, a fact which might be clearly ascribed to the development of the mechanized sector.

IMPACT OF MECHANIZATION ON FISH PRODUCTION

Mechanization has had its impact on the quantity and value of landings. The species composition of total landings has also changed considerably.

In Gujarat, Bhadbhut is an estuarine village where there were some landings of prawns and lobsters even without the operations of mechanized craft. Comparison of landings in Hirakot and Chorwad indicated that introduction of trawlers

TABLE 3.10

Distribution of gill nets owned by households according to the mesh size in different villages, Gujarat and Karnataka

Mesh size (in inch)	Gujarat				Karnataka			
	Chorwad	Hirakot	Bhadbhut	Total	Kadekar	Bengre	Idya	Total
0-1.0	1 (0.9)	—	—	1 (0.3)	5 (20.8)	5 (29.4)	6 (66.7)	16 (32.0)
1.1-2.0	—	—	—	—	12 (50.0)	12 (70.6)	2 (22.2)	26 (52.0)
2.1-3-0	—	—	—	—	6 (25.0)	— —	—	6 (12.0)
3.1-4.0	51 (47.2)	45 (40.6)	47 (32.4)	143 (39.3)	1 (4.2)	—	—	1 (2.0)
4.1-5.0	19 (17.6)	1 (0.9)	65 (44.8)	85 (23.3)	—	—	1 (11.1)	1 (2.0)
5.1-6.0	7 (6.5)	17 (15.3)	16 (11.1)	40 (11.0)	—	—	—	—

TABLE 3.10 (*Contd.*)

6.1-7.0	29 (26.9)	1 (0.9)	10 (6.9)	40 (11.0)	—	—	—	—
7.1-8.0	1 (0.9)	47 (42.3)	7 (4.8)	55 (15.1)	—	—	—	—
8.1-9.0	—	—	—	—	—	—	—	—
Total	108 (100)	111 (100)	145 (100)	364 (100)	24 (100)	17 (100)	9 (100)	50 (100)

Note: 1. (—) indicates nil.

2. Figures in parentheses are percentages to column total.

Source: Based on data given in the case studies (Chapters 5 to 10).

TABLE 3.11

Lengthwise distribution of gill nets owned by households in different villages, Gujarat and Karnataka

Length (in feet)	Gujarat				Karnataka			
	Chorwad	Hirakot	Bhadbhut	Total	Kadekar	Bengre	Idya	Total
Less than 1000	5 (4.6)	8 (7.2)	38 (26.2)	51 (14.0)	24 (100.0)	17 (100.0)	9 (100.0)	48 (100.0)
1001-2000	38 (35.2)	26 (23.4)	58 (40.0)	122 (33.5)	—	—	—	—
2001-3000	40 (37.1)	21 (18.9)	30 (20.7)	91 (25.0)	—	—	—	—
3001-4000	20 (18.5)	13 (11.7)	10 (6.9)	43 (11.8)	—	—	—	—
4001-5000	—	13 (11.7)	6 (4.1)	19 (5.2)	—	—	—	—
5001-6000	3 (2.8)	18 (16.2)	3 (2.1)	24 (6.6)	—	—	—	—

TABLE 3.11 (*Contd.*)

6001-7000	—	1 (0.9)	—	1 (0.3)	—	—	—	—
7001-8000	—	6 (5.5)	—	6 (1.6)	—	—	—	—
8001-9000	1 (0.9)	1 (0.9)	—	2 (0.6)	—	—	—	—
9001-10000	1 (0.9)	4 (3.6)	—	5 (1.4)	—	—	—	—
Total	108 (100)	111 (100)	145 (100)	364 (100)	24 (100)	17 (100)	9 (100)	48 (100)

Note: 1. (—) indicates nil.

2. Figures in parentheses are percentages to column total.

Source: Based on data given in the case studies (Chapters 5 to 10).

resulted in catches of high-value prawns and lobsters on the one hand and large catches of low-value species often termed as "trash" on the other. Catch composition has, therefore, changed substantially in the post-mechanization period mainly due to the introduction of trawlers. Introduction of OBM boats, however, did not affect the species composition, but resulted in increased levels of catches. On the whole, mechanization has led to an overall increase in the production level. The total catch increased by about 5.5 per cent per annum in the post-mechanization period.

In Karnataka, the increase in landing in terms of quantity on the whole was not very substantial. There were some increases in the landings of prawns and lobsters with the introduction of trawlers. The substantial part of the catches of purse-seiners introduced in the post-mechanization period were offset by the reduction or disappearance of catches from traditional rampanis. Mechanization, therefore, has not led to substantial increases in fish production in Karnataka (Table 3.12).

Comparing Gujarat and Karnataka, it then appears that the type of boats introduced has been responsible for the variations. Introduction of trawlers, mechanized gillnetters and OBMs led to substantial increases in the catch in both value and quantity. In the case of Karnataka, introduction of purse-seiners, on the other hand, did not lead to any increase in the catch. In fact, catch per unit effort declined in the post-mechanization period in Karnataka. This is also confirmed by the capital-output ratio which is considerably higher in the case of Karnataka as compared to Gujarat. This aspect is analysed later.

In terms of value, while the catches have gone up substantially in Gujarat and Karnataka, a substantial increase in the value of landings with a marginal increase in the catch in the Karnataka villages points to the price rise factor reflected in such values only (Table 3.13).

In the selected villages of Karnataka, there have been less fluctuations in catches during the post-mechanization period. One contribution of mechanization has, thus, been perhaps greater stability in production.

TABLE 3.12

Specieswise estimated marine fish landings during pre-mechanization (1968-69) and current (1981-82) periods of villages, Gujarat and Karnataka

(Quantity in tonnes)

	Gujarat (Landings during current period)									Karnataka (Landings during current period)					
	Chorwad		Hirakot		Bhadbhut		Pre-mechanization								
Species	Total	% share of MB owners	Total	% share of MB owners	Total	% share of MB owners	Kadekar Total	Bengre Total	Idya Total	Kadeker Total	% share of MB owners	Bengre Total	% share of MB owners	Idya Total	% share of MB owners
1. Pomfret	188.4	81.6	280	95.00	—	—	8	2	1	75	82 67	7	85.71	4	100.00
2. Seer fish	115.9	73.86	113	93.80	—	—	46	4	2	57	43.86	12	73.00	12	75.00
3. Hilsa	106.7	74.79	92	94.57	108.26	—	—	—	—	—	—	—	—	—	—
4. Clupeids	130.6	84.76	61	95.08	94.79	—	—	—	27	—	—	—	—	18	66.67
5. Sharks and rays	80.70	93.06	71	91.55	9.69	—	—	87	—	—	—	24	66.69	—	—
6. Prawns and Lobsters	25.80	100.0	—	—	74.88	—	8	3	—	37	94.59	17	94.12	7	100.00

7. Dhoma	396.9	100.0	—	—	—	—	—	—	—	—	—	—	—	—	—
8. Eel	30.1	100.0	—	—	—	—	—	—	—	—	—	—	—	—	—
9. Sardines	—	—	—	—	—	—	908	506	242	1257	95.78	345	59.42	295	89.15
10. Mullets	—	—	—	—	57.09	—	—	—	—	—	—	—	—	—	—
11. Mackerel	—	—	—	—	—	—	576	124	129	628	87.58	111	37.84	163	82.82
12. Bombay Duck	—	—	—	—	54.93	—	—	—	—	—	—	—	—	—	—
13. Catfish	—	—	—	—	52.24	—	188	103	59	350	93.71	115	68.70	95	92.63
14. Jew fish	—	—	—	—	52.78	—	—	—	—	—	—	—	—	—	—
15. Carangids	—	—	—	—	—	—	—	54	42	—	—	25	60.00	76	94.74
16. Silver belly	—	—	—	—	—	—	—	3	21	—	—	61	100.00	39	82.05
17. Others	66.6	81.33	119	93.61	33.94	—	418	206	105	692	98.12	258	42.25	58	81.03
Total	1141.7	88.67	736	94.00	538.60	—	2162	1092	628	3096	93.12	975	57.23	767	87.22

Note: (—) indicates nil.

Source: Based on data given in the case studies.

TABLE 3.13

Specieswise estimated value of landings during pre-mechanization (1968-69) and current (1981-82) periods of villages, Gujarat and Karnataka

(in '000 Rupees)

Species	Gujarat (Landings during current period)						Pre-mechanization period		
	Chorwad		Hirakot		Bhadbhut				
	Total	% share of MB owners	Total	% share of MB owners	Total	% share of MB owners	Kadekar Total	Bengre Total	Idya Total
1. Pomfret	1653.20	86.14	2291.0	94.54	—	—	7.7	2.26	0.51
2. Seer fish	695.40	73.86	678.0	93.81	—	—	66.5	5.17	2.07
3. Hilsa	483.50	82.52	460.0	94.56	784.89	—	—	—	—
4. Clupeids	587.70	84.76	274.5	95.08	450.25	—	—	—	24.81
5. Sharks and rays	261.46	93.04	284.0	91.55	29.07	—	—	71.69	—
6. Prawns and Lobsters	645.00	100.00	—	—	433.99	—	33.3	6.26	—
7. Dhoma	198.45	100.00	—	—	—	—	—	—	—
8. Eel	82.78	100.00	—	—	—	—	—	—	—
9. Sardines	—	—	—	—	—	—	158.9	118.91	37.70
10. Mullets	—	—	—	—	371.09	—	—	—	—

11. Mackerel	—	—	—	—	—	—	592.7	113.58	52.41
12. Bombay Duck	—	—	—	—	123.59	—	—	—	—
13. Catfish	—	—	—	—	52.24	—	118.1	63.14	41.72
14. Jew fish	—	—	—	—	448.63	—	—	—	—
15. Carangids	—	—	—	—	—	—	—	50.44	11.81
16. Silver belly	—	—	—	—	—	—	—	0.96	8.43
17. Others	133.20	81.83	238.0	89.92	84.85	—	188.1	54.71	24.55
Total	4740.69	86.77	4225.50	94.00	3096.75	—	1165.3	487.12	240.01

TABLE 3.13 (*Contd.*)

Species	Karnataka (Landings during current period)					
	Total	% share of MB owners	Total	% share of MB owners	Total	% share of MB owners
1. Pomfret	467.3	82.67	44.74	85.72	41.56	100.00
2. Seer fish	313.5	43.86	43.91	74.99	46.31	74.99
3. Hilsa	—	—	—	—	—	—
4. Clupeids	—	—	—	—	72.00	66.67
5. Sharks and rays	—	—	87.62	66.67	—	—
6. Prawns and Lobsters	512.5	94.60	216.07	94.12	105.00	100.00
7. Dhoma	—	—	—	—	—	—
8. Eel	—	—	—	—	—	—
9. Sardines	729.1	95.79	178.37	59.42	167.50	89.15
10. Mullets	—	—	—	—	—	—
11. Mackerel	2346.7	87.66	289.93	37.84	605.15	82.82
12. Bombay Duck	—	—	—	—	—	—
13. Catfish	420.0	93.71	100.74	68.69	83.27	92.63

14. Jew fish	—	—	—	—	—	—
15. Carangids	—	—	78.00	60.62	108.31	94.74
16. Silver belly	—	—	63.14	100.00	59.86	82.06
17. Others	539.8	98.11	274.51	42.25	108.16	81.04
Total	5330.9	83.92	1377.03	61.28	1397.12	85.63

Note: (—) indicates nil.
Source: Based on data given in the case studies (Chapters 5 to 10).

MECHANIZATION AND CHANGES IN MARKETING PATTERN

Motorization of traditional craft has led neither to any major changes in the catch composition nor in the use flow. However, after the introduction of trawlers in Chorwad three major changes seemed to have taken place in the use flow. First, a small percentage of exportable varieties has developed. Second, a very large portion of the catch has begun to go for fishmeal and oil extraction in the post-mechanization period. Third, it has also resulted in the overall decline in fresh fish consumption as well as in sun-drying and salt-curing. It may be noted that in Hirakot the fresh consumption has increased while the sun-drying and salt-curing has decreased. These findings are in consonance with the macro analysis. Earlier studies have pointed out that in Gujarat the share of fishmeal has considerably increased and so also the share of exports but the share of fresh fish consumption has decreased owing to the nature of mechanization of the fishing craft.

In Karnataka it was observed that there had been an increase in the percentage of fish going for fresh fish consumption during the post-mechanization period particularly in Kadekar and Idya villages. In the case of Bengre, however, the share of fresh fish consumption declined to 52.98 per cent from 60.59 per cent in the post-mechanization period. Thus, on the whole there seems to be a general increase in the share of fish going for fresh consumption and reduction in the share of fish going for sun-drying and salt-curing. The share of fish going for fishmeal and oil extraction has also declined during the post-mechanization period. Further, there has been an increase in the share of exportable varieties in all the three villages of Karnataka (Table 3.14).

While the general increase in the share of exportable varieties in total landings during the post-mechanization period over the pre-mechanization period may be attributed to the mechanization of fishing craft, particularly the introduction of trawlers, the increase in the share of fresh fish consumption might not be directly attributed to the mechanization of fishing craft. It is our contention that the increase in the share of fresh fish consumption during the post-mechanization period has occurred mainly because of the improvements in the infrastructure such

TABLE 3.14

Percentage share of marine fish utilization during pre- and post-mechanization periods of different villages, Gujarat and Karnataka

Particulars	Gujarat						Karnataka					
	Chorwad		Hirakot		Bhadbhut		Kadekar		Bengre		Idya	
	Pre-mech. period	Post-mech. period	Pre-mech. period	Post-mech. period	Pre-mech. period	Post-mech. period	Pre-mech. period	Post-mech. period	Pre-mech. period	Post-mech. period	Pre-mech. period	Post-mech. period
1. Fresh consumption	62.5	50.7	70.0	80.0	—	71.2	42.5	54.5	60.59	52.98	42.86	52.55
2. Drying/curing	37.5	14.5	30.0	17.0	—	18.4	32.8	25.6	20.76	21.00	32.86	26.35
3. Fishmeal/oil extraction	—	32.5	—	—	—	5.6	23.4	16.3	18.63	23.76	23.22	19.35
4. Export (freezing/canning/ drying)	—	2.3	—	3.0	—	4.8	1.3	3.6	0.02	2.26	1.05	1.75
Total	100	100	100	100	—	100	100	100	100	100	100	100

Note: (—) indicates nil.

Source: Based on data given in the case studies (Chapters 5 to 10).

as extensive availability of ice and cold storage facilities, faster transport and better handling facilities. Further, the share has increased at the expense of a decline in dry fish through sun-drying and salt-curing. It may further be argued that the major impetus for the development of ice and cold storage has been received from the bulk landings of centralized fishing harbours as a result of the mechanization programme. Therefore, the mechanization of fishing craft has only indirectly contributed to the increase in the share of fresh fish consumption.

The analysis presented in the village studies indicated that the mechanization has brought many changes in the marketing practices also.

First, the sale of fish by weight has become the generally accepted practice in the case of precious varieties such as prawns, lobsters, pomfrets and seer fish in most of the selected villages. It is, however, not to suggest that the sale of fish by other means such as count or lot has completely vanished from the marketing system. In fact some of the varieties such as mackerel and scienide are still generally sold either by count or by lot. However, there is a definite shift to weighing and grading. It is a very welcome development from the fisherman's point as it has resulted in a considerable improvement in the fishermen's share of the consumer rupee.

Second, it has been observed that introduction of mechanized craft particularly trawlers in Gujarat and trawlers and purse-seiners in Karnataka caused a shift in the marketing activity. New assembly-cum-landing centres have been developed. In Karnataka, a substantial portion of the marketing activity shifted to Malpe or Mangalore, the nearest ports with modern landing and berthing facilities for mechanized craft. As a result of this, the number of marketing intermediaries operating in the selected villages declined in the post-mechanization period. In almost all the villages, a large number of intermediaries belonging to the fishermen community shifted to the marketing centres. Often there was now a stronger interlocking between production and marketing. The commission agents and wholesalers who do not often belong to the fishermen community tend to dominate the scene now for reasons of supply of capital required for the mechanized craft and for developing distant markets for the produce. Although data in regard to disposal of catch could not be analysed, it appeared that almost 70 to 80 per cent of the catch in various use flows passed through commission agents and wholesalers.

In spite of the presence of wholesalers/commission agents in the village community for several decades, the fishermen were ready to develop ties with a co-operative organization which offered similar facilities as offered by the commission agents/wholesalers on more reasonable terms. This is thus a significant change in the attitude towards the intermediaries.

Another important feature was the introduction of transportation facilities. In the pre mechanization period, the predominant mode of transportation was either headloads or bicycles/rickshaws. In the post-mechanization period, owing to more centralized landings, motors, trucks and other automobiles have been introduced. The necessity for a faster and larger means of transport has arisen mainly because of large landings of fish which have to be sent to the interior markets as fast as possible so that the freshness of fish may be preserved.

Owing to the shift in the location of landings and changes in the marketing activity, two changes in the structure of fish markets were noted. As stated earlier, the volume of the catch in the village landing centres particularly in Karnataka declined and attracted very few traders. Thus, an oligopolistic market situation resulted in reduced prices for the fishermen. On the other hand a sort of glut situation[5] has been created in the landing-cum-assembly centres, to which the operations of the mechanized craft have shifted. The glut has also resulted in reduced prices to the fishermen. Thus, in both cases, mechanization has resulted in either less prices or less catches or both for non-mechanized boat owners. Reduced prices have also effected the realization of the mechanized boat owners. What needs to be stressed here is the fact that market risks have become higher for the traditional craft owners as compared to mechanized boat owners. The traditional small fishermen located away from market centres get bypassed and are often at a greater disadvantage today.

ACCRUAL AND DISTRIBUTION OF INCOME

We attempted to estimate incomes from various types of boats in selected villages. The income from non-fishing sources for the boat-owning households were also estimated. Finally, the incomes of the crew member households working on mechanized and non mechanized boats were also obtained on the basis of the village data and economics of different types of boats in thev illage. Villagewise net incomes for different types of boats for both Gujarat and Karnataka are presented in Table 3.15. In the case of boat-owning households, lowest incomes were earned by non-mechanized boat owners having the boats of lengths less than 25 feet in the Karnataka villages. The highest net incomes were earned by purse-seiner owners of the Karnataka villages. Further, trawler owners of Chorwad in Gujarat earned more than their counterparts in all Karnataka villages, because of both higher unit value realization and higher catches.

In almost all cases the mechanized boat owners earned higher per capita and per household income. The second highest per capita income was earned by non-mechanized boat owners both in Gujarat and Karnataka villages except in Hirakot village, where the crew working on mechanized boats earned higher per capita and per household income. It was also observed that average per capita incomes of crew member households in mechanized villages were substantially higher than those of control villages except in Idya in Karnataka. Per capita and per household incomes were generally higher in Gujarat compared to Karnataka villages (Table 3.16). Further, a break-up of the total earnings of crew member households from non-mechanized craft and mechanized craft revealed that the crew households working on mechanized craft particularly on trawlers and purse-seiners earn more than those working on non-mechanized craft.

For comparing the incomes of crew in mechanized craft and non-mechanized boat owners we have computed annual earnings[6] and presented in Table 3.17. Such a comparison of incomes indicated that the earnings of crew members of mechanized craft were significantly higher as compared to the earnings of non-mechanized boat owners. In the case of Gujarat villages the earnings of the crew even in OBM boats were higher than the earnings of smaller size non-mechanized craft. However, owners of larger size non-mechanized craft (25 feet and above)

TABLE 3.15

Net Income from different types of boats of different villages, Gujarat and Karnataka

State/Village	NMB of length		OBM of length		Rampani	Trawler	Purse-seiner
	less than 25 ft.	more than 25 ft.	less than 25 ft.	more than 25 ft.			
I. *Gujarat*							
Chorwad	5622.65	5622.65	8566.25	9641.25	—	27289.25	—
Hirakot	7220.25	3575.50	8898.00	8898.00	—	—	—
Bhadbhut	3813.00	6827.50	—	—	—	—	—
II. *Karnataka*							
Kadekar	2358.00	—	—	—	—	15143.25	94575.00
Bengre	2018.00	2018.00	—	—	—	14271.00	78754.00
Idya	2519.00	—	—	—	—	4602.00	90267.00

Note: (—) indicates nil.

Source: Based on data given in the case studies (Chapters 5 to 10).

TABLE 3.16

Distribution of per capita and per household income according to occupation in Gujarat and Karnataka

Occupation	Gujarat						Karnataka					
	Chorwad		Hirakot		Bhadbhut		Kadekar		Bengre		Idya	
	PC	PH	PC	PH	PC	PH	PC	PH	PC	PH	PC	PH
1. MBO	4181	36182	2780	24690	—	—	3653	49159	3144	19915	1973	14886
2. NMBO	1914	13736	1590	9530	2392	16363	2095	19435	1864	12428	1398	9923
3. CRM	1947	11873	1890	11390	796	3866	1611	10817	1194	7229	1328	10922
4. Others	—	—	1760	3970	3750	7500	1010	8078	1666	8957	1021	7102
Total	3059	22330	2910	15220	2017	12516	2719	21385	1700	11189	1418	10329

Note; 1. (—) indicates nil.

2. PC=Per Capita Income.

3. PH=Per Household Income.

Source: Based on data given in the case studies (Chapters 5 to 10).

TABLE 3.17

Estimated annual earnings of crew in mechanized boats and owners of non-mechanized boats in selected villages, Gujarat and Karnataka

(*in Rupees*)

State/Village	Estimated earnings of				
	Crew in purse-seiner	Crew in trawler	Crew in OBM boat	NMB owner* of boat size up to 25 ft.	NMB owner* of boat size 25 ft. and above
I. *Gujarat*					
Chorwad	—	6600	7164	—	10908 (5622)
Hirakot	—	—	8444	7592 (4872)	10271 (6696)
Bhadbhut	—	—	—	6535 (3813)	10554 (6827)
II. *Karnataka*					
Kadekar	6065	6616	—	5335 (2358)	—
Bengre	5677	6918	—	5196 (1034)	—
Idya	5720	6760	—	6199 (2519)	—

Note: 1. (–) indicates not applicable.

2. *includes the earnings of one crew (owner-operator of boat).

3. Figures in parentheses of last two columns indicate the earnings of non-mechanized boat owners excluding the returns to family members working as crew.

Source: Compiled from the data given in case studies (Chapters 5 to 10).

earned significantly higher than those of the crew in OBM boats. It is quite interesting to note that the returns to the crew in trawlers of Chorwad were lower than those of the crew in OBM boats. The crew in trawlers worked for less than the going wage rate in OBM boats, perhaps because of the following reasons:

The trawler crew of Gujarat usually is employed on a fixed wage while the crew in OBM boats had a share in the catch. The fluctuations in the catch from day to day induced a certain degree of risk in the case of the earnings of the OBM boat crew while the trawler crew faced no such uncertainties. It appears that the earnings are related to the amount of risk undertaken. Further, earnings of the OBM crew of Gujarat were higher compared to the earnings of the trawler and purse-seiner crew in Karnataka.

When we look at the overall income distribution in the villages, the picture is as follows:

About 46.9 per cent households owning mechanized craft generated and controlled 70.35 per cent of the total village income in Chorwad. On the other hand, 15.71 per cent households owning non-mechanized craft generated and controlled only 9.7 per cent of the village income. In the case of Hirakot village 35 per cent of the households owning mechanized craft controlled 58.1 per cent of the total village income. Similarly, 6.3 per cent non-mechanized boat owners generated and controlled only 3.9 per cent of the village income. In the case of Karnataka village in Kadekar 22.3 per cent owning mechanized craft generated and controlled 51.3 per cent of the village income. It was more or less same in other villages. On the whole, the share of mechanized boats in the total village income was higher in Karnataka than in Gujarat (Table 3.18).

Savings and investments

In Gujarat, the savings rate was 24.08 per cent in the Chorwad village, while it was 27.83 per cent in Bhadbhut—the non-mechanized village. The poorest in the savings rate was Hirakot having only 9.8 per cent. As stated earlier, the comparison should in fact be only between Chorwad and Hirakot as Bhadbhut represented an exceptionally high rewarding, high income fishing operations in estuarine fishing. In Karnataka the savings rate in Kadekar—the highly mechanized village—was 55.1 per cent. On the whole the Karnataka villages had a higher savings rate compared to the Gujarat villages. It may be hypothesized that larger disparities in income and assets distribution at relatively low levels of developments led to higher rates of savings.

Further, within the villages, the mechanized boat owners

TABLE 3.18

Distribution of income and consumer expenditure by occupation of different villages, Gujarat and Karnataka (1981-82)

(in '000 Rupees)

State/Village	Income					Expenditure				
	MBO	NMBO	Crew	Others	Total	MBO	NMBO	Crew	Others	Total
1	2	3	4	5	6	7	8	9	10	11
I. *Gujarat*										
Chorwad	1680.91	233.51	474.91	—	2389.34	1038.81	236.90	528.10	—	1813.81
	(70.36)	(9.77)	(9.88)		(100)	(57.27)	(13.61)	(29.12)		(100)
Hirakot	1530.86	104.79	922.17	75.40	2633.22	1095.82	134.50	956.91	186.85	2374 17
	(58.14)	(3.98)	(35.02)	(2.86)	(100)	(46.16)	(5.66)	(40.31)	(7.87)	(100)
Bhadbhut	—	1750.79	181.71	7.50	1940.00	—	1092.11	298.16	9.28	1399.55
		(90.25)	(9.37)	(0.38)	(100)		(78.03)	(21.30)	(0 67)	(100)
II. *Karnataka*										
Kadekar	1130.67	553.05	454.31	64.62	2202.65	266.95	299.46	344.57	77.09	988.07
	(51.38)	(25.11)	(20.63)	(2.93)	(100)	(27.02)	(30.31)	(34.87)	(7.80)	(100)
Bengre	119.49	484.71	130.12	143.32	877.64	84.13	369.36	154.38	142.72	750.59
	(13.61)	(55.23)	(14.83)	(16.33)	(100)	(11.21)	(49.21)	(20.57)	(19.01)	(100)
Idya	491.25	99.23	48.30	333.80	1022.58	267.36	89.60	80.65	393.77	831.38
	(48.04)	(9.70)	(9.62)	(32.64)	(100)	(32.16)	(10.78)	(9.70)	(47.36)	(100)

TABLE 3.18 (*Contd.*)

State/Village	Savings				
	MBO	NMBO	Crew	Others	Total
	12	13	14	15	16
I. *Gujarat*					
Chorwad	642.10	—3.39	—53.19	—	575.53
Hirakot	435.04	—29.80	—34.74	—111.45	259.05
Bhadbhut	—	658.68	16.45	—1.78	540.45
II. *Karnataka*					
Kadekar	863.72	253.59	109.74	—12.47	1214.58
Bengre	35.36	115.35	—24.26	8.60	127.05
Idya	223.89	9.63	17.65	—59 59	191.20

Note: 1. (—) indicates nil.
2. Figures in parentheses represent percentages to row total.

Source: Based on data given in the case studies (Chapters 5 to 10).

had a relatively much higher rate of savings as compared to non-mechanized boat owners as well as crew members. In fact in the case of Chorwad and Hirakot these segments had dis-savings (Table 3.18).

The higher savings rate also manifested in higher investments. The highly mechanized village of Chorwad having the highest savings rate had also the highest growth in the investments as depicted by the growth of mechanized fishing craft. A similar pattern was observed in the case of Karnataka.

Income distribution

The income distribution according to occupation classes does not throw much light on the impact of mechanization in selected villages. We have computed the Gini ratios for understanding the income distribution and are presented in Table 3.19.

TABLE 3.19

Gini ratios for income distribution in selected villages, Gujarat and Karnataka (1982)

State/Village	Gini ratio for income distribution
I. *Gujarat*	
Chorwad	0.3207
Hirakot	0.1973
Bhadbhut	0.2345
II. *Karnataka*	
Kadekar	0.5048
Bengre	0.3136
Idya	0.3135

Two important observations can be made. First, the income inequality in the Gujarat villages was much less than in the Karnataka villages. Second, the income inequality in each of the villages was lower than the asset inequality in the respective villages. This may be explained by the fact that mechanized boats give rise to employment of crew who while not possessing the assets in the same measure, share in the income generated through the assets. Further, the income inequality was more in the highly mechanized villages compared to less mechanized villages in Gujarat and Karnataka, as would be expected.

The Gini ratios of income distribution in Chorwad, Hirakot, Bhadbhut, Bengre and Idya were comparable to another agricultural village in Uttar Pradesh in the process of agricultural development.[7] Our ratios are lower than the ratios estimated for developing countries.[8] In brief it can be concluded that mechanization of fishing industry did not lead to larger than expected income inequalities. However, there seems to be an exception in the case of the highly mechanized Kadekar which has a relatively high income inequality. It may be noted that the village has an average 17.7 h.p. per household which was almost of the village Chorwad—the highly mechanized village in Gujarat. It can be postulated, therefore, that perhaps high degree of mechanization which results in concentration of productive assets leads to disparities in the distribution. The observation relates to investments in purse-seiners, trawlers vs. outboard motor boats.

ITEMWISE ANNUAL CONSUMPTION EXPENDITURE

Itemwise annual consumption expenditure of all households alongwith the share of MB owner households in the selected villages of Gujarat and Karnataka is presented in Table 3.20. The consumer expenditure on food items ranged between 73 per cent of the total in Chorwad and 77 per cent in Hirakot. Among the food items foodgrains, edible oils and fish accounted for the bulk of the total. In the case of Karnataka villages the expenditure on food items accounted for over 77 per cent of total in the case of Kadekar and Bengre and about 70 per cent in the case of Idya. Further, it was observed that the share of MB owners in the total consumer expenditure was greater than average in almost all the selected villages of Gujarat and Karnataka.

In terms of per capita and per household consumer expenditure, it was observed that villages with medium and higher degrees of mechanization in Gujarat and Karnataka had a higher per capita and per household expenditure than those in the non-mechanized or no-mechanization villages. The per capita consumer expenditure in both Gujarat and Karnataka

TABLE 3.20

Itemwise annual consumption expenditure (by total households with percentage share of MB owners) of different villages, Gujarat and Karnataka

(in '00 Rupees)

Item	Gujarat						Karnataka					
	Chorwad		Hirakot		Bhadbhut		Kadekar		Bengre		Idya	
	Total	% share MB owner	Total	% share MB owner	Total	% share MB owner	Total	% share MB owner	Total	% share MB owner	Total	% share MB owner
I. Food Items:												
Foodgrains	364.78	58.56	651.72	47.08	306.85	—	346.53	23.32	232.18	10.75	294.27	35.87
Milk and milk products	45.50	53.14	88.82	46.89	51.64	—	29.48	31.58	31.51	14.19	26.57	24.65
Edible oils	310.35	56.56	425.00	49.36	179.25	—	50.49	29.35	49.29	7.28	26.47	27.31
Meat and Chicken	11.70	35.13	66.87	44.86	5.62	—	—	—	—	—	—	—
Eggs	—	—	2.34	33.33	—	—	—	—	—	—	—	—
Fish	276.07	68.27	432.07	48.12	225.15	—	144.97	28.19	147.11	12.37	93.97	35.64
Vegetables	35.15	55.02	77.00	41.47	48.16	—	36.92	30.28	21.57	5.28	33.13	33.44
Fruits and Nuts	21.32	76.83	1.61	16.15	23.46	—	31.24	36.78	14.19	19.80	19.81	28.62

TABLE 3.20 (*Contd.*)

Sugar, Gur and Khandsari	112.89	54.86	182.41	43.10	98.28	—	16.69	26.03	15.70	7.96	16.54	24.85
Salt and Spices	74.67	55.36	83.92	43.74	80.28	—	43.16	27.23	45.09	13.37	55.01	31.57
Beverages	4.89	94.68	32.91	53.24	1.56	—	121.06	28.99	85.01	12.84	62.66	22.98
Pan, Tobacco and Supari	72.07	48.20	120.33	45.12	42.64	—	48.47	28.76	43.82	12.80	27.20	41.88
Sub-total	1329.37 (73.29)	57.34	2165.00 (77.15)	46.94	1062.89 (73.16)	—	869.11 (77.49)	26.88	685.47 (77.03)	11.52	632.23 (69.81)	31.95
II. Non-food Items:												
Entertainment	2.53	43.48	2.79	48.49	4.33	—	4.73	33.19	2.02	19.31	4.29	29.60
Travel and Transport	16.85	54.24	15.10	43.58	13.60	—	9.85	24.67	6.50	7.69	9.90	33.33
Education	1.47	64.63	0.35	42.86	11.91	—	16.12	48.58	7.16	3.49	11.73	28.13
Medicines	102.46	54.92	86.33	45.96	64.78	—	16.85	30.98	13.35	13.11	12.67	29.36
Domestic utensils	4.95	34.34	5.94	54.54	9.28	—	7.72	39.51	4.55	20.08	2.37	32.49
Clothes	132.50	59.06	159.18	47.59	145.90	—	41.87	33.43	81.57	10.54	39.55	30.16
Footwear	5.02	69.32	11.87	46.93	9.25	—	5.43	39.97	3.96	25.25	6.39	31.30
Ornaments	—	—	—	—	—	—	6.33	40.33	1.33	45.11	2.57	22.18
Fuel and Light	218.76	57.72	359.32	43.13	130.37	—	143.62	24.62	179.55	11.70	183.15	35.18
Others	—	—	0.36	16.67	—	—	—	—	1.45	—	0.79	12.66
Sub-total	484.44 (26.71)	57.11	641.24 (22.85)	44.83	389.92 (26.84)	—	252.52 (22.51)	29.38	201.44 (22.64)	11.59	273.41 (30.19)	33.43
Total	1813.81 (100)	57.27	2806.24 (100)	46.46	1452.81 (100)	—	1121.63 (100)	27.44	886.91 (100)	11.54	905.64 (100)	32.38

Note: 1. (—) indicates nil.
2. Figures in parentheses represent percentages to row total.

Source: Based on data given in the case studies (Chapters 5 to 10).

villages showed a similar pattern as the total expenditure. Between 72 and 77 per cent of the per capita consumer expenditure was spent on food items in Gujarat and 69 and 79 per cent of the per capita consumer expenditure went for buying food items in Karnataka. This pattern showed hardly any difference between the mechanized and non-mechanized villages. Among non-food items, expenditure on education was small (say less than 0.5 per cent) in Gujarat as compared to the Karnataka villages. This, however, reflected the difference between literacy rate of Gujarat and Karnataka villages (Table 3.21).

The per capita and per household consumer expenditure indicated that almost all the villages were above poverty line at current prices. This, however, conceals the aspect of income distribution and, therefore, cannot be generalized for all occupations/groups in the villages.

CAPITAL OUTPUT AND LABOUR RATIOS

With the mechanization of fishing craft it was expected that both capital labour and output labour ratios will rise. We did not have a sufficient data to compute these ratios for all the selected villages. Therefore, we have computed such ratios for different types of boats in operation in the selected villages with a view to understanding the employment aspects of mechanization. Capital requirement for generating employment[9] for one person was highest for trawlers with a requirement of Rs. 32,750 per workplace and was followed by OBM boats and non-mechanized boats with Rs. 13,530 and Rs. 8,900 respectively in the case of Gujarat villages. Similarly, the output-labour ratio was the highest for trawlers with 8.58 tonnes per man-year and was followed by OBM boats and non-mechanized boats with 5.23 and 3.07 tonnes per man-year respectively.

In Karnataka it has been noted that capital requirement for generating one workplace was highest again for trawlers with 29,360 and was followed by purse seiners, dug-out canoes and rampani units with Rs. 25,050, Rs. 7,010 and Rs. 3,920 respectively. Similarly, output-labour ratio was 10.66 tonnes per labourer for rampanis, 15.41 tonnes per labourer for

TABLE 3.21

Itemwise per capita and per household consumer expenditure of different villages, Gujarat and Karnataka

Items	Gujarat						Karnataka					
	Chorwad		Hirakot		Bhadbhut		Kadekar		Bengre		Idya	
	PC	PH	PC	PH	PC	PH	PC	PH	PC	PH	PC	PH
I. Food Items:												
(a) Foodgrains	467	3410	541	3767	319	1980	427.96	3364.40	471	2939	408.14	2972.40
(b) Milk and milk products	59	426	74	513	54	333	36.39	286.00	64	399	36.85	268.40
(c) Edible oils	398	2901	353	2457	183	1156	62.40	490.36	100	624	36.71	267.35
(d) Meat and Chicken	15	110	58	387	6	36	—	—	—	—	—	—
(e) Eggs	—	—	2	14	—	—	—	—	—	—	—	—
(f) Fish	354	2581	359	2497	234	1453	178.88	1407.64	299	1863	130.32	949.13
(g) Vegetables	46	328	64	445	50	311	45.76	358.28	44	272	45.94	335.59
(h) Fruits and Nuts	27	200	1	9	24	151	38.48	303.16	29	180	27.48	200.12
(i) Sugar, Gur and Khandsari	145	1055	152	1054	102	634	20.80	163.28	32	199	22.95	167.03
(j) Salt and Spices	96	698	70	485	83	518	53.04	419.12	92	571	43.85	319.35
(k) Beverages	7	46	27	190	2	10	149.24	1175.20	173	1077	86.91	632.93
(l) Pan, Tobacco and Supari	92	674	100	695	44	275	59.8	407.60	89	555	37.72	274.71
Sub-total	1701 (76.54)	12424 (73.29)	1799 (77.18)	12513 (77.15)	1105 (73.15)	6857 (73.16)	1072.76 (77.47)	8438.04 (77.47)	1393 (77.91)	8680 (77.86)	876.85 (69.83)	6388.01 (69.82)

II. Non-food Items:												
(a) Entertainment	3.25	23.71	2	16	4.50	28	5.83	45.87	4.11	25.62	5.96	43.42
(b) Travel and Transport	21.58	158	13	87	14.13	88	12.16	95.63	13.18	82.27	13.73	99.99
(c) Education	1.89	13.79	—	2	12.38	77	19.92	156.62	14.53	90.70	16.26	118.42
(d) Medicines	131.19	957.57	72	499	67.33	418	20.81	163.69	27.09	169.06	17.56	127.88
(e) Domestic utensils	6.34	46.26	5.9	34	10.16	63	9.54	75.0	9.24	57.66	3.27	23.84
(f) Clothes	169.65	1238.32	132	920	151.66	941	51.64	406.5	76.22	475.63	54.84	399.39
(g) Footwear	6.43	46.96	10	69	9.61	60	6.72	52.82	8.05	50.25	8.85	64.44
(h) Ornaments	—	—	—	—	—	—	7.82	61.50	2.71	16.90	3.54	25.81
(i) Fuel and Light	281.00	2045.00	298	2076	136	841	177.32	1394.64	250.00	1564.00	253.76	1850.16
(j) Others	—	—	—	—	—	—	0.15	1.17	2.94	18.35	1.00	7.88
Sub-total	521.33	4527.48	532	3706	405.64	2516	311.91	2453.44	394.89	2468.16	378.86	2761.24
	(27.96)	(26.71)	(22.82)	(22.85)	(26.85)	(26.84)	(22.53)	(22.53)	(22.09)	(22.14)	(30.17)	(30.18)
Total	2222.33	16951.50	2331	16219	1580.64	9373	1384.67	10891,48	1787.89	11148.16	1255.74	9149.25

Note: 1. (—) indicates nil.

2. Figures in parentheses represent percentages to column total.

Source: Based on data given in the case studies (Chapters 5 to 10).

purse-seiners, 2.61 tonnes for dug-out canoes and 9.2 tonnes for trawlers.

LABOUR DISPLACEMENT AND LABOUR MOBILITY

The above data reveal that the capital-output ratio for trawlers is less than the similar ratio for non-mechanized boats both in Gujarat and Karnataka. Given the fact that in Karnataka there was a negative growth rate in landings of fish over the past five years, such a mechanization as is highly capital intensive and labour displacing should have resulted in large unemployment or labour displacement. However, an estimate of demand and supply of labour for fishing in different selected villages of Gujarat and Karnataka indicated that, in fact, there was a shortage of labour for fishing particularly in high and medium mechanized villages. An exception to the above was Hirakot in Gujarat where there was a marginal surplus. Similarly, among less mechanized/non-mechanized villages, Bhadbhut was an exception where the average fishing household faced labour shortage to the extent of 1.19 man-years. Amongst the mechanized villages the shortage of labour per household was higher in the case of villages having purse-seiners in Karnataka, i.e. Kadekar and Bengre, as compared to Chorwad—a highly mechanized village with few trawlers and a large number of OBM boats in Gujarat (Table 3.22).

It seems to us that such a phenomenon can be explained only through two facts. First, the overall number of boats in all the mechanized villages increased at a faster rate than in the non-mechanized villages. Further, the induction of mechanized boats was higher than the labour displacement rate on the one hand and the entry of new labourer in the market on the other. Second, mechanization of fisheries creates several ancillary activities resulting in increased employment. For instance, development of exportable varieties has led to the development of freezing, canning, packaging and transportation activities. Similarly, other fish varieties have started moving to distant markets which were not serviced before mechanization. It may also be noted that the type of mechanization is also a factor in improving capital- and labour-output ratios. Chorwad where

TABLE 3.22

Estimates of surplus labourers of different villages (Gujarat and Karnataka)

Particulars	Gujarat				Karnataka			
	Chorwad	Hirakot	Bhadbhut	Total	Kadekar	Bengre	Idya	Total
1. No. of households	107	173	155	435	103	79	99	281
2. No. of able bodied adult male members of family	217	295	284	706	293	146	238	677
3. No. of adult male members with occupations other than fishing	23	34	14	71	42	36	86	164
4. No. of adult male members who have not yet entered the working force (students)	1	2	16	19	31	12	36	79
5. No. of members actively engaged in fishing or at best having no occupation	203	259	254	716	220	97	116	433
6. No. of members required for operating the fishing equipment	227	225	438	890	326	134	79	608
7. Surplus labourers in the fishing workforce	−24	+34	−184	−174	−106	−37	+39	−175
8. Surplus labourers per household	−0.22	+0.20	−1.19	−1.21	−1.03	−0.47	+0.39	−1.90

Note: 1. (—) indicates nil.
2. Negative surpluses indicate deficits.

Source: Based on data given in the case studies (Chapters 5 to 10).

OBM boats were preferred over large trawlers had a better capital-output ratio compared to non-mechanized boats.

The resultant labour shortage particularly in high and medium mechanized villages improved the economic condition of crew members particularly in the mechanized boats, through bargaining for higher wages and more favourable sharing patterns. However, this has not resulted in a very high labour mobility ratios for crew members on the mechanized craft. It is interesting to note that the non-mechanized crew had a lower labour mobility ratio[10] compared to mechanized crew both in Gujarat and Karnataka (Table 3.23). In a large number of cases where crew changed their employers, the reason was to improve their income, and was followed by disputes with the boat owners in Gujarat villages. In the case of Karnataka villages disputes with the boat owners accounted for the maximum and were followed by the hope to get better wages. The reason for a change of employer by crew was neutral for the level of mechanization (Table 3.24).

FAMILY AND HIRED CREW

Mechanized boats require a larger crew which often cannot be met from amongst the family members. Employment of crew thus becomes necessary in these boats. Family members contributed only 17.96 per cent of the total crew in trawler families of Chorwad village. However, in the case of OBMs and non-mechanized boats family members contributed about 65 per cent of the crew force in Gujarat. The situation in this regard was similar in the case of Karnataka where family members formed only 30 per cent of the crew force in spite of the partnership basis of ownership of purse-seiners and trawlers (Table 3.25). It can, therefore, be stated that a higher level of mechanization transgresses the family boundary. Fishing no longer remains a family enterprise.

In Gujarat, with the introduction of trawlers, the wage payment system has changed from a share in the total catch to fixed money wages. However, OBM boats still continue with the traditional system of sharing the catch. In the case of Karnataka villages the crew in all types of craft participated on the basis of a share in total landings. The reason for the similar

TABLE 3.23

Distribution of sample crew members according to labour mobility ratios and type of craft in different villages of Gujarat and Karnataka

State/village	No. of MB crew with labour mobility				No. of NMB crew with labour mobility			
	High (0.81 and above)	Medium (0.41 to 0.80)	Low (Less than 0.41)	Total	High (0.81 and above)	Medium (0.41 to 0.80)	Low (Less than 0.41)	Total
I. *Gujarat*								
Chorwad	—	3 (30.00)	7 (70.00	10 (100.00)	—	—	—	—
Hirakot	—	7 (35.00)	13 (65.00)	20 (100.00)	—	—	—	—
Bhadbhut	—	—	—	—	—	—	10 (100.00)	10 (100.00)
Aggregate	—	10 (33.33)	20 (66.67)	30 (100.00)	—	—	10 (100.00)	10 (100.00)
II. *Karnataka*								
Kadekar	—	7 (21.88)	25 (78.12)	32 (100.00)	—	—	—	—

TABLE 3.23 (*Contd.*)

B. Bengre	—	—	22 (100.00)	22 (100.00)	—	—	—	—
Idya	—	—	1 (100.00)	1 (100.00)	—	1 (20.00)	4 (80.00)	5 (100.00)
Aggregate	—	7 (12.73)	48 (87.27)	55 (100.00)	—	1 (20.00)	4 (80.00)	5 (100.00)

Notes: 1. (—) indicates nil.

2. Figures in parentheses indicate percentages to total.

3. The labour mobility ratio for each individual has been computed by dividing the number of times the labourer changed the employer by the number of years for which he has been working as crew in the same type of craft.

Source: Compiled on the basis of information in the respective case studies (Chapters 5 to 10).

TABLE 3.24

Reasons for change of employer by the crew members during their immediate past change of different villages, Gujarat and Karnataka

Reasons	Gujarat				Karnataka			
	Chorwad	Hirakot	Bhadbhut	Total	Kadekar	Bengre	Idya	Total
1. Dispute with the boat owner	4	4	3	11	14	2	—	21
2. Hope of getting higher returns due to efficient working of the craft	5	6	3	14	12	1	2	18
3. Household head wanted the member to join the own enterprise	2	—	—	2	—	—	—	—
4. Invitation to join a new craft/disposition of fishing equipment by boat owner	3	3	2	8	—	—	—	—
5. Need of higher advance to clear debt	3	3	—	6	—	—	—	—
6. Others	—	4	8	12	26	—	—	—
Total	17	20	16	53	52	3	2	39

Note: (—) indicates nil.

Source: Based on data given in the case studies (Chapters 5 to 10).

TABLE 3.25

Estimated[1] labourer (crew), employment pattern (family and hired) for operating different type of boats of different villages, Gujarat and Karnataka

Type of boat	Source	Gujarat				Karnataka			
		Chor-wad	Hira-kot	Bhad-bhut	Total	Kade-kar	Bengre	Idya	Total
1. NMB (25 ft.)	Family	29	10	13	52	52	56	20	128
	Hired	15	6	24	47	28	34	25	87
2. NMB (25 ft.)	Family	—	4	169	173	—	—	—	—
	Hired	—	3	232	235	—	—	—	—
3. OBM (25 ft.)	Family	56	—	—	56	—	—	—	—
	Hired	27	—	—	27	—	—	—	—
4. OBM (25 ft.)	Family	34	105	—	139	—	—	—	—
	Hired	38	95	—	133	—	—	—	—
5. Rampani	Family	—	—	—	—	—	—	—	—
	Hired	—	—	—	—	—	—	—	—
6. Trawler	Family	5	—	—	5	10	5	—	19
	Hired	23	—	—	23	37	10	5	52
7. Purse-seiner	Family	—	—	—	—	21	2	23	46
	Hired	—	—	—	—	168	27	4	199
Total	Family	124	119	182	425	83	63	43	189
	Hired	103	106	256	465	233	71	34	388

Note : 1. Estimated on the basis of information from sample respondents.

2. (—) indicates nil.

pattern of sharing irrespective of the type of boat may be the predominance of partnership basis of owning trawlers and purse-seiners.

DEVELOPMENT OF ENTREPRENEURS

Internalization of the mechanization programme can be judged from the growth of crew members graduating to boat owner entrepreneurs. Particularly in this respect the time taken to move to the position of boat owner becomes important. The important factors involved in internalization of the mechanization process are the confidence to fish in the high seas, and ability to perform the leadership function in terms of identification of fishing grounds, keeping the crew motivated and making the economics of the boat favourable.

It also involves capacity to take risks and ability to find necessary capital. A successful mechanization programme should lead to such a graduation of crew members to boat owners at a relatively faster pace. We had a sample of 100 boat owners in Gujarat and 87 owners in Karnataka who had graduated from crew to boat owners. We found that the majority in both states took between 6 and 15 years to move from crew to a boat owner. Considering the fact that our sample did not include hereditary succession, this period may be considered as normal. In a few exceptional cases crew members progressed into owning boats in a much shorter span of time. However, these included hereditary successions and other factors (Table 3.26).

INDEBTEDNESS AMONG FISHING HOUSEHOLDS

The Gujarat villages together had a total loan outstanding of Rs. 18,50,085 in which the share of mechanized boat owners was 50.64 per cent. Thus, 26 per cent households in Gujarat commanded about 50.64 per cent of the loans. It was more favourable in Karnataka where the total loan outstanding was Rs. 19,51,650. The share of mechanized boat owners was 80.30 per cent. Thus only 22.06 per cent households commanded 80.30 per cent of the loan outstanding. It was observed that in the highly mechanized villages of Gujarat and Karnataka about 33.64 per cent and 66.31 per cent households respectively were debt free. The non-mechanized villages had a relatively lesser number of households which were debt free in both states. On the whole the analysis revealed that a larger percentage of households were debt free in Karnataka (44.98 per cent) as compared to Gujarat (19.31 per cent), the non-mechanized boat owners constituted a majority in the debt-free group in both states (Table 3.27).

Private or informal sources of borrowing were quite

TABLE 3.26

Distribution of sample boat owners according to the pace[3] of becoming entrepreneurs in different villages of Gujarat and Karnataka

State/Village	No. of MB owners with a pace of				No. of NMB owners with a pace of			
	High	Medium	Low	Total	High	Medium	Low	Total
1. *Gujarat*								
Chorwad	1 (4.55)	1 (4.54)	20 (90.91)	22 (100)	—	1 (10.00)	9 (90.00)	10 (100.00)
Hirakot	—	—	18 (100.00)	18 (100.00)	—	—	5 (100.00)	5 (100.00)
Bhadbhut	—	—	—	—	—	—	39 (100.00)	39 (100.00)
Aggregate	1 (2.50)	1 (2.50)	38 (95.00)	40 (100.00)	—	1 (1.85)	53 (98.15)	54 (100.00)
2. *Karnataka*								
Kadekar	4 (19.05)	1 (4.76)	16 (76.19)	21 (100.00)	1 (9.09)	—	10 (90.91)	11 (100.00)
Bengre	1 (14.29)	—	6 (85.71)	7 (100.00)	1 (4.35)	1 (4.35)	21 (91.30)	23 (100.0)

Idya	—	—	16 (100.00)	16 (100.00)	—	—	9 (100.00)	9 (100.00)
Aggregate	5 (11.36)	1 (2.28)	38 (86.36)	44 (100.00)	2 (4.65)	1 (2.32)	40 (93.03)	43 (100.00)

Note: 1. (—) indicates nil.

2. Figures in parentheses are percentages to column total.

3. The pace of graduation has been categorized into three levels, viz. high, medium and low. Crew members who have graduated within a short span (say less than 1.5 years) were treated as high pace. Similarly, those who have graduated within a period between 1.5 and 3 years were treated as medium pace. Finally, those who have taken time between 3 and 15 years were treated to have low pace.

Source: Compiled on the basis of information in respective village studies (Chapters 5 to 10).

TABLE 3.27

Size distribution of households according to the total outstanding debts in different villages, Gujarat and Karnataka

	Gujarat							
	Chorwad		Hirakot		Bhadbhut		Total	
	Total	% share of MB owners	Total	% share of MB owners	Total	% share of MB owners	Total	% share of MB owners
Zero outstanding	36 (33.64)	19.44	31 (17.92)	9.68	20 (12.90)	—	87 (20.0)	11.49
Up to 1000	12 (11.22)	16.67	16 (9.25)	12.50	17 (10.97)	—	45 (10.34)	8.89
1001-3000	25 (23.36)	52.00	39 (22.54)	10.26	56 (36.13)	—	120 (27.59)	14.17
3001-6000	15 (14.02)	80.00	45 (26.01)	51.11	40 (25.81)	—	100 (22.99)	35.00
6001-10000	7 (6.54)	71.43	26 (15.03)	61.54	15 (9.68)	—	48 (11.03)	43.75

10001-15000	1 (0.94)	—	11 (6.36)	90.91	6 (3.87)	—	18 (4.14)	55.56
15001-25000	7 (6.54)	100.00	6 (2.89)	80.00	1 (0.64)	—	13 (2.99)	84.62
25001-35000	2 (1.87)	100.00	—	—	—	—	2 (0.46)	100.00
35001 and above	2 (1.87)	100.00	—	—	—	—	2 (0.46)	100.00
Total	107 (100.00)	46.73	173 (100.00)	35.84	155 (100.00)	—	435 (100.00)	25.75

TABLE 3.27 (*Contd.*)

	Karnataka							
	Kadekar		Bengre		Idya		Total	
	Total	% share of MB owners	Total	% share of MB owners	Total	% share of MB owners	Total	% share of MB owners
Zero outstanding	58 (56.31)	1.72	29 (36.70)	3.45	38 (38.39)	2.63	125 (44.48)	2.40
Up to 1000	7 (6.80)	—	16 (20.25)	—	6 (6.06)	—	29 (10.32)	—
1001-3000	10 (9.71)	10.00	21 (26.58)	4.76	18 (18.18)	11.11	49 (17.44)	8.16
3001-6000	6 (5.83)	50.00	5 (6.33)	—	4 (4.04)	—	15 (5.34)	20.00
6001-10000	3 (2.91)	33.33	5 (6.33)	80.00	3 (3.03)	66.66	11 (3.91)	63.64
10001-15000	6 (5.83)	83.33	1 (1.27)	—	11 (11.11)	100.00	18 (6.41)	88.89
15001-25000	4 (3.88)	100.00	1 (1.27)	—	10 (10.10)	100.00	15 (5.34)	93.33

25001-35000	1 (0.97)	100.00	—	—	2 (2.02)	100.00	3 (1.07)	100.00
35001 and above	8 (7.76)	87.50	1 (1.27)	—	7 (7.07)	100.00	16 (5.69)	87.50
Total	103 (100.00)	22.33	79 (100.00)	7.60	99 (100.00)	33.33	281 (100.00)	22.06

Note: 1. (—) indicates nil.

2. Figures in parentheses represent percentages to column total.

Source: Based on data given in the case studies (Chapters 5 to 10).

TABLE 3.28

Distribution of households according to source of borrowing and their outstanding debts as on December 1981 of different villages, Gujarat and Karnataka

Source of borrowings	Gujarat											
	Chorwad			Hirakot			Bhadbhut			Total		
	No.	Outstanding debt (Rs.)	% share of MB owners	No.	Outstanding debt (Rs.)	% share of MB owners	No.	Outstanding debt (Rs.)	% share of MB owners	No.	Outstanding debt (Rs.)	% share of MB owners
I. Formal landing agencies:												
Commercial banks	6	12550	74.50	3	6500	46.15	9	17100	—	18	36150	34.10
Co-operative societies/banks	1	5000	100.00	1	2500	—	—	—	—	2	7500	66.67
Sub-total	7	17550	81.77	4	9000	33.33	9	17100	—	20	43650	36.75
II. Private or informal sources:												
Friends/relatives	7	23000	65.22	17	74900	13.35	3	7000	—	27	104900	23.83
Moneylenders	—	—	—	26	133000	15.03	2	4000	—	28	137000	14.60
Fish merchants/boat owners	27	185600	92.73	60	292400	79.10	51	165300	—	138	643300	62.71
Sub-total	34	208600	89.69	103	500300	52.24	56	176300	—	193	885200	50.66
III. From multiple sources	30	270750	83.53	35	314200	77.98	73	336285	—	131	921235	51.14
Total	71	496900	86.05	142	823500	61.85	138	829685	—	344	1850085	50.64

TABLE 3.38 (*Contd.*)

	Karnataka											
	Kadekar			Bengre			Idya			Total		
	No.	Outstanding debt (Rs.)	% share of MB owner	No.	Outstanding debt (Rs.)	% share of ME owner	No.	Outstanding debt (Rs.)	% share of MB owner	No.	Outstanding debt (Rs.)	% share of MB owner
I. Informal lending agencies:												
Commercial banks	40	746250	94.94	25	136250	18.50	54	764800	89.30	116	1647300	86.00
Co-operative banks	1	50000	—	2	2100	28.57	—	—	—	3	52100	1.15
Village funds	—	—	—	4	2400	—	—	—	—	4	2400	—
Sub-total	41	796250	88.98	31	140750	18.33	54	764800	89.30	123	1701800	83.28
II. Informal sources:												
Friends and relatives	2	5250	—	10	26200	—	3	11500	—	15	42950	—
III. Multiple sources	2	10400	—	9	37000	—	4	159500	99.73	17	206900	72.26
Total	45	811900	87.26	50	203950	12.65	61	935800	88.96	155	1951650	80.28

Note: (—) indicates nil.

Source: Based on data given in the case studies (Chapters 5 to 10).

TABLE 3.29

Distribution of households according to the purpose of borrowing of the outstanding debt and occupations of different villages, Gujarat and Karnataka

Reasons for borrowing the outstanding debt	Gujarat				Karnataka			
	Chorwad	Hirakot	Bhadbhut	Total	Kadekar	Bengre	Idya	Total
1. No outstanding debt	36 (19.44)	31 (9.68)	17 (—)	84 (23.81)	58 (1.72)	28 (3.45)	38 (2.63)	125 (2.40)
2. Replacement of gear	16 (62.59)	17 (70.59)	79 (—)	112 (19.64)	21 (71.43)	—	5 (100.00)	26 (46.15)
3. Purchase of fishing equipment	36 (83.33)	50 (80.00)	30 (—)	116 (60.34)	16 (46.67)	30 (16.67)	35 (74.29)	80 (57.50)
4. To meet household expenditure	12 (8.33)	48 (—)	25 (—)	85 (1.18)	8 (—)	11 (—)	14 (7.14)	33 (3.03)
5. To meet expenditure for social functions	—	23 (26.09)	3 (—)	26 (23.08)	—	9 (—)	1 (—)	10 (—)
6. Others	7 (28.57)	4 (25.0)	1 (—)	12 (25.00)	1 (—)	—	6 (—)	7 (—)
Total	107 (46.73)	173 (41.63)	155 (—)	435 (28.05)	103 (22.33)	79 (7.59)	99 (33.33)	281 (22.06)

Note: 1. (—) indicates nil.

2. Figures in parentheses represent percentages of MB owners.

Source: Based on data given in the case studies (Chapters 5 to 10).

predominant (95 per cent) compared to formal sources in Gujarat. In Karnataka only 2.46 per cent of the borrowings came from informal sources (Table 3.28).

The distribution of households according to the purpose of borrowing of the outstanding debt (share of MB owners) of different villages of Gujarat and Karnataka is presented in Table 3.29. It can be observed that mechanized boat owners had primarily borrowed for the purchase of fishing equipment and replacement of gear. On the other hand the non-mechanized boat owner and crew member households had borrowed for meeting the household expenditure, particularly in the medium and high mechanized villages.

The credit and marketing linkages seemed to have disappeared to a large extent in the Karnataka villages as institutional finance replaced the traditional sources. However, in Gujarat, because of the dominance of informal sources of credit, this linkage was still predominant. It is indeed an interesting question as to why institutional credit is weak in Gujarat.

REFERENCES

1. The traditional craft of Karnataka and Kerala were assumed to be unsuitable for motorization for the following reasons. Firstly, the vast majority of the traditional craft in these two states are dugout canoes, which are technically unsuitable for motorization. Secondly, it is alleged that with the then existing species composition of traditional craft and their respective price structure motorization would not have been economically viable.
2. Typically, most of the mechanized craft in Karnataka in general and in the selected villages in particular were owned on partnership basis. Often all the partners of a craft may not be from the same villages after discounting for partners from other villages.
3. The Gini coefficient is a ratio computed for quantifying the distributive inequality and is widely used for studying the extent of inequality in assets or income distribution. The Gini ratio ranges between 0 and 1. The zero value of the ratio indicates the perfectly equitable distribution while the value one indicates most inequitable distribution. For further details see Sen, A.K., *On Economic Inequality* (Delhi: Oxford University Press, 1974), p. 29.
4. The value of assets included the value of both boats and gear. For making adjustments in the value of assets purchased at different points of time by different households, we have computed the value of assets at 1980 prices.

5. For details about the market situation in various landing-cum-assembly centres, see Gupta *et. al.*, *Marine Fish Marketing in India: Current Situation*, Volume II (Ahmedabad: Indian Institute of Management, 1984).
6. While computing the annual earnings of non-mechanized boat owners we have assumed that one family member of NMB owner works on the boat as crew. The earnings of NMB owner include the returns to the boat and the labour of owner working as crew in the boat.
7. Bliss and Stern have calculated the Gini ratio for income distribution in the case of Palanpur to be 0.326. For details see Bliss, C.J., and Stern, N.H., *Palanpur: The Economy of Indian Village* (London: Oxford University Press, 1982), p. 209.
8. Anand has found the Gini ratio of income inequality for Malaysia to be 0.4 in 1976 and Atkinson found it to be 0.5 for another developing country in 1970. For details, see Anand, S., *Inequality and Poverty in Malaysia: Measurement and Decomposition* (Mimeo.), D.Phil dissertation (London: Oxford University, 1978) and Atkinson, A.B., "On the Measurement of Inequality", *Journal of Economic Theory*, Nov.-Dec. 1979, pp. 1370-86.
9. Here we have taken employment in only the production sector and the employment in forward and backward linkages was omitted.
10. Ideally the labour-turnover ratio should have been computed in terms of the share of crew which changed employer in the total requirement for a given type of craft. However, in view of the paucity of information, the labour-turnover ratio for each crew member has been computed by dividing the number of times the labourer changed the employer by the number of years for which he has been working as crew in the given type of craft.

4

Summary of Findings and Policy Implications

THE MARINE fisheries sector has experienced rapid changes and has moved to highly complex and capital-intensive technologies. In the process of this transition several concerns have been expressed. Keeping in view the interests of small fishermen, some important concerns were in relation to (i) disadvantages occurring due to competition from mechanized boats, particularly those fishing in shallow waters, (ii) dominance of non-fishermen households, who were presumed to have invested on mechanized boats as an economic strategy aimed at rapid enrichment in the fishing sector, (iii) unemployment or underemployment in fisheries presumably because of the labour displacement due to mechanization of fishing craft and (iv) unfavourable assets and income distribution after mechanization. Yet another concern has been with respect to the observation that the existing type of mechanization of fishing craft has led to overcapitalization of fishing craft and its impact on the socio-economic status of fishermen with small means has been discussed in earlier chapters and in the in-depth village studies. Here we present a brief summary of our findings and the corresponding policy implications.

DATA AND METHODOLOGY

The study used both primary and secondary data. The primary data for the study were obtained through a four-stage stratified sampling with the state as the first-stage unit, district as second-stage unit, village as third-stage unit, and fishermen as ultimate sampling unit. Keeping in mind the intensity of mechanization and types of mechanized boats in operation, Gujarat and Karnataka were selected in the first stage. Using the intensity of mechanization as a criterion Junagadh in Gujarat and South Canara in Karnataka were selected at the second stage.

The control village Bhadbhut, however, was drawn from Bharuch district in Gujarat because of some physical constraints in identifying the control village from Junagadh district.

The villages in the selected districts were analysed according to the ratio of mechanized to non-mechanized boats keeping the horse power of motor/engine of the mechanized craft in consideration. From this, three villages each from Gujarat and Karnataka were selected representing different levels of mechanization. By following this procedure three villages selected in Gujarat were Chorwad (with a high level of mechanization), Hirakot (with a medium level of mechanization), and Bhadbhut (a non-mechanized village). In the case of Karnataka the selected villages were Kadekor (a highly mechanized village), Bokkapatna Bengre (a medium mechanized village) and Idya (a low mechanized village). After selecting the villages a complete enumeration of all 716 households was carried out. Of these 230 households were selected for an in-depth survey.

Based on this data and data from village records and discussions with village elders detailed case studies of the selected villages were prepared. These studies give an insight into the process of mechanization and changes in the important socio-economic variables in the selected villages. The case studies from the selected villages were also subjected to inter-village and inter-state comparisons to gain an insight into the changes in socio-economic variables at different levels and types of mechanization.

SUMMARY OF FINDINGS

Evidence from macro data

Before analysing data from the village studies, impact of mechanization was analysed with the help of macro data. This analysis presented the following findings:

The type of mechanization and its pace in Gujarat and Karnataka were different. In Gujarat, the introduction of trawlers was preceded by fitting outboard motors to traditional fishing craft. In Karnataka there was a quantum jump from traditional dugout canoes and rampanis to trawlers and purse-seiners.

The number of mechanized craft in Gujarat increased from 411 in 1961 to 3,732 in 1980 and the composition consisted of 1,047 OBM boats and 2,685 IBE boats in 1980. Junagarh district of Gujarat had the highest intensity of mechanization and accounted for over 61 per cent of the mechanized boats in the state in 1980. The share of non-fishermen owning mechanized craft was only 15.21 per cent in the state in 1980. On the other hand in Karnataka the number of mechanized craft increased from 2 in 1957 to over 1,500 in 1977 and thereafter to 2,004 in 1980. In 1980 the composition of the total mechanized craft in Karnataka consisted of 1,553 trawlers, 325 purse-seiners, 28 gill netters and 18 others. Further, South Canara district of Karnataka had the highest intensity of mechanization. The trawlers in the state increased at a rapid rate after 1975 while purse-seiners increased at a faster rate between 1977 and 1980. The rapid increase in the number of purse-seiner boats in the state was accompanied by a sharp decline in the number of rampani boats—a traditional mode of production—and this has resulted in a total shift in the catch composition, employment and income. The incidence of ownership of mechanized craft by non-fishermen was relatively high in Karnataka as compared to Gujarat and accounted for 46.51 per cent of the boats in the state. Further, a large number of mechanized boats in Karnataka were owned on a partnership basis while such ownership was completely absent in Gujarat. Here it should, however, be emphasized that the share of mechanized boats owned by non-fishermen in Karnataka may go down, if we take the community background of all the partners in the groups owning mechanized boats into account.

Despite the mechanization of fishing craft mainly characterized by the large-scale introduction of shrimp trawlers the growth rate of fish production has accelerated during the post-mechanization period in Karnataka. However, in the case of Gujarat mechanization of fishing craft has contributed to the accelerated growth of fish production. Further, the growth rate of production in the country has increased from 1.50 per cent during the pre-mechanization period (1956-69) to 2.32 per cent during the post-mechanization period (1970-80).

In Karnataka deceleration in output during the post-mechanization period was associated with acceleration in effort and decrease in productivity. In the case of Gujarat the accelerated growth rate in production during the post-mechanization period was generally associated with the accelerated growth in the effort and productivity. Further, the states showing a higher growth rate of fish production during the post-mechanization period were the states where the level of mechanization was low.

It was also observed that mechanization of fishing craft has contributed substantially to increased fish production in Gujarat, while in Karnataka there was only a marginal increase. The different outcomes may be due to the difference in the type of mechanization. For example, both OBM and trawlers in Gujarat had an augmenting effect on the output, while the purse-seiners had a replacing effect on production in Karnataka due to the disappearance of catches from traditional rampanies during the post-mechanization period.

Now turning to the specieswise growth rate of production, it was found that most of the species which experienced accelerated growth rates during the post-mechanization period usually were demersal species while species which experienced decelerating or negative growth rate were pelagic. The above trend may again be due to the large-scale introduction of demersal shrimp trawlers in all the maritime states or as part of the mechanization programme. A similar trend was observed in Gujarat and Karnataka in terms of the specieswise growth of output. However, the rate of increase or decrease was relatively steep in these two states as compared to all India.

Our analysis indicated that the contribution of the mechanized fishing craft in the country to total fish production may range between 60,000 and 122,000 tonnes. The contribution of mechanization of fishing craft in Gujarat accounted for the entire increase in fish production and may be to the tune of about 148,000 tonnes, while in the case of Karnataka such contribution was almost negligible.

Mechanization of fishing craft has contributed to a reduction in the seasonal variations in total landings in Gujarat and Karnataka. Further, introduction of purse-seiners in Karnataka has reduced the fluctuation in production, while in Gujarat no such phenomenon was observed.

Some of the important factors which have contributed to the rapid increase in the number of mechanized boats are described here. First, mechanization was encouraged by the institutional credit on liberal terms and the introduction of a large amount of subsidy, in some cases amounting even to one-third of the capital invested. Second, the high profitability of investment on mechanized boats also contributed to the rapid progress in the mechanization of fishing craft, particularly in the initial period. Third, given the fact that wage payment for crew members is in terms of a pre-determined share of the total catch. Fourth, fish prices rose at a faster rate making it worthwhile for crew members and boat owners. Further, it should be emphasized here that the growth in OBM boats in Gujarat was rapid only due to their higher profitability and lower rate of investment.

Findings from village studies

In understanding the impact of mechanization as detailed in the case studies several diversions need to be highlighted here. These include the impact of mechanization of fishing craft on the socio-economic conditions of fishermen, production technology, production, utilization and marketing pattern of fish landings, and savings and investment behaviour of fishermen households alongwith the regular feature of indebtedness. We have already stated that the village studies also supported most of the findings based on the macro evidence.

Impact on socio-economic characteristics : It was observed that the boat-owning households particularly mechanized boat owners had a tendency to live in extended households with a larger than average family size. It is also felt that this might have been dictated by the economic necessities in terms of supply of skilled and loyal labour for manning the large-size mechanized fishing vessels. The analysis of literacy rate in selected villages indicated that mechanization of fishing craft was not the cause nor a consequence of higher education.

However, the rate of literacy in general was high for all the selected villages in Karnataka as compared to Gujarat villages.

Mechanization of fishing craft did not induce large-scale long-term migration of fishermen. It has also not led to the induction of non-fishermen into fishing activity in the two states selected. As has been indicated earlier the higher incidence of non-fishermen owning mechanized craft in Karnataka needs to be understood from a different angle. In Karnataka most of the mechanized boats are owned on a partnership basis and such a boat is generally classified as owned by non-fishermen if an individual owned a major share. However, in most such groups the aggregate share of non-fishermen may be lower than the share of fishermen partners. It is our feeling that the incidence of non-fishermen owning mechanized craft may thus be quite low even in Karnataka when all partners are taken into account.

Further, our analysis indicated that mechanization induced the fishermen in Gujarat to move around the coast and seek temporary landing facilities in other villages. Such mobility around the coast was high in the case of mechanized craft with smaller crew requirement particularly OBMs.

A major portion of households in the selected villages was dependent on fishing and allied activities. There was no relationship between the level of mechanization and the proportion of non-fishing households in the total households in the case of Gujarat villages while in Karnataka villages the number of non-fishing households have decreased with the increased level of mechanization. This might have been mainly because of the wider employment opportunities in fishing and allied activities in the mechanized villages.

Introduction of mechanized craft in Karnataka has led to the development of partnership enterprises while there was no change in Gujarat villages and most of the boats were owned on a proprietary basis. However, despite the partnership enterprise development in Karnataka the proportion of boat-owning households was low as compared to Gujarat villages. The variation in the type of mechanization in two states may be responsible for the above pattern. It was observed that in general the inequality in owning of fishing assets was less in all the villages of Gujarat as compared to Karnataka villages, may be due to the differences in the type of mechanization in the two states. The higher level of mechanization generally transgresses the family boundary. It does not remain a family enterprise which is built around family labour and skills.

In Gujarat the wage payment system has changed from a share in total catch in the case of non-mechanized and OBM boats to fixed money wages and some perquisites in the case of trawlers. In the case of Karnataka villages the crew in all types of craft worked on the basis of a share in the total catch. The predominance of partnership basis of owning of trawlers and purse-seiners might have been the main reason for the continuance of the old wage payment system in Karnataka.

Our analysis confirmed the general belief that the mechanized boat owners possessed assets of much higher value than the non-mechanized boat owners and crew members in both the states. The only exception to it is Bhadbhut village in Gujarat which is completely non-mechanized but is engaged in high value estuarine fishing.

Impact on the traditional technology of production: Our analysis in the village studies indicated that the mechanization of fishing craft resulted in various changes in the technology of production in the traditional sectors also. There were two main changes which have taken place after the mechanization of fishing craft. First, the introduction of purse-seiners in Karnataka resulted in the general routing of the rampani operations—a traditional mode of fish production. The total routing was mainly because of the competition between purse-seiners and rampanis for the same resource, i.e. shoaling pelagic fishes and the capability of purse-seiners to fish on the high seas. Second, the gear technology has been diversified in terms of the material used for mending and repairing the various types of nets. The introduction of mechanized craft has encouraged the use of synthetic and nylon yarn for mending and repairing the nets used by both mechanized and non-mechanized boats in place of cotton yarn. This has resulted in the closure of village industry producing cotton yarn, and providing subsidiary employment particularly to the womenfolk and non-seaworthy men. Further, the above change to a capital-intensive material for net mending and repairing has resulted in the complete dependence of boat owners and other families on the fish merchants for the supplies of yarn and credit. Such a dependence furthered interlocked transactions often unfavourable to fishermen. It is also felt that a major burden of such interlocked transactions usually fell on the traditional sector with smaller economic means. On the other hand, the technological change in the use of yarn has increased the life of the net and improved the profitability of both mechanized and non-mechanized boats.

The operations of shrimp trawlers in shallow waters have resulted in conflicts of interest of traditional small fishermen. Several fishermen reported occasional damages to nets in addition to loss of catch. However, the operation of OBM boats did not usually result in any negative effects on the traditional sector. Thus, the effect of purse-seiners on the traditional sector may be treated as competitive in nature while the effect of trawlers to be complementary with occasional conflicts and OBMs with completely complementary effect.

Impact on production sector : Turning to the question of impact of mechanization on fish production, we found changes in respect of quantity and value of landings and species composition of total landings. The introduction of trawlers in both states has changed the species composition in favour of exportable varieties, which assured better returns to fishermen on the one hand and a large catch of low-value demersal species often termed as trash on the other. Introduction of OBM boats did not affect the species composition, but result in increased levels of harvest. In the case of Karnataka the increased level of landings due to purse-seiners not offset by the reduction or disappearance of catches from traditional rampants. Further, the introduction of purse-seiners did not change the species composition.

In terms of value, the total landings have increased substantially. Further, it was found that the increase in the value of landings of Karnataka was mainly due to inflated prices. In Gujarat, however, while the value of landings improved due to prices, total landings also incr?ased considerably.

Changes in utilisation pattern and marketing : Early motorization of traditional fishing craft in Gujarat did not lead to any major change in the catch composition or in the use flow.

With the introduction of trawlers, changes in the use flow of fish seemed to have taken place in favour of the exportable varieties and fish meal and oil extraction at the expense of fresh-fish consumption and fish going for sun-drying and salt-curing. The introduction of purse-seiners has contributed to the increased availability of fish for fresh consumption in Karnataka, though they did not contribute to increased landings through better handling methods. On the whole, in Gujarat the share of fishmeal and exportable varieties has increased considerably but the share of fresh-fish consumption has decreased owing to the nature of mechanization of fishing craft with the induction of a large number of trawlers. On the other hand, in Karnataka there seems to be a general increase in the share of fish going for fresh consumption and a reduction in the share of fish going for sun-drying, salt-curing, and fishmeal extraction. Further, there has been an increase in the share of exportable varieties.

The major contribution of mechanization was observed to be the development of assembly-cum-landing centres and a shift in the marketing activity. This has aided in the development of market yards, ice and cold storage facilities, freezing and canning plants, fishmeal plants and transport facilities. Another development in Karnataka included the development of a cold chain. The development of market infrastructure in assembly-cum-landing centres in turn contributed to the linking of distant markets on a sustained basis, and in this manner increased availability of fish in the domestic markets was assured. Further an increase in the value added due to processing began to be realized. The development of the assembly-cum-landing centres also contributed to the changes in the structure of fish markets at the small landing centres and assembly-cum-landing centres. The lower volume of catches in the village landing centres now attracted very few traders and this contributed to the development of an oligopolistic market situation. Such an effect was more predominant in the case of Karnataka villages compared to Gujarat villages. Small landing centres are still thriving. On the other hand, a sort of glut was often experienced at the large landing-cum-assembly centres. In both situations the price realization of the fishermen was adversely effected. Further, market intermediaries such as commission agents and wholesalers, while they are essential for reasons of finance and development of distant markets, controlled the flows to the markets and thus prices in the primary and terminal markets. In this process the traditional small fishermen usually get by-passed and often are at a disadvantage.

The role of market intermediaries in financing the production operation and the consequent interlocking of marketing and credit has declined considerably in Karnataka after the mechanization of fishing craft. Such a reduction in the interlocking of marketing and credit can be attributed to the increased presence of mechanized craft particularly purse-seiners in Karnataka totally financed by commercial banks and other financial institutions. However, no such reduction in the interlocking of marketing and cradit was observed after the mechanization of fishing craft in Gujarat because traders still play an important role in financing fishing operations. After the mechanization of fishing craft the sale of fish by weight has become the generally accepted practice in the case of major varieties. Such a trend has contributed to the improvement in the fishermen's share in the consumer rupee.

Before the mechanization of fishing craft, often there was an integration between production and marketing of fish. The shift in the marketing activity from village landing centres to assembly-cum-landing centres after the mechanization of fishing craft has resulted in separation of production and marketing activities, particularly in Karnataka.

Impact on income distribution and savings : The comparison of incomes of crew in mechanized craft and the non-mechanized boat owners indicated that the former earned a much higher income as compared to the latter. Further the returns to crew in trawlers were lower than those of OBM boats in Gujarat. The mechanized-boat owners commanded a much higher share in the total village income as compared to their population and number of households. Such a disparity was higher in Karnataka compared to Gujarat.

The analysis of the village studies indicated that the rate of saving has improved because of mechanization of fishing craft. Further, the rate of saving in Karnataka villages was much higher compared to Gujarat villages. The higher rate of saving due to mechanization of fish craft also manifested in higher investment indicated by the sustained growth of mechanized craft and development of infrastructure facilities in mechanized villages.

The per capita per household incomes for mechanized boat owner households were higher compared to non-mechanized boat owners and crew members. Within the crew member households the crew in mechanized craft earned higher per capita and per household incomes as compared to their counterparts in non-mechanized craft, even the owners of non-mechanized craft earned less than the crew member of mechanized boat. The per capita and per household incomes were generally higher in Gujarat compared to Karnataka villages. The lower rate of savings with higher per capita and per household incomes in Gujarat villages indicated the spendthrift nature of Gujarat fishermen.

The income inequality, as measured by the Gini ratios, was found to be lower in Gujarat villages as compared to Karnataka villages. Further, the income inequality was in direct proportion to the level of mechanization in both states. While mechanization of craft aided the inequitable distribution of income we found that it did not lead to larger than the expected income inequalities on a comparison of the income distribution in selected villages and other studies dealing with income distribution in agricultural societies in developing countries. However, there seems to be an exception in the case of Kadekar—a highly mechanized village—in Karnataka which has a relatively high income inequality. The Kadekar case points that, perhaps, a high degree of mechanization results in the concentration of production assets and leads to larger disparities in the income distribution. This observation relates to investments in purse-seiners vs. trawlers and OBM boats. On the other hand, mechanization has assured better incomes to the crew. Usually crew members earlier owned non-mechanized craft.

An analysis of the annual consumption expenditure indicated that the mechanization of fishing craft has improved the standard of living of not only mechanized boat owners but also of all the other segments of the population in village society. Expenditure on food items accounted for over 70 per cent of total expenditure in all the villages under study.

Impact on employment and entrepreneurship development: Judging from the capital-output and output-labour ratios, the mechanization of fishing craft should have resulted in large-scale unemployment and underemployment in mechanized villages. However an estimate of demand and supply of labour in the selected villages did not support the above hypothesis. In fact our analysis indicated a shortage of labour for fishing in high and medium mechanized villages. The above feature may occur due to the increase in the number of mechanized craft at a faster rate than the displacement of labour and large employment opportunities in ancillary activities in the mechanized villages due to increased landings. Further, it was found that the type of mechanization in Gujarat with a large number of OBM boats had superior impact on the employment situation as compared to the impact in the case of Karnataka. Thus, the type of mechanization programme followed in Gujarat seemed a better process in relation to production, productivity and employment as compared to the process in Karnataka, where purse-seiners dominated.

The observed labour shortage situation particularly in high and medium mechanized villages improved their economic conditions, through bargaining for higher wages and more favourable sharing patterns. This also led to lower labour mobility rates for crew members on mechanized craft.

The mechanization of fishing craft also contributed to the entrepreneurship development among the fishermen community. Most of the sample mechanized boat owners graduated from crew member or non-mechanized boat owner. However, the pace at which the graduation took place was relatively slow and was anywhere between 6 and 15 years. It was also found that the participation of fishermen and the rate of graduation was constrained not only by the scarcity of crucial inputs but also due to lack of ability to perform the leadership functions and other managerial abilities.

Impact on sources of borrowing and indebtedness: The mechanization of fishing craft has also brought about changes in the sources of borrowing and pattern of indebtedness. First, the mechanization of fishing craft has reduced indebtedness among the fishermen, particularly mechanized boat owners. This, perhaps, might have been possible because of better returns. In spite of the presence of merchants in the village community for several decades, the fishermen were ready to develop ties with a co-operative organization not only for finance but also for marketing. It was also found that the share of formal institutions in total outstanding loans in the case of non-mechanized boat owners was quite low as compared to mechanized boat owners. It is hypothesized that the low level of participation of formal institutions in loans to non-mechanized boat owners may be mainly because of the small size of their loan requirement.

POLICY IMPLICATIONS

The overall findings of the study indicate several advantages in favour of OBM boats such as economic efficiency, favourable income and asset distribution, increased employment and increased availability of fish for domestic consumption. The introduction of OBM boats also did not change the structure of the output market at village landing centres. Further the mechanization of fishing craft with OBMs also increased landings without any effect on the landings of non-mechanized craft. Therefore, a policy must be evolved to encourage OBM boats particularly where gill netting is the major type of fishery. This will also increase landings and consequently improve the marketing environment in the depleting village landing centres. This, in turn, will contribute to better price realization of small fishermen. Such a policy, however, should take into account the bottlenecks in relation to the supply of motors and increasing cost of construction of boats, mainly because of paucity of quality wood.

While trawlers and purse-seiners have contributed to increased landings, there were indeed a few negative effects. First, the introduction of trawlers and purse-seiners has contributed to greater disparities in income and ownership of fishing assets. Therefore, a policy must be evolved to encourage partnership enterprises particularly in relation to owning of trawlers and purse-seiners. Second, with the introduction of trawlers a considerable portion of the catch is going for fish-meal and oil extraction. Much of this can be used for human consumption through better methods of handling and value-added processing. Several fish products have already been developed and more experimentation in product development and marketing is required. Third, the introduction of purse-seiners in Karnataka with their relatively high level of capital investment did not contribute to increased landings. Therefore, the future policy in relation to purse-seiners in Karnataka must be guided by the increased level of exploitation through their effective operations in distant waters, which are not accessible to the traditional fishermen operating with rampanis. To increase the level of landings and consequently the availability of fish in domestic markets, it is necessary to adopt an allocative policy, on fishing grounds. Further, conscious policy measures must also be taken to rehabilitate fishermen displaced from the traditional rampani sector, in the production and processing segments of the fishing industry. In this context, there is a need for training of traditional fishermen particularly in the rampani sector to take up work as crew in large mechanized vessels and in processing and marketing activities. It is also recommended to accelerate the growth of fishing with purse-seiners in view of their being a cause for changes in the structure and pattern of output marketing with several advantages to both mechanized and non-mechanized craft owners in terms of price realization and their ability to reduce the annual fluctuations in total landings. However, the recent indications of reduced productivity of purse-seiners should also be kept in view.

In order to accelerate the growth of mechanization it would also be necessary to consider changes in the policies relating to the training and marketing infrastructure. First, as of now the process of entrepreneur development amongst fishermen is quite slow. In order to accelerate change, it would be essential that more and more entrepreneurs come forward from within the community. Therefore, training should be imparted to accelerate the process of entrepreneur development and growth of mechanization. Such a training may be highly required particularly in view of the possibility of the development of deep sea fishing, which will require large-sized crew fully trained in the different mechanical operations. Non-availability of trained manpower is even today considered as one of the important impediments in the development of marine fisheries. Second, it is important to take appropriate policy decisions for development of marketing infrastructure facilities. In this context, the efforts being made to set up Fish Terminal Authorities (FTAs) at major landing and landing-cum-assembly centres and very important to regulate the markets and provide necessary market infrastructure to boat owners and fish traders. This will benefit non-mechanized boat owners as well.

Efforts must be made to increase the presence of institutional finance in the fishing sector. This can be done through a feasible policy approach in the matter of the working capital requirement and off-season maintenance to mechanized boat owners. Such a step may also assist in reducing the interlocked credit and marketing transactions in the fishing villages, particularly in Gujarat.

Asset distribution worsens with the introduction of mechanized boats. Deep sea vessels are highly capital intensive and a worsening of asset distribution is inevitable with the new plans of mechanization. However, it has also been observed that income distribution in the fishing villages need not worsen that much. While introduction of large-sized mechanized vessels is necessary for the exploitation of deep sea fishery resources, income distribution can be considerably improved by taking appropriate policy measures.

There is an urgent need for improving the economic conditions of non-mechanized boat owners, particularly in view of the possibility of such a trend resulting in a state of stagnation or even depletion in the non-mechanized sector. First, the poor economic conditions of non-mechanized boat owners and crew members may be due to unemployment and underemployment during off-season. Employment opportunities during the off-season must, therefore, be created. The available evidence suggests that in Idya making of beedi is undertaken as a part-time activity and almost all the households had savings during the period under consideration. Second, necessary policy measures may be taken to motorise the fishing craft and consequently improve their productivity which in turn will bring better economic conditions and reverse the trend in the savings pattern. Third, the dis-savings of non-mechanized boat owners may not be necessarily due to poor economics of non-mechanized boats and may be even due to the spendthrift nature of this segment of population with their fatalistic nature and gambling spirits to spend excessively on feasts and other functions during the days of plenty of catch without bothering for "bad" days. Development of social education programmes in such circumstances is absolutely necessary to educate fishermen in regard to the need and importance of savings.

Such a step will not only improve their economic condition but also contribute to the sustained growth of investments in non-mechanized craft.

5

Chorwad Bander Village, Junagarh District, Gujarat

CHORWAD BANDER, a coastal village, is situated in Junagarh District. The village is bounded by Veraval taluk towards the north-east, Chorwad main village towards the west, Gadu towards the north-west and the Arabian sea towards the south (see Figure 5.1). The village is popularly known and identified as Chorwad Holiday Camp and is recognized as a tourist centre by the Government of Gujarat. Chorwad Main which is the revenue village and the Gram Panchayat headquarters for Chorwad Bander is situated at a distance of 4 km. to the west.

The principal language in the village is Gujarati. A few individuals of the village understand Hindi also but none understands English.

Population and caste

The livestock census of 1977 indicates the population of the fishing hamlet to be 895 and the total number of households to be 116.[1] The population and the number of households when we conducted household enumeration in 1981 were 781 and 107 respectively. Though the data may suggest a decrease in the number of households and population in the village between 1977 and 1981, there is no clear evidence to conclude, there is, a decreasing trend in the population of the village.

The main castes in the fishing village are Kharwa, Koli and Machhiyara. The traditional occupation of Kharwas and Machhiyaras is fishing and fishery-related occupations. The Kolis otherwise known as Koli-Kharwas are traditionally a

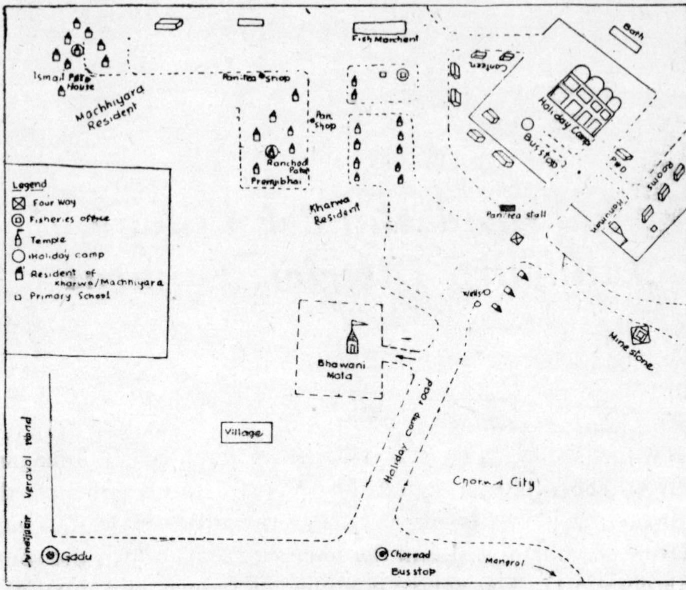

FIG. 5.1: *Map of Chorwad Bander*.

land owning/cultivating community and agricultural labourers, and have their origins in the interior parts of Saurashtra and Diu.

Village amenities and infrastructure

The infrastructure in the village can be broadly classified into: general and fishery related.

General infrastructure: For an easy analysis, the facilities including civic facilities are classified into five sub-groups. They are as follows: (i) transport and communication facilities, (ii) civic amenities, (iii) trading facilities, (iv) institutional services and (v) social, cultural and religious organizations.

The village has an all-weather road with a direct bus service to important places like Ahmedabad, Veraval and Mangrol. Three-wheeler vehicles are also available from the village for the nearby Chorwad main village. The nearest railway station Chorwad Road is about 12 km. away from Chorwad Bander. Transportation of fish is done through private transport. Before the introduction of the bus and three-wheelers, bullock-carts were used to transport fish. Cycles were also used, particularly for retail sale. There is no transportation problem after the Gujarat Government declared Chorwad Holiday Camp as a tourist centre.

Drinking water is obtained from draw wells which are 1 km. away from the village. It is also available on the campus of the Holiday Camp which is part of the village. The village is electrified and about 44 per cent of the households in the village have electricity.

The village has only two small refreshment stalls and two "pan" shops. Vegetable vendors visit the village for retail sales. The fishermen community has to go all the way to the main village for purchasing their regular requirements. Services of blacksmiths, goldsmiths, carpenters and others are available only in the main village.

The village has a primary school. The post office, primary health centre, commercial banks and police station are all located in the main village. The educational facility was made available to village in 1955 with the setting up of a primary school which has a strength of 99 children and 2 teachers. The nearest upper primary/secondary school is in the main village, which is not attended by any children from the fishing village.

The political set-up in Chorwad consists of both caste panchayats and a democratically elected panchayat. The fishermen caste panchayats are powerful governing authorities in all matters affecting the fishermen code of behaviour and there are two caste panchayats, one for the Kharwas and the other for the Machhiyaras. The composition of these panchayats varies according to caste and type. The intra-village matters of dispute within a caste are looked after by the caste panchayat in the village of origin; for example, the intra-village matters in the Koli community are looked after by the Patel of Vanakbara—the place of origin of the Koli community. The position of a Patel or headman in the Machhiyaras is hereditary or confined to a single lineage. The lineage which is eligible for holding the position of Patel is Pateliya, which is indicated as surname. In the case of the Kolis and Kharwas, the Patel is selected in an informal election which may take place in some ritual function. The tenure of a Patel varies from person to person, though the informal

TABLE 5.1

Distribution of households and population according to occupational pattern and caste, Chorwad

Occupational pattern	Caste				Total No. of persons
	Kharwa	Koli	Machhiyar	Total	
1. MB	34 (47.89)	1 (100)	15 (42.86)	50 (46.73)	402 (51.47)
2. NMB	8 (11.27)	—	9 (25.71)	17 (15.89)	122 (15.62)
3. Crew	29 (40.84)	—	11 (31.43)	40 (37.38)	257 (32.91)
Total	71 (100)	1 (100)	35 (100)	107 (100)	781 (100)

election or opinion gathering from elders takes place in this regard annually. In the case of the Kharwas and Kolis, all lineages are treated equally, while some weightage is given to the social status of the person to be elected for the caste panchayat. Discussions with the villagers indicated that competition for the position of Patel in the case of Kharwas has developed recently, particularly after the mechanization of fishing craft. The power of a Patel in the case of both castes has been decreasing in recent years.

The village is under the jurisdiction of the Chorwad Nagar Palika. Currently, one member from the village is on the Municipal Council of Chorwad.

Fishery-related infrastructure: The fishery-related infrastructure can be particularly classified into infrastructure for the supply of inputs and infrastructure for marketing of output. Infrastructure for supplies of inputs include the boat-building yards, supplies of motors or engines, ice-plants, cold storages, repair facilities for boats, motors and engines, and fuel outlets. The output marketing infrastructure comprises marketing organizations (from wholesalers to vendors), freezing plants, canning plants, fishmeal plants, fish pulverizers and transport facilities.

Infrastructure for supply of inputs is available either at Chorwad main village or at Veraval. For example, boat-building yards and cold storage facilities are available at Veraval, repair facilities for motors and ice-plants are available in Chorwad main village. Infrastructure related to processing and marketing is also available mainly in Veraval. Some wholesalers and commission agents, however, come to the village for purchase of fish.

A fisheries office was opened in the village with a fisheries assistant as its in-charge. He is normally expected to guide fishermen and conduct fish catches surveys. It was observed that the fishermen had developed some skills to undertake minor repairs of motors. The nets are usually repaired by the fishermen family members. Yarn is procured from Veraval. Curing and sun-drying of fish is undertaken on open beaches.

There are two separate fishermen co-operative societies in the village. One was set up in 1954 and the other in 1977.

Occupation of village households and production equipment

All the economic activities of the village are related to marine fishing. Occupationwise distribution of village population, according to caste, is presented in Table 5.2 About 31.11 per cent of the village population was involved in fishing and fishery-related activities.

To facilitate easy analysis, all occupations were grouped into three broad categories: (i) Mechanized Boat Owners (MBO), (ii) Non-Mechanized Boat Owners (NMBO) and (iii) Crew Members (CM). Out of 107 households in the village 50 were classified as mechanized boat owners, 17 as non-mechanized boat owners, and the remaining 40 as crew members. The castewise distribution of households according to the occupational pattern at Chorwad Bander showed that the maximum number of mechanized boats were owned by Kharwas. Only one mechanized boat was owned by a Koli. It was also observed that a large number of Kharwas and Machhiyaras were also crew members.

Mechanized and non-mechanized craft are used in Chorwad Bander. Mechanized craft can be further sub-divided into Out

TABLE 5.2

Occupationwise distribution of population according to castes, Chorwad

Occupation	No. of persons from the Kharwa	Koli	Machhiyara	Total
I. *Economic activities: Fishery*				
1. Fishing with OBM	82 (16.17)	3 (37.50)	35 (13.16)	120 (15.36)
2. Fishing with NMB	10 (1.97)	—	8 (3.01)	18 (2.30)
3. Crew with gear	20 (3.94)	—	6 (2.26)	26 (3.33)
4. Crew without gear	16 (3.16)	—	11 (4.13)	27 (3.46)
5. Net mending/repairing	38 (7.50)	1 (12.50)	12 (4.51)	51 (6.53)
6. Fish retailing	1 (0.20)	—	—	1 (0.13)
Sub-total	167 (32.94)	4 (50.00)	72 (7.07)	243 (31.11)
II. *Economic activities: Non-fishing*		—	—	—
III. *Non-economic activities:*				
1. Dependants/Not working	217 (42.80)	—	134 (50.38)	351 (44.94)
2. Students	18 (3.55)	2 (25.00)	2 (0.75)	22 (2.82)
3. Housewife	104 (20.51)	2 (25.00)	58 (21.80)	164 (21.00)
4. Others	1 (0.20)	—	—	1 (0.13)
Sub-total	340 (67.06)	4 (50.00)	194 (72.93)	538 (68.89)
Total	507 (100)	8 (100)	266 (100)	781 (100)

Note: 1. (—) indicates nil.
2. Figures in parentheses are percentages to column total.

Board Motors (OBM) and In Board Engine (IBE) boats. The IBE boats were usually 40 footers, the OBM boats were usually plank-built or dugout canoes fitted with Out Board Motors of 5—8 h.p. depending upon the length of the boat. Non-mechanized boats in the village are canoes dugout or plank-built which are generally smaller in length than the mechanized boats with OBMs. The major source of supply of labour was the crew member households.

SOCIO-ETHNOGRAPHIC PROFILE OF FISHERMEN

The social characteristics analysed in this section relate to family size and structure, level of education, age groupwise distribution, migration pattern and social participation of the fishermen and their households.

Size and structure of households

The size of the households at Chorwad varies considerably. This, to some extent, may reflect the difference in reproduction and death rates but there are a few other factors as well. One factor responsible for considerable variation is the tendency among some households[2] to live in large extended households and of others to live in small households.

The family size is analysed according to its occupation pattern. The average family size was about seven members as per our census taken in 1981. The distribution of households, according to family size and occupation, is presented in Table 5.3. It was observed that the mechanized boat owners usually had larger families than the non-mechanized boat owning households and the crew member households. More than two-thirds of the mechanized boat owning households had seven and above members as against 50 per cent in the above category in the case of crew member households and non-mechanized boat owning households with the family size of over 13 persons. Uncertainty of availability of crew may perhaps be the main reason for the tendency of the equipment owners (particularly the mechanized boat owners) to have a larger family size. The mode values of the family size were 7, 9 and 7 for mechanized boat owners, non-mechanized boat owners and crew member households respectively. There was

TABLE 5.3

Occupationwise distribution of households according to family size, Chorwad

Family size (members)	Number of households of MBO	NMBO	CM	Total
1	—	—	1(2.5)	1(0.94)
2	—	1(5.89)	1(2.5)	2(1.87)
3	—	—	1(2.5)	1(0.94)
4	1(2.0)	1(5.89)	5(12.5)	7(6.54)
5	6(12.0)	2(11.76)	7(17.5)	15(14.02)
6	8(16.0)	2(11.76)	5(12.5)	15(14.02)
7	10(20.0)	2(11.76)	11(27.6)	23(21.50)
8	6(12.0)	2(11.76)	2(5.0)	10(9.34)
9	7(14.0)	6(35.29)	1(2.5)	14(13.08)
10	7(14.0)	1(5.89)	3(7.5)	11(10.28)
11	—	—	2(5.0)	2(1.87)
12	2(4.0)	—	1(2.5)	3(2.80)
13	3(6.0)	—	—	3(2.80)
Total	50(100)	7(100)	40(100)	107(100)

Note: 1. (—) indicates nil.
2. Figures in parentheses are percentages to column total.

only one single-member household in the case of crew households.

The family structure in the village consists of single, nuclear and joint families. It was observed that the predominant form of family structure in the village was nuclear family with 83 households. Out of 23 families in the village which had joint family structure, it was observed that MBO households were predominant in this group (Table 5.4).

Agentwise distribution and education level of fishermen

The age and sex distribution of the village population according to occupation is given in Table 5.5. It was observed that in the

TABLE 5.4

Distribution of households by occupational pattern and type of family, Chorwad

Occupation	No. of household with family structure			Total
	Single	Nuclear	Joint	
1. MBO	—	31 (37.35)	19 (82.61)	50 (46.73)
2. NMBO	—	16 (19.28)	1 (4.35)	17 (15.89)
3. CM	1 (100)	36 (43.37)	3 (13.04)	40 (37.38)
Total	1 (100)	83 (100)	23 (100)	107 (100)

Note: 1. (—) indicates nil.
2. Figures in parentheses are percentages to column total.

village as a whole the ratio of males to females is more than one. It is substantially higher in the case of mechanized boat owners particularly OBM boat owner households. There was an excess of male over female members in the age group of 13-20 years and 21-30 years. This may be partly because of the early marriage of girls as compared to boys. The number of male members per household between the ages of 13 and 55 years (the normal age group during which an individual gets involved in active fishing) were 3, 2.69, 1.64 and 1.62 for trawler owner, OBM boat owner, NMB boat owner and crew households respectively. The tendency of equipment owning households, particularly MB owners, to live in extended households with a higher number of male members in active fishing age group (13-55 years) indicates labour shortage for fishing in the village.

We calculated for each family the age gaps between surviving children, only for whom it was possible[3] to observe the age gap. More than 70 per cent of the children had less than three years' gap between the two surviving children. There was no difference between various occupations in this respect. Only in the case of crew members it was observed that there was a gap

TABLE 5.5

Age and sex distribution of villagers according to occupational pattern, Chorwad

Age / Occupation	0-12		13-20		21-30		31-45		46-55		56 and above		Total	
	M	F	M	F	M	F	M	F	M	F	M	F	M	F
1. MB (OBM)	70 (40.18)	71 (39.44)	55 (55.0)	35 (53.85)	30 (46.88)	22 (38.60)	25 (52.08)	25 (53.19)	11 (64.71)	12 (66.67)	5 (55.56)	3 (50.00)	196 (48.04)	168 (45.04)
2. MB (IBE)	3 (1.76)	12 (6.67)	8 (8.00)	3 (4.62)	2 (3.12)	—	4 (8.34)	4 (8.51)	1 (5.88)	1 (5.56)	—	—	18 (4.41)	20 (5.36)
3. NMB	35 (20.39)	29 (16.11)	13 (13.00)	9 (13.85)	6 (9.38)	8 (14.18)	7 (14.58)	7 (14.89)	2 (11.76)	1 (5.56)	2 (22.22)	3 (50.0)	65 (15.93)	57 (15.28)
4. CRM	62 (38.47)	68 (37.78)	24 (24.08)	18 (27.68)	26 (40.62)	27 (47.36)	12 (25.00)	11 (23.41)	3 (17.65)	4 (22.23)	2 (22.22)	—	129 (31.62)	128 (34.32)
Total	170 (100)	180 (100)	100 (100)	65 (100)	64 (100)	57 (100)	48 (100)	47 (100)	17 (100)	18 (100)	9 (100)	6 (100)	408 (100)	373 (100)

Note: 1. (—) indicates nil.
2. Figures in parentheses are percentages to column total.

of at least two years between the two surviving children for 75 per cent of the households (Table 5.6).

TABLE 5.6

Frequency distribution of age gaps between surviving children of same parents according to occupation pattern, Chorwad

Age gap interval	No. of instances in which the age gap falls in the state interval for			Total
	MBO	NMBO	CM	
1—1.9	38 (33.04)	20 (43.48)	28 (25.23)	86 (31.62)
2—2.9	40 (34.78)	15 (32.61)	56 (50.45)	111 (40.81)
3—3.9	16 (13.91)	5 (10.87)	16 (14.41)	37 (13.60)
4—4.9	7 (6.09)	1 (2.17)	7 (6.31)	13 (5.52)
5—5.9	6 (5.22)	4 (8.70)	2 (1.80)	12 (4.41)
6 and above	8 (6.96)	1 (2.17)	2 (1.80)	11 (4.04)
Total	115 (100)	46 (100)	111 (100)	272 (100)

Note: Figures in parentheses are percentages to column total.

The educational level of the village population varied considerably. To some extent this reflects difference in the access to educational facilities in the village. In addition the caste structure and mechanization of fishing craft might have influenced the variations in the education level of the fishermen in the village. While it is certain that the mechanization of fishing craft has influenced the education level of fishermen, it is difficult in practice to determine whether technology is a cause or consequence of the educational facilities. The highest level of education in the village as per the census taken in 1981 was only primary.[4] About 50 per cent of the MBO households could read and write but this percentage was only 40 and 45 in the case of NMBOs and CM households respectively. The proportion of households without any education was accordingly higher in the case of NMBOs and CM households (Table 5.7).

TABLE 5.7

Distribution of households according to occupational pattern and highest level of education in the household, Chorwad Bander

Level of education	Number of households of			Total
	MBO	NMBO	CM	
1. Illiterate	25 (50.0)	10 (58.83)	22 (55.00)	57 (53.27)
2. Read and Write	1 (2.0)	1 (5.88)	—	2 (1.87)
3. Primary	24 (48.0)	6 (35.29)	18 (45.00)	48 (44.86)
Total	50 (100)	17 (100)	40 (100)	107 (100)

Note: 1. (—) indicates nil.
2. Figures in parentheses are percentages to column total.

Migration and typology of migrants

Migration is generally defined in terms of space and time and in the former category the migrant is usually defined as the one who crosses a specific geographical, political or administrative boundary to live in or take up work. Determination of the migration pattern basically involves the identification of places of origin and current residence, and type of those areas. In terms of time the migration is defined as long-term and short-term. In addition there is another type of migration known as circular migration in which the migrant changes the place of residence for various reasons in a set pattern in a given time frame and returns to the normal place of residence. In this section we identify the structure of migrant population.

Long-term migration : Long-term migration was analysed on the basis of the place of birth of the head of the household. Accordingly, migrants have been defined as those who have moved out at least once at any time during their life-time from their normal place of residence. Table 5.8 shows that 80.4 per cent of the household heads have indicated their

TABLE 5.8

Distribution of households by occupational pattern and birthplace location of the household head, Chorwad Bander

Location of birth-place	Number of households which had their heads birthplace indicated for			Total
	MBO	NMBO	CM	
1. Same village	39 (78.0)	13 (76.47)	34 (85.0)	86 (80.38)
2. Outside the village	11 (22.0)	4 (23.53)	5 (12.50)	20 (18.69)
3. Outside the district	—	—	1 (2.50)	1 (0.93)
Total	50 (100)	17 (100)	40 (100)	107 (100)

Note: 1. (—) indicates nil.
2. Figures in parentheses are percentages to column total.

birthplaces to be in the same village and only 19.5 per cent of the households had migrated and settled in the village from outside. Immigrant households accounted for about 22 per cent in the case of MBO households, 23.5 per cent in the case of NMBO households and 15 per cent in the case of crew member households. Further, our discussions with the villagers have indicated that all the long-term migrations were immigrations only and were inter-rural.

Short-term migration : Short-term migration is very common among fishermen. Unlike long-term migration, short migration is in the nature of out-migration from the village. One important reason is the migratory nature of fish. Migration is intensified because of the open access to harvesting of the resource.

During the census we took in late 1981, we found that eight households were looked. We also found that these households had migrated to various parts of Saurashtra during the fishing season. Though these households included both equipment (fishing) owners and crew members, they were dominated by boat owners. Seven households had got back to the village with their equipment on and off during the fishing season. We have taken the census of these seven households during their short visits to the village. These households comprised 1 trawler owner, 4 OBM boat owners and 2 crew member households.

Social participation of fishermen

Social participation of fishermen households is analysed in terms of their membership of various organizations. In addition the duration of membership and membership in multiple organizations are also analysed.

Participation in fishermen co-operative societies : Two fishermen co-operative societies function in the village. The oldest society to be organized was the Chorwad Bhavani Lodhi Sahakari Mandali Ltd. Both Hindu and Muslim fishermen used to be the members of the society. However, due to some differences, members of the one community organized another society, namely, Chorwad Sagar Utapadak Sahakari Mandali, in 1977. The total membership of these two societies was 353 in 1981. However, our census gave the membership as only 172.[6]

Membership of the co-operative societies according to occupation pattern is presented in Table 5.9. Members accounted for 22.02 per cent of the village population. Membership of the co-operatives is dominated by MBO households and poorly represented by NMBO and crew member households. The number of co-operative society members per household was the highest for MBO households with 2.1 members per household.

TABLE 5.9

Distribution of co-operative societies members and their households according to occupation pattern, Chorwad (1981)

Occupation	Number of HH with at least one member	% share in total	Number of members	% share in total
1. MB owner	105	48.5	49	61.0
2. NMB owner	22	14.9	15	12.8
3. Crew members	45	36.6	37	26.2
Total	101	100.0	172	100.0

MECHANIZATION: ITS IMPACT ON PRODUCTION SYSTEM

Mechanization of fishing craft and its impact on the production system will be taken up in this section. The contents include: technology of production; ownership of production assets; production pattern, current and past; output and incomes; distribution of gains; and disposal of fish landings.

Technology of production

We find a mix of modern, intermediary and traditional technologies in the village. The technology of accessories is either traditional or intermediate. The craft consist of In Board Engine (IBE) boats and dugout or plank-built canoes of length ranging from 15 to 25 feet with or without motors. The plank-built or dugout canoes fitted with Out Board Motors (OBM) with the horse power ranging between 3 and 8 are called OBM boats while canoes without motors are called traditional or non-mechanized boats. The only type of IBE boats in the village are called trawlers, after the type of the net used for catching fish.

The use of traditional canoes for catching fish is age-old. Motorization of the traditional fishing craft in the village began with the induction of first OBM in 1961 by the Gujarat Fisheries Central Co-operative Association (GFCCA) on demonstration basis.[7] The introduction of motorized boats in 1961 was subjected to initial resistances[8] by the fishermen. After observing for a year the fishermen of the village started buying motors. A capital subsidy[9] of Rs. 500 per motor also contributed to motorization. The progress was even during the period 1970 to 1980.

The introduction of IBE boats, particularly trawler [10], in 1967 was quite smooth. First, the introduction of IBE boats was preceded by the introduction of OBM boats. Second, the introduction of trawlers was quite sometime after its performance was observed in other areas. Trawlers first introduced in the village were 14 metres long and were fabricated from wood. Subsequently, trawlers were introduced mainly during early 1970s.

Distribution of different types of boats is presented in Table 5.10. In 1981 there was 5 IBE boats, 59 OBM boats and 22 non-mechanized boats. Of the 59 OBM boats 35 were in the length range of 15 to 25 feet and the rest above 26 feet. An overwhelming percentage (90.9) of the non-mechanized boats was less than 25 feet in length. All the five existing[11] IBE boats in the village were purchased between 1970 and 1974. An important characteristic of the OBM boats is that non-mechanized boats in both length ranges are more or less equally preferred for motorization. The non-mechanized boats are usually small as compared to OBM boats and pedalling is used for steering and propelling with an occasional use of sails.

Both OBM and non-mechanized boats in the village used gill nets while the IBE boats used trawl-nets. Thus, the trawl nets were introduced in the village with the purchase of an IBE trawler in 1967. There were both set and drift type of gill nets in the village. The mesh size of gill nets, a deciding factor in determining the type of fish to be caught, varied from 1 to 9 inch and the maximum concentration was observed in the range of 3.1 to 8 inch. Maximum (70 out of 108) number of gill nets[12] are owned by OBM owners. The crew owned 20 and the non-mechanized boat owners owned 18 gill nets. The nets with the mesh sizes in the range of 3.1 to 4 inch account for the maximum number of gill nets in the village and are usually used for catching pomfret, seer, hilsa and tuna fish (Table 5.11).

Gill nets with 7.1 to 8 inch mesh size usually used for

TABLE 5.10

Distribution of different types of boats according to the year of purchase, Chorwad (1981)

Year of acquiring	Mechanized boat*			NMB (Dugout of length)	
	Trawler	OBM of length			
		15 ft to 25 ft.	26 ft. and above	15 ft. to 25 ft.	26 ft. and above
Up to 1965	—	11	3	4	—
1966	—	—	—	—	—
1967	—	1	—	—	—
1968	—	1	1	—	—
1969	—	—	—	1	—
1970	1	1	1	2	—
1971	2	1	—	—	—
1972	1	3	2	3	—
1973	—	—	1	—	—
1974	1	2	1	2	—
1975	—	2	1	1	—
1976	—	—	1	1	—
1977	—	1	1	1	—
1978	—	5	2	1	—
1979	—	3	3	3	1
1980	—	2	1	1	1
1981	—	2	6	—	—
Total	5	35	24	20	2

Note: 1. (—) indicates nil.
2. *Indicates the year of purchase of boat but not the year of motorization.

catching bigger varieties of fish such as shark, ray, ghol, dhara, and sea fish account for about 35.7 per cent of the total gill nets owned by OBM and IBE boat owners. In the case of non-mechanized boat owners and crew the mesh size of the gill nets is concentrated in the range of 3.1 to 4 inch. The ownership of gill nets with more than one mesh size by the boat

TABLE 5.11

Distribution of gill nets owned by different households according to the mesh size, Chorwad (1981)

Mesh size (in inch)	Households		
	OBM (IBE)	NMB	CRM
0—1.0	1 (1.44)	—	—
1.1—2.0	—	—	—
2.1—3.0	—	—	—
3.1—4.0	34 (48.57)	7 (38.88)	10 (50.00)
4.1—5.0	5 (7.14)	6 (33.33)	8 (40.00)
5.1—6.0	5 (7.14)	1 (5.56)	1 (5 00)
6.1—7.0	—	—	—
7.1—8.0	25 (35.71)	3 (16.67)	1 (5.00)
8.1—9.0	—	1 (5.56)	
Total	70 (100)	18 (100)	20 (100)

Note: 1. (—) indicates nil.
2. Figures in parentheses are percentages to column total.

owners is also observed and the incidence is high in the case of OBM boat owners. The owning of gill nets with different mesh sizes by a boat owner is for the year-round production.

The lengthwise distribution of gill nets indicates that nets owned by the non-mechanized boat owners and crew members are smaller than those owned by the mechanized boat owners. However, most of the gill nets operated by the boat owners in the villages were less than 5,000 feet. The length of the two gill nets owned by OBM boat owners was in the range of 800 to 10,000 feet (Table 5.12).

TABLE 5.12

Lengthwise distribution of gill nets owned by different households, Chorwad (1981)

Length (in feet)	Households		
	OBM (IBE)	NMB	CRM
Up to 5000	65 (92.85)	18 (100)	20 (100)
5001-6000	3 (4.29)	—	—
6001-7000	—	—	—
7001-8000	—	—	—
8001-9000	1 (1.43)	—	—
9001-10000	1 (1.43)	—	—
Total	70 (100)	18 (100)	20 (100)

Note: 1. (—) indicates nil.
2. Figures in parentheses are percentages to column total.

All the five IBE boat owners owned trawl nets only. The mesh size of trawl net varies from 15 inch at the mouth of the net to ½ inch at the cord end.[13] The pattern of mesh size for different trawl nets is more or less the same and decreases from the mouth of the net to the cord end of the net. The lengthwise classification of the existing trawl nets indicates that all the nets have a length between 22 and 25 metres.

In addition to the gill nets, the non-mechanized boat owners also operated cast nets during the off-season for fishing. In 1981 the number of cast nets owned by non-mechanized boat owners was about 22. The mesh size and length of these nets did not vary much. The yarn used for mending all the above types of nets was either monafilament or nylon, and cotton yarn was not used for mending any type of nets. The significant technological changes in relation to gear after the mechanization of fishing craft are the shift from cotton yarn to either monafilament or nylon and the induction of trawl nets.

Ownership of production assets

In Chorward there are 5 IBE boats,[14] 44 OBM boats and 17 non-mechanized boats between 57 boat-owning households indicating the ownership of more than one boat in the case of some households.

Looking now at the situation as we found in 1981, 40 out of 107 households accounting for 33 per cent of the population in the village did not have any fishing equipment (except some nets), whereas the top 15 per cent households owned more than one boat along with nets and accessories. The Gini coefficient for the distribution of value of productive assets over the households was found to be 0.6025. Since the calculated value is over 0.6, it indicates an inequitable distribution of assets in the village. Figure 5.2 shows the Lorenz curve of the distribution of fishing assets.[15]

Pattern of production: Present and past

Fishing is a joint enterprise in the sense that it requires participation of more than one person. The number of fishermen varies from as small as two in some of the non-mechanized boats to six or seven in trawlers.

Although fishing is a joint enterprise in the sense described above, the ownership pattern of fishery assets—craft and gear—in the village is basically individual.[16]

In addition to the ownership of the craft and gear, the nature and character of owner (in terms of active fishing) and the status of non-owner workers in the boat play an important role in the organization of production. Taking these dimensions into account John Kurien[17] has identified six possible combinations of ownership and status of owner and worker, and found the combination of joint ownership, owner worker and non-owner partner to be the most egalitarian. In the village there are four patterns of ownership:

(i) Individual owner, owner worker and non-owner partner (IO, OW and NOP);
(ii) Individual owner, owner non-worker and non-owner partner (IO, ONW and NOP);
(iii) Individual owner, owner worker and non-owner labour (IO, OW and NOL); and

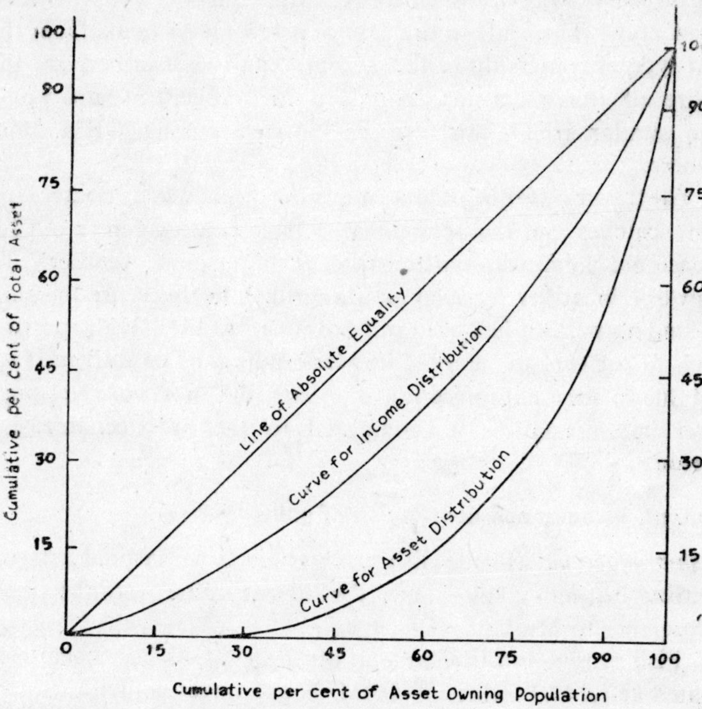

	Asset	Income
Gini ratio	0.6025	0.3207

FIG. 5.2: *Lorenz curve for asset and income distribution, Chorwad (1981-82)*

(iv) Individual owner, owner non-worker and non-owner labour (IO, ONW and NOL).

The first has been the predominant mode and was observed in all the non-mechanized boats and a substantial number of OBM boats. The second, third and fourth types of ownership pattern have come into existence for mechanized boats. The second type of ownership pattern is, however, only confined to a few OBM boat owners. The third and fourth types are more prominent in the case of trawler owners, wherein the boat is operated by the owner with the help of either totally (in one out of five trawlers) or partially (four out of five trawlers) hired crew. The shift in the case of a few OBM boats from the first type of ownership to the second can be ascribed to the desire of the fishermen to reduce the drudgery of hard work. The similar trend can also be noticed among OBM boat owners.

All trawlers, OBM boats and non-mechanized boats land their catches on the traditional village landing centre but for occasional landings, particularly during rough weather, by trawlers in either Veraval or Mangrol.[18] In this sense the shift in landing pattern has been only confined to the small portion (say 5 per cent of total) of trawler landings. The shift in landing due to seasonal migration of boats did not change much after mechanization as compared to the pre-mechanization period.

Output, incomes and distribution of gains

Fish production: Marine fish production is a seasonal activity. Active fishing takes place for about nine months from September to May.

Fish production in Chorwad during 1981-82 has been estimated at 1,142.7 tonnes.[19] OBM boats have contributed the maximum to production with 516 tonnes and are followed by trawlers and non-mechanized boats with 497 and 129 tonnes respectively. Landings of the mechanized boats, both trawlers and OBM, account for about 89 per cent of the landings. Total landings in the village have at least doubled after mechanization. There has been a marked change in the variety of fish caught after the addition of trawlers to the fishing fleet; high-value prawns and lobsters have been added to the catch and large quantities of dhoma and other small demersal species have been caught after trawlers have been introduced.

Varietywise fish production is presented in Table 5.13. Dhoma accounts for the maximum with 396.9 (34.6 per cent) tonnes and accounted for about 80 per cent of the trawler landings. The landings of dhoma are followed by white pomfret, clupeids, seer and hilsa with 148.4, 130.6, 115.9, and 106.4 tonnes respectively. The specieswise distribution of the OBM and non-mechanized boat landings indicates that it is quite even compared to the landings of trawlers.

TABLE 5.13

Specieswise estimated marine fish landings by mechanized and non-mechanized boats, Chorwad (1981-82)

(in tonnes)

Species	Fish landings of stated+ variety by			
	Mechanized boats		Non-mechanized boats	Total
	Trawlers	OBM		
1. White pomfret	12.5 (2.5)	106.5 (20.7)	19.4 (15.0)	148.4 (13 0)
2. Black pomfret	3.6 (0.7)	31.3 (6.1)	5.1 (3.9)	40.0 (3.5)
3. Seer fish	—	85.6 (16.6)	30.3 (23.4)	115.9 (10.2)
4. Hilsa	—	79.8 (15.5)	16.9 (13.1)	106.7 (9.3)
5. Clupeids	—	110.7 (21.4)	19.9 (15.4)	130.6 (11.4)
6. Sharks and Rays	18.6 (3.7)	56.5 (11.0)	5.6 (4.3)	80.7 (7.1)
7. Prawns and Lobsters	25.8 (5.2)	—	—	25.8 (5.2)
8. Dhoma	396.9 (79.9)	—	—	396.9 (34.8)
9. Eel	28.6 (5.8)	1.5 (0.3)	—	30.1 (2.6)
10. Others*	10.8 (2.2)	43.7 (8.4)	32.1 (24.9)	66.6 (5.8)
Total	496.8 (100)	515.6 (100)	129.3 (100)	1141.7 (100)

Notes: 1. +Excluding the household consumption in the village and gifts.
2. (—) Indicates nil.
3. *Includes ribbon fish, cat fish, silver bar, etc.
4. Figures in parentheses are percentages to column total.

Output values: Estimates of output in the village are based on the price information obtained by us during the survey and output estimates. As there were sharp fluctuations in prices received by the fishermen for different varieties, we have used average prices. The annual gross value of output has been estimated at Rs. 47,406,90. About 62 per cent of this is contributed by the landings of OBM boats. Pomfret landings by OBM account for 44 per cent of the catch value. Trawlers contribute about 24 per cent of the value. Prawns and lobsters constitute about 55 per cent of the value of catch by trawlers. The value of catch of non-mechanized boats comes only to 13 per cent (Table 5.14). Pomfrets, prawns and lobsters account for about 49 per cent of the output value. Thus, the economic well-being of the fishermen depends largely on the landings of pomfrets, prawns and lobsters.

Measurement of household's income from fishing : In this section we will estimate the incomes of each household, which can be defined as the net returns on the fishing assets owned by the households and family labour. These data were collected by using questionnaires and checking was done with the fish merchants in the mini village.

For working out the returns, it is necessary to estimate the economics of the fishing craft and gear. Table 5.15 shows the quarterwise gross value of output (GVO) for different types of boats. The GVO per trawler is estimated to be Rs. 1,88,133. The GVO for OBMs up to 25 feet is estimated at Rs. 44,402 and for OBMs above 25 feet show a GVO of Rs. 67,274. Non-mechanized boats of feet up to 25 give a GVO of Rs. 24,898. The quarterwise distribution of GVO is similar for OBM and non-mechanized boats and trawlers. For example, the quarter October-to-December accounts for 41 per cent of the catch value in the case of trawlers, 31 per cent in the case of OBM boats up to 25 feet, 43 per cent in the case of OBM boats more than 25 feet and 41 per cent in the case of non-mechanized boats.

The cost of operations can be classified into variable costs and fixed costs. Variable costs include the cost of fuel, wages, expenditure on ice and water, food expenditure on crew (if any), cost of net yarn and others. Typically these costs are incurred only when the boat is in operation and may change

TABLE 5.14

Average prices and annual gross value of output by different types of boats, Chorwad (1981-82)

(in '000 Rupees)

Varieties	Price per kg. (Rs.)	Annual gross value of output by			
		Trawlers	OBM boats	NM boats	Total
1. White pomfret	10.50	131.25 (11.4)	1118.25 (37.8)	203.70 (32.5)	1453.20 (30.7)
2. Black pomfret	5.00	18.00 (1.6)	156.50 (5.3)	25.50 (4.1)	200.00 (4.2)
3. Seer fish	6.00	—	513.60 (17.3)	181.80 (29.0)	695.40 (14.7)
4. Hilsa	5.00	—	399.00 (13.5)	84.50 (13.4)	483.50 (10.2)
5. Clupeids	4.50	—	498.15 (16.8)	89.55 (14.3)	587.70 (12.4)
6. Sharks and rays	3.25	60.45 (5.2)	182.81 (6.2)	18.20 (2.9)	261.46 (5.5)
7. Prawns and Lobsters	25.00	645.00 (55.9)	—	—	645.00 (13.6)
8. Dhoma	0.50	198.45 (17.2)	—	—	198.45 (4.2)
9. Eel	2.75	78.65 (6.8)	4.13 (0.1)	—	82.78 (1.7)
10. Others	2.00	21.60 (1.9)	87.40 (3.0)	24.20 (3.8)	133.20 (2.8)
Total		1153.40 (100)	2959.84 (100)	627.45 (100)	4740.69 (100)

Note: 1. (—) indicates nil.
2. Figures in parentheses are percentages to column total.

from day to day. Fixed costs are incurred irrespective of whether the boat is operating or not and include expenditure on repairs and maintenance of boats, dry-docking and oil-painting,

TABLE 5.15

Quarterwise gross value of output per boat of different types of boats, Chorwad (1981-82)

(in Rupees)

Quarter	Gross value of output of			
	Trawler	OBM boat with length		NMB of length
		Up to 25 ft.	25 ft. and above	up to 25 ft.
July-September	18343 (9.75)	6685 (15.06)	9370 (13.93)	1056 (4.24)
October-December	77887 (41.40)	16550 (34.27)	29450 (43.78)	10254 (41.18)
January-March	52640 (27.98)	11887 (26.77)	15994 (23.77)	8916 (35.81)
April-June	39263 (20.87)	9280 (20.90)	12460 (18.52)	4672 (18.77)
Total	188133 (100)	44402 (100)	67274 (100)	24898 (100)

Note: Figures in parentheses are percentages to column total.

depreciation, interest on borrowed capital and others. Strictly speaking, payment to crew is variable, but in our calculation we have included this item in fixed costs in view of the permanent nature of employment. Further, it is easy to calculate yearly salaries of the crew which is estimated on the share basis.

The itemwise average variable costs per day for operating different types of boats in the villages during 1981-82 are given in Table 5.16. The variable cost per day for a trawler works out to Rs. 353 which is 3 to 5 times that of the cost per day of OBM boat depending on the size. OBM boats up to 25 feet incur Rs. 56 towards the variable cost a day. OBM boats of over 25 feet have a variable cost of Rs. 109 a day. The total variable cost of a non-mechanized boat is about one-third of an OBM boat of a comparable size. In the case of trawlers

TABLE 5.16

Average variable costs per day for operating various types of boats, Chorwad (1981-82)

(*in Rupees*)

Items of cost	Cost incurred on the stated item per day per trip by			
	Trawler owner	OBM Boat (of length from 15 ft. to 25 ft.) owner	OBM Boat (of 25 ft. and above) owner	NMB (of less than 25 ft.) owner
1. Fuel oils	263.50	42.50	73.80	4.25+
2. Mobile oil and other lubricants	15.60	3.50	9.25	—
3. Wages to casual labourers	—	4.50*	6.25*	3.50*
4. Ice and water	26.50	—	—	—
5. Food expenditure for crew	28.50	2.50	2.00	3.00
6. Cost of net twine	6.65	9.75	13.50	7.50
7. Others	12.40	3.50	4.50	4.50
Total	353.25	66.25 (61.75)	109.30 (103.05)	22.75 (19.25)

Note: 1. +Indicates expenditure incurred for lighting devices during the fishing trip.
2. *Mostly in kind (fish) for putting the boat into and out of the sea before and after the fishing trip.
3. Figures in parentheses in total row indicate cash expenditure.

and OBM boats the cost of fuel oil is the most important single item in the variable cost.

Annual fixed costs incurred per boat for different types of boats are presented in Table 5.17. Salaries to crew members account for the large part of expenditure, followed by depreciation and other items. Crew salary differs depending on the type

TABLE 5.17

Annual fixed costs incurred per boat by different types of owners, Chorwad (1981-82)

(*in Rupees*)

Items of expenditure	Cost incurred on the stated item for boat			
	Trawler	OBM boat of less than 25 ft.	OBM boat of 25 ft. and above	NMB of less than 25 ft.
1. Salaries to the crew members*	39600.00	16980.50	28307.50	10572.10
2. Repairs and maintenance	7658.00	1384.50	1700.00	806.00
3. Dry docking and oil painting	2167.00	360.50	482.00	296.50
4. Depreciation**	17250.00	4534.00	6180.00	3267.80
5. Interest*** on borrowed capital	2184.00	330.00	660.00	330.00
6. Others	3445.00†	205.00	181.50	250.00
	91960.00	23794.50	37511.00	15521.60

Note: * For working out the salaries of the crew it has been assumed that all the required (5 per trawler, 3 for OBM boat of 25 ft. and above, 2 for OBM of less than 25 ft. and 2 for NMB of less than 25 ft.) is hired.

** For estimating the depreciation we have taken the economic lifetime of the boat gill nets, trawlers, motor/engine and winch to be 15, 3, 1, 12, and 10 years respectively. The investment on these items was taken at 1981 prices.

*** For working out the interest on borrowed capital only borrowings from formal sources for investments on boats and gears are considered.

† Includes the insurance premium of Rs. 1997.

of boat. In general crew salary in mechanized boats is higher than in non-mechanized boats.

The net returns are the highest in the case of trawlers (Rs. 27,289.25), followed by OBM boats of 25 feet and above (Rs. 9,641.25), OBM boats of less than 25 feet (Rs. 8,566.85) and non-mechanized boats (Rs. 5,672.65). However, the return on investment is the highest for non-mechanized boats and the least for trawlers (Table 5.18).

TABLE 5.18

Gross and net returns of different types of boats, Chorwad (1981-82)

(in Rupees)

Particulars	Returns on			
	Trawler	OBM boat of length less than 25 ft.	OBM boat of length 25 ft. and above	NMB of less than 25 ft.
I. Annual gross returns	188133.00	44402.00	67274.00	24898.00
II. Annual expenditure				
(a) Fixed costs	91960.00	23794.00	37511.00	15521.60
(b) Variable costs	68888.75	12041.25	20094.75	3753.75
Sub-total	160843.75	35835.75	57605.75	19275.35
III. Net returns	27289.25	8566.25	9641.25	5622.65
IV. Return on investment (%)	13.99	28.55	22.58	33.07

Note: Annual variable costs have been estimated by multiplying the per day/trip expenditure by the number of fishing days. The number of fishing days for all types of boats was found to be 195 in a year.

Distribution of income: While the primary source of income is fishing, a few households also derived some income from non-fishing sources. We have computed the income accruing to each of the households. The income derived from fishing is obtained from the economies of different types of fishing craft. Data on the income derived from professions other than fishing was obtained from the heads of households during the census taken in 1981.

The distribution of income by occupation and source is presented in Table 5.19. The income generated from occupations

TABLE 5.19

Distribution of income according to occupation, Chorwad (1981-82)

(in Rupees)

Occupation	Income			Per household	Per capita
	Fishery related	Non-fishery	Total		
1. IBM	212901 (8.91)	3000 (0.13)	215901 (9.04)	43180.20	5681.61
2. OBM	1415512 (59.24)	49500 (2.07)	1465012 (61.31)	32555.83	4024.76
3. NMB	218014 (9.13)	155.00 (0.65)	233514 (8.77)	13736.13	1914.05
4. CRP	447912 (18.74)	27000 (1.13)	474912 (19.88)	11872.80	1847.91
Total	2294339 (96.02)	95000 (3.98)	2389339 (100)	22330.28	3059.33

Note: Figures in parentheses represent percentages to column total.

other than fishing as related by the villagers is small and accounts for less than 4 per cent of the income of all households. As expected, the boat-owning households are richer than non-owning. Among the boat-owning households, the per capita income is the highest in the case of trawler owners and was followed by OBM boats and non-mechanized boat-owning households. Maximum income (61 per cent) is generated by households owning boats.

The estimated Gini ratio and Lorenz curves for the distribution of productive assets and incomes are given in Figure 5.2. The Gini ratio for the inequality in income is 0.3207 as against the computed ratio for assets of 0.6025. As expected, income distribution is more equal than asset distribution. The large gap between the inequalities indicates the favourable factor share of labour.

The Gini ratio of income inequality is low as compared to the Gini ratio of incomes in developing countries which has been computed to be 0.4 and 0.5 by Anand and Atkinson respectively.[20] However, the computed ratio is more or less comparable to a recent estimate by Bliss and Stern in relation to an agricultural village in Uttar Pradesh.[21]

Disposal of fish

The landings can be channelized into: (a) fresh consumption in domestic market, (b) sun-dried and salt-cured for domestic consumption purposes, (c) extraction of fishmeal and oil, and (d) freezing, canning and drying for exports.[22]

Trawlers have brought about a major change in prawn catches for exports. At the same time, the catch of low-value species has also gone up. In the pre-mechanization period the entire landings were disposed of either fresh or after sun-drying and salt-curing. After mechanization fresh consumption and sun-drying and salt-curing have gone down. A substantial portion is set aside for fishmeal extraction. Presently (1981-82) the utilization pattern is as follows: fresh consumption (50.7 per cent); sun-drying and salt-curing (14.5 per cent); fishmeal extraction (32.5 per cent) and exports (2.3 per cent).

MARKETS IN THE VILLAGE

In this section, we shall examine the markets for inputs, labour, credit and output in the village. The major purpose is to understand the changes which have taken place with technological developments.

Markets for inputs

With mechanization, fishermen require such inputs as service facilities for motors/engines, fuel, lubricants, ice and construction facilities for landing and berthing which were otherwise unkown to the traditional fishermen. In addition, the fishermen depend on facilities for boat building and suppliers of nets and yarn for net mending and repairing, which form the core input sector.

Table 5.20 shows the distribution of boats according to the place of purchase/construction of boats. Sixteen boats were

TABLE 5.20

Distribution of boats owned by sample respondents according to place of purchase/ construction, Chorwad

Location of source of purchase	Stated source of purchase for						Total	
	Trawlers		OBM Boats		NMB			
	New	Old	New	Old	New	Old	New	Old
1. Within the village	—	—	—	—	—	—		—
2. Outside the village but within the district	—	—	—	4	—	5	—	9
3. Outside the district but within the state	3	—	4	3	2	3	9	6
4. Outside the state	2	—	11	—	3	—	16	—
Total	5	—	15	7	5	8	25	15

Note: (—) indicates nil.

purchased from sources outside the state. Not one new boat was constructed within the district. Two trawlers were constructed in boat-building yards outside the state. It was understood that almost all types of boats which had origins outside Gujarat were purchased from Karnataka. Some of the boats were purchased from unorganized boat-building yards or carpenters from other villages. Further, it appears that transaction of boats particularly in the case of OBM and NBM between the fishermen is very common.

There are a few carpenters in Mangrol (which is about 5.7 km. from Chorwad) who construct NMB and OBM boats. The fishermen of the village do not go to Mangrol but prefer organized boat-building yards.

In the last 10-15 years the prices of wooden boats have gone up because of the short supply of timber suitable for construction of wooden boats. In order to minimize the cost, many fishermen developmental agencies have tried alternative material for constructing boats. So far, no boats constructed with material other than wood are used by the fishermen in the village.

Supply of motors/engines is another important aspect of the construction of mechanized/motorized boats. It is the supply of motors which is of interest to us. Motorization of fishing craft started with the installation of British Anjani motors. However, this motor did not gain the confidence of fishermen due to the very low horse power of the motor less than 4. Later on Yamaha motors of 8 h.p. were imported by the Gujarat Fisheries Central Co-operative Association (GFCCA). The demand for Yamaha increased considerably from 1975 onwards. Now, British Anjani and Yamaha are the only motors used by the fishermen in the village while various brands are available in the market. Yamaha motors are supplied by both co-operatives and private entrepreneurs.

The supply of motors by co-operatives is very limited. Motor suppliers are in a monopolistic situation. Thair hands have been strengthened by the granting of only one import licence to the state agency to import Yamaha motors. Hence supplies of motors are made at a very high price (Rs. 12,000) as against the normal price of Rs. 8,000 in 1981. The prices are uniform for different buyers and there is no evidence of discriminating monopoly. In the initial stages the supply of motors was entirely through co-operatives only. With the increased demand for motors, which could not be sustained by the supply system in the co-operative set-up, the private entrepreneur started importing the motors. The two sources of supply of motors, GFCCA and the private importer, are located outside the village but within the district.

Important changes in the gear and gear material after motorization are:

(i) the technology of production of yarn for net mending and repairing has changed from decentralized village level industries producing cotton yarn to centralized large-scale industries to produce nylon and synthetic yarn and machine mended nets,

(ii) bulk of the sales of material for net mending are by a few large-scale merchants.

There are two main yarn supply sources available in the village for net mending and repairing. One of them is a co-operative society and the other is a private trader. Both of them also extend credit facilities to the fishermen. Fishermen, particularly trawler owners, also purchase yarn from Veraval and Chorwad (main) village. It is observed that a considerable share of the purchases is from private traders and on credit.

The private trader purchases yarn from Veraval and sells to the fishermen. The price of the yarn charged by the trader appears to be 15-20 per cent higher than the price charged by co-operatives. Neither the trader nor the co-operatives stock yarn with them, but they procure it only after an order is placed. The private trader procures the yarn during his regular visits to Veraval.

Petrol and kerosene are used for operating motorized boats. Most of the OBM boats are operated on kerosene only. However, all motors use petrol for starting. A few are run throughout with petrol alone while others switch over to kerosene immediately after start. The number of motors which run entirely on petrol has decreased over time in the village. Currently, there are only three motors which are run on petrol. Kerosene supplied through the co-operative society is available right in the village while the supplies through the private trader are arranged in the nearly main village. Boat owners usually turn to the private trader when supplies through the co-operatives are inadequate. The entire supply of petrol is met by private traders in the nearby village or Veraval. Trawlers require diesel for their operation which is supplied by private traders in the main village. Trawler owners normally do not find it difficult to get diesel. Service facilities for motors and engines though inadequate are available in Veraval and Mangrol.

Market for labour

In this section we deal with the supply-demand conditions of labour, and occupational mobility in the village.

Two types of labour contracts are prevalent. The first is the wage system and the second is share contract in which the labourer receives a share in the fish caught during his working. In the former system, wages are paid in cash and kind. Wages in kind are usually paid to labourers involved in putting OBM and NM boats into sea and for taking out while wages in cash are paid to the crew in trawlers. During normal fishing trips the crew are not provided with food in either of these contracts. However, during long trips and night fishing they are provided with food.

The sharing system is standard and is worth describing in detail to understand the employer-employee relations. The fishing labourers go fishing with their own gear or with the gear of the owners of the craft. Each of the crew member in an OBM boat which requires three persons for its operation is given one-sixth share and the equipment owner gets one-half of the gross value of output. The operating expenditure on the boat, gear and motor is borne by the equipment owner. The general principle of sharing is that each of the crew member gets one share each and the boat, gear and motor get one share each in the gross value of output.

There are certain variations in the pattern of operation. One or more of the family members of the equipment owner may go fishing. In such cases the equipment owner(s) also gets share(s) for the labour of his or his family member in addition to the equipment share. In some other cases, which is very rare, the crew member gets the share for his gear in proportion to the size of the gear in the total gear. The sharing pattern in the case of non-mechanized boats is similar to that of the OBM boats but for the difference that there will not be any share for the engine/motor. Thus, the total gross value of output of a NMB in which three crew members are employed, the share of the boat and gear is two-fifths and the share of each crew member is one-fifth. The variations equally apply to the patterns in the case of non-mechanized boats. Thus, we find that the system of payment to the labourer has not changed even after motorization while the absolute incomes of the labourers might have increased due to improved economics of boats after motorization. However, in the case of the crew in trawler (mechanized boat) the returns to labour are paid in terms of fixed wages. Thus, on the one hand, motorization has not altered the wage pattern and, on the other, introduction of trawlers has paved the way for fixed wages in cash.

Supply and demand pattern for labour : In order to understand the employment situation we have attempted to estimate surplus labourers[23] in the village. Before we get down to the details we give a brief description of the supply and demand patterns for labourers in the village.

The supply of labourers in the village is more or less constant throughout the year, while the requirement fluctuates widely from day to day. The fluctuations mainly depend upon the weather and the decision of the boat owners to put out their boats for fishing. Once the boat decides to go fishing, the labour requirement is fixed. From about June to August, no boat owner may be prepared to go fishing and bear the risk even if the labourers are willing. Thus, during the monsoon period, the demand is the lowest. However, some fishing labourers are employed for repairing nets during the off-season. During the fishing season the fishing labourers have occasional forced idleness owing to religious beliefs[24] and non-seaworthiness of the craft. However, this does not affect all the labourers in the village at a time.

Table 5.22 gives the estimates of surplus labourers.[25] The deficit in short supply accounts for about 12 per cent. In a situation where demand exceeds supply, the equipment owners tend to allocate the work to family members until all family members are fully employed and then only allocate work to hired labourers. The study of demand-supply relations of labour in the village on the basis of the wage rates could not be undertaken in view of the non-availability of ruling wages.[26]

The estimated labour participation, in terms of family and hired labourer, in the operation of different types of fishing craft, is presented in Table 5.22. We notice that the family member participation in actual fishing is maximum possible in the case of NM boat owner households, and to near complete in the case of OBM boat owners. However, in the case of trawler owner households only five were involved in actual fishing while the availability was about 14 members. As expected, the share of family labour in total crew required for the operation of boats was maximum (65.91 per cent) in the case of NM boats and minimum (17.96 per cent) in the case of trawlers.

The structure of the labour force has not changed with the

TABLE 5.21

Estimates of surplus labourers according to occupations, Chorwad (1982-83)

Particulars	No. of members in households of				Total
	Trawler owners	OBM boat owners	NMB owners	Crew	
1. Number of households	5	45	17	40	107
2. Number of able-bodied adult male members of family	15	121	29	62	217
3. Number of adult male members with occupations other than fishing	1	16	—	6	23
4. Number of members actively engaged in fishing or at best having no occupation	14	104	29	56	203
5. Number of adult male members who have not yet entered the working force (students)	—	1	—	—	1
6. Number of members required for operating the fishing equipment	—30	153	40	—	227
7. Surplus labourers in the fishing workforce	—16	—49	—15	56	—24
8. Surplus labourers per household	—3.40	—1.09	—0.88	—1.40	—0.22

Note: 1. (—) indicates nil.
2. Negative surpluses indicate the deficits.

introduction of mechanized/motorized boats. Over 98 per cent of the labour force for fishing is employed on a permanent basis. Casual labourers are a relatively unknown phenomenon.

Employment effect of the technological development in the village: Employment in fisheries can be divided into (i) employment in actual fishing, and (ii) employment in forward and backward linkages.

TABLE 5.22

Estimated labour participation pattern, family and hired, for operating different types of boats, Chorwad (1981-82)

Type of boat	Total No. of boats	Estimated avg. crew size required per boat	Total crew required	Estimated source of crew		
				Family	Hired	
					Sharing	Salary
1. Trawlers	5	5.6	28 (100)	5 (17.96)	—	23 (82.14)
2. OBM boats:						
(a) Up to 25 ft.	35	2.37	83 (100)	56 (67.47)	27 (32.53)	—
(b) 25 ft. and above	24	3.00	72 (100)	34 (47.22)	38 (52.78)	— —
3. NM boats	22	2.00	44 (100)	29 (65.91)	15 (34.09)	—
Total	86	—	227 (100)	124 (54.63)	80 (35.24)	23 (10.13)

Notes: 1. Estimated on the basis of information from sample respondents.
2. Figures in parentheses indicate the share of family hired labourers in total crew required.

We have computed the capital-labour and output-labour ratios for different types of boats in the village (Table 5.23). The amount of capital required for creating one workplace in the non-mechanized sector is estimated to be only Rs. 8,900 while it is as high as Rs. 13,533 for OBM boats and Rs. 32,750 for trawlers. Further, the output-labour ratio was 3.07 tonnes for non-mechanized boats and 5.23 tonnes for OBM boats. Thus, for every six tonnes of output in the OBM boat sector there is a displacement of three potential workplaces in the non-mechanized sector.

TABLE 5.23

Estimated capital-labour and output labour ratios for different types of boats, Chorwad (1981)

Type of boat	Capital invest-ment (Rs.)	Employ-ment in terms of persons	Output (tonnes)	Capital-labour ratio (Rs.)	Output-labour ratio (tonnes)
1. Non-mechanized	26700	3	9.2	8900	3.07
2. OBM	40600*	3	16.7	13533	5.23
3. Trawlers	196500+	6	51.5	32750	8.58

Note: 1. *Including the investment on gear.
2. +Taking the ration price of the motor into account.

Labour mobility: Distribution of the sample OBM boat crew members according to the labour mobility ratio[27] is presented in Table 5.24. Of the 10 crew working in OBM boats seven were found to be having low mobility and three medium mobility. There is a tradition that the labourers do not change the employer during the fishing season. The reasons for mobility may vary from labourer to labourer.

From the above analysis, we may conclude that the supply and demand conditions for labourers can impede the movement of labourers, but this is usually not an insurmountable obstacle. In fact crew mobility among the skilled and healthy crew is very high in view of the strong competition among employers. Crew are attracted by the employers through non-

TABLE 5.24

Distribution of sample OBM boat crew members according to the labour-mobility ratio, Chorwad (1981-82)

Labour mobility	Number of crew with stated mobility	% share in total
1. High (0.81 and above)	—	—
2. Medium (0.41 to 0.80)	3	30.00
3. Low (up to 0.41)	7	70.00
Total	10	100.00

price mechanisms since the remuneration is not a fixed wage in the majority of cases. The mechanisms include the condition of the fishing equipment, employer-labourer relations, granting of free loans by craft owners, and fishing techniques.

The distribution of crew according to the main reason for change of an employer is presented in Table 5.25. Hope of

TABLE 5.25

Reasons for change of employer by the crew members during their immediate past change, Chorwad (1981-82)

Reasons for change of employer	No. of crew who indicated the stated reasons	% share in total
1. Dispute with the boat owner	4	23.53
2. Hope of getting higher returns due to efficient working of the craft	5	29.41
3. Household head wanted the member to join the own enterprise	2	11.76
4. Invitation to join a new craft/disposition of fishing equipment by boat owner	3	17.65
5. Others	3	17.65
Total	17	100.00

getting higher returns accounts for the maximum of changes. A new employer is identified owing to disputes with the present boat owner. Many wanted to start their own ventures.

The interlocking of credit and labour, though weak, takes the form of lending money to the crew by equipment owners. Generally, it is in the form of advance wage or to meet the credit needs of the crew.[28] The reasons behind the interlocking of credit and labour are quite obvious in a labour shortage situation. In addition interlocking of credit and labour helps in attracting skilled, experienced and healthy labourer for fishing.

The details pertaining to the amount borrowed and outstanding are presented in Table 5.26. It may be noticed that

TABLE 5.26

Size distribution of sample crew members according to the amount borrowed at the time of joining from and outstanding debt to the employer owner as on December 31, 1981, Chorwad

Frequency interval (Rs.)	Number of crew with stated range of borrowings	% share in total	Number of crew with outstanding debt in the stated range	% share in total
No borrowwing/outstanding debt	4	40.00	9	90.00
1—500	2	20.00	1	10.00
501—1000	4	40.00	—	—
1000—2000	—	—	—	—
2001—2500	—	—	—	—
Total	10	100	10	100

six out of 10 sample crew members have borrowed from the employer at the time of joining, the amount borrowed being less than Rs. 1,000. It may also be observed that the tendency of repaying loans among the crew is showing an encouraging trend. At the time of our survey, i.e. December 1981, only 10 per cent of the crew members are faced with an outstanding debt of less than Rs. 500. The tendency of non-returning of loan borrowed may be attributed to two reasons: (1) a system wherein the employer deducts the amount from his salary, (2) pressure tactics adopted by the employer. It is gathered that the skilled labourer hardly finds it difficult to get a loan as the employer cannot afford to relieve him in any case.

Occupational mobility : Taking the economic and social status into account the fishing occupations in the village can be ranked, in descending order, as follows: (a) Trawler owner, (b) OBM boat owner, (c) Non-mechanized boat owner, (d) Crew in trawler, (e) Crew in OBM boat, and (f) Crew in non-mechanized boat. It is also true that the individual at the lower rung of the occupational ladder is always ambitious to reach the higher rung and this is how the occupational changes take place. This is, however, not to suggest that the sliding down the ladder of occupation is not possible or is not observed. But the sliding down the ladder may be mainly due to some unavoidable circumstances and may not be an invited change. For example, two of the non-mechanized boat owners changed to crew in OBM boat/NM boat as they lost their craft during a cyclone in the village. We have computed the occupational mobility ratio[29] for the sample respondents.

The distribution of working population in sample households according to the pace of graduation to the current position is given in Table 5.27. The occupational mobility ratio in the village is not very high as compared to other villages. About 75 per cent of the villagers have the pace of graduation as low, while over 14 per cent had the same as medium and 11 per cent as high. The table also indicates that the pace of graduation is quite low in the MB owners compared to that of crew in MB.

Market for credit

Credit is not an input like labour and mechanical power but it enables the fishermen or boat owner to buy inputs[30] and therefore plays an important role.[31] Therefore, it is very essential to understand the credit market and its influence on the mechanization of fishing craft. We shall first describe the

TABLE 5.27

Distribution of working population in sample households according to pace of graduation to current status, Chorwad (1981-82)

Pace of graduation	Current status					Total
	MB owner	NMB owner	Crew in MB	Crew in NMB	Others	
1. High (0.81 and above)	1 (4.54)	—	5 (16.67)	2 (25.00)	—	8 (11.27)
2. Medium (0.51 to 0.81)	1 (4.54)	1 (10.00)	6 (20.00)	2 (25.00)	—	10 (14.08)
3. Low (up to 0.51)	20 (90.91)	9 (90.00)	19 (63.33)	4 (50.00)	1 (100.0)	53 (74.65)
Total	22 (100.00)	10 (100.00)	30 (100.00)	8 (100.00)	1 (100.0)	71 100.00)

Note: 1. (—) indicates nil.
2. Figures in parentheses are percentages to column total.

structure and assess how easy it is to obtain credit for individuals in different occupations. In addition, the terms and conditions of credit from various sources are also analysed alongwith the study of interlinkages of credit, labour and marketing relations, and equilibrium/disequilibrium of the credit market.

Credit facility is extended by sources such as co-operatives, commercial banks, fish merchants, professional moneylenders, friends, etc. However, it is observed that the fishermen of this village borrow from two main sources: fish merchants and friends and relatives.

The pattern of loans advanced and their recovery by the fish merchants is quite typical. These loans are not purpose tied and are advanced throughout the year. The majority of the fishermen borrow for off-season maintenance. The advancing of loans to the fishermen entitles the fish trader to buy off the entire fish catch of the fishermen at mutually negotiated prices. The trader deducts about 25 per cent of the sale proceeds of the fishermen towards the recovery of the loan. These loans do not carry any interest. Further, leniency in recovering loans by fish traders is shown mainly to keep the fishermen in a credit-market interlocked situation for the benefit of the fish trader. The credit on similar lines is also available from the Gujarat Fisheries Central Co-operative Association, but the co-operative society in the village did not avail of the facility.

The commerical banks advanced loans to fishermen only for the purchase of gear with the condition that the fishermen should route their loan applications only through their co-operative society. The banks charge an interest rate of 4 per cent (under DRI scheme) on these loans. Further, these loans are repayable in 24 easy monthly intalments. However, off-season for fishing is treated as recovery holiday.

Loans by moneylenders and friends and relatives are advanced only after seeking a security. Further, these loans were observed to be quite costly with the rate of interest ranging from 24 to 36 per cent.

The credit economy of the village shows some intensity characteristics. For, the main credit agencies to which majority of the borrowers turn are existing in the private market with the exception of moneylenders who are from the fishermen community itself and a few of these lenders themselves are the borrowers. This is particularly true in the case of fish merchants and boat owners who are lending to boat owners and crew members respectively. This is quite complicated when we consider the lender who himself is a borrower.

From Table 5.28 we can observe that 71 households out of total of 107 have borrowed from some or the other source. Of the total outstanding debt of Rs. 4.97 lakhs, 42 per cent is borrowed from private or informal sources by 34 households; of which 89 per cent is borrowed from fish merchants only. The average outstanding debt per household in the village was reported to be Rs. 6,999. In the case of trawler owner households it was Rs. 33,000 while in the case of crew it was reported to be only Rs. 1,753. OBM boat owner households were having the maximum outstanding debt in the village

TABLE 5.28

Distribution of households according to the source of borrowing and occupation and their outstanding debt as on December 31, 1981, Chorwad

(*in Rupees*)

Sources of borrowing	Number of households having debts to the stated lender of									
	Trawler owner		OBM boat owners		NMB owners		Crew		Total	
	No.	O/s Debt	No.	O/s Debt	No.	O/s Debt	No.	D/s Debt	No.	O/s Debt
I. Formal Landing Agencies										
(a) Commercial Banks	—	—	3	9350 (3117)	1	2000 (2000)	2	1200 (600)	6	12550 (4183)
(b) Co-op. Societies/Banks	1	5000 (5000)	—	—	—	—	—	—	1	5000 (5000)
(c) Sub-total	1	5000	3	9350	1	2000	2	1200	7	17550
II. Private or Informal Source										
(a) Friends and Relatives	—	—	3	15000 (5000)	3	3000 (1000)	1	5000 (5000)	7	23000 (3286)
(b) Moneylenders										
(c) Fish Merchants/Boat Owners	3	110000 (36667)	14	62100 (4436)	4	6000 (1500)	6	7500 (1250)	27	185600 (6874)
Sub-total	3	110000	17	77100	7	9000	7	12500	34	208600
III. From Multiple Sources	1	50000 (50000)	17	171650 (10362)	4	28500 (7125)	8	16100 (2683)	30	270750 (9025)
Total	5	165000 (33000)	37	262600 (7097)	12	33500 (2792)	17	29800 (1753)	71	496900 (6999)

Note: 1. (—) indicates nil.
2. Figures in parentheses indicate per household outstanding debt. 3. O/s: Outstanding.

(Rs. 2,62,600) but per household the debt comes to almost equal to that of the average in the village.

Though we could not assess the supply and demand conditions, the fragmentary loans for the same purposes indicate credit shortage in the village. This is also indicated by the distribution of debts outstanding according to the rate of interest. The moneylenders who are the main source were observed to be lending at an interest rate as high as 40 per cent. Nevertheless, the borrower tends to go to the moneylender only when he cannot get a loan from any other source where the interest rate is low or even zero. However, in view of the disequilibrium in the credit market of Chorwad the non-market mechanisms play a significant role in securing loans by borrowers.[32]

Occupationwise distribution of the households according to the purpose of borrowing is presented in Table 5.29. Of the total (107) households in the village, 66 per cent are borrowers. Majority of them are OBM owners. It is interesting to know that 65 per cent of the crew households do not have any outstanding debt. Majority of all types of boat owners have borrowed for the purchase of fishing craft and gear. Four out of five trawler owner households have borrowed for the same purpose. Of the borrower crew, about 65 per cent have borrowed for meeting the household expenditure. None of them have borrowed for any kind of social function. Hence, we can say that the cause of borrowing for boat owners is their fishing equipment and for non-boat owners it is household expenditure.

Size distribution of households according to occupation and total outstanding debt is presented in Table 5.30. It can be seen that about 33.64 per cent of the total households did not have any outstanding debt. Over 51 per cent of the total households had their total outstanding debt less than Rs. 6,000. Of the total 19 households with an outstanding debt of over 6,000, four households had an outstanding debt of over Rs. 25,000 and these four households were trawler owner households. The outstanding debts of all OBM boat owners, NMB owner and crew were less than Rs. 10,000 but for one NMB owners whose debt was between Rs. 10,000 and Rs. 15,000.

TABLE 5.29

Distribution of households according to the purpose of borrowing of the outstanding debt and occupations, Chorwad (1981)

Reasons for borrowing the outstanding debt	Number of households for stated reason of borrowing of				
	Trawler owners	OBM boat owners	NMB owners	Crew	Total
1. No outstanding debt	—	7 (15.56)	3 (17.65)	26 (65.00)	36 (33.64)
2. Replacement of gear	1 (20.00)	9 (20.00)	2 (11.76)	4 (10.00)	16 (14.95)
3. Purchase of fishing craft and gear	4 (80.00)	26 (57.78)	6 (35.30)	—	36 (33.64)
4. To meet household expenditure	—	1 (2.22)	2 (11.76)	9 (22.50)	21 (11.22)
5. To meet the expenditure for social functions	—	—	—	—	—
6. Others	—	2 (4.44)	4 (23.53)	1 (2.50)	7 (6.54)
Total	5 (100)	45 (100)	17 (100)	40 (100)	107 (100)

Note. 1. (—) indicates nil.
2. Figures in parentheses are percentages to column total.

Market for product

The discussion in this section is going to be around the historical evolution of the fish market in the village and its structure, costs and returns of the traders and the changes brought about by motorization.

Historical evolution in fish marketing

In early 1930s there were no fish traders in the village and no trader outside the village was coming to buy the fish. The fish was taken to Veraval by fishermen themselves, which is

TABLE 5.30

Size distribution of households according to the total outstanding debts, Chorwad (1981)

Range of outstanding debt (Rs.)	Number of households with outstanding debt in stated ranges of				
	Trawler owners	OBM boat owners	NMB owners	Crew	Total
Zero outstanding	—	7 (15.56)	3 (17.75)	26 (65.00)	36 (33.64)
Up to 1000	—	3 (4.44)	2 (17.65)	7 (17.50)	12 (11.22)
1001—3000	—	13 (28.89)	6 (35.29)	6 (15.00)	25 (23.37)
3001—6000	—	12 (26.67)	2 (11.76)	1 (2.50)	15 (14.02)
6001—10000	—	5 (11.11)	2 (11.76)	—	7 (6.54)
10001—15000	—	—	1 (5.89)	—	1 (0.93)
15001—25000	1 (20.00)	6 (13.33)	—	—	7 (6.54)
25001—35000	2 (40.00)	—	—	—	2 (1.87)
35001 and above	2 (40.00)	—	—	—	2 (1.87)
Total	5 (100)	45 (100)	17 (100)	40 (100)	107 (100)

Note: 1. (—) indicates nil.
2. Figures in parentheses are percentages to column total.

some 10 km. far from Chorwad. During that period no transport or any other type of conveyance was available, hence, the fishermen used to carry fish as headloads.[33] During the late 1930s and early 1940s the fish trade underwent considerable changes. However, we did not have enough information to study the historical evolution of fish marketing in the village.

Changes in the number of different marketing intermediaries with the mechanization of fishing craft are presented in Table 5.31. There are only two major intermediaries working in the village since the pre-mechanized period. These are retailers/vendors and commission agents. The number of commission agents has been the same in all these 20 years whereas the number of retailers/vendors has gone up from 7 (1960-61) to 15 (1980-81). It is interesting to note that all these retailers are from the fishermen community itself. In addition to this, currently two persons from non-fishermen community are involved in fish business. Of them one is working as fishmeal variety supplier and the other as dry fish wholesaler and fish-meal variety supplier.

Channel members and structure of fish market

The channels of marine fish marketing in the village Chorwad consist of commission agents, wholesalers, fish processors and retailers/vendors. Before discussing the structure of the fish market in the village an attempt is made to understand the functions of the channel members, viz. commission agents, wholesalers, fish processors and retailers/vendors.

The commission agents in the village are mainly dealing with fresh fish. They play a central role in the fish market. Their functions also include moneylending to fishermen/boat owners. They collect fish from the fishermen, pay the sale value of the same and then take the fish to the nearest assembling centre (Veraval) for sale. The expenditure incurred for collection of fish from various fishermen and transportation of the catch to the buyers in Veraval is borne by the commission agents. Generally, the fishermen are paid as and when the commission agent receives money from the fish merchants of the assembling centre, which is not more than 15 days in any case. But as and when fishermen need money, they ask the commission agents for immediate payment. Normally, price fixation and account settlement is made every fortnight.

There is only one wholesaler in the village who is working as dry fish wholesaler as well as wholesaler of fishmeal variety. He buys low-price fish variety for sun-drying and salt-curing and the varieties which are not consumed in fresh form (leftouts) for fishmeal extraction. He generally purchases directly from

TABLE 5.31

Change in the number of different marketing intermediaries with mechanization of fishing craft, Chorwad (1960-1982)

Marketing intermediaries	Number of stated persons/organizations during					
	Pre-mechanization period (1960-61)			Current period (1981-82)		
	Fishermen community	Non-fishermen community	Total	Fishermen community	Non-fishermen community	Total
1. Retailers/Vendors	7	—	7	15	—	15
2. Wholesalers:	—	—	—	—	—	—
(a) Fresh fish	—	—	—	—	1	1*
(b) Dry fish	—	—	—	—	—	—
(c) Fishmeal	—	—	—	—	—	—
3. Commission agents	3	2	5	3	2	5
4. Semi-wholesalers	—	—	—	—	—	—
5. Processing variety suppliers	—	—	—	—	—	—
6. Fishmeal variety suppliers	—	—	—	—	1	1

Notes: 1. (—) indicates nil.

2. *The dry fish wholesaler is also involved in the supply of fish for fishmeal extraction.

fishermen/boat owners and sells in the assembling market. There is only one supplier of processable variety in the village who is involved in pre-processing and supplying the same to processing houses.

In all there are 15 retailers/vendors in Chorwad. They normally buy directly from fishermen and sell in their nearby locations. Compared to other channel members, the number of retailers/vendors is high but the sale through them is very low. The fishermen/boat owners who do not have any linkage with the commission agents sell their fish catch to these intermediaries. Transactions with these intermediaries are always on a cash basis. Hence, as and when other boat owners need hard cash, they directly sell to retailers/vendors without the knowledge of fish merchants. All the retailers/vendors are from the same village. The fish distribution channel is presented in Figure 5.3.

We find that the commission agents handle over 80 per cent of the total landings in terms of quantity. The remainder is handled by retailers/vendors, wholesalers of dry fish and fishmeal varieties, and processable variety suppliers. As already indicated earlier, there are five commission agents. All the five commission agents are having credit marketing interlinkages with fishermen. The number of fishermen with credit marketing linkage with each commission agent was in the range of 5 to 15. The two largest commission agents account for about 55 per cent of the total quantity handled by the commission agents. With the introduction of motorized and mechanized craft two major changes have occurred in the product market of the village. First, the extent of competition for output has increased considerably. The sales pattern has changed from count to weight. Second, two new product market segments have been developed for processable varieties and fishmeal extraction varieties.

THE VILLAGE ECONOMY

In this section we intend to study the economic balances in the village. However, before we take up the issue of economic balance in the village we shall briefly describe the assets structure of fishermen households.

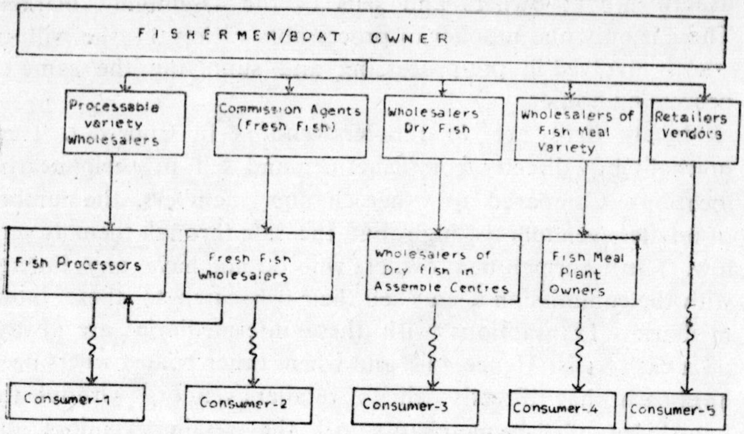

Note 1. ~~~ indicates the existence of the channel members whose details are not available.

2. The subscript for consumers indicates the consumer segmentation according to the number of channel members in between and from which fish is secured.

FIG. 5.3: *Channel of distribution for marine fish, Chorwad (1981-82)*

Assets structure of fishermen

As already discussed in an earlier section, the most remarkable feature of the assets structure is that the production equipment constitutes the major part of the capital and are owned individually. Nevertheless, there are few rich fishermen who have invested in various household goods and immovable properties. The incidence of animal ownership such as bullocks, cows, buffaloes, sheep and goats is completely absent. The only form of the domestic livestock of the village households is the ownership of few poultry birds. Thus, besides the fishing equipment, the general ownership of fishermen households are only thatched huts or tiled houses, household utensils and some real and personal chattels. However, a few households own such items as radios, tape recorders and stereos.

As already indicated, the ownership of a thatched hut or tiled house is the most important form of asset of the fishermen households in the village. However, there are 11 out of a total 107 households in the village without any type of own house and are staying in rented houses. Of these 11 households

9 are crew households. It is interesting to find that there are two motorized boat owner households residing in rented houses, which indicates the tendency of the fishermen to own fishing equipment before investing house and other similar assets. This may be due to the availability of interest-free loan from fish merchants to buy fishing equipment and not for any household items.

As indicated in Table 5.32 more than 80 per cent of the households staying in rented houses are crew households and

TABLE 5.32

Distribution of households according to occupations and value of owned house, Chorwad (1981)

Value range (Rs.)	Number of houses in the stated range of value of			
	MB owners	NMB owners	Crew	Total
No owned house	2 (18.18)	—	9 (81.82)	11 (100)
Less than 1000	—	3 (100)	—	3 (100)
1001—3000	8 (32.00)	5 (20.00)	12 (48.00)	25 (100)
3001—5000	14 (58.33)	4 (16.67)	6 (25.00)	24 (100)
5001—10000	14 (53.85)	4 (15.38)	8 (30.77)	26 (100)
10000 and above	12 (66.67)	1 (5.55)	5 (27.78)	18 (100)
Sub-total of owned houses	48 (50.00)	17 (17.71)	31 (32.29)	96 (100)
Total households	50 (46.73)	17 (15.89)	40 (37.38)	107 (100)

Note: 1. (—) indicates nil.
2. Figures in parentheses are percentages to row total.

the remaining are MB owners. Among the crew members owning houses, 45 per cent own houses valued at less than Rs. 5,000. In the case of motorized boat owners, more than 50 per cent own houses valued at more than Rs. 5,000. All the non-mechanized boat owners own a house. Maximum of the NMB owners own a house valued between Rs. 1,001 and Rs. 3,000.

The incidence of ownership of various items by households of different occupations is given in Table 5.33. It is observed that most of the advanced entertainment items are owned by MB owners. More than 50 per cent of the MB households own radios as well as wrist-watches. The only one cycle available in the village is also owned by an MB owner. In the case of cooking apparatus and kitchenware also, more than 50 per cent of the steel items are owned by MB owners and more than 80 per cent of the MB households own some or other form of steel kitchenware.

Table 5.34 presents size distribution of households according to the value of household articles in the village. More than 70 per cent of the households own articles valued at less than Rs. 1,000 and less than 5 per cent households own articles costing more than Rs. 10,000. Of the total 45 OBM boat owner households 53 per cent were in the category of less than Rs. 1,000, whereas in the case of trawler, NMB owner, and crew member households the same size class accounted for 80 per cent, 82 per cent and 78 per cent respectively.

Consumption and expenditure pattern of fishermen households

Items of consumption can broadly be classified into: food items and non-food items. Food items include foodgrains, milk and milk products, edible oils, meat and chicken, eggs and vegetables and non-food items include fuel and light, entertainment, education, travel and transport, clothes and medicines. The pattern of consumption of all these items and the corresponding expenditure pattern is likely to be affected by the habits, social customs, income and other household characteristics such as household size, education, etc. Therefore, we shall discuss the itemwise expenditure pattern for different households of different occupations.

As shown in Table 5.35, of the total consumer expenditure

TABLE 5.33

Ownership of different households items according to occupation, Chorwad (1981-82)

Items	No. of households owning the stated items						Total	
	MB owner		NMB owners		Crew members			
	NI	HH	NI	HH	NI	HH	NI	HH
I. Transport vehicles:								
Cycle	1	1	—	—	—	—	1	1
II. Communication/ Entertainment:								
Radio/Transistor	28	28	3	3	15	15	46	46
TV/2 or 3-in-one	3	3	—	—	1	1	4	4
III. Office Equipment								
Chairs	2	1	—	—	1	1	3	2
Tables	3	3	—	—	1	1	4	4
Wooden Almirah	7	7	1	1	2	2	10	10
IV. Time Indicators:								
Wrist-watches	32	28	4	4	17	16	53	48
Clock	4	4	—	—	4	3	8	7
V. Cooking Apparatus:								
Non-kerosene stove	58	47	16	14	45	37	119	98
Kerosene stove	38	35	8	8	21	21	68	64
VI. Kitchenware:								
Earthen	121	50	38	17	93	38	252	105
Aluminium	294	48	120	17	202	35	616	100
Steel	215	41	48	11	139	32	402	84
Others	288	43	62	12	187	29	537	84

Note: 1. NI: Number of items.
2. HH: Number of households owning the items.

TABLE 5.34

Size distribution of households according to the value of the household articles, Chorwad (1981-82)

Frequency interval (Rs.)	No. of households with the value of household articles in stated range of				Total
	IBE	OBM	NMB	CRM	
Up to 500	2 (40.00)	13 (28.90)	12 (70.59)	25 (62.50)	52 (48.60)
501—1000	2 (40.00)	11 (24.44)	2 (11.77)	6 (15.00)	21 (19.63)
1001—1500	—	4 (8.90)	1 (5.88)	2 (5.00)	7 (6.54)
1501—2000	—	2 (4.44)	—	2 (5.00)	4 (3.74)
2001—2500	—	4 (8.90)	1 (5.88)	—	5 (4.67)
2501—3000	—	1 (2.22)	1 (5.88)	2 (5.00)	4 (3.74)
3001—3500	—	1 (2.22)	—	—	1 (0.94)
3501—4000	—	1 (2.22)	—	—	1 (0.93)
4001—5000	—	1 (2.22)	—	—	1 (0.94)
5001—5500	—	1 (2.22)	—	1 (2.50)	2 (1.87)
5501—6000	—	—	—	—	—
6001—6500	—	2 (4.44)	—	1 (2.50)	3 (2.80)
6501—7000	—	—	—	—	—
7001—7500	—	—	—	1 (2.50)	1 (0.93)
7501—8000	—	—	—	—	—
8001—8500	—	1 (2.22)	—	—	1 (0.93)
8501—9000	—	—	—	—	—
9001—9500	—	—	—	—	—
9501—10000	—	1 (2.22)	—	—	1 (0.94)
10001 and above	1(20.00)	1 (2.22)	—	—	2 (1.87)
Total	5 (100)	45 (100)	17 (100)	40 (100)	107 (100)

Note: 1. (—) indicates nil.
2. Figures in parentheses represent percentages to column total.

of Rs. 19,13,810 the expenditure by MB owner households accounts for Rs. 10,38,810 (57.27 per cent) while they account for 46.73 per cent of the households and 51.47 per cent of the population.

TABLE 5.35

Itemwise annual consumption expenditure by occupation, Chorwad (1981-82)

(in '000 Rs.)

Item	Expenditure on the stated item by			Total
	MB house-holds	NMB house-holds	Crew	
1	2	3	4	5
I. Food Items:				
(a) Foodgrains	213.62 (58.56)	49.24 (13.00)	101.92 (27.94)	364.74 (100)
(b) Milk and milk products	24.18 (53.14)	6.60 (14.51)	14.72 (32.35)	45.50 (100)
(c) Edible oils	175.50 (56.55)	40.97 (13.20)	93.86 (30.25)	310.33 (100)
(d) Meat and Chicken	4.11 (35.13)	4.47 (38.21)	3.12 (26.66)	11.70 (100)
(e) Eggs	—	—	—	—
(f) Fish	166.40 (60.27)	37.13 (13.45)	72.54 (26.28)	276.07 (100)
(g) Vegetables	19.34 (55.02)	4.32 (12.29)	11.49 (32.69)	35.15 (100)
(h) Fruits and Nuts	16.38 (76.83)	3.90 (18.29)	1.04 (4.88)	21.32 (100)
(i) Sugar, Gur and Khandsari	61.93 (54.86)	18.82 (16.67)	32.14 (28.47)	122.89 (100)
(j) Salt and Spices	41.34 (55.36)	9.98 (13.37)	23.35 (31.27)	74.67 (100)
(k) Beverages	4.63 (94.68)	—	0.26 (5.32)	4.89 (100)
(l) Pan, Tobacco and Supari	34.74 (48.20)	9.88 (13.71)	27.45 (38.09)	72.07 (100)
Sub-total	762.17 (57.34)	185.31 (13.93)	381.89 (28.73)	1329.37 (100)

TABLE 5.35 (*Contd.*)

1	2	3	4	5
II. Non-food Items:				
(a) Entertainment	1.10 (43.48)	0.35 (13.83)	1.08 (42.69)	2.53 (100)
(b) Travel and Transport	9.14 (54.24)	1.86 (11.04)	5.85 (33.12)	16.85 (100)
(c) Education	0.95 (65.63)	0.10 (6.80)	0.42 (28.57)	1.47 (100)
(d) Medicines	55.76 (54.92)	13.90 (13.57)	32.80 (32.01)	102.46 (100)
(e) Domestic utensils	1.70 (34.34)	1.00 (20.20)	2.25 (45.46)	4.95 (100)
(f) Clothes	78.25 (59.06)	16.60 (12.53)	37.65 (28.41)	132.50 (100)
(g) Footwear	3.48 (69.32)	0.38 (7.57)	1.16 (23.11)	5.02 (100)
(h) Fuel and light	126.26 (57.72)	27.40 (12.52)	65.10 (29.76)	218.76 (100)
(i) Others	—	—	—	—
Sub-total	276.64 (57.11)	61.59 (12.71)	146.21 (30.18)	484.44 (100)
Total	1038.81 (57.27)	246.90 (13.61)	528.10 (29.12)	1813.81 (100.00)

Note: 1. (—) indicates nil.
2. Figures in parentheses are percentages to row total.

A major part of the total expenditure is spent on food items in all the types of households. An overwhelming per cent (73.29) of the total consumer expenditure is accounted by food items which is 73 per cent in MB households followed by 75 per cent in NMB households and 72 per cent in crew households respectively. Of the total expenditure on food items (Rs. 13,29,370) expenditure on foodgrains, edible oils and fish together accounts for 72 per cent and is 73 per cent, 69 per cent and 71 per cent in MB, NMB and crew households respectively. Expenditure on edible oils accounts for more than 80 per cent of the expenditure on foodgrains.

Expenditure on non-food items accounts for only 26.71 per cent with Rs. 4,84,440 for all occupations together. The expenditure on non-food items by MB households accounts for 57 per cent of the total expenditure on non-food items in the village. The main non-food items which account for maximum expenditure (93.66 per cent together) are clothes, fuel and light and medicines.

Itemwise per capita and per household annual consumer expenditure is presented in Table 5.36. The per capita expense of MB owner household is slightly higher (Rs. 2,583.11) than that of the average in the village (Rs. 2,322.33) while the same is quite low in the case of NMB owner and crew households. The picture is the same for both the cases, i.e. expenditure on food and non-food items, by MB households is little higher than that of average in the village, and loss in the case of NMB owners and crew households. Per capita expenditure on entertainment and domestic utensils by crew households is higher than that of MB households otherwise the expenses on all the items by MB households are higher than any other category.

Income and savings

Table 5.37 presents the occupationwise income, expenditure and savings in the village. The net saving of the fishermen is 24.09 per cent of the total income (Rs. 23,89,340). In the case of MB households it is 38.20 per cent while NMB and CRM households incur a loss of Rs. 13,390 and Rs. 53,190 respectively. However, the actual dis-savings of these households may be quite less than this as they receive gifts and remuneration in kind which are usually consumer items. In some cases the crew are recruited on a share basis where they get part of fish catch instead of cash. Hence, the actual income (moneywise) goes down and the amount of dis-savings increases.

Moreover, it should be noticed that the savings estimated above relate to catches in a normal fishing year. However, the savings may be very nominal or even negative when we consider the savings during fish famine years, usually once in three

TABLE 5.36

Itemwise per capita and per household consumer expenditure by occupation, Chorwad (1981-82)

(in Rupees)

Item	Per capita (per household) annual consumer expenditure on stated item by			For all village total households
	MB owners	NMB owners	Crew	
1	2	3	4	5
I. Food Items:				
(a) Foodgrains	531 (4272)	404 (2897)	397 (2548)	467 (3410)
(b) Milk and Milk products	60 (484)	54 (388)	57 (368)	59 (426)
(c) Edible oils	437 (3510)	336 (2410)	365 (2347)	398 (2910)
(d) Meat and Chicken	10 (82)	36 (263)	12 (78)	15 (110)
(e) Fish	414 (3328)	304 (2184)	282 (1814)	354 (2581)
(f) Vegetables	48 (387)	35 (254)	45 (288)	46 (328)
(g) Fruits and Nuts	41 (328)	32 (229)	4 (26)	27 (200)
(h) Sugar, Gur and Khandsari	154 (1239)	154 (1107)	125 (803)	145 (1055)
(i) Salt and Spices	103 (827)	82 (587)	91 (584)	96 (698)
(j) Beverages	11 (93)	—	1 (6)	7 (46)
(k) Pan, Tobacco and Supari	86 (695)	81 (581)	107 (686)	92 (674)
Sub-total	1895 (15245)	1518 (10900)	1486 (9548)	1701 (12480)

1	2	3	4	5
II. Non-food Items:				
(a) Entertainment	2.75 (22.08)	2.89 (20.71)	4.21 (27.02)	3.25 (23.71)
(b) Traval and Transport	22.74 (182.80)	15.25 (109.41)	22.77 (146.25)	21.58 (158)
(c) Education	2.36 (19.00)	0.82 (5.88)	1.65 (10.63)	1.89 (13.79)
(d) Medicines	138.71 (1115.20)	113.93 (817.65)	127.63 (820.00)	131.19 (957.57)
(e) Domestic Utensils	4.23 (34.0)	8.20 (58.82)	8.75 (56.25)	6.34 (46.26)
(f) Clothes	194.65 (1565.0)	136.07 (976.47)	146.50 (941.25)	169.65 (1238.32)
(g) Footwear	8.67 (69.70)	3.11 (22.35)	4.51 (29.00)	6.43 (46.96)
(h) Fuel and Light	314.0 (2525)	225.0 (1612)	253.0 (1628)	281.0 (2045)
Sub-total	688.11 (5532.78)	505.27 (3623.29)	569.02 (3658.4	621.33 (2505.06)
Total	2583.11 (20777.78)	2023.27 (14523.29)	2055.02 (13206.40)	2322.33 (2629.86)

Note: 1. (—) indicates negligible.
2. Figures in parentheses represent per household expenditure.

TABLE 5.37

Occupationwise income, expenditure and savings of fishermen in Chorwad

(*in '000 Rupees*)

Occupation	Income	Expenditure	Savings
1. MB	1680.91	1038.81	642.10
2. NMB	233.51	246.90	—13.39
3. CRM	474.91	528.10	—53.19
Total	2389.34	1813.81	575.53

years. The hypothesis of aggregate negative savings in the village is supported by the observed high rate of indebtedness of the villagers and low value of household articles.

REFERENCES

1. Even the Census does not give the disaggregated villagewise information. Population figures for the village in 1977 were obtained from the Office of the Commissioner of Fisheries, Government of Gujarat, Ahmedabad.
2. The test for whether a particular household should be treated as a separate household or single is quite often based on commensal pattern. The number of people which the kitchen of a particular household serves on a normal day is treated as the size of that household.
3. In some cases it was not possible to observe the age gap between children because of the joint family structure in which two or more married brothers stayed together. Thus, we could calculate the age gaps in about 272 cases while there are 350 cases in which two or more children of same parents under 12 are still in residence.
4. The education level of fishermen has been classified into: illiterates and literates. An individual who cannot read and write any one language has been classified as illiterate and the remaining as literates. The latter category of literates had been further sub-divided on the basis of the level of education attained.
5. For an elaborate discussion on different types of migration partners and the review of literature on migration patterns, see Hugo, G., *New Conceptual Approaches to Migration in the Context of Urbanisation: A Discussion based on Indonesia*, paper presented at IUSSP meeting, Bellegie, Italy, July 1978; Pryor, R.J., *Residence History Analysis Studies in Migration and Urbanisation No. 3* (Canberra: Department of Demography, Australian National University, 1979) and Kamble, N.D., *Labour Migration in Indian States*, New Delhi).
6. The large gap between the official records and our census is mainly because of the dual membership of the majority of the members of the Chorwad Sagar Utapadak Sahakari Mandali.
7. In promoting mechanization of fishing craft the co-operatives have played a significant role. For promoting the motorization of non-mechanized craft in the state, GFCCA has acquired five OBMs of 5 h.p. from British Anjani and distributed them to the village heads or Patels in Hirakot, Domlez, Chorwad, and Sutrapada for demonstrating the performance of the motors.
8. The fishermen were not inclined to use motors for propulsion of boats mainly because of the fear that the resources may deplete faster. In the initial period, the officials of the Department of

Fisheries and GFCCA were subjected to lot of hardships to carry out the demonstration trips as the fishermen were not even willing to talk to them. The time taken for convincing the fishermen of various villages ranged between 12 and 18 months.

9. In order to promote the use of motors the Government of Gujarat released a subsidy of Rs. 500 through GFCCA on each motor purchased till 1975. The amount of subsidy was constant over the period from 1961 to 1975. In the initial stage the rate of subsidy worked out to be as high as 20 per cent due to lower cost of motor during that period.
10. The trawler acquired by the fishermen of the village in 1967 has been sold. Thus, the existing information on IBE boats in the village does not take this into account.
11. In addition to the five existing trawlers, two more trawlers were purchased by the fishermen of the village and disposed off during 1967 and 1977.
12. It should be noted that each gill net consists of many pieces, which are joined to make one set of gill net. As we can see the sizes of the pieces may be more or less equal and the length of net used by different boat owners varies according to the number of pieces in each net.
13. The trawl net is a bell-shaped bag type net which is dragged along the seabed for catching fish. The mesh size of the net varies along the length of the feet. The portion which is tied to the boat is called the mouth and where the fish entangled in the net gets accumulated is called as the cord end.
14. All the IBE boats are trawlers and therefore hereafter referred to as trawlers.
15. The value of fishing assests has been estimated by taking the constant prices (at 1980 prices) for different types of boats irrespective of their year of purchase, with a view to neutralizing the trend in the prices of similar type of craft and gear over time.
16. The ownership of the boat and gear would either be individual or joint. Individual ownership implies that only one person owns the craft and gear. In joint ownership, more than one person from different households invests, not necessarily in equal amount per head, in the boat.
17. For further details, see Kurien, J., "Towards an understanding of the Fish Economy of Kerala State", 1978, op. cit.
18. Shift in fish landings may take place because of lack of infrastructure. The trawler owners have preferred to land their catches in the village though the infrastructure is inadequate, in view of other difficulties such as management and input supply during normal days.
19. Data collected on sample days for some boats permit the calculation of quantity and species composition of landings of different types of boats. For estimating the total landings in the villages

we have multiplied the number of different types of boats by the products of average landing per boat per day and the number of fishing days for different types of boats.

20. See Anand, S., *Inequality and Poverty in Malaysia: Measurement and Decomposition* (Mimeo.) D.Phil. dissertation, Oxford University, 1978; and Atkinson, A.B., "On the measurement of Inequality", *Journal of Economic Theory*, Nov.-Dec. 1979, pp. 1370-86.
22. Bliss and Stern have calculated the Gini ratio for income distribution in the case of Palanpur to be 0.326. See Bliss, C.J. and Stern, U.H., *Palanpur: The Economy of an Indian Village* (London: Oxford University Press, 1982), p. 209.
22. It should be noticed that each type of utilization has different economic impact on the producers and the overall utilization pattern varies with the change in the species composition.
23. There is considerable difference between surplus labourers and labour. The distinction between labourers and labour has been brought out very clearly by A.K. Sen, "Peasants and Dualism With and Without Surplus Labour", *Journal of Political Economy*, 74(5), Oct. 1956.
24. There are few religious beliefs which may not permit the fishermen to go fishing on particular days. For example, on the eleventh day of the moon and dark moon day, caste Hindu fishermen do not go for fishing.
25. The methodology is based on Rudra, A., "Direct Estimation of Surplus Labour in Agriculture", *Economic and Political Weekly*, Annual Number, Feb. 1973, pp. 277-280.
26. In fisheries there is no ruling wage rate which may freely respond to relative pressure of demand and supply on the labour market, as the remuneration of the labourer is calculated as a proportion of catch value. For details, see Platteau, J. Ph., *et al.*, "Rural Credit Market in a Backward Area: A Kerala Fishing Village", *Economic and Political Weekly*, Special Number, October 1980, p. 1974.
27. The labour mobility ratio is defined as the ratio of number of times the labourer changed the employer and the total number of years during which the labourer has been working as crew in a given type of boat.
28. For a detailed description of the system and its effectiveness in relation to a village in Kerala, see Platteau, J. Ph., *et al.*, op. cit., pp. 182-212.
29. The occupational mobility ratio is defined in the similar way that of labour mobility.
30. A similar view has been expressed by Bliss and Stern, in relation to agriculture, op. cit., p. 106.
31. It has been argued elsewhere that mechanization of fishing craft has been made artificially cheap through subsidies and credit on liberal term in some cases and in other cases the affluent fishermen invested

in mechanization of boats in view of the fairly comparable (to other forms of investments particularly in industry) returns on investment. Thus, availability of credit has played a central role in mechanization.

32. For a similar view in the case of a fishing village in Kerala, see Platteau, op. cit., p. 1773.
33. Fish was transported from the village by headloads because the individual quantities for sale were small and it was not economical to hire a horse-cart.

6

Hirakot Village, Junagarh District, Gujarat

HIRAKOT, a fishing hamlet, is in Junagarh district, and is 15 km. south-west of Veraval. Junagarh, the district headquarters, is 80 km. to the north-east of Hirakot. The nearest metalled road is about 2 km. from the village. The nearest railway station is Veraval town. Kadvar, which is the revenue village and gram panchayat headquarters, is situated at a distance of 2 km. to the north. The village is stretched all along a long sandy beach (Fig. 6.1). Most houses are constructed from dried mud or sand stone. In most of the houses the flooring is of sand.

The fishermen in Hirakot acquired the right of fishing by an agreement between some immigrant Muslim families from Sind (Pakistan) and Rasul Khan, the erstwhile ruler of Prabhas Patan. One of the conditions of the agreement was that the families engaged in fishing would pay Rs. 500 a year directly to the ruler. The fishing activity was begun with the immigration of Muslim families, who are called Machhiyaras, about 100 years ago with a single dugout canoe and a pair of hand-made cotton gill nets. Prior to 1940 the fishing activity of Hirakot was completely in the hands of Muslim fishermen. During the partition of the country about 20 Hindu fishermen families mainly belonging to Koli and Kharwa communities migrated to Hirakot, who initially worked as crew members in the boats owned by the Muslim fishermen.

Gujarati and Sindhi are the two languages of communication. The former is spoken by both Hindu and Muslim fishermen while the latter is used for conversation by Muslims only. A few individuals understand Hindi also.

which is the main location for buying and selling and contacting fisheries department personnel.

The four wells, which were dug at the time of the village formation, are the primary source of potable water for the villagers. The water from these wells is drawn out manually. There is no electricity in the village and efforts are being made by villagers to get power supply.

The facilities included in the village industry and trade are the services of barber, tailor, washerman, blacksmith, carpenter, goldsmith, etc., grocer stores, general stores and medical stores. It was observed that most of the services and trade facilities, but for a few essential services of barber, tailor, provision stores and a small hotel, are not available within the village. Depending upon the type of the service/facility needed the villagers have to commute a distance ranging from 4 to 15 km. to reach the service/trading centre.

The institutional services include the facilities for education, communication, health and hygiene, banking and law and order maintenance. The primary school in the village was established in 1969 and has a strength of one teacher and 48 pupils as on 31 March, 1981. The school building has a simple structure with only one room, and is provided with two black boards, two maps and a first-aid box. The current enrolment of the school is about 15 per cent of the children in the school-going age group (i.e. 5 to 12 years). The nearest upper primary/secondary school is in Sutrapada, about 6 km. from the village. During our survey it was, however, found that none of the households was availing the facility of a higher secondary school in Sutrapada or in any other place.

The postal communication facilities for the villagers are available in Kadvar village. The post office in Kadvar was established in 1979 and is managed by a single person. It extends all the window facilities such as sale of letters, stamps, etc. But, telephone and telegraphic facilities are available only in Sutrapada, located about 6 km. from the village. The post office at Kadvar operates an extension counter for about an hour in the village in addition to the regular clearance of the post box in Hirakot. Our discussions with the post master in Kadvar, however, indicate that the utilization of postal services for communication by the villagers is negligible.

Turning to health facilities, we find that Hirakot is under the jurisdiction of the Primary Health Centre (PHC) at Patan, located about 11 km. from the village. PHC, Patan, has set up a sub-centre at Sutrapada to serve the villagers of Hirakot, among others. Despite the availability of PHC sub-centre within a distance of less than 5 km., fishermen of Hirakot were observed to be consulting/getting treatment only from private doctors, who periodically visit the village, mainly for the reasons of inadequate and irregular services at PHC. There is only one private doctor (RMP) in Kadvar who periodically visits the village.

The nearest bank for the villagers is located in Sutrapada where there are two branches of the nationalized commercial banks. The banks provide the normal facilities of savings bank accounts, and extend short- and medium-term loans to the fishermen of Hirakot.

The police station located at Sutrapada looks after law and order in Hirakot and provides security for the fishing equipment. Often the fishermen ensure law and order through caste panchayats under the leadership of their caste Patel.

The political system of Hirakot consists of both caste panchayat and elected panchayat. The fishermen caste panchayats are the governing authorities in all matters affecting the fishermen code of behaviour. There are two caste panchayats—one for the Kolis and the other for Machhiyaras—in the village. The procedure of election of caste Patels and their powers and functions of the village are similar to those explained in the last case study (Chorwad Bander).

The gram panchayat for Hirakot and Kadvar is common and the headquarters is at Kadvar. It consists of 12 elected members and the sarpanch is selected from among the elected members. Currently, the gram panchayat of Kadvar is represented by the sarpanch and three members from the fishermen community of Hirakot. The secretary, a paid employee of the gram panchayat, is stationed at Kadvar and assists the sarpanch in day-to-day administration. Its main functions are to collect some taxes and spend the money on the day-to-day administration. The village, by and large, is an autonomous political unit linked to the wider state political system only through the few gram panchayat members and the fisheries inspector. In sum, the villagers of Hirakot are oblivious of the political changes in the state while they are much involved in the caste panchayats. The village has two temples, a mosque and a Dargah. The caste association and the mosque trust are very active and powerful.

Fishery-related infrastructure: Most of the fishery-related infrastructure facilities are not available in the village and the nearest facility is as far as 16 km. from the village. Currently, the existing boat-building yards in the region, in particular, or in the country, in general, are involved in the construction of larger wooden mechanized boats for trawling only. The construction of non-mechanized boats and OBM boats is undertaken by unorganized private builders with less capital. It is noticed that fishermen of the Saurashtra coast get most of their non-mechanized wooden boats constructed from Karnataka and Kerala. The repair of these motorized or non-mechanized boats is generally undertaken by the local carpenters. The organized service facilities for motors are located very far. Therefore, it is noticed that the fishermen of the village have developed the skills to undertake minor motor repairs. The fishermen of Hirakot do not use ice or cold storage for preservation of fish. The small quantity of ice needed by the fish merchants is procured from Veraval and transported by their own/hired transport to the village. The nets are usually mended by the fishermen family members. The necessary yarn is procured from Veraval. Two of the fish merchants also undertake the supply of yarn for nets and fuel for the motors.

The curing and sun-drying of fish in the village is done on the open beaches by two individuals and there are no construction facilities of fish-curing and sun-drying. The supply infrastructure and marketing facilities for fish are controlled by the few fish merchants. For undertaking the functions of supply of inputs and to market the fish catches two fishermen's co-operative societies also operate in the village.

Production equipment and occupations

All economic activities in Hirakot centre around marine fishing. The village population consists of the owners of fishing equipment, labourers in fishing, fish wholesalers (including retailers and vendors) and village functionaries. The equipment owners use their own gear for fishing. In few cases the smaller equipment owners, however, supplement their income from the operation of their own equipment by working as labourers.

There are two types of fishing craft in use in Hirakot—mechanized and non-mechanized. All the mechanized boats in Hirakot are Out Board Motor (OBM) boats and there are no In Board Engine (IBE) boats owned by the villagers. The OBM boats are usually plank-built canoes or dugout canoes fitted with outboard motors of 5 to 8 h.p. depending upon the length of the boat. The length of the OBM boats was in the range of 18 to 33 feet. The non-mechanized boats in the village are canoes—dugout or plank-built—and are generally smaller in length than OBM boats.

The mechanized and non-mechanized craft owners of Hirakot use only gill nets for fishing. These nets are single-walled nets which may be of the "set" or the "drift" type. The set type are further classified as "surface" or "bottom set" nets. However, majority of the set gill nets in the village are bottom set gill nets. The gill nets may be made of cotton or nylon or synthetic yarn. However, an overwhelming majority of the gill nets in operation in the village are made from the synthetic or nylon yarn. For the year-round productivity the fishermen of Hirakot were observed to own gill nets of varying mesh size for operation from a given fishing craft. The number of persons required for the operation of a gill net depends upon the length and weight of the net and it is in the range of 2 to 4 persons in Hirakot.

The distribution of the village population according to occupation and caste is presented in Table 6.2. Dependants or retired or not working population accounts for the maximum (50.58 per cent) of the total population of 609. The dependant category is followed by housewives, fishing with OBM, crew without gear, students, and persons engaged in net mending/repairing with 216 (17.94), 113 (9.39), 95 (7.89), 61 (5.07) and 46 (3.82) respectively (Table 6.2). The Machhiyara community accounts for over 60 per cent of the population involved in fishing with OBM boats while they account for about 40 per cent of the village population.

Taking the major sources of income into account, the

TABLE 6.2

Occupationwise distribution of population according to castes, Hirakot

Occupation	Number of persons from the caste				
	Kharwa	Koli	Muslim	Macchiyara	Total
1. *Economic activities: Fishery*					
(i) Fishing with OBM	3(10.34)	33(5.87)	9(7.50)	68(13.79)	113(9.39)
(ii) Fishing with NMB	2(6.90)	—	—	14(2.84)	16(1.33)
(iii) Crew with gear	—	3(0.53)	—	2(0.41)	5(0.42)
(iv) Crew without gear	1(3.45)	70(12.46)	7(5.83)	17(3.45)	95(7.89)
(v) Net mending/repairing	—	36(6.40)	—	10(2.03)	46(3.81)
(vi) Fish retailing	—	5(0.89)	—	1(0.20)	6(0.50)
(vii) Fish wholesaling	—	—	—	1(0.20)	1(0.08)
Sub-total	6(20.69)	147(26.15)	16(13.33)	113(22.92)	282(23.42)
2. *Economic activities: Non-fishery*					
(a) Service	—	2(0.36)	4(3.33)	—	6(0.50)
(b) Agricultural labour	—	1(0.18)	1(0.83)	3(0.61)	5(0.42)
Sub-total	—	3(0.54)	5(4.16)	3(0.61)	11(0.92)
3. *Non-economic activities:*					
(a) Dependants/not working	13(44.83)	297(52.85)	42(35.00)	257(52.13)	609(50.57)
(b) Students	4(13.79)	33(5.87)	10(8.33)	14(2.84)	61(5.07)
(c) Housewives	5(17.24)	77(13.70)	29(24.18)	105(21.30)	216(17.94)
(d) Others	1(3.45)	5(0.89)	18(15.00)	1(0.20)	25(2.08)
Sub-total	23(79.31)	412(73.31)	99(82.51)	377(76.47)	911(75.66)
Total	29(100.00)	562(100.00)	120(100.00)	493(100.00)	1204(100.00)

Note: 1. (—) indicates nil.
2. Figures in parentheses are percentages to column total.

households in Hirakot can broadly be classified into four categories: (i) owners of mechanized boats; (ii) owners of non-mechanized boats; (iii) crew members; and (iv) others. About 56.80 per cent of the total 173 households in Hirakot at the time of our census were not owning any fishing equipment, i.e. boat or gear. The population of these households accounts for about 48.80 per cent of the total village population. Of the households without any fishing equipment no more than one-fifth derive their major income from occupations other than fishery-related activities; the remainder are the households whose major income is derived from the sale of labour to the fisheries equipment owners. Thus, these households represent the potential source of fishery labour force in Hirakot. The households whose major source of income is from occupations other than fishery-related activities are either agricultural labour households, or village functionaries. The village functionaries cater either for the fishermen households' needs or they are involved in trading of fish and other commodities. None of these village functionaries have a hereditary relationship, i.e. they have not branched out to these occupations during the current generation. These functionaries are paid in cash for their services.

The households which are the major source of supply of fishery labourers, or otherwise called as crew member households, account for about 40.80 per cent of the total households with a population of 489 (40.6 per cent of the total). These households supply the labour input necessary for the operation of both mechanized and non-mechanized boats alongwith the gear in the village. The fishery equipment-owning households of Hirakot account for about 42.20 per cent households in the village and for about 51.20 per cent of the village population. Of the equipment-owning households over 80 per cent own mechanized fishing craft alongwith the necessary fishing gear; the remaining are owners of non-mechanized fishing craft. We notice that the Machhiyaras account for 40.95 per cent of the village population and own about 62 per cent of the fishing craft (Table 6.3). However, it was noticed that the distribution of fishing craft within each caste is uneven.

TABLE 6.3

Distribution of households and population according to the occupational pattern and caste, Hirakot

Occupation	Caste					Total No. of persons
	Kharwa	Koli	Machhiyar	Muslim/ Others	Total	
1. MB	2 (40.00)	24 (27.91)	35 (53.85)	1 (5.89)	62 (35.84)	550 (45.7)
2. NMB	1 (20.00)	—	10 (15.38)	—	11 (6.36)	66 (5.5)
3. CRM	1 (20.00)	5 (5.81)	18 (27.69)	6 (35.29)	81 (46.82)	489 (40.6)
4. Others	1 (20.00)	6 (6.98)	2 (3.08)	10 (58.82)	19 (10.98)	99 (8.2)
Total	5 (100)	86 (100)	65 (100)	17 (100)	173 (100)	1204 (100)

SOCIO-ETHNOGRAPHIC PROFILE OF FISHERMEN

Size and structure of households

The distribution of households according to family size and occupation is presented in Table 6.4. There are 10 households with 13 or more members in a household. Of these 8 (80 per cent) are mechanized boat owner households. The maximum family size was 23. This is the case of several brothers and their families living together and fishing jointly. The average family size of the households in the village is 6.96, while it is over 8.87 for mechanized boat owner households. The model family sizes of the households are 10, 6, 5, 4 and 5 for MBO, NMBO, CM, other and total households respectively. There are two households, one each in CM and other households with single member. The uncertainty of the availability of crew members for operating the fishing equipment is perhaps the main reason for the tendency of the equipment owners to have a larger family size.

TABLE 6.4

Occupationwise distribution of households according to family size, Hirakot

Family size (members)	Number of households of				Total
	MBO	NMBO	CM	Others	
1	—	—	1(1.2)	1(5.3)	2(1.2)
2	—	1(9.1)	3(3.7)	3(15.8)	7(4.1)
3	1(1.6)	—	4(4.9)	1(5.3)	6(3.5)
4	3(4.8)	1(9.1)	15(18.5)	6(31.6)	25(14.5)
5	8(12.9)	2(18.2)	20(24.7)	1(5.3)	31(17.9)
6	7(11.3)	3(27.3)	10(12.4)	2(10.6)	22(12.7)
7	8(12.9)	1(9.1)	8(9.9)	—	17(9.8)
8	4(6.5)	2(18.2)	4(4.9)	1(5.3)	11(6.4)
9	6(9.7)	1(9.1)	9(11.2)	1(5.3)	17(9.8)
10	10(16.1)	—	3(3.7)	2(10.6)	15(8.7)
11	2(3.2)	—	2(2.4)	1(5.3)	5(2.9)
12	5(8.1)	—	—	—	5(2.9)
13+16	8(12.9)	—	2(2.4)	—	10(5.9)
Total	62(100.00)	11(100.00)	81(100.00)	19(100.00)	173(100.00)

Note: Figures in parentheses are percentages to total.

The family structure in Hirakot consists of three categories. They are single, nuclear and joint families. There are two households, one each in crew and other households in the village, which are of single-type of family structure. Joint family structure is relatively more predominant in MBO households, while it is nuclear family structure which is more common among the crew and NMBO (Non Motor Boat Owner) households. In MBO households joint family structure accounts for over 38 per cent while it is only 25 per cent for all the households. In the case of NMBO households all the 11 households are having a nuclear family structure (Table 6.5).

TABLE 6.5

Distribution of households by occupational pattern and type of family, Hirakot

Occupation	No. of households with family structure			Total
	Single	Nuclear	Joint	
1. NBO	—	38(61.3)	24(38.7)	62(100.00)
2. NMBO	—	11(100.0)	—	11(100.00)
3. CM	1(1.2)	66(81.5)	14(17.3)	81(100.00)
4. Others	1(5.3)	12(63.1)	8(31.6)	19(100.00)
Total	2(1.2)	127(73.4)	44(25.4)	173(100.00)

Note: Figures in parentheses indicate percentages to row total.

Agewise distribution and education level of fishermen

The age distribution of village population according to occupation is given in Table 6.6. It is interesting to note that the ratio of males is more than females for crew member households while it is relatively lower for other occupations and for the village as a whole. Further, it was also observed that there is a surplus of males over the females in the age groups of 13-20 and 21-30 years while the converse is true in other cases. This may be mainly because of the usual occurrence of marriage of girls at a younger age. The number of male members per household in the age group between 13 and 55 years (the normal age group during which an individual is fit for active fishing) were 2.2, 1.2, 1.5 and 1.3 for MBO, NMBO, CRM and other households respectively. The tendency of MBO households to live in extended families with highest number of male members per household in the normal active fishing age group of 13 to 55 years indicates the existence of labour shortage for fishing in the village.

The frequency distribution of age gaps between the surviving children of same parents according to occupational pattern is presented in Table 6.7. In the case of MBO, the frequency of age gap interval of 1—1.9 years accounts for 30.9 while it is

TABLE 6.6

Age and sex distribution of villagers according to occupational pattern, Hirakot

Age→	0—12		13—20		21—30		31—45		46—55		56 and above		Total	
Occupation ↓	M	F	M	F	M	F	M	F	M	F	M	F	M	F
1. MBO	135 (45.8)	148 (48.7)	47 (50.0)	34 (38.6)	42 (38.5)	43 (42.2)	37 (50.0)	40 (52.0)	11 (55.0)	9 (39.1)	3 (30.0)	4 (26.7)	272 (45.8)	278 (45.6)
2. NMBO	15 (5.2)	22 (7.2)	1 (1.1)	6 (6.8)	8 (7.3)	7 (6.9)	2 (2.7)	3 (3.9)	2 (10.0)	— —	— —	— —	28 (4.7)	38 (6.3)
3. CRM	122 (42.2)	116 (38.2)	37 (39.4)	39 (44.3)	48 (44.1)	44 (43.1)	33 (44.6)	29 (37.6)	4 (20.0)	11 (47.9)	2 (20.0)	4 (26.7)	246 (41.3)	243 (39.9)
4. Others	19 (6.6)	18 (5.9)	9 (9.6)	9 (10.2)	11 (10.1)	8 (7.8)	2 (2.7)	5 (6.5)	3 (15.0)	3 (13.0)	5 (50.0)	7 (46.6)	49 (8.2)	50 (8.2)
Total	288 (100)	304 (100)	94 (100)	88 (100)	109 (100)	102 (100)	74 (100)	77 (100)	20 (100)	23 (100)	10 (100)	15 (100)	595 (100)	609 (100)

Note: 1. (—) indicates nil.
2. Figures in parentheses are percentages to column total.

TABLE 6.7

Frequency distribution of age gaps between surviving children of same parents according to occupation pattern, Hirakot

Age gap interval	No. of instances in which the age gap falls in the stated interval for				Total
	MBO	NMBO	CM	Others	
1—1.9	60(30.9)	7(23.3)	55(28.8)	3(11.6)	125(28.3)
2—2.9	97(50.0)	16(53.4)	101(52.8)	15(57.7)	229(51.9)
3—3.9	24(12.4)	6(20.0)	17(8.9)	5(19.2)	52(11.8)
4—4.9	8(4.1)	—	8(4.2)	1(3.8)	17(3.9)
5—5.9	3(1.5)	—	3(1.5)	2(7.7)	8(1.8)
6 and above	2(1.1)	1(3.3)	7(3.8)	—	10(2.3)
Total	194(100.0)	30(100.0)	191(100.0)	26(100.0)	441(100.0)

Note: 1. (—) indicates nil.
2. Figures in parentheses are percentages to column total.

less than 29 per cent for all occupational groups together. The model frequency for all occupational patterns is 2 to 2.9 years age gap interval.

Table 6.8 shows the distribution of households according to occupation and highest level of education in a house. The households without any education for any member account for about 58 per cent of the MBO households while it is over 67 per cent of the total households in the viilage. The households with primary as the highest education in a household account for about 40 per cent in the case of MBO huseholds while it is only 22 per cent in the case of CM households. The highest education level in the village in 1981 was only higher secondary, and there was one household of this category in MBO households, and two in crew member households.

Migration and typology of migrants

Long-term migration: In addition to the information relating to the place of birth of the head of the household, we have

TABLE 6.8

Distribution of households according to occupational pattern and highest level of education in the household, Hirakot

Highest level of education	Number of households of				Total
	MBO	NMBO	CM	Others	
1. Illiterate	36(58.1)	8(72.7)	60(74.1)	12(63.2)	116(67.1)
2. Primary	25(40.3)	3(27.3)	18(22.2)	6(31.6)	52(30.1)
3. Middle	—	—	1(1.2)	—	1(0.5)
4. Secondary	1(1.6)	—	2(2.5)	1(5.2)	4(2.3)
Total	62(100.0)	11(100.0)	81(100.0)	19(100.0)	173(100.0)

Note: 1. (—) indicates nil.
2. Figures in parentheses are percentages to column total.

also collected information about the time of their immigration to Hirakot. But we have not tabulated the information because of relatively less variation[5] in the time of immigration to the village by individual households. Therefore, the groups of immigrants were quite homogeneous within each segment and were having similar initial conditions. Further, all the long-term migrants were intra-rural migrants, i.e. immigrants who settled in Hirakot, a rural location, were having their origin in a rural location.

Table 6.9 shows the distribution of households by occupational pattern and the location of the birthplace of the household heads. It could be noticed that about 42.2 per cent of the household heads have indicated their birthplace to be in the same village while the rest have immigrated to the village after the birth of the household head. Of the total immigrated not more than 20 per cent are from Gujarat state; the remainder are migrants from Sind (Pakistan) or Diu, the erstwhile French territory. Crew member households account for the maximum of the total immigrant households from other states with 48. MBO households account for maximum of the native households with 37 and are followed by a crew member, NMBO

TABLE 6.9

Distribution of households by occupational pattern and birthplace location of the household head, Hirakot

Location of birth place	Number of households which had their heads' birthplace indicated for				Total
	MBO	NMBO	CRM	Others	
1. Same village	37(59.7)	10(90.9)	24(29.6)	2(10.5)	73(42.2)
2. Outside the village	1(1.6)	—	7(8.6)	10(52.6)	18(10.4)
3. Outside the district	—	—	2(2.5)	—	2(1.2)
4. Outside the state	24(38.7)	1(9.1)	48(59.3)	7(36.9)	80(46.2)
Total	62(100.0)	11(100.0)	81(100.0)	19(100.0)	173(100.0)

Note: 1. (—) indicates nil.
2. Figures in parentheses are percentages to column total.

and other households with 24, 10 and 2 households respectively.

Short-term migration: During the census we took in late 1981 we found that about 49 of the total 196 households were locked. On further probing about these households we found that these households migrate to different parts of Saurashtra during the fishing season and go back to the village during the off-season. These households include both owners of fishing equipment and crew members. Though we do not have an exact information we found that the majority of the households are MBO households. Of the 49 households there are about 26 which go back to the village with their equipment on and off during the fishing season. We have taken the census of these 26 households which go out on very short migration visits. These comprised 14 MBO, 2 NMBO and 10 crew member households.

Social participation of fishermen

The social participation of the fishermen households is analysed in terms of their membership of various organizations such as fishermen co-operative society, caste association and gram panchayat. In addition, the duration of their single and multiple of these organizations is analysed according to occupation.

Fishermen co-operatives: There are two fishermen co-operative societies in the village. The oldest of these two societies was organized[6] in 1975 and the other one in 1977. The records of these two societies indicated that the total membership of these societies was over 260 as on October 1981. However, our census taken in 1981 indicated that the total number of members in the co-operative societies is only 130.[7] These 130 members of the co-operative societies represent only 93 (53.8 per cent) of the total 173 households in the village.

The distribution of the members of the co-operative societies according to the occupation pattern is presented in Table 6.10. The total members of the co-operative societies account

TABLE 6.10

Distribution of co-operative societies' members and their households according to occupation pattern, Hirakot (1981)

Occupation	Number of members	% share in Total	Number of HH with at least one member	% share in Total
MBO	81	62.3	54	56.1
NMBO	14	10.8	10	10.8
CRM	31	23.8	27	29.0
Others	4	3.1	2	2.1
Total	130	100.0	93	100.0

for only 10.8 per cent of the total population in the village. The MBO members of the co-operative society account for over 63 per cent of the total members while the population of MBO households account for less than 46 per cent of the total population. The membership of co-operatives in terms of population or number of households is over-represented by MBO population/households and is under-represented by crew and other population/households.

About two-thirds of the households had membership of the co-operative society for about five years or less and the remainder for over five years but less than eight years. Of the 27 crew households 19 enrolled with the society during the past five years only.

Membership of caste association/Mosque trust and gram panchayat: There is one Mosque trust in the village and it is represented by five members. These five are drawn from four households, one from MBO households, and two each from crew and other households. The Mosque trust came to the village quite long ago. However, the current members of the trust are holding the membership only for the past five years.

The Gram Panchayat at Kadvar is represented by two members one of whom is the Sarpanch. The Sarpanch of the Gram Panchayat belongs to an MBO household and the Machhiyara community. The other member is from a crew member household and also belongs to the Machhiyara community. These members/sarpanch had been holding the membership for the past three years.

The distribution of households according to the number of memberships of organizations indicated that 77 of the total 173 households do not have a single active member in any of the three organizations, three households have membership of two or three of these organizations of which two are MBO households and one crew member household. These three households are of the Machhiyara community.

MECHANIZATION: ITS IMPACT ON PRODUCTION SYSTEM

The contents of this section can be outlined as follows: The Technology of Production; Ownership of Productive Assets; Production Pattern: Current and Past; Output and Incomes and Distribution of Gains; and Disposal of Fish Landings.

Technology of production

Turning to the question of the technology of fishing, in the broader context of boats, gear and accessories, in the village we find that it is an intermediate and traditional technology in relation to boats and gear. The technology in relation to accessories is very traditional and is based on the long experience of fishermen. The craft technology consists of dugout or plank-built canoes of lengths ranging from 15 to 35 feet with or without motors. The non-mechanized boats, very few in number, are small in size and use pedal for steering and propulsion. Occasionally, the non-mechanized boats use sails for propulsion. The other type of boats called OBM boats are propelled by motors of 3 to 5 h.p. As indicated earlier, motorized boats were introduced in the village in 1961 by the Gujarat Fisheries Central Co-operative Association (GFCCA) on a demonstration basis. However, the motorization of fishing craft gained the acceptance of the fishermen only in 1963 after an initial resistance during 1961-62. In 1963 about three OBMs were acquired by the fishermen of the village at a subsidized rate. And though the motorization of the fishing craft started in 1961 it was only during the early seventies that it gained momentum and currently over 80 per cent of the fishing craft are motorized.

In 1981, there were 70 OBM boats and 13 non-mechanized boats. Of the total 70 OBM boats 66 were of the length of 20 feet and above and the rest less than 20 feet. Majority (10 out of 13) of the non-mechanized boats were of the length up to 20 feet, and the non-mechanized boats of over 20 feet account for only 23.07 per cent of the total non-mechanized boats (Table 6.11). Though we could not collect information to analyse the trends in the number of OBMs and non-mechanized boats our discussions with the villagers reveal that a rapid increase in the motorization of fishing craft during early 1970s was accompanied by a decrease in the number of non-mechanized boats since motorization was only a case of conversion.

Only one type of net (namely, gill net)[8] is used for fishing by both OBM and non-mechanized boat owners during the fishing season. The mesh sizes of the nets vary from 3 to 8 inch. The distribution of nets according to mesh size is shown in Table 6.12. It can be seen that about 92 of the total 111 gill nets are owned by OBM boat owners. Of the rest 14 are owned by non-mechanized boat owners and 5 by crew members. The nets with 7.1 to 8 inch mesh size, usually used for catching sharks, ray fish, ghol, dhara and sheer, account for maximum of the total nets with 47 (42.3 per cent) followed by nets with mesh sizes of 3.1 to 4 inch (used for catching pomfrets, cat

TABLE 6.11

Distribution of different types of boats according to the year of purchase, Hirakot (1981)

Year of purchase	Number of boats purchased in the stated year			
	OBM[1] boats of length		Non-mechanized boats	
	Up to 20 ft.	20 ft. and above	Up to 20 ft.	20 ft. and above
Up to 1965	—	9	—	—
1966	—	—	—	—
1967	—	1	1	—
1968	—	2	—	—
1969	—	1	—	—
1970	2	8	—	—
1971	—	4	1	—
1972	1	4	1	—
1973	—	2	1	—
1974	—	3	—	—
1975	—	4	2	1
1976	—	6	1	—
1977	—	2	—	—
1978	1	7	2	—
1979	—	4	—	1
1980	—	5	—	—
1981	—	4	1	1
Total	4	66	10	3

Note: 1. The year of purchase of OBM is based on the year of purchase of boat and not on the basis of year of motorization which may be different.

2. (—) indicates nil.

fish, etc.), 5.1 to 6 inch and others with 45 (40.6 per cent), 17 (15.3 per cent) and 2 (1.8 per cent) respectively. It can also be noticed that the total nets in the village are more than the number of boats indicating ownership of more than one net per boat but the nets are usually of different mesh sizes, for the year-round productivity.

TABLE 6.12

Distribution of gill nets owned by different occupational households according to mesh size, Hirakot (1981)

Mesh size interval (in inches)	Number of nets owned by			
	OBM boat owners	NMB owners	Crew members	Total
3.1—4.0	37(40.2)	6(42.9)	2(40.0)	45(40.6)
4.1—5.0	1(1.1)	—	—	1(0.9)
5.1—6.0	12(13.0)	3(21.4)	2(40.0)	17(15.3)
6.1—7.0	—	1(7.1)	—	1(0.9)
7.1—8.0	42(45.7)	4(25.6)	1(20.0)	47(42.3)
Total	92(100)	14(100)	5(100)	111(100)

Note: 1. Figures in parentheses represent percentages to column total.
2. (—) indicates nil.

The lengthwise distribution of the nets indicates that the nets owned by NMB owners and crew members are smaller than the ones owned by OBM owners. The length of the nets owned by OBM boat owners in the range of 500 to 10,000 feet while of the ones owned by NMB owners is in the range of less than 500 to 6,000 feet, and of the crew members from 1,000 to 2,500 feet. The average length per net for OBM owners is 3,913 feet while it is only 1,929 feet for NMB owners and 1,900 feet for crew (Table 6.13).

In addition to the gill nets, the non-mechanized boat owners operate cast nets during off-season. Three of the non-mechanized boat owners own cast net sets in addition to gill nets. These three nets are mended with nylon yarn.

The yarn used in mending the nets consisted of both nylon and monofilament. The nets made out of monofilament account for over 54 per cent of the total with 60 nets and the remaining are nylon nets. It is interesting to notice that there are now no cotton gill nets in the village, whereas they used to be the predominant type of nets during the pre-motorization period in the village.

TABLE 6.13

Lengthwise distribution of gill nets owned by different occupational households, Hirakot (1981)

Length interval (Feet)	No. of nets in the stated range owned by			Total
	OBM owners	NMB owners	Crew	
Less than 1000	2(2.2)	6(42.9)	—	8(7.2)
1001—2000	21(22.8)	2(14.4)	3(60.0)	26(23.4)
2001—3000	16(17.4)	3(21.4)	2(21.4)	21(18.9)
3001—4000	12(13.0)	1(7.1)	—	13(11.7)
4001—5000	12(13.0)	1(7.1)	—	13(11.7)
5001—6000	17(18.5)	1(7.1)	—	18(16.2)
6001—7000	1(1.1)	—	—	1(0.9)
7001—8000	6(6.6)	—	—	6(5.5)
8001—9000	1(1.1)	—	—	1(0.9)
9001 and above	4(4.3)	—	—	4(3.6)
Total	92(100)	14(100)	5(100)	111(100)

Note. 1. (—) indicates nil.
2. Figures in parentheses represent percentages to column total.

Ownership of productive assets

In Hirakot there are 68 OBM and 14 NMB boats between 73 households, indicating more than one boat owner[9] in a household in some cases. Looking now at the situation as we found in 1981, there were more than 100 households consisting of about 45.42 per cent of the total village population without any fishing equipment whereas the top 15 per cent of the households owned more than one boat alongwith the necessary gear and accessories. The inequality in the ownership of boats is measured by the Gini coefficient. The value of Gini coefficient for the distribution of value of productive assets over the households was found to be 0.5648. The estimated value of Gini ratio indicates inequitable distribution of assets. Figure 6.2 shows the Lorenz curve of the distribution of fishery assets in terms of value.

Pattern of production: Present and past

Although fishing is a joint enterprise, the ownership pattern of fishery assets—craft and gear—in the village is basically individual ownership. In addition to the ownership of craft and gear, the nature and character of the owner (in terms of active fishing) and the status of non-owner workers in the boat play an important role in the organizatio of production.

In the village there are only two patterns of ownership. These are: (i) Individual owner, owner-worker and non-owner partner (IO, OW and NOP), and (ii) Individual owner, owner non-worker and non-owner partner (IO, ONW, NOP).

The first pattern is the most predominant, and traditional types of ownership patterns account for more than 90 per cent of the boats and gear for OBM boats and for all the non-mechanized boats. Further, our discussions with the villagers indicated that the ownership pattern did not change with the introduction of motorized boats int he village.

The fish landings in the village take place on the open sandy beach. In view of the intermediate level of technology introduced in the village, the shift in the place of landing did not occur in the village.[10] Thus, both non-mechanized boats and mechanized boats land their catches in the traditional village landing centre.

Output and income and distribution of gain

Fish production : The marine fish production in the village has been estimated to be about 680 tonnes during 1980-81.[11] Table 6.14 shows the quarterwise marine fish production in Hirakot vis-a-vis in Veraval region consisting of seven fishing centres. The total marine fish production in the village has decreased from 1,065 tonnes during 1977-78 to 680 tonnes during 1980-81, while the production in the region increased from 64,502 tonnes to 89,294 tonnes during the same period. The decrease may be due to the recent trend in migration of boats from the village during the fishing season. Turning to the seasonality of fish production, we find that the quarter starting from October to December accounts for about 50 per cent of the annual landings of the region while it is more evenly spread over the remaining quarters of the year with

TABLE 6.14

Quarterwise marine fish production in Hirakot vis-a-vis Veraval region (1977-78 to 1980-81)

(Quantity in tonnes)

Quarter	Fish production during							
	1977-78 in		1978-79 in		1979-80 in		1980-81 in	
	Hirakot	Veraval	Hirakot	Veraval	Hirakot	Veraval	Hirakot	Veraval
July-September	218 (20.5)	44639 (7.2)	14 (1.4)	4787 (5.3)	96 (14.1)	5874 (6.8)	124 (18.2)	3241 (3.6)
October-December	260 (24.8)	40179 (62.3)	368 (35.8)	44470 (48.9)	253 (37.3)	38469 (44.2)	354 (52.1)	38747 (43.4)
January-March	411 (38.6)	10729 (16.6)	381 (37.1)	25771 (28.4)	127 (18.7)	24957 (28.7)	100 (14.7)	28824 (32.3)
April-June	172 (16.1)	8955 (13.9)	264 (25.7)	15850 (17.4)	203 (29.9)	17653 (20.3)	102 (15.0)	18482 (20.7)
Total	1065 (100)	64502 (100)	1027 (100)	90878 (100)	679 (100)	86953 (100)	680 (100)	89294 (100)

Note: Figures in parentheses represent percentages to column total.

Source: Compiled on the basis of information obtained from the Office of the Assistant Director (Projects) of Fisheries, Veraval.

some concentration during October to March in the village. The contrasting seasonal variations in the village against the pattern in the region may be mainly because of the technological variations; the fishing activity in the region is dominated by the presence of more trawlers while the technique of fishing in the village is predominantly gill-net fishing.

Fish production in the village during 1981-82 has been estimated to be 736 tonnes of which the contribution of OBM boats is about 689 tonnes (93.6 per cent) and the remaining is the production by non-mechanized boats.[12] White pomfret is the single most important variety of the fish landings in the village which accounts for about 20 per cent of the OBM landings and 21 per cent of the NMB landings. It should be noted that the species composition of OBM landings and NMB landings is similar but for a moderate variation in relation to black pomfret, sharks and others. Further, if we want to find out a single contrasting characteristic of the species composition of the landings in the village compared to the Veraval region it is prawns and shrimps, and small demersal fish. Whereas the landings of prawns and shrimps and small demersal fish particularly small sciaenids account for majority of the total landings in the region, there are no landings of these varieties in the village. This is also a contrasting feature of the fishing techniques with trawl nets, and gill nets (Table 6.15).

As already indicated, the gear technology in the village did not change due to introduction of motorized boats, while the number of OBM boats have increased very rapidly from one boat in 1961 to over 70 in 1980. Consequently, the species composition of fish landings did not change much with the introduction of OBM boats in the village. A rough calculation indicates that the total landings have increased from about 200 tonnes during 1960-61 (the year before the motorization of the first boat) to about 1,065 tonnes during 1977-78.[13]

Output value : The value estimates of output in the village are based on the price information obtained by us during the survey and the estimates of output. The price information used related to the specieswise prices received by the fishermen on different days during the period of our survey. As there

TABLE 6.15

Specieswise estimated marine fish landings by mechanized and non-mechanized boats, Hirakot (1981-82)

(*in tonnes*)

Species	Fish landings of stated variety by					
	OBM boats		NMB boats		Total	
	Quantity	% share	Quantity	% share	Quantity	% share
1. White Pomfret	152	20.1	10	21.3	162	22.0
2. Black Pomfret	114	16.6	4	8.5	118	16.0
3. Seer Fish	106	15.4	7	14.9	113	15.3
4. Hilsa	87	12.6	5	10.6	92	12.5
5. Clupeids	58	8.4	3	6.4	61	8.3
6. Sharks	65	9.4	6	12.8	71	9.7
7. Others*	107	15.5	12	25.5	119	16.2
Total	689	100	47	100	736	100

Note: 1. Excluding the household consumption and gifts.
2. *Includes mainly cat fish, thread fin, eel, silver bar, etc.

were sharp fluctuation, we used average prices of major varieties to estimate the value of output. The information was obtained from the records of fish merchants. Average prices for the major varieties of fish which are used for estimating the gross value of output (GVO) alongwith the annual GVO are presented in Table 6.16.

The annual gross value of output (GVO) in the village has been estimated to be Rs. 42,25,500 during 1981-82, of which the contribution of OBM boats was Rs. 39,72,000 (94 per cent of the total) and the remainder was the value of output of non-mechanized boats. Pomfret accounts for over 40 per cent of the annual GVO of OBM boats, NMBs and aggregate. Thus, the economy of the fishermen in the village is centred on pomfret landings. The ranking of the species in terms of GVO is: white pomfret, seer fish, black pomfret, hilsa and others. The average unit values of output were Rs. 5.76 per kg. for the output of OBM boats, Rs. 5.39 per

TABLE 6.16

Average price and annual gross value of output by OBM boats and NMBs, Hirakot (1981-82)

(in '000 Rupees)

Species	Price Rs./kg.	Annual gross value of output by					
		OBM boats		NBM boats		Total	
		Value	% share	Value	% share	Value	% share
1. White Pomfret	10.50	1596.0	40.2	105.0	41.3	1701.0	40.3
2. Black Pomfret	5.00	570.0	14.4	20.0	7.9	590.0	14.0
3. Seer Fish	6.00	636.0	16.0	42.0	16.6	678.0	16.0
4. Hilsa	5.00	435.0	10.9	25.0	9.9	460.0	10.9
5. Clupeids	4.50	261.0	6.6	13.5	5.3	274.5	6.5
6. Sharks	4.00	260.0	6.5	24.0	9.5	284.0	6.7
7. Others	2.00	214.0	5.4	24.0	9.5	238.0	5.6
Total	—	3972.0	100.0	253.5	100.0	4225.5	100.0

kg. for the output of NMBs and Rs. 5.74 per kg. for the combined output in the village.

Measurement of household incomes from fishing: For working out the returns on the capital invested in fishing equipment and labour, it is necessary to estimate the economics of the fishing craft and gear. Table 6.17 shows the quarter-wise gross value of output (GVO) per boat for different types of boats. The GVO per OBM boat has been estimated at Rs. 64,675 while it is Rs. 33,481 for an NMB boat of 20 feet length. The quarterwise distribution of GVO is similar for all the three types of boats; the pariod between October and December accounts for the maximum in all the cases. The two quarters (October-March) account for more than three-fourths of the total annual GVOs for all the three types of boats, while the remaining half year's production accounts for less than one-fourth of the annual GVOs in all cases. Thus, the quarterwise distribution of GVOs indicates the highly seasonal nature of the production.

The itemwise average variable costs per day for operating different types of boats are presented in Table 6.18. The total

TABLE 6.17

Quarterwise gross value of output per OBM boat and NMB, Hirakot (1981-82)

(in Rupees)

Quarter	Gross value of output of non-mechanized boat of		OBM boat of 20 ft. and above
	Less than 20 ft.	20 ft. and above	
July-September	1589 (8.2)	2243 (6.7)	4690 (7.2)
October-December	9482 (48.6)	15468 (46.2)	29852 (46.2)
January-March	5965 (30.5)	9442 (28.2)	18135 (28.0)
April-June	3454 (17.7)	6328 (18.9)	12018 (18.6)
Total	19490 (100)	33481 (100)	64675 (100)

Note: 1. Figures in parentheses represent percentages to column total.
2. Average sizes were 18 ft. for NMB less than 20 ft., 24 ft. for NMB above 20 ft. and 28 ft. for OBM boats of 20 ft. and above.

variable cost per OBM boat was more than three times that of the NMB boat of comparable length. Expenditure on fuel is the single most important cost for operating of an OBM boat and accounts for over 75 per cent of the total variable cost per day. In the case of the non-mechanized boats, the expenditure on net twine and sundry items accounts for an overwhelming (say, over 70 per cent) share of the daily expenditure.

Annual fixed costs incurred per boat for different types in Hirakot during 1981-82 are presented in Table 6.19. The total fixed costs per boat for OBM boats and NMB boats of less than 20 feet, 20 feet and above are Rs. 39,076, Rs. 13,640, and Rs. 25,830 respectively. In the case of all types of boats the salaries of the crew account for a large part of the fixed costs. The depreciation is the next most

TABLE 6.18

Average variable costs per day for operating various types of boats, Hirakot (1981-82)

(*in Rupees*)

Items of cost	Costs incurred by boat owners of		
	NMB of		OBM of
	Less than 20 ft.	20 ft. and above	20 ft. and above
1. Fuel oils	2.50+	3.90+	50.80
2. Mobile oil and other lubricants	—	—	10.50
3. Wages of daily labourers	3.50*	4.00*	5.60*
4. Ice and water	—	—	—
5. Food expenditure for crew	1.75	2.25	3.25
6. Cost of net twine	6.80	7.50	10.20
7. Others	5.00	7.25	8.75
Total	19.55 (16.05)	24.90 (20.90)	89.10 83.50)

+indicates expenditure incurred on lighting devices during fishing trips.

*indicates mostly in kind (fish) for putting the boat into and out of the sea before and after the fishing trip.

Note: Figures in parentheses represent percentages to total cash expenditure.

important component of the fixed cost in eash case. The annual salary of a crew member in an OBM boat works out to be Rs. 8,444. In the case of crew in a non-mechanized boat the salary per crew member is lower than that of the OBM crew; it is Rs. 6,696 for crew in an NMB boat of 23 feet and above and Rs. 4,872 in the case of crew in an NMB boat of length less than 20 feet. The wide variations in the remuneration of crew in different types of boats may be because of the difference in the level of technology and skill of the crew. Usually, the crew members in non-mechanized boats, particularly of length less than 20 feet, are trainees and, therefore, are

TABLE 6.19

Annual fixed cost incurred per boat for different types of boats, Hirakot (1981-82)

(in Rupees)

Items of cost	Costs incurred on stated item per boat		
	NMB of		OBM boat of
	Less than 20 ft.	20 ft. and above	20 ft. and above
1. Salaries to the crew members*	9745.00	20089.00	25332.50
2. Repairs and maintenance	315.00	450.00	1925.00
3. Dry docking and oil painting	275.00	360.00	458.50
4. Depreciation**	2700.00	4067.00	9742.00
5. Interest on borrowed capital***	300.00	450.00	1200.00
6. Others	305.00	414.00	418.00
Total	13640.00	25830.00	39076.00

Note: *For working out the salaries of the crew it has been assumed that all the required crew is hired. The required crew for NMBs of less than 20 ft. and 20 ft. and above are 2 and 3 respectively while for OBM boats of 20 ft. and above it is 3.

**For working out the depreciation we have taken the economic lifetime of the boat, gear and motor to be 15, 3 and 12 years respectively. The total investment on these components was taken at 1981 prices.

***For working out interest on the borrowed capital only borrowings from the formal sources for investment on boats and gear are considered.

less skilled. In other words, the non-mechanized boats in the village are used for training the fishermen youth and for teaching the technique of fishing.

The annual gross and net returns of different types of boats are presented in Table 6.20. The pattern of net returns of different types of boats is similar to that of the gross returns. The net returns of OBM boats are the highest with Rs. 8,898,

TABLE 6.20

Gross and net returns of different types of boats, Hirakot (1981-82)

(*in Rupees*)

Particulars	NMB boats		MB
	Less than 20 ft.	20 ft. and above	20 ft. and above
1. Annual gross returns	19490.00	33481.00	64675.00
2. Costs:			
Annual fixed costs	13640.00	25830.00	39076.00
Annual variable costs*	3129.75	4075.50	16700.00
Total costs	16769.75	29905.50	55776.00
3. Net returns	2720.25	3575.50	8898.00
4. Returns on investment (%)	16.48	13.24	14.95

Note: *Annual variable costs have been estimated by multiplying the per day expenditure by the number of fishing days in a year. The total fishing days for different types of boats have been estimated to be as follows: Number of working days of OBM of 20 ft. and above=200, and Number of working days for non-mechanized boats=195.

followed by NMB boats of 20 feet and above and less than 20 feet, with Rs. 3,545 and Rs. 2,720 respectively. The Return on Investment (ROI) is the highest for non-mechanized boats with a length less than 20 feet with 16.48 per cent, is followed by OBM boats of 20 feet and above and non-mechanized boats of 20 feet and above with 14.75 per cent and 13.24 per cent respectively.

Distribution of income: We have computed the income accruing to each of the households taking the occupation of every person gainfully employed within each house into account. The distribution of income by occupation and source is given in Table 6.21. Income generated from occupations

TABLE 6.21

Distribution of income according to occupations, Hirakot (1981-82)

(in '000 Rupees)

Occupation	Income			Income per household	Per capita income
	From fishery related	Non-fishing activities	Total		
1. OBM boat owners	1521.11 (60.24)	9.75 (9.02)	1530.86 (58.14)	24.69	2.78
2. NMB owners	104.04 (4.12)	0.75 (0.69)	104.79 (3.98)	9.53	1.59
3. Crew	888.67 (35.19)	33.50 (30.98)	922.17 (35.02)	11.39	1.89
4. Others	11.25 (0.45)	64.15 (59.31)	75.40 (2.86)	3.97	0.76
Total	2525.07 (100)	108.15 (100)	2633.22 (100)	15.22	2.19

Note: Figures in parentheses represent percentages to column total.

other than fisheries is negligible and accounts for less than 4.11 per cent of the total income of all the households. As expected, the OBM boat owning households are richer. They share 58.14 per cent of the total income and 60.24 per cent of the income from fishery-related activities, although they account for only 35.84 per cent of households and 45.68 per cent of population. The NMB owners and crew households are roughly close to each other in terms of per capita income. The income per household for OBM boat owner households is maximum with Rs. 24,090 and is followed by crew, NMB owner and other households. The ranking of households according to per capita income is similar to that based on income per household. All the households except OBM boat owner households have below average per household and per capita income with the poorest being the other households.

The estimated Gini ratios and the Lorenz curves for the distribution of productive assets and incomes are shown in Figure 6.2. The Gini ratio of inequality for income is 0.1973 while it is over 0.5648 for the assets. As expected, the income distribution is more equal than the distribution of productive assets. The large gap between the Gini ratio of inequality for assets and incomes indicates the favourable factor shares for labour in the village.

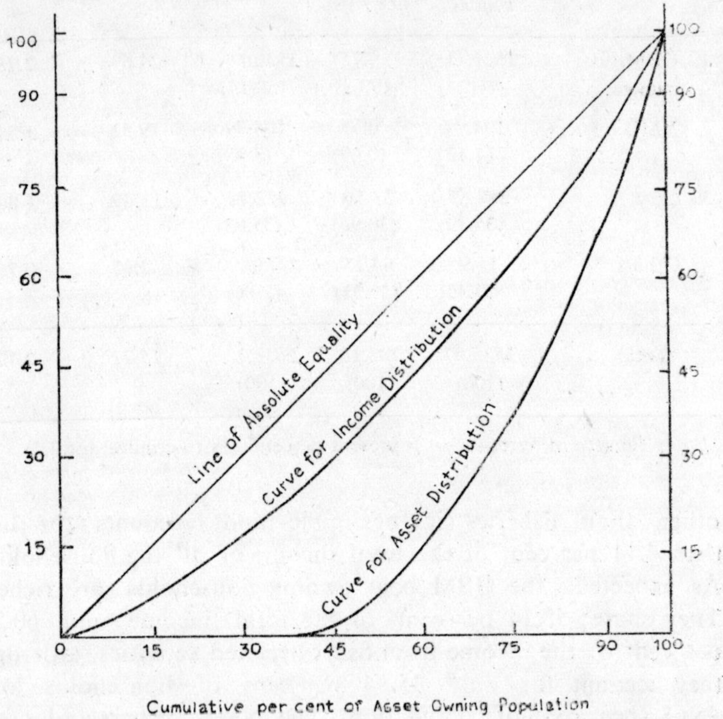

	Assets	Income
Gini ratio	0.5648	0.1973

FIG. 6.2: *Lorenz curve for assets and income distribution, Hirakot (1981-82)*

It should be emphasized that inequality of income is on the basis of household income. When we consider individual personal income the inequality may be slightly lower, because larger households usually have higher incomes. Thus, the income is evenly distributed in the village.

Disposal of fish landings

The techniques of fishing and consequently the species composition of fish landings and the availability of infrastructure facilities for processing of fish largely determine the pattern of fish utilization in the given region. As there are no landings of prawns, which is a major marine product for export, the contribution of village landings for export is almost negligible. The village landings are mainly used for fresh consumption and sun-drying or salt-curing.

Our observations with regard to the utilization of marine fish are summarized in Table 6.22. It can be seen that fresh

TABLE 6.22

Estimated utilization pattern of marine fish landings, Hirakot

Utilization	Per cent share of state utilization during	
	Pre-mechanization period (1960-61)	Current period (1981-82)
1. Fresh consumption	70	87
2. Drying and Salt-curing	30	10
3. Fishmeal extraction	—	—
4. Exports (frozen and canned)	—	3
Total	100.0	100.0

fish consumption accounts for the maximum of landings during pre-motorization periods and post-mechanization. The share of fresh fish and exports has increased while the share of drying and salt-curing has decreased. The changes in the utilization pattern are mainly because of the availability of different infrastructure facilities. Exports mainly consist of the pomfret. The detailed marketing pattern of different types/forms of fish is given in the next section.

MARKETS IN THE VILLAGE

In this section, we will examine the market for inputs, labour, credit and output in the village and their influence on the production system. Our examination is with a view to uncovering the changes in these markets as a result of mechanization.

Markets for inputs

Both non-mechanized and mechanized boats require facilities such as boat-building yards, net yarn supplies, etc., while the mechanized craft require inputs such as service facilities for motor/engines, fuel oil, lubricants and landing and berthing facilities.

The major sources for boats—both non-mechanized and OBM—are boat-building yards outside the village, particularly outside the state. The distribution of sample boats according to the place of construction/purchase is presented in Table 6.23. Of the total 21 new boats purchased/constructed, 11 (52.4 per cent) were purchased from sources outside the state. Another 9 were constructed within the district. Transaction of boats between the fishermen is very common in the case of non-mechanized boats. The construction of boats within the district and outside the state (mainly Karnataka) is by unorganized boat builders. A few carpenters at Mangrol construct NMB and OBM boats. Hence, the carpenters, in theory, operate in an oligopolistic market and one might expect them to charge higher prices. However, the real situation is different and the monopoly element is too weak owing, perhaps, to the presence of organized boat-building yards.

The market situation for motors in the village is similar to the one in Chorwad village. Of the 70 motors in the village, in 1982, 55 were Yamaha make. Other brands which have an established market in the village are Johnson and British Anjani.

There are two principal sources for supply of yarn for mending and repairing of nets: co-operative societies and the private trader who is also a fish merchant. In addition, fishermen themselves purchase net material from Veraval. Most purchases from the private trader are on credit and the price is fixed by bargaining.

TABLE 6.23

Distribution of boats owned by sample respondents according to place of purchase/construction, Hirakot

Location of source	Stated source for					
	OBM boats		NMB		Total	
	New	Old	New	Old	New	Old
1. Within the village	1 (5.0)	3 (75.0)	—	1 (14.3)	1 (4.8)	4 (36.4)
2. Outside the village but within the district	8 (40.0)	1 (25.0)	1 (100.0)	5 (71.4)	9 (42.8)	6 (54.5)
3. Outside the district but within the state	—	—	—	—	—	—
4. Outside the state	11 (55.0)	—	—	1 (14.3)	11 (52.4)	1 (9.1)
Total	20 (100.0)	4 (100.0)	1 (100.0)	7 (100.0)	21 (100.0)	11 (100.0)

Note: 1. (—) indicates nil.
2. Figures in parentheses are percentages to column total.

Over one-half of the requirements of nylon and synthetic twine is supplied by the private trader who also trades in fish. Neither the trader nor the co-operatives keep stocks of yarn but procure in small quantities as and when needed. The prices charged by the trader appear to be higher by about 15 to 20 per cent.

Most of the motors in the village use petrol for starting and switch over to kerosene afterwards; some are operated on petrol only. Only eight OBMs are operated on petrol, the remaining use petrol for starting and switch over to kerosene later.

The principal source of supply of kerosene are the co-operative societies. Lubricants are supplied by the fish trader in the village. Usually the OBM boat owners ensure petrol requirements for a couple of weeks from Veraval. Petrol brought by the OBM boat owners at one time was about 20 litres. Kerosene is supplied at the rate of 15 litres per boat per week. Additional requirements are met from the nearby village or town by individual fishermen. It is also supplied, though in small quantities, by the fish trader. The fish trader also supplies oil. He is a monopolist as far as the supply of oil is concerned and charges relatively higher prices for oil. There is nothing like mobile oil.

Market for labour

The productive assets are owned by less than 40 per cent of the households while majority of the rest of the households derive an overwhelming share of their income by selling labour. Of the total households which derive their income by selling labour over 90 per cent are involved in fishing. Thus, the hiring of wage-paid or partnership labour to undertake fishing is widespread and in a large number of cases all their income is derived from fishery labour. In this section we will examine the selling of labour time by the households with particular attention to fishing labour in the village. Only two of the total 63 labour households have generated most of their income from selling of labour outside the village and fishing activity.

In general, two types of labour contracts are observed: fixed wage and catch sharing. The fixed wage system is restricted to shore-based activities such as transportation of fish from landing centre to market and putting the craft to sea and taking it out. Payment to labourers on a share basis is prevalent in actual fishing operations. The system of paying to crew members is standard and is the same as mentioned in the last profile (see page 160).

Demand for and supply of labour in the village: The supply and demand pattern of labour in the village was similar to the one explained in the last chapter (see page 162). As indicated earlier, to understand the employment situation in the village we have attempted to estimate the surplus labourers in the village.

Table 6.24 shows the estimates of surplus labourers. Surplus labourers in the village account for about 11.52 per

TABLE 6.24

Estimates of surplus labourers according to occupation, Hirakot (1981-1982)

Particulars	No. of members in households of				Total
	MB owners	NMB owners	Crew	Others	
1. Number of households	62	11	81	19	173
2. Number of able-bodied adult male members of family	134	14	122	25	295
3. Number of adult members with occupations other than fishing	5	—	8	21	34
4. Number of adult male members who have not yet entered the workforce (students)	1	—	—	1	2
5. Number of members actively engaged in fishing or at best having no other occupation	128	14	114	3	259
6. Number of members required for operating the fishing equipment	200	25	—	—	225
7. Surplus labourers in the fishing workforce	—72	—11	114	3	34
8. Surplus labourers per household	—1.16	—1.00	1.41	0.16	0.20

Note: 1. (—) indicates nil.
2. Negative surplus indicates deficits.

cent of the availability of labourers. The boat owners tend to withdraw family labourers from fishing particularly in view of odd conditions during fishing trips. This tendency may be more in the case of motorized boats because of the higher rate of return on investment which could be sufficient for the maintenance of the family. In the case of non-mechanized boat owners the return on investment may not be sufficient to maintain the family and therefore the owners tend to go fishing in order to augment income. The demand-supply relation of labour in the village cannot be studied on the basis of wage rates since no ruling wage rate can be computed. However, at the same time, we find the village is seemingly labour abundant.

The estimated (on the basis of our sample information) labour participation, in the operation of different types of fishing equipment, is presented in Table 6.25. We notice that only 105 fishermen family members of the OBM boat owners are involved in actual fishing while the households have a potential for supply of 128 hands, with a total working force of 134 members. As expected, the deficit of working force is maximum in the case of MB owner households with 72 crew requirement over and above the theoretical supply of labourers from the family. The total deficit of fishing hands in equipment-owning households is 83 while the availability of labourers from the supplying households is about 117 hands. Under the optimal allocation model[14] the total surplus labourers should be from the labour supplying households but the reality is quite different. This aspect can be looked into closely when we consider the pattern of labour participation. Further, our estimates are global and are computed with an assumption that all the craft are in operation during the season. Therefore, the actual surplus labour may be higher than the computed value if we take the seasonal variations into account. Thus, we find there is no scarcity of labourers during any season in the village.

In the case of non-mechanized boats all the able-bodied adult members are involved in fishing and the hiring of crew is done only after all the family labourers are fully employed. Thus, there is a clear evidence that fishermen tend to withdraw family labour from active fishing as the level of fishing technology increases. The share of hired crew in the total crew required is maximum for OBM boats with 47.5 per cent and is followed by NMBs up to 20 feet and 20 feet and above with 44.4 and 42.9 per cent respectively.

The structure of the labour force in terms of casual and permanent labourers did not change with mechanization in the village. An overwhelming part of labour force is employed on a permanent basis. Casual labourers are relatively unknown.

TABLE 6.25

Estimated labour participation, pattern, family and hired for operating different types of boats, Hirakot (1981-82)

Type of boat	Total boats in the village	Estimated average crew size required per boat	Total crew required	Estimated source of crew	
				Family	Hired
1. Dugout canoes					
(a) up to 20 ft.	10	1.80	18 (100.0)	10 (55.6)	8 (44.4)
(b) 20 ft. and above	3	2.25	7 (100.0)	4 (57.1)	3 (42.9)
2. OBM boats	70	2.85	200 (100.0)	105 (52.5)	95 (47.5)
Total	83	2.71	225 (100.0)	119 (52.89)	106 (47.11)

They are employed only when permanent labourers are not available.

Displacement of labourers by motorization of fishing craft: The employment in fisheries is of two kinds: (a) employment in actual fishing and (b) employment in forward and backward linkages. We shall try to estimate the displacement of labour due to motorization of fishing craft only in the actual fishing, mainly because of lack of data to estimate the situation in forward and backward linkages.

The net displacement of labour is measured in terms of man-months per tonne of output in both mechanized and non-mechanized sectors. Table 6.26 shows the monthwise employment per tonne of output in both OBM and non-mechanized sectors for the year 1981-82. Employment per tonne of output fluctuates widely from month to month. During 1981-82 the employment per unit of output was 1.771 man-months for OBM boats and 2.960 for non-mechanized boats. With motorization, employment is reduced by about 1.183 man-months per tonne of output. The net displacement accounts for about 39.97 per cent of the employment per tonne of output in non-mechanized boats. The increased employment in forward linkages due to an increase in the output may not be generating employment to offset the displacement in the production system. Thus, there may be a net displacement of labour due to motorization of fishing craft. The estimated displacement of labour village due to motorization is of the order of 815.09 man-months.

Labour mobility : Let us now consider labour mobility in the village. Distribution of sample OBM boat crew members[15], according to the labour mobility ratio, is presented in Table 6.27. Out of the 20 sample crew members, 13 (65 per cent) have been found to be having low mobility and the remaining (7) were having a medium mobility ratio. Each of the crew members worked for at least one year before he changed the employer. It is the common practice that labourers do not change employer during the fishing season. The changing of employer takes place only during the rough or off-season for fishing. Crew mobility for the skilled and healthy crew is very high in view of the strong competition among employers. The crew attraction by the employers is mainly through the non-price mechanisms as the remuneration of the crew members is

TABLE 6.26

Monthwise output and employment per tonne of output in both mechanized and non-mechanized sectors, Hirakot (1981-82)

Month	For OBM boats				For NM boats			
	Output (tonnes)	Number of boats in operations**	Manpower* employed (Man-months)	Employment per tonne of output (Man-months)	Output (tonnes)	No. of boats in operation**	Manpower* employed (Man-months)	Employment in tonne of output (Man-months)
1	2	3	4	5	6	7	8	9
July	—	—	—	—	—	—	—	—
August	48.83	27	76.95	1.575	—	—	—	—
September	45.36	27	76.95	1.696	2.14	6	11.52	5 383
October	109.62	54	153.90	1.404	6.85	12	23.04	3.363
November	43.56	27	76.95	1.767	19.80	12	23.04	1.164
December	203.11	54	153.90	1.320	3.41	5	9.60	2.815
January	66.40	54	153.90	2.318	6.51	42	23.04	3.539
February	48.22	54	153.90	3.192	2.13	12	23.04	10.817

TABLE 6.26 (*Contd.*)

1	2	3	4	5	6	7	8	9
March	27.28	54	153.90	5.641	5.21	12	23.04	4.422
April	29.28	54	153.90	5.442	—	—	—	—
May	139.97	70	199.50	1.425	—	—	—	—
June	—	—	—	—	—	—	—	—
Total	761.63	—	1353.75	1.777	46.05	—	136.32	2.960

Note: *Estimated on the basis of the average crew size required per boat; 2.85 persons for OBM boat and 1.92 persons for NM boat.

**Estimates based on our observations in the operations during our data collection.

Source: The data on output has been obtained from the Office of the Commissioner of Fisheries, Government of Gujarat, Ahmedabad.

TABLE 6.27

Distribution of sample OBM boat crew according to labour mobility ratio, Hirakot (1981-82)

Mobility ratio	Number of crew with stated ratio	% share in total
High	—	—
Medium	7	35.00
Low	13	65.00
Total	20	100.00

not a fixed wage. The particular variation which may attract a skilled crew member includes the condition of the fishing equipment, employer-labourer relations and the granting of free loans by the equipment owners and the fishing technique of the craft.

We notice that the crew often changed their employer in search of better incomes or better relations with the employer. Distribution of crew members according to the main reason[16] for the change of employer during the immediate past change is presented in Table 6.28. We notice that the hope of getting better returns is one reason which accounts for the maximum of changes. In about 50 per cent of the cases, the new employer is identified before the crew member breaks away from the old employer while in the other 50 per cent of the cases the labourers search for jobs after having decided to leave the current employer. We now egress briefly to present an interesting case of labour mobility due to non-market and non-price reason below.

Mr. M. K. Pathan is a crew member in an OBM boat and started fishing at the age of 20 as a crew member in a non-mechanized boat. He worked with the first owner for about two years and shifted to work in an OBM boat in order to increase his income and skill of fishing. He became a skilled fisherman, opted for a third owner-employer after quarrelling with the second owner. However, the second owner-employer was very much impressed with the skills of Pathan and tried successfully to re-employ him on his boat after a year. Pathan's

TABLE 6.28

Reasons for change of employer by the crew members for their immediate past change, Hirakot (1981-82)

Reasons for change of employer	Number of crew who indicated the stated reason	% share in total
1. Dispute with the owners	4	20 0
2. Need of high advance to clear debt	3	15.0
3. Hope of getting higher returns due to efficient working of the craft and gear	6	30.0
4. Invitation to join a new craft/ deposit of fishing equipment by the owner	3	15.0
5. Others	4	20.0
Total	20	100.0

last change of job (from the third owner to the second owner) was mainly because of non-market or non-price[17] links such as loyalty[18] to the second owner-employer and appreciation of work by the owner-employer.

The interlocking of credit and labour, though weak, takes the form of lending money to the crew by equipment owners, towards wage advance or credit needs of the crew.

The distribution of crew members according to the amount borrowed at the time of joining and outstanding debt are presented in Table 6.29. We notice that only 13 of the total sample crew members have borrowed from their employers at the time of joining the boat owner-employer. One-half of the crew members borrowed less than Rs. 1,000. Only 2 (20 per cent) members borrowed over Rs. 2,000, but less than Rs. 2,500. We can also find the tendency of crew members to repay the loan taken from the owner-employer as soon as the repayment capacity exists; 10 of the 15 borrower crew members have cleared the debt to the employer-owner. The tendency of

TABLE 6.29

Size distribution of sample crew members according to the amount borrowed at the time of joining and outstanding debt to the employer/owner, as on December 31, 1981, Hirakot

Frequency interval (Rs.)	Number of crew with stated range of borrowings	% share	Number of crew with outstanding debt in the stated range	% share
No borrowing/outstanding debt	5	25.0	15	75.0
1—500	4	20.0	1	5.0
501—1000	3	15.0	1	5.0
1001—1500	—	—	1	5.0
1501—2000	6	30.0	1	5.0
2001—2500	2	10.0	1	5.0
Total	20	100.0	20	100.0

crew members to clear debt may be mainly due to the pressure by the lender. This aspect may be brought out clearly when we consider the borrowing pattern of crew members from the moneylenders: most credit requirements of crew are met by the moneylenders who charge an interest of 36 per cent or more. If the taking of loan from the owner-employer at no interest were easy the crew members would not have borrowed from the moneylenders at such a high rate of interest.

Occupational mobility: The occupational mobility path for the village with an intermediate level of technology was indicated in the last chapter (see page 168). In Hirakot, we found that five non-mechanized boat owners had turned into crew in OBM boats mainly because of the destruction of boats in a cyclonic storm.

The pace of graduation to the current occupation is presented in Table 6.30. The pace is quite slow in the case of

TABLE 6.30

Distribution of working population of sample households according to the pace of graduation to current occupation, Hirakot (1981-82)

Pace of graduation	Number of individuals with stated pace in occupation					Total
	MB owner	NMB owner	Crew in MB	Crew in NMB	Others	
High	—	—	7 (18.92)	2 (100.00)	—	9 (13.43)
Medium	2 (11.11)	—	18 (48.65)	—	—	20 (29.85)
Low	16 (88.89)	5 (100.00)	12 (32.43)	—	5 (100.00)	38 (56.72)
Total	18 (100.00)	5 (100.00)	37 (100.00)	2 (100.00)	5 (100.00)	67 (100.00)

Note: 1. (—) indicates nil.
2. Figures in parentheses are percentages to column total.

OBM boat owners and high in the case of crew in OBM boats. The high pace of graduation for two of the crew in non-mechanized boats indicates that it is a very transitory occupation. Our discussions with non-mechanized boat owners indicated that the crew members tend to move to OBM boats after they have acquired proficiency and skill.

Market for credit

The important sources of credit in the village are co-operative societies, commercial banks, fish merchants, moneylenders and friends and relatives. The fishermen of Hirakot were observed to borrow from two or three sources simultaneously. Fish merchants play a dominant role, some of whom are from the fishermen community itself. Since credit obtained from co-operative societies on a short-term basis is quite common, we will explain the procedure.

The Gujarat Fisheries Central Co-operative Association

(GFCCA) used to advance short-term loans to fishermen for off-season maintenance during the late sixties. However, owing to bad recovery it has stopped advancing such loans, though it has once again started lending from June 1982. GFCCA provides cash loans on a short-term basis for off-season maintenance of boats and nets and net-making yarn. Generally credit is provided only to member boat owners of GFCCA through primary co-operative societies. Borrowing is subject to a maximum of Rs. 5,000 for OBM boat owners and Rs. 2,500 for NMB owners. The amount is interest free and is recoverable during the succeeding fishing season in which the borrower is expected to market fish through GFCCA. The procedure of recovery is as follows:

During the fishing season following immediately after the lending, GFCCA's fish collection van goes to the village every day to buy fish from the boat owners who have borrowed from GFCCA. The sales value of the catch is paid to the boat owners on the same day (of purchase) after deducting 25 per cent of the sales value towards the repayment of the loan. Interestingly, it was observed that the facility to borrow from GFCCA was availed of by the members of the Bharat Matsya Udyog Sahakari Mandali. The reasons for non-borrowing of off-season loans by the members of the other society, the Kismat Matsya Udyog Mandali (KMUM), were not quite clear. However, the puzzle was simple to solve when we came to know that KMUM was headed by one of the leading fish merchants in the village. This merchant discouraged the members to borrow from GFCCA fearing an unexpected cut into his own captured market for credit and output. As the lending by GFCCA had started only in June 1982 we could not obtain information about the loans advanced and outstanding. However, during the first phase of loan-advancing in June 1982, about Rs. 60,000 was advanced to the fishermen of Hirakot.

The lendings by commercial banks to the villagers are mainly for the purchase of gear. Each of the fishermen can get a loan of Rs. 3,000 in kind for gear.

The private market, consisting of fish merchants, moneylenders and friends and relatives, is the most important source of credit in the village. The loans from these sources are not purpose tied and the repayment schedule is highly flexible. Fish merchants are the dominant lenders and their lending operations are similar to those of GFCCA but for the difference that the lending by GFCCA is only during the off-season while the merchants extend loans round the year as and when needed irrespective of the purpose.

Moneylenders and friends and relatives extended loans on varying terms and conditions. Also these sources occasionally want security, in most cases jewellery. Also these loans are quite expensive as compared to the loans from the organized financial market. The rate of interest ranges from 25 to 38 per cent. The amount of loan borrowed by a fisherman also varies widely, from Rs. 500 to Rs. 7,000.

The distribution of households according to the source of borrowing and the amount outstanding per household as on December 31, 1981, is presented in Table 6.31. It can be noticed that 142 (80.1 per cent) of the total 173 households are borrower households with outstanding debts and have a total debt of Rs. 8,23,000 or a debt of Rs. 5,789 per borrower household. Interestingly, an overwhelming share (over 85 per cent) of the outstanding loan is from the private market. Of the total outstanding debt in the private market loan borrowed from the fish merchants accounts for three-fourths.

It was not possible to assess the supply and demand conditions for credit in the village but credit shortage was observed. Some of the households were paying interest up to 40 per cent on the money borrowed from moneylenders.

The distribution of households according to the purpose of borrowing and occupations in Table 6.32 indicates that most of the OBM boat owner households have borrowed for investing in boats, or gear or both, while the borrowing for household expenditure particularly in off-season accounts for a maximum of cases in crew households. It is also interesting to note that none of the households of OBM boat owners and NMB owners have borrowed for household expenditure.

Table 6.33 gives the size distribution of outstanding debt according to occupation. It can be seen that there are four households of OBM boat owners whose outstanding debt is more than Rs. 15,000 while there is only one household of NMB owners with an outstanding debt of Rs. 15,000 and

TABLE 6.31

Distribution of households according to the sources of borrowing and occupations and their outstanding debt as on December 31, 1981, Hirakot

Source of borrowing	No. of Households having outstanding debts of									
	MBO		NMBO		Crew		Others		Total	
	No.	Outstanding debt	No.	Outstanding debt	No.	Outstanding debt	No.	Outstanding debt	No.	Outstanding debt
1	2	3	4	5	6	7	8	9	10	11
I. Formal Lending Agencies:										
(a) Commercial banks	1	3000 (3000)	—	—	2	3500 (1750)	—	—	3	6500 (2133)
(b) Cooperative societies/bank	—	—	—	—	1	2500 (2500)	—	—	1	2500 (2500)
Sub-total	1	3000	—	—	3	6000	—	—	4	9000
II. Private or informal sources										
(a) Friends and relatives	1	10000 (10000)	1	2000 (2000)	13	61200 (4708)	2	1700 (850)	17	74900 (4406)

TABLE 6.31 (*Contd.*)

1	2	3	4	5	6	7	8	9	10	11
(b) Moneylenders	2	20000 (10000)	2	7500 (3750)	18	88500 (4917)	4	17000 (4250)	26	133000 (5115)
(c) Fish merchants/ Boat owners	32	231300 (7228)	6	19500 (3250)	19	36100 (1900)	3	5500 (1833)	60	292400 (4873)
Sub-total	35	261300	9	29000	50	185800	9	24200	103	500300
III. From both the sources	23	245000 (10652)	2	30000 (15000)	8	32700 (4087)	2	6500 (3250)	35	314200 (8977)
Total	59	509300 (8532)	11	59000 (5365)	61	224500 (3680)	11	30700 (2791)	142	823500 (5799)

Note: Figures in parentheses are the outstanding debt per household.

TABLE 6.32

Distribution of households according to purposes of borrowing of the outstanding debt and occupations, Hirakot (1981)

Reasons for borrowing the outstanding debt	Number of households with the stated reason of				Total
	OBM boat owners	NMB owners	Crew	Others	
1. No outstanding debt	3 (4.8)	—	20 (24.7)	8 (42.1)	31 (17.9)
2. Replacement of gear	12 (19.4)	2 (18.2)	3 (3.7)	—	17 (9.8)
3. Purchase of fishing equipment	40 (64.5)	9 (81.8)	1 (1.2)	—	50 (28.9)
4. To meet household expenditure	—	—	41 (50.6)	7 (36.8)	48 (27.8)
5. To meet social expenditure	6 (9.7)	—	16 (19.8)	1 (5.3)	23 (13.3)
6. Others	1 (1.6)	—	—	3 (15.8)	4 (2.3)
Total	62 (100)	11 (100)	81 (100)	19 (100)	173 (100)

Note: Figures in parentheses indicate the percentages to column total.

above. The modal values of the frequency distribution of the size of outstanding debt are Rs. 3001—6000 for OBM boat owners, Rs. 1001—3000 for NMB owner households and crew households and non-borrowers or households with zero outstanding debts for other households. Further, the outstanding debts to moneylenders were predominant in the case of crew and other households while in the case of boat owner households it was the outstanding debt to fish merchants.

Market for product

The contents of this section include the historical evolution of fish marketing in the village, fish market structure, and cost and returns of market intermediaries.

TABLE 6.33

Size distribution of households according to occupation on the total outstanding debt, Hirakot (Dec. 1981)

Range of outstanding debt (Rs.)	Number of households with outstanding debt in stated range of				Total
	OBM boat owners	NMB owners	Crew	Others	
Zero outstanding	3 (4.8)	—	20 (4.7)	8 (42.1)	31 (17.9)
Up to 1000	2 (3.2)	—	12 (14.8)	2 (10.5)	16 (9.2)
1001—3000	4 (6.5)	5 (45.5)	24 (29.6)	6 (31.6)	39 (20.5)
3001—6000	23 (37.1)	4 (36.3)	16 (19.8)	2 (10.5)	45 (26.1)
6001—10000	16 (25.8)	—	9 (11.1)	1 (5.3)	26 (15.0)
10001 –15000	10 (16.1)	1 (9.1)	—	—	11 (6.4)
15001+	4 (6.5)	1 (9.1)	—	—	5 (2.9)
Total	62 (100)	11 (100)	81 (100)	19 (100)	173 (100)

Note: Figures in parentheses are percentages to column total.

Historical evolution of fish marketing: During the early stages of fishing activity in the village, i.e. in early 1930s, there were no fish traders in the village nor any trader visited Hirakot to buy fish. Therefore, fisherwomen used to carry fish for sale to Prabhas Patan, a town about 19 km. from the village. They carried fish on their heads as there was no other mode of conveyance available at that time excepting the horse-cart. But this was not used as the fish quantity to be sold by individual fisherwomen was too small to bear the hiring charge. On the other end, at Patan, there was only one fish merchant who undertook multiple functions such as collection of fish from fishermen, wholesaling, retailing, and occasionally vending. By 1955 there were three fish merchants in Patan who brought fish from the boat owners in Hirakot. These three merchants used to send their men with horse-carts to collect fish from the boat owners in the village. The inter-linkage of credit and marketing of fish started sometime in late 1950s, with the purchase of fish by the three traders of Patan. They used to advance short-term loans ranging from Rs. 100 to Rs. 500 in order to have direct access to the fish lendings with a stipulation that the catch should be sold to them at a pre-fixed price, throughout the season.

In 1955, one fish merchant, Husen Rahim, started a commission agency in the village. And he was the only commission agent who could continue in the fish trading business from 1955 to 1973. Between 1955 and 1962 seven other fish traders also started the business particularly commission agency for selling fish. All these seven, including GFCCA, stopped their operations in the village after a period ranging from one to four years.

The trend in the number of commission agents in the village from 1962 to 1982 is presented in Table 6.34. Currently there are five commission agents operating in the

TABLE 6.34

Trend in the number of commission agents, Hirakot (1962-82)

Year	Total number of agents	% change from previous period
1962	2	—
1967	3	+33.33
1973	2	—50.00
1976	3	+33.33
1979	5	+40.00
1982	5	Nil

village of which only two operate from the village and the rest from places outside the village—two are from Patan and one is from Sutrapada. The number of commission agents in the village has increased from two in 1962 to five in 1979. There is no addition to or reduction in the number of commission agents from 1979 to 1982. Of the total five commission agents two are the oldest in the trade.

The direct retailing or vending of fish by fisherwomen in the village or outside the village is negligible. Currently there are two vendors in the village who are involved in door-to-door selling in the nearby village. In addition, four retailers buy fish from Hirakot for selling in their areas.

Channel members and structure of fish market : The channels of fish marketing in the village consisted of commission agents, semi-wholesalers, retailers/vendors and dry fish merchants. The functions of these channel members have already been explained in the profile of Chorwad (see page 175). The channels of fish distribution in the village are presented in Figure 6.3. An overwhelming percentage of the total

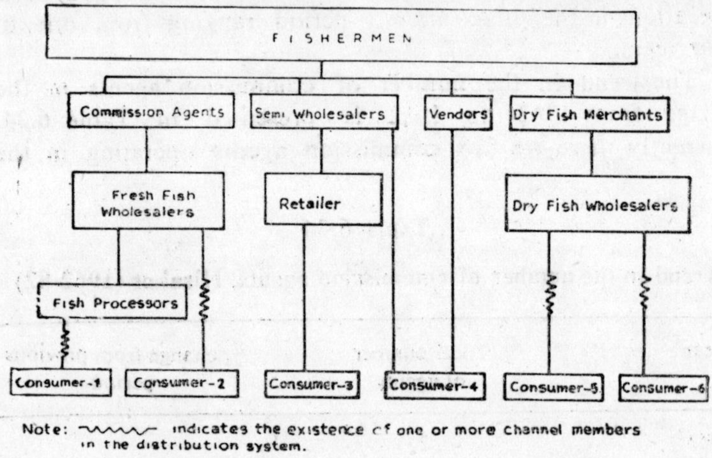

FIG. 6.3: *Channel of marine fish distribution, hirakot (1981-82).*

landings in the village is marketed through the commission agents.

The quantum of business handled by each of the merchants usually depends on the number of boat owners with whom a merchant has credit-marketing linkage. About 57 (66.7 per cent) of the total 63 boat owners were having marketing-credit linkage with the merchants/commission agents. The number of boat owners with marketing-credit linkage, with each of the merchants/commission agents was in the range of 6 to 15. Of the total 57 boat owners having credit-marketing linkages, 29 were having with the commission agents of Hirakot and the remainder with the agents of Patan and

Sutrapada. As on December 31, 1982, the total outstanding loan advanced to the boat owners by the commission agents was about Rs. 2,75,000. The first two commission agents account for over 48 per cent of the outstanding loan advanced. The outstanding loan advanced per boat owners was about Rs. 4,820 (Table 6.35).

TABLE 6.35

Number of boat owners having credit-marketing linkage with each of the commission agents, Hirakot (1981-82)

Agent	Location of the agent	Number of boats contracted*	Outstanding loan with boat owners (Rs.)
A	Hirakot	15(26.3)	65800(23.9)
B	Hirakot	14(24.6)	68500(24.9)
C	Patan	12(21.1)	49300(18.0)
D	Patan	12(17.5)	40900(14.9)
E	Sutrapada	6(10.5)	50400(18.3)
	Total	57(100.0)	274900(100.0)

*Includes the number of boats owned by a merchant.
Note: 2. Figures in parentheses are percentages to column total.

Table 6.36 shows the turnover in terms of quantity and value of the commission agent operating in the village during 1981-82. It can be seen from the table that the volume of turnover of largest two commission agents accounts for over 61 per cent in terms of quantity and over 65 per cent in terms of value. This, however, does not indicate any concentration or monopolistic or oligopolistic nature of the product market in the village.

Costs and returns of the commission agents are based on the data obtained from two local commission agents. The average estimates of costs and returns for these commission agents are presented in Table 6.37. The commission charged by the commission agents was in the range of 25 to 50 paise

TABLE 6.36

Turnover of the commission agents, Hirakut (1981-82)

Agent	Turnover in terms of	
	Quantity (tonnes)	Value ('000 Rs.)
A	225.22(30.6)	1182.1(28.0)
B	231.10(31.4)	1564.5(37.0)
C	121.44(16.5)	782.5(18.5)
D	90.53(12.3)	394.8(9.3)
E	67.71(9.2)	301.6(7.2)
Total	736.00(100.0)	4225.5(100.0)

Note: Figures in parentheses are percentages to column total.

TABLE 6.37

Average costs and returns of commission agents, Hirakot (1981-82)

Particulars	Amount (in Rs.)
I. Total turnover:	
Quantity (tonne)	235.52
Value ('000 Rs.)	2746.58
II. Gross returns	86300
III. Expenditure:	
(a) Salaries and wages	15865
(b) Transportation+	6375
(c) Ice	4390
(d) Others	2940
(e) Depreciation*	3075
Sub-total	32655
IV. Net returns (II—III)	53645
V. Return on investment	83.17%

Note: +Includes repair charges for the three-wheeler vehicles owned by the commission agents and fuel charges.

*Worked out on the basis of linear depreciation of assets owned by the commission agents for running the business. The items included for calculating depreciation are three-wheeler vehicles, equipment for transporting and weighing and office equipment.

per kg. depending upon the amount of loans advanced to the boat owners. The estimated gross return of the agents during 1981-82 was Rs. 86,300 and expenditure Rs. 32,655. Thus, the average annual net return of the agents was Rs. 53,645, and the return on investment about 83.17 per cent.

Changes in output marketing: The modernization of fishing craft in the village has brought about four important changes. These changes relate to the replacement of fish wholesalers by commission agents in the channels of distribution, increase in the amount of loan advanced to the boat owners, the purpose for which the loans are advanced and the mode of transportation. In addition, the pattern of selling has also changed from count to weight.

The replacement of fresh fish wholesalers by the commission agents in the channels of distribution of fish in the village is not accidental, but mainly because of the unwillingness of the traders to take risk in the violently fluctuating marketing conditions. The trend to replace the wholesaling by commission agency has also been aided by the increased credit requirements of fishermen after mechanization of the fishing craft. The average amount of credit advanced by the traders to the boat owners has increased from Rs. 500 in 1961 to Rs. 6,000 in 1981. During the pre-mechanization period the loans by the traders were advanced only for meeting the capital needs of the boat owners. Currently, the traders also advance credit for meeting the working capital requirements. The demand for credit from non-formal sources has increased considerably in view of the non-availability of credit for purchase of fishing equipment, particularly OBM and NM boats, from formal financial agencies.

The mode of transportation of fish from the village to the different distribution centres has changed from predominantly head-load transportation to transportation by horse-cart and subsequently to transportation by automobiles. The changes in the transportation system were affected by the increased quantum of landings due to mechanization of fishing craft. During the pre-mechanization period the selling of fish was predominantly by count while currently all the varieties are sold by weight. Again, the use of weighing machines was not there in the village during the pre-mechanized period mainly because of the smaller daily landings and dominance of traders from locations other than the fishing village.

THE VILLAGE ECONOMY

It is intended to study the economic balance of fishermen of the village in this section. However, before we take up the issue of economic balances in the village we shall briefly describe the assets structure.

Assets structure of fishermen

Investment on items other than fishing equipment was relatively less in the village. Of course, a few richer fishermen spent their money on luxury household items. In addition to the fishing equipment, generally fishermen owned small houses and household items. The fishermen do not own any livestock like bullocks, cows, sheep, goats, etc. The only form of domestic livestock in the village is poultry birds. Almost all the fishermen owned some or the other kind of a house.

The distribution of households according to the value of owned house and occupation in Table 6.38 indicates that an overwhelming percentage of MB households own houses. Of the total 60 owned houses of MB owners about 31 are valued also between 5,001 and Rs. 10,000 and eight more than Rs. 10,000. Seven of the 19 other community households are residing in rented houses. Houses valued of less than Rs. 10,000 account for most NMB households. Generally, the average value of crew member owned house is higher than the average value of a house owned by an NMB owner.

As shown in Table 6.39 most of the modern items/equipments are mainly owned by MB owners. This is true in the case of transport vehicles, radio-cum-tape recorders, and watches. On an average one out of four houses owns a radio in the village while in the case of MB owner households one out of two households owns a radio. Further, the cooking apparatus is predominantly kerosene stove in the case of MB owners. The MB owners account for more than 50 per cent of the total modern items owned by the village while they account for only 35.84 per cent of the total households.

TABLE 6.38

Distribution of households according to the occupations and value of owned houses, Hirakot (1981)

Value range (Rs.)	No. of houses in the stated range of value of				Total
	MB owners	NMB owners	Crew	Others	
No own houses (Nos.)	2 (6.90)	—	20 (68.86)	7 (24.14)	29 (100)
Less than 1000	1 (11.11)	4 (44.45)	2 (22.22)	2 (22.22)	9 (100)
1001—3000	6 (26.09)	2 (8.70)	12 (52.17)	3 (13.04)	23 (100)
3001—5000	14 (31.11)	4 (8.89)	23 (51.11)	4 (8.89)	45 (100)
5001—10000	31 (54.39)	1 (1.75)	23 (40.35)	2 (3.51)	57 (100)
10001 and above	8 (80.00)	—	1 (10.00)	1 (10.00)	10 (100)
Sub-total of owned houses	60 (41.67)	11 (7.4)	61 (42.36)	12 (8.33)	144 (100)
Total households	62 (35.84)	11 (6.36)	81 (46.82)	19 (10.98)	173 (100)

Note: Figures in parentheses represent percentages to row total.

On an average, the value of household items did not exceed Rs. 3,000 (at cost price) but for two cases of MB owners. In these cases, autorickshaws owned by them are the major household articles. However, these autorickshaws are mainly used for transportation of fish.

Consumption and expenditure pattern of fishermen households

The consumption habits and expenditure pattern of the fishermen vary from house to house depending upon features like the size of household, community, etc.

TABLE 6.39

Ownership of different household items according to occupation, Hirakot (1981-82)

Items	Number of households owning the stated items								Total	
	MB owners		NMB owners		Crew members		Others			
	No. of items	House-holds	No. of items	House-holds	No. of items	House-holds	No. of items	House-holds	No. of items	House-holds
I. Transport Vehicles:										
(a) Cycle	3	3	—	—	—	—	1	1	4	4
(b) Motorcycle/Rickshaw	2	2	—	—	—	—	—	—	2	2
II. Communication/Ent.:										
(a) Radio/Transistor	27	27	4	4	22	22	3	3	56	56
(b) Radio-cum-Tape Recorder	4	4	—	—	—	—	—	—	4	4
III. Office Equipment:										
(a) Chairs	8	4	—	—	1	1	1	1	10	6
(b) Tables	1	1	—	—	—	—	8	3	9	4
(c) Wooden Almirah	9	9	—	—	2	1	1	1	12	11

IV. Time Indicators										
(a) Wrist-watches	38	28	2	2	25	22	7	5	72	57
(b) Clock	10	10	1	1	3	3	1	1	15	15
V. Cooking Apparatus:										
(a) Non-kerosene Stove	69	56	10	9	93	77	18	17	190	159
(b) Kerosene Stove	34	33	3	3	20	12	5	5	62	53
VI. Kitchenware:										
(a) Earthen	148	47	17	8	126	45	47	16	338	118
(b) Aluminium	436	61	79	11	469	79	82	15	1066	1166
(c) Steel	188	37	15	3	129	33	22	5	354	78
(d) Others	194	31	23	3	170	33	42	11	429	78

The itemwise annual consumer expenditure by occupation in the village is presented in Table 6.40. An overwhelming percentage (77.15) of the total consumer expenditure is accounted by food items. Of the total expenditure of Rs. 21,63,000 on food items, expenditure on foodgrains, edible oils and fish together accounts for about Rs. 15,08,790 (69.69 per cent). The expenditure on edible oil seems to be quite high compared to foodgrains as it accounts for almost 65 per cent of the expenditure on foodgrains. The total expenditure on non-food items accounts for just 22.85 per cent of the total consumer expenditure with Rs. 6,41,240 for all occupations together.

The MB owner households account for about 46.94 per cent of the total consumer expenditure on food items and 44.83 per cent of the total consumer expenditure on non-food items. Of the total consumer expenditure of Rs. 28,06,240, the expenditure by MB owner households accounts for Rs. 13,03,720 (46.48 per cent) while they account for 34.34 per cent of the households and 45.65 per cent of the population of the village. The other households which receive an income less than the share in terms of households and population account for 7.29 per cent of the total consumer expenditure. The consumer expenditure of different households is more or less in proportion to the income received by them.

The per capita income for boat owner households is marginally higher than the average per capita income for all households while it is less than the average for crew and other households. Correspondingly, per capita annual consumer expenditure is also higher in the case of boat owners than that of other households. It is only Rs. 2,099 for other households while it is Rs. 2,331 for all the households. The per capita expenditure on food items for MB owners is higher than that of all households. The per capita annual consumer expenditure in the households other than MB owners is less than the average consumer expenditure in the village. While in the case of non-food items it is less than the average, per capita annual consumer expenditure in the households other than MB owners is less than the average consumer expenditure in the village. This indicates that the boat-owning households particularly MB owners tend to spend more on food items as compared to all other categories of households (Table 6.41).

TABLE 6.40

Itemwise annual consumption expenditure by occupation, Hirakot (1981-82)

(*in '000 Rupees*)

Items	Expenditure on the stated item by				
	MB households	NMB households	Crew	Others	Total
1	2	3	4	5	6
I. *Food Items*:					
(a) Foodgrains	306.85	34.84	258.39	51.64	651.72
	(47.08)	(5.35)	(39.65)	(7.92)	(100)
(b) Milk and Milk Products	41.65	7.02	31.88	8.27	88.82
	(46.89)	(7.90)	(35.89)	(9.32)	(100)
(c) Edible Oils	209.77	22.46	165.21	29.56	425.00
	(49.36)	(5.28)	(38.87)	(6.49)	(100)
(d) Meat and Chicken	30.00	4.99	24.34	7.54	66.87
	(44.86)	(7.46)	(36.40)	(11.28)	(100)
(e) Eggs	0.78	—	0.78	0.78	2.34
	(33.33)		(33.33)	(33.34)	(100)
(f) Fish	207.90	25.79	180.39	17.99	432.07
	(48.12)	(5.97)	(41.75)	(4.16)	(100)
(g) Vegetables	31.93	3.84	31.25	9.98	77.00
	(41.47)	(4.99)	(40.58)	(12.96)	(100)

TABLE 6.40 (*Contd.*)

1	2	3	4	5	6
(h) Fruits and Nuts	0.26 (16.15)	0.73 (45.34)	—	0.62 (38.51)	1.61 (100)
(i) Sugar, Gur and Khandsari	78.62 (43.10)	10.04 (5.50)	78.10 (42.82)	15.65 (8.58)	182.41 (100)
(j) Salt and Spices	36.71 (43.74)	4.16 (4.96)	38.01 (45.29)	5.04 (6.01)	83.92 (100)
(k) Beverages	17.52 (53.24)	0.36 (1.09)	13.16 (39.99)	1 87 (5.08)	32.91 (100)
(l) Pan, Tobacco and Supari	54.29 (45.12)	9.00 (7.48)	48.67 (40.44)	8.37 (9.96)	120.33 (100)
Sub-total	1016.28 (46.94)	123.23 (5.69)	870.18 (40.19)	155.31 (7.18)	2165.00 (100)
II. *Non-food Items*:					
(a) Entertainment	1.45 (48.49)	0.07 (2.34)	1.10 (36.69)	0.17 (5.68)	2.79 (100)
(b) Travel and Transport	6.58 (43.58)	6.98 (6.09)	6.05 (40.07)	1.55 (10.26)	15.10 (100)
(c) Education	0.15 (42.86)	—	0.10 (28.57)	0.10 (28.57)	0.35 (100)

(d) Medicines	39.68 (45.96)	8.00 (9.27)	33.60 (38.92)	5.05 (5.85)	86.33 (100)
(e) Domestic Utensils	3.24 (54.54)	0.30 (5.05)	2.13 (35.86)	0.27 (4.55)	5.94 (100)
(f) Clothes	75.75 (47.59)	10.00 (6.28)	59.30 (37.25)	14.13 (8.88)	159.18 (100)
(g) Footwear	5.57 (46.93)	0.60 (5.05)	4.78 (40.27)	0.92 (7.75)	11.87 (100)
(h) Fuel and Light	154.96 (43.13)	17.26 (4.80)	160.06 (44.54)	27.04 (7.53)	359.32 (100)
(i) Others	0.06 (16.67)	—	—	0.30 (83.33)	0.36 (100)
Sub-total	287.44 (44.83)	37.15 (5.79)	367.12 (41.66)	49.53 (7.72)	641.24 (100)
Total	1303.72 (46.46)	160.38 (5.72)	1137.30 (40.53)	204.84 (7.29)	2806.24 (100)

Note: Figures in parentheses represent percentages to row total.

TABLE 6.41

Itemwise per capita and per household consumer expenditure by occupation, Hirakot (1981-82)

(in '000 Rupees)

	Per capita (per household) annual consumer expenditure on stated item by				Total
	MB owners	NMB owners	Crew	Others	
I. *Food Items*:					
(a) Foodgrains	558(4949)	528(3167)	528(3190)	522(2718)	541(3767)
(b) Milk and Milk Products	76(672)	106(638)	65(394)	84(435)	74(513)
(c) Edible Oils	381(3383)	341(2842)	338(2039)	76(397)	353(2457)
(d) Meat and Chicken	55(484)	75(454)	50(301)	76(397)	56(387)
(e) Eggs	2(12)	—	2(10)	8(41)	2(14)
(f) Fish	378(3353)	391(2345)	369(2227)	181(947)	359(2497)
(g) Vegetables	58(515)	58(350)	64(386)	101(526)	64(445)
(h) Fruits and Nuts	1(4)	11(66)	—	6(33)	1(9)
(i) Sugar, Gur and Khandsari	143(1268)	152(913)	160(964)	158(824)	152(1054)
(j) Salt and Spices	67(592)	63(378)	77(469)	51(266)	70(485)
(k) Beverages	32(283)	6(33)	27(162)	19(98)	27(190)
(l) Pan, Tobacco and Supari	99(876)	136(818)	99(606)	85(440)	100(695)
Sub-total	1850(16391)	1867(11204)	1779(10748)	1599(8175)	1799(12513)

II. *Non-food Items*:					
(a) Entertainment	3(23)	1(6)	2(14)	2(9)	2(16)
(b) Travel and Transport	12(106)	14(64)	12(75)	15(82)	13(87)
(c) Education	—(2)	—	—(1)	1(5)	—(2)
(d) Medicines	72(640)	121(727)	69(415)	51(266)	72(499)
(e) Domestic Utensil	6(52)	5(27)	4(26)	3(14)	5(34)
(f) Clothes	138(1223)	152(909)	122(732)	143(743)	132(920)
(g) Footwear	10(90)	9(55)	10(59)	9(48)	10(69)
(h) Fuel and Light	282(2500)	262(1569)	327(1976)	276(1439)	298(2079)
Sub-total	523(4636)	564(3377)	546(3298)	500(2606)	532(3706)
Total	2373(21027)	2431(14581)	2325(14046)	2099(10781)	2331(16219)

Note: 1. (—) indicates negligible.
2. Figures in parentheses are per household expenditure.

Income and savings of fishermen households

The distribution of annual incomes and expenditure by occupation is shown in Table 6.42. The total income of the village

TABLE 6.42

Distribution of income and consumer expenditure by occupations, Hirakot (1981-82)

(in '000 Rupees)

Occupation	Income	Consumer expenditure*	Savings
1. MB owners	1530.86 (2.78)	1095.82 (2.37)	435.04
2. NMB owners	104.79 (1.59)	134.59 (2.43)	—29.80
3. Crew	922.17 (1.89)	956.91 (2.33)	—34.74
4. Others	75.40 (1.76)	186.85 (2.10)	—111.45
Total	2633.22 (2.19)	2374.17 (2.33)	259.05

Note: 1. *Excluding the consumption value of fish. We have excluded it from the consumer expenditure mainly because none of the households in the village purchase fish. They usually consume fish caught by themselves or obtained free of cost. Further, the income generated has been worked out after allowing for the own consumption and gifts.

2. Figures in parentheses are per capita incomes, consumer expenditures and savings for different occupations.

during 1981-82 has been estimated to be Rs. 26,33,220 while the consumer expenditure to be Rs. 23,74,170, leaving a net saving of Rs. 2,59,030 (9.84 per cent). However, the net saving is only Rs. 1,59,050 when the income generated from the marketing of fish by two commission agents is excluded from the incomes of the MB owner households. Further, only MB owner households had savings while all others had dissavings in the range of Rs. 1,11,450 for other households to

TABLE 6.43

Size distribution of households according to the value of the household articles, Hirakot (1981-82)

Frequency Interval	No. of households with the value of household articles in the stated range of				Total
	MB	NMB	CRM	Others	
Up to 500	13(20.97)	6(54.55)	54(66.67)	13(68.42)	86(49.71)
501—1000	8(12.90)	3(27.27)	16(19.75)	1(5.26)	28(16.18)
1001—1500	9(14.52)	1(9.09)	4(4.94)	1(5.26)	15(8.67)
1501—2000	5(8.06)	1(9.09)	2(2.47)	1(5.27)	9(5.20)
2001—2500	8(12.90)	—	2(2.47)	1(5.26)	11(6.36)
2501—3000	—	—	1(1.24)	—	1(0.58)
3001—3500	3(4.84)	—	1(1.23)	1(5.26)	5(2.89)
3501—4000	2(3.23)	—	—	—	2(1.16)
4001—4500	1(1.61)	—	1(1.23)	1(5.27)	3(1.73)
4501—5000	3(4.84)	—	—	—	3(1.73)
5001—5500	—	—	—	—	—
5501—6000	—	—	—	—	—
6001—6500	1(1.61)	—	—	—	1(0.58)
6501—7000	3(4.84)	—	—	—	3(1.73)
7001—7500	2(3.23)	—	—	—	2(1.16)
7501—8000	1(1.61)	—	—	—	1(0.58)
8001—8500	—	—	—	—	—
8501—9000	1(1.61)	—	—	—	1(0.58)
9001—9500	—	—	—	—	—
9501—10000	—	—	—	—	—
10001 and above	2(3.23)	—	—	—	2(1.16)
Total	62(100.00)	11(100.00)	81(100.00)	19(100.00)	173(100.00)

Note: 1. (—) indicates nil.
2. Figures in parentheses are percentages to column total.

Rs. 29,800 for NMB owner households. Further, the actual dissavings if we calculate will not be so much as majority of the crew and other households receives some consumer items towards their wages which is in fact their income, but monetarily not counted as income. The savings estimated above may not be the same for all the years as they even calculated on the basis of the fish catch in a normal fishing year. They may be much less or even negative during the periodical fish famine years. The hypothesis of aggregate negative savings in the village is supported by the observed high rate of indebtedness of the villagers and is strengthened by the size distribution of households according to the value of household articles as presented in Table 6.43. Over 49 per cent of the households have their value of household articles less than Rs. 500. The mechanized boat owner households generally have household articles of a higher value as compared to other households.

REFERENCES

1. According to our census taken in 1981, our figures are, however, incomplete due to some houses which were locked throughout our stay of six months in the village. The inhabitants of the locked houses are generally boat owners who migrate to different parts of the Saurashtra coast during the fishing season and go back to Hirakot in off-season.
2. "Bigamous" relationships, and owning of two or more houses by one owner in some cases and consequent double accounting tend to overestimate the population unless a mechanism is built in to check on the accuracy of the information. However, the long stay of ours has made it possible.
3. During our stay in the village, the claim of superiority of the fishermen belonging to the Muslim religion over the Machhiyaras was noticed in terms of their caste ranking. Further, it was also indicated that the Muslims engaged in fishing are ranked lower than the Muslims in other occupations.
4. The public transport buses, though very infrequent, used to come to the village till 1978. From 1978 onwards the bus service connecting Hirakot with other towns and villages was suspended as a result of land, under the road, dispute between the inhabitants in Kadvar and Hirakot.
5. The immigration of households from different places was in groups at two or three points of time. Thus, there is no much variation in the time of immigration by different households.
6. The name of the fishermen co-operative society organized in 1975 is the Bharat Matsya Udyog Co-operative Society. Both Hindu and Muslim (including Machhiyara) fishermen used to be the members of the Society. However, due to some differences, the Machhiyara community members in particular Pateliyas of the Society organized

another society, namely, the Kismat Matsya Udyog Co-operative Society in 1977.

7. The large gap between the official records and our census information is mainly because of the reason that almost all the members of the Kismat Matsya Udyog Co-operative Society are still having the nominal membership in the Bharat Matsya Udyog Co-operative Society. It is also noticed that these members have requested the transfer of their share capital to Kismat Matsya Udyog Co-operative Society which could not be done due to some procedural difficulties. Thus, these members are inactive members of the Bharat Matsya Udyog Co-operative Society.
8. Gill nets in the village consisted of both set and drift types.
9. All the boats in the village are owned by individual owners and they mostly acquired the title through a transactlon with the boat builders.
10. The shift in the location of the landing centre may take place because of the non-availability of infrastructure, particularly landing and berthing facilities. However, for OBM boats the landing and berthing facilities are not essential; nevertheless, the fishermen experience difficulty due to non-availability of these facilities.
11. Most of the data on production of marine fish in the village has been obtained from the office of the Assistant Director (Projects) of Fisheries, Veraval. The villagewise catch data have been estimated for seven selected villages in Veraval from the year 1977-78. Hirakot is one of these seven villages.
12. Our data collected on sample days for some boats permit the calculation of the quantity and species composition of landing per boat per day. The information on the number of fishing days per annum has been obtained from the sample respondents. For estimating the total fish landings in the village we have multiplied the number of boats operated from the village by the product of the average daily catch and number of fishing days for different type of boats. For estimating the landings of boats migrating often to different places the number of fishing days have been adjusted accordingly.
13. Our discussions with some of the villagers indicated that there were about 30 non-mechanized boats and the average catch per boat has decreased by about 60 to 75 per cent. Using this information we have roughly calculated the output in the village to be approximately 200 tonnes.
14. The optimal allocation of labourers is assumed in the following fashion. During the fishing season the work is allocated to the family members until all the family members without any other occupation are fully employed and only then work is allocated to hired labourers.
15. No sample of crew members for the study of labour mobility of crew has been drawn because of the following reasons. First, the

households with a crew in non-mechanized boat alone in the village are relatively insignificant in number and were very difficult to contact. Second, our discussions with few of the crew members in non-mechanized boats indicated that the mobility ratio in this segment is quite high. In fact fishing in non-mechanized boats becomes a training for moving into OBM boats.

16. It should be noticed that the crew members do not change the employer just for one or two reasons. It is usually a combination of three or more reasons which lead to the breaking away of the crew members. Nevertheless there is one reason which has a very strong effect on the decision of the crew member. The sample crew members indicated an average of 2.5 reasons per crew for change of employer. The distribution is based on the one major reason for change.
17. For a detailed analysis of the interlocking of several (product and factors) markets in fisheries and agriculture, see Platteau, op. cit; Bharadwaj, K., *Production Conditions in Indian Agriculture: A Study Based on Farm Management Studies* (Cambridge: Cambridge University Press, 1974), pp. 2-5; and Bardhan, P., and Rudro, A., "Interlinkage of Land, Labour and Credit Relations: An Analysis of Village Survey Data in East India", *Economic and Political Weekly*, 12 (6-7), Annual Number 1976, pp. 367-384.
18. The loyalty of the Pathan to the second owner employer was mainly because of the following two reasons. First, the owner provided him an opportunity to learn the skill; secondly, he advanced over Rs. 1500 and helped him to get married.

7

Bhadbhut Village, Bharuch District, Gujarat

BHADBHUT village is located in Bharuch district. It is situated on the bank of river Narmada and on the road passing through Bharuch to Daheg. In view of its location, Bhadbhut is more of an estuarine fishing village than a marine fishing village. It is 22 km. away from Bharuch and Daheg west. Mahegam is another village in the north-eastern direction (Fig. 7.1).

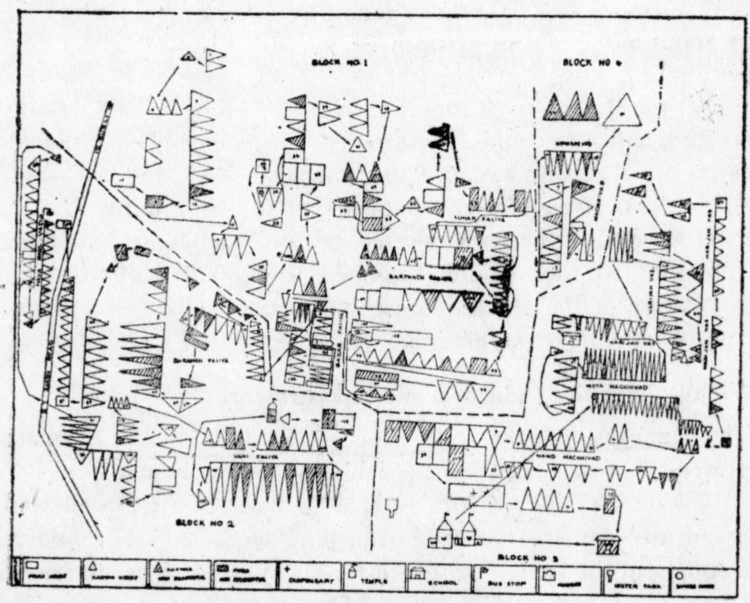

FIG. 7.1: *Village Bhadbhut*

Bhadbhut is popular all over Gujarat as a religious place. A famous temple called Bhadbhuteshwar Mahadev is located there and a Kumbh mela is organized once here every 18 years. The fishermen of Bhadbhut originally belonged to Bhavnagar and were engaged in small trade. It was about 100 years back these fishermen migrated from Bhavnagar to pursue their business. They entered into fishing and allied activities and for this reason they are called "Machhi", while they were known as Hindu Rajput earlier.

The principal language of communication is Gujarati. However, some residents are fairly conversant with Hindi and a few could talk in English also. The Gujarati spoken in the village is called Surati or Valsadi Gajarati.

Population and castes

According to the livestock census taken in 1977 the population of Bhadbhut fishermen village was 886. Out of the total 458 were males and 428 females. The enumeration carried out for the purpose of this study during 1981 indicated the population of the village to be 962 residing in 155 households. The comparison[1] of the population of the village in 1977 and 1981 indicates that the population of the village has increased by about 6.08 per cent between 1977 and 1981 or 1.52 per cent per annum.

All the fishermen of Bhadbhut village belong to the Hindu religion. All households are involved in fishing. The different castes are Kharwa, Vasava Patel, Machhi, Koli and Kothari. All but two of the households of the village belong to Vasava Patel Machhi—otherwise referred to as Machhi—community. The other two households belonged to Koli or Kothari. The population of the Machhi households accounts for over 99 per cent of the village population.

Village amenities, industries and infrastructure

The analysis of the infrastructure in the village is again presented in two categories: general and fishery related.

General village infrastructure: Bhadbhut is well connected by an all-weather road and transport facilities are available throughout the year. The nearest railway station is Bharuch, about 22 km. away. Fish catches from the village are normally carried in private vehicles and sometimes by bus. Usually the fish merchants make their own arrangements for transportation. In earlier days the fishermen themselves carried the fish on their head. Some of the boats landed their catches directly at Bharuch and the fish was sold in the Bharuch market. A few tractors were also available and were occasionally used as transport. There are sight wells which cater to the needs of drinking water for both fishermen and other villagers. The village has been recently electrified. Fishermen houses have got power connection. A distinct lack of cleanliness, however, was observed in the home surroundings. Diseases like malaria, dysentery, diarrhoea and some skin infections were quite common among the fishermen.

Almost all facilities are available in the village. Vendors visit the village once a week to sell clothes and domestic utensils. For facilities not available in the village, the villagers go to Bharuch. Most of the industry and trade facilities in the village came up sometime in late sixties or early seventies.

A primary school was established in 1878 in the village by the District Parishad to cater to the educational needs of the villagers, and is located in that part of the village which is predominated by population other than the fishing community. Till recently normally the children from the Brahmin and Patel communities only attended the school. Later in 1958, a Government Matsyodyog Primary School was also established to cater to the needs of children from the fishermen community. The school also imparts practical training in fisheries, home science and carpentry. The school has a strength of 350 children, 9 teachers and 3 supporting staff and runs classes up to the seventh standard. The school is well equipped and a new building has just been constructed to accommodate the children. Most of the teachers stay in the village. One of the supporting staff members belongs to the fishermen community.

The post office in the village is manned by a single person and is assisted by two extra-departmental mail-carrier-cum-delivery agents. It provides all postal facilities. However, no telegraphic or telephone facilities are available at the village post office.

There is no police station in the village. Therefore, the

police station located at Amleshwar, about 5 km. away, is entrusted with the functions of law and order in Bhadbhut.

A Primary Health Centre set up in 1966 is located at Haldar, about 7 km. from Bhadbhut. The nearest sub-centre of the Primary Health Centre is at Navathal, 3 km. away from the village. The fishermen normally prefer to visit doctors who have their clinics in the village itself. Three such clinics have been functioning for the past 25 years. The Family Planning Centre at Bharuch organises camps once or twice a month in the village.

The political system consists of both caste panchayats and elected panchayat. There is one caste panchayat for the Machhis. The head of the caste panchayat known as Patel is usually elected during informal or religious gatherings of the fishermen.

The elected Gram Panchayat is common for the fishermen and non-fishermen community of the village. The Panchayat consists of 11 members and a Sarpanch elected from the members. The President and three members of the Panchayat are from the fishermen community. There are no cultural organisations in the village.

Fishery-related infrastructure: Major fishery-related facilities are available only at Bharuch. For repairing boats there is one carpenter in the village. In the absence of any facilities for the preservation of fish, the fishermen of the village sell fish immediately after landing. There are five fish merchants operating from the village since 1951. In addition to the fish merchants there were few retailers and vendors in the village for the retail sale of fresh fish. However, we did not have the information about the number of retailers/vendors in the village.

Turning to the institutional infrastructure relating to fisheries we find that a branch of the Office of the Department of Fisheries, Government of Gujarat, is located in the village. The office is staffed with one Jal Sewak and one Gram Sewak to help the fishermen in the fishing and related activities. They are also involved in collection of the catch data from the village. These two fishery officials belong to the fishermen community. In addition, the fishermen have a co-operative society for undertaking various fishery-related activities. It was established in 1951.

The general infrastructure in the village is well developed as compared to the fishery-related infrastructure.

Production equipment and occupation

The main economic activities relate to agriculture and related industries. However, the economic activities of the fishermen in the village[2] are centred around fishing and allied activities. The village population consists of fishing equipment owners, fishing labourers, fish marketing intermediaries and other village functionaries. All the fishing boats in the village are non-mechanized flat-bottom boats. The equipment owners operate their own as well as leased boats. In some cases the boat-owning households supplement their income by working as labourers in other boats.

All the non-mechanized boats in the village are flat bottom type plank-built canoes. The length of the boats in the village varied between 15 and 35 feet. The non-mechanized boats in the village used gill nets and bag nets[3] for fishing. The majority of the gill nets in the village are bottom-set gill nets with mesh sizes varying between 2 and 8 inch. Most of the gill nets and bag nets in the village are mended by synthetic or nylon yarn.

The distribution of village population is presented in Table 7.1. Over 69 per cent of the village population was estimated to be either non-working or engaged in non-economic activities. People involved in economic activities other than fisheries accounted for only 1.66 per cent of the population. And people involved in economic activities relating to fisheries accounted for 29 per cent, almost all of them belonging to the Machhi community. The economic activities relating to fisheries were further divided into seven sub-groups. Fishing with non-mechanized boats accounted for the maximum, followed by crew with gear (42), fishing in leased boat (25), net mending and repairing (20), crew without gear (10), retailing/vending (3) and wholesaling.

All the households, however, had already at least one member involved in fishery-related economic activities. This indicates that most of the households derived their incomes from fishery and non-fishery related economic activities. The occupational pattern in the village, therefore, is fishery biased. The households according to their occupational pattern can

TABLE 7.1

Occupationwise distribution of population according to caste, Bhadbhut

Occupation	No. of persons from the caste		Total
	Machhi	Others	
1. *Economic Activities: Fishery*			
(i) Fishing with NMB	178(18.66)	—	178(18.50)
(ii) Fishing in leased boat	25(2.62)	—	25(2.60)
(iii) Crew with gear	42(4.40)	—	42(4.37)
(iv) Crew without gear	8(0.84)	2(25.00)	10(1.04)
(v) Net Mending/Repairing	20(2.10)	—	20(2.08)
(vi) Rampani purse-seiner	3(0.32)	—	3(0.31)
(vii) Fish wholesaling	1(0.10)	—	1(0.10)
Sub-total	277(29.04)	2(25.00)	279(29.00)
2. *Economic Activities: Non-Fishery*			
(a) Business	2(0.21)	—	2(0.21)
(b) Service	6(0.63)	—	6(0.62)
(c) Agricultural labour	7(0.73)	1(12.50)	8(0.83)
Sub-total	15(1.57)	1(12.50)	16(1.66)
3. *Non-Economic Activities:*			
(a) Dependants/Retired/Not working	327(34.28)	3(37.50)	330(34.31)
(b) Students	81(8.49)	—	81(8.42)
(c) Housewife	253(26.52)	2(25.00)	255(26.51)
(d) Others	1(0.10)	—	1(0.10)
Sub-total	662(69.39)	5(62.50)	667(69.34)
Total	954(100.00)	8(100.00)	662(100.00)

Note: 1. (—) indicates nil.
2. Figures in parentheses are percentages to column total.

broadly be divided into three categories: non-mechanized boat owner households, crew member households and others.[4] The distribution of households and population according to the occupational pattern and castes in Bhadbhut is presented in Table 7.2. The non-mechanized boat owner households accoun-

TABLE 7.2

Distribution of households and population according to occupational pattern and caste, 1981, Bhadbhut

Occupation	Caste			Total No. of persons
	Machhi	Others	Total	
1. NMB	107	—	107	732
	(69.93)		(69.03)	(76.1)
2. CRM	45	2	47	228
	(29.42)	(100.0)	(30.32)	(23.7)
3. Others	1	—	1	2
	(0.65)		(0.65)	(0.2)
Total	153	2	155	962
	(100 0)	(100.0)	(100.0)	(100.0)

Note: 1. (—) indicates nil.
2. Figures in parentheses are percentages to column total.

ted for maximum of the total households with 107 households, and are followed by crew households and others with 447 (30.3 per cent) and 1 (0.65 per cent) respectively. The non-mechanized boat owner household population was 732 persons and accounted for 76.1 per cent of the population. The non-mechanized boat owner households are densely populated with 6.84 per household. All boat owners belonged to the Machhi caste.

SOCIO-ETHNOGRAPHIC PROFILE OF THE FISHERMEN

The socio-ethnographic profile of the fishermen includes family size and structure, level of education, age groupwise distribution of village population, migration pattern, and social participation of the fishermen and their households.

Size and structure of the households

The average family size in the village was 6.2 persons per household. Fourteen households accounting for about 9 per cent of the households were having a family size of three or less. The occupationwise distribution of households according to family size in the village indicates that an overwhelming percentage (68.45 per cent) of the households had the family size between four and seven members. Further, the non-mechanized boat owner households usually had larger sizes as compared to crew member households. Of the 51 households which had the family size of six or more 44 (86.1 per cent) were boat-owner households while they have accounted for only 69 per cent of the total households. Four of the NMB owner households had more than 13 members in their households. One of the total 155 households belonged to another caste and it has a family size of less than five members in its household (Table 7.3).

The distribution of the households by occupational pattern and the type of family is presented in Table 7.4. It can be seen from the table that the village had a nuclear family structure in 99 (63.87 per cent) of the 155 households. The crew member households had predominantly a nuclear family structure, as compared to NMB owner households. Similar was the case of castewise distribution of households according to family structure. Of the 153 households of the Machhi caste, 98 households had nuclear family structure.

Agewise distribution and educational level of fishermen

Data relating to age of fishermen population were classified into six different age groups and then it was analysed according to their occupational pattern and sex. The agewise and sex distribution of the village population according to occupational pattern is presented in Table 7.5. The male population was more than the female population in the case of NMB owner households while the converse was true in the case of crew member households. However, at an aggregate level the number of males in the village outnumbered the females by 24. The male population is in excess of or equal to female population in the case of all age groups except in the case of 56-and-above

TABLE 7.3

Occupationwise distribution of households according to family size, Bhadbhut (1981-82)

Family size (members)	Number of households of NMB	CRM	Others	Total
1	—	—	—	—
2	1(0.93)	2(4.25)	1(100.00)	4(2.58)
3	2(1.87)	8(17.02)	—	10(6.45)
4	16(14.95)	12(25.53)	—	28(18.06)
5	17(15.89)	14(29.79)	—	31(20.00)
6	27(25.23)	4(8.51)	—	31(20.00)
7	12(11.22)	1(2.13)	—	13(8.39)
8	8(7.48)	4(8.51)	—	12(7.74)
9	7(6.54)	1(2.13)	—	8(5.16)
10	8(7.48)	1(2.13)	—	9(5.81)
11	2(1.87)	—	—	2(1.29)
12	3(2.80)	—	—	3(1.94)
13	4(3.74)	—	—	4(2.58)
Total	107(100.00)	47(100.00)	1(100.00)	155(100.00)

Note: 1. (—) indicates nil.
2. Figures in parentheses are percentages to column total.

TABLE 7.4

Distribution of households by occupational pattern and type of family, Bhadbhut

Occupation	Nuclear	Joint	Total
1. NMB	59(59.60)	48(85.71)	107(69.03)
2. Crew	39(39.39)	8(14.29)	47(30.32)
3. Others	1(1.01)	—	1(0.65)
Total	92(100.00)	56(100.00)	155(100.00)

Note: 1. (—) indicates nil.
2. Figures in parentheses are percentages to column total.

TABLE 7.5

Age and sex distribution of village population according to occupational pattern, Bhadbhut

Occupation/ Age	0—12		13—20		21—30		31—45		46—55		56 and above		Total	
	M	F	M	F	M	F	M	F	M	F	M	F	M	F
1. NMB	139	114	70	62	76	77	60	52	26	26	14	16	385	347
	(75.54)	(69.51)	(88.61)	(77.50)	(74.51)	(75.49)	(77.92)	(74.29)	(89.66)	(81.25)	(63.64)	(76.19)	(78.09)	(73.09)
2. Crew	45	50	9	18	25	24	17	18	3	6	8	5	107	121
	(24.46)	(30.49)	(11.39)	(22.50)	(24.51)	(23.53)	(22.08)	(25.71)	(10.34)	(18.75)	(36.36)	(23.81)	(21.71)	(25.80)
3. Others	—	—	—	—	1	1	—	—	—	—	—	—	1	1
	—	—	—	—	(0.98)	(0.98)	—	—	—	—	—	—	(0.20)	(0.21)
Total	184	164	79	80	102	102	77	70	29	32	22	21	493	469
	(100.0)	(100.0)	(100.0)	(100.0)	(100.0)	(100.0)	(100.0)	(100.0)	(100.0)	(100.0)	(100.0)	(100.0)	(100.0)	(100.0)

Note: 1. (—) indicates nil.
2. Figures in parentheses are percentages to column total.

age group for NMBO households. The high ratio of male population in the case of NMB owner households particularly up to the age group of 13 to 20 years indicates the tendency of boat owner households to have male children and the early marriage of female children.

Frequency distribution of age gaps between surviving children of same parents according to the occupational pattern in the village at the time of our census in 1981 is presented in Table 7.6. About 63 per cent of the parents in the village had

TABLE 7.6

Frequency distribution of age gaps between surviving children of some parents according to occupational pattern, Bhadbhut (1981-82)

Age gap interval	Number of instances in which the age gaps fall in the stated interval for		Total
	NMB owners	Crew	
1—1.9	32(19.75)	8(10.13)	40(16.60)
2—2.9	65(40.12)	48(60.76)	113(46.89)
3—3.9	28(17.29)	10(12.66)	38(15.77)
4—4.9	15(9.26)	6(7.59)	21(8.71)
5—5.9	11(6.79)	3(3.80)	14(5.81)
6 and above	11(6.79)	4(5.06)	15(6.22)
Total	162(100.00)	79(100.00)	241(100.00)

Note: Figures in parentheses are percentages to column total.

more than three-year gap between the surviving children. In terms of occupation it was observed that a large number of parents belonging to crew member households (71.7 per cent) had less than three-year gap between their surviving children, while in the case of parents of non-mechanized boat owner households it was only 40 per cent.

At the village level 39.4 per cent of the households had at least one person educated up to primary, 18.1 per cent up to higher secondary. Of the 28 households with at least one person educated up to higher secondary 24 were NMB owner households with all the family members as illiterate was highest (32 out of 47) in the case of crew member households, and in the case of NMBO households it was only 24.30 per cent with 26 out of 107 households. The non-mechanized boat owner households appear to be having a large number of educated. There was one household with graduation as the highest level of education in the case of NMBO households (Table 7.7).

TABLE 7.7

Distribution of households according to occupational pattern and highest level of education in the household, Bhadbhut (1981-82)

Highest level of education	Number of households of			Total
	NMB	CRM	Others	
1. Illiterate	26(24.30)	32(60.09)	—	58(37.42)
2. Read and write	1(0.93)	—	—	1(0.65)
3. Primary	51(47.66)	10(21.28)	—	61(39.35)
4. Middle	4(3.74)	2(4.25)	—	6(3.87)
5. Higher Secondary	24(22.43)	3(6.38)	1(100.00)	28(18.06)
6. Graduate and above	1(0.94)	—	—	1(0.65)
Total	107(100.00)	47(100.00)	1(100.00)	155(100.00)

Note: 1. (—) Indicates nil.
2. Figures in parentheses are percentages to column total.

Migration pattern of fishermen

An analysis of the migration pattern of fishermen in this section is undertaken to understand long-term and short-term migration. To analyse the long-term migration we have elicited the information about the birthplace of the head of the household.

A close look at the location of birthplace of the household head indicates that out of 155 households 154 had the birthplace of the household head in the same village. Thus, the phenomenon of long-term migration was almost non-existent in the village.

Like long-term migration, short-term migration is also in-migration to the village. As fishing activity in the village is highly seasonal and labour is in short supply, there is a large in-migration to the village. The crew member households from nearby villages migrate to the village during the fishing season, which lasts for three to four months, from June to October.

Social participation of fishermen

The social participation of the fishermen households was analysed by looking into their membership in the organization such as fishermen co-operative society, youth club, Gram Panchayat and Bhajan Mandali.

Fishermen co-operative society: Twenty-six per cent of the total households are members of the co-operative society and majority of these are NMBO households. Of the total members 5.1 per cent became members 6 to 15 years back, 34 per cent have been members for the past 16 to 25 years and only 15 per cent had enrolled themselves as members during the past five years.

Youth clubs: A Youth Club was established a year back and six households were members of this club. They were the youths from NMBO households, except one from the crew member households.

Bhajan mandalis: The Bhajan Mandali has been in existence at the village for the past 25 years. A quarter of the households in the village were members of this Mandali and at least a half of them have been members for the past 16 to 25 years.

ANALYSIS OF THE PRODUCTION SYSTEM

The contents of this section include the technology of production, ownership of productive assets, current and past production patterns, output, incomes and distribution of gains, and disposal of fish landings.

Technology of production

The technology of fishing in relation to boats in the village is traditional and all boats are non-mechanized. Further, the basic technology of fishing gear is only traditional while the material used for mending the fishing gear has undergone many improvements. These improvements in the yarn for mending the gear have contributed mainly to an extended life of the gear without any marked change in the productivity of the gear.

The craft technology in the village consists of plank-built canoes with flat bottoms. The length of these boats ranged between 15 and 35 feet. As the distance between the fishing grounds and the shore is less the boats use only paddlers for steering and propulsion. The gear technology in the village consists of synthetic/nylon gill nets and bag nets. Before we undertake the analysis of the current situation with regard to the number of boats and gear a brief write-up about the operation of both types of fishing gear in the village is given below.

The gill nets are wall type nets and are operated at various levels. The gill nets are operated throughout the fishing season by a few boat owners while some boat owners operate them during the lean season for bag-net fishing. The net resembles a walled mesh. The net is hauled into the boat by crew after allowing it to drift in the water. The boat owners in the village take one or two hauls during a normal fishing trip. The operation of the bag net is quite different to that of a gill net. As its name indicates it is bag-shaped. The operation of the net is mainly during the monsoon months. For operating the net, two bamboo poles are fixed and the net is tied to the poles so that its mouth is opened during the water current, and water filters out leaving fish at the end. When the tide changes direction the fish caught in the net is hauled into the boat and the net is fixed in the opposite direction. The number of hauls taken in the case of bag nets depends upon the duration of the high and low tides.

Depending upon the number of crew employed for the operation of the boat and its length boats can be divided into two categories. The first category of boats were of length of between 15 and 25 feet and normally three crew members were employed for their operation. The length of the second category ranged between 26 and 35 feet and employed about four crew members per boat. In 1981 there were 10 boats in the first category and 109 boats in the second category. These boats were acquired over a long period of 20 years or so. However, majority of them were purchased between 1970 and 1978. Of the total 119 boats only 17 were purchased after 1978 (Table 7.8).

TABLE 7.8

Distribution of different types of boats according to the year of purchase, Bhadbhut (1981)

Year of acquiring	Type of boat NMB flat bottom	
	15 to 25 ft. length	26 ft. and above length
Up to 1965	1	12
1966	—	—
1967	—	2
1968	—	1
1969	—	—
1970	3	13
1971	—	1
1972	—	16
1973	—	4
1974	1	7
1975	—	14
1976	1	7
1977	—	4
1978	1	14
1979	2	8
1980	1	4
1981	—	2
Total	10	109

Note: (—) indicates nil.

The mesh size of the gill nets in the village varied between 3 and 8 inches. The distribution of gill nets, according to mesh size in the village, is shown in Table 7.9. It can be seen from the table that out of the 145 gill nets in use in the village, 91 were owned by non-mechanized boat owners, and 40 were owned by the crew member households, the remaining 14 were

TABLE 7.9

Distribution of gill nets owned by different households according to the mesh size, Bhadbhut (1981-82)

Mesh size (in inch)	Households		Hired boat
	NMB	CRM	
0—1.0	—	—	—
1.1—2.0	—	—	—
2.1—3.0	—	—	—
3.1—4.0	28(30.77)	16(40.00)	3(21.43)
4.1—5.0	43(47.25)	13(32.50)	9(64.29)
5.1—6.0	8(8.79)	8(20.00)	—
6.1—7.0	7(7.69)	1(2.50)	2(14.28)
7.1—8.0	5(5.50)	2(5.00)	—
8.1—9.0	—	—	—
Total	91(100.00)	40(100.00)	14(100.00)

Note: 1. (—) Indicates nil.
2. Figures in parentheses are percentages to column total.

owned by the households hiring in the boats particularly during the lean season for fishing. It can also be seen from the table that majority of the gill nets were of the mesh size of 3 to 5 inches, which were primarily used for catching pomfret, seer fish, catfish, mullet, etc. It was also observed that the total number of nets in the village were more than the number of boats indicating ownership of more than one net per boat. As observed elsewhere on Gujarat, the nets are usually of different mesh sizes for the year-round productivity. The length-wise distribution of nets indicates that the nets owned by the non-mechanized boat owners were larger in size than those owned by the crew member households. While the length of the nets owned by non-mechanized boat owners varied between 500 and 5,000 feet and above, the length of nets owned by the crew members varied only between 500 and 4,000 feet. The length of the gill nets in the case of hired-in boats was similar to that of crew member households (Table 7.10). It

TABLE 7.10

Lengthwise distribution of gill nets owned by different households, Bhadbhut (1981-82)

Length (in feet)	Household		Hired boat
	NMB	CRM	
Below 500	6(6.59)	9(22.50)	2(14.29)
501—1000	7(7.69)	12(30.00)	2(14.29)
1001—1500	20(21.98)	9(22.50)	2(14.29)
1501—2000	17(18.68)	6(15.00)	4(28.58)
2001—2500	13(14.29)	1(2.50)	2(14.29)
2501—3000	13(14.29)	1(2.50)	—
3001—3500	3(3.30)	—	1(7.14)
3501—4000	4(4.39)	2(5.00)	—
4001—4500	1(1.10)	—	1(7.14)
4501—5000	4(4.39)	—	—
5001 and above	3(3.30)	—	—
Total	91(100.00)	40(100.00)	14(100.00)

Note: 1. (—) indicates nil.
2. Figures in parentheses are percentages to column total.

was observed that these nets were usually made of nylon synthetic yarn. There were no cotton gill nets in the village. We were told by the villagers that a few years back the predominant number of gill nets were made out of cotton yarn. This is one area where a major change has occurred over time.

Ownership of productive assets

In the village there were 119 boats owned by 107 households, indicating that a few households owned more than one boat. All the non-mechanized boats in the village were owned by the Machhi community which has been traditionally involved in fishing. All the crew members in the village (45 households with 228 members) also belong to the Machhi community. As mentioned earlier, the 45 households of crew members owned only 40 nets.

The inequality of ownership of the productive fishing assets is measured also by Gini coefficient. The value of Gini coefficient for the distribution of value of productive assets for the households was found to be 0.3277. The estimated value of the Gini coefficient indicates a much more equitable distribution of productive assets in the village as compared to the previous two villages. The Lorenz curve of distribution of fishery assets in the village is presented in Figure 7.2.

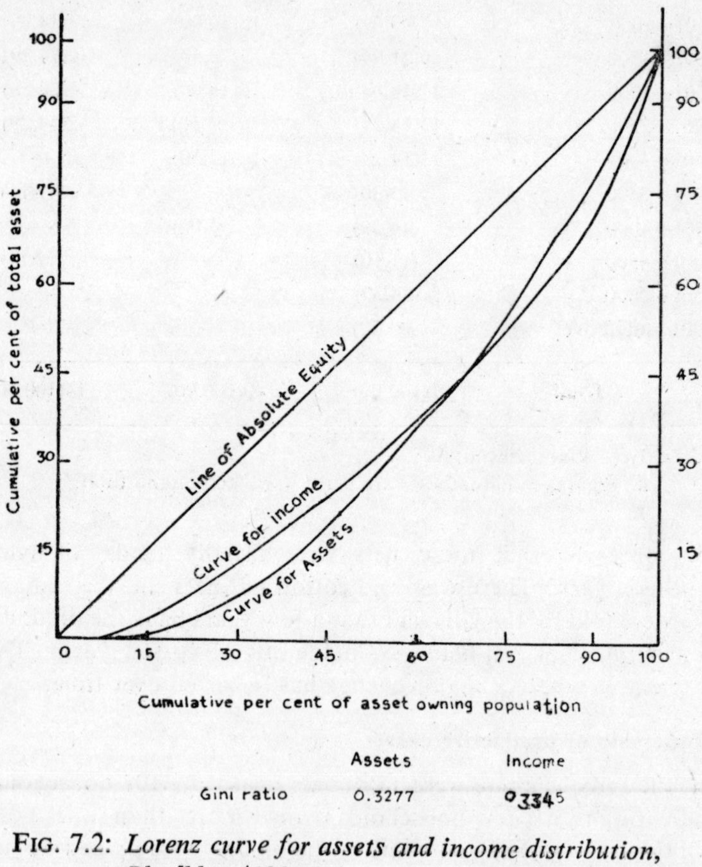

FIG. 7.2: *Lorenz curve for assets and income distribution, Bhadbhut (1981-82)*

It was observed that the fishing craft and gear in the village are basically individually owned. In addition to the ownership of craft and gear, the nature and character of owner (in terms of active fishing) and the status (in terms of labourer or partner) of non-owner worker in the boat also pay an important role in the organization of fish production. As indicated earlier, the ownership pattern of fishing craft and gear can be classified into six categories. The six ownership patterns are as follows: (i) IO, OW, NOL; (ii) IO, OW, NOP; (iii) IO, ONW, NOL; (iv) CO, OW, NOL; (v) CO, OW, NOP; and (vi) CO, ONW, NOL, where IO=Individual Owner, OW=Owner, Worker, NOP=Non-Owner Partner, CO=Collective Owner, ONW=Owner Non-Worker, NOL=Non-Owner Labourer.

In the village we have observed primarily two types of ownership patterns. These are: (i) Individual owner, owner worker, non-owner labourer (IO, OW, NOL), and (ii) Individual owner, owner worker, non-owner partner (IO, OW, NOP).

The first pattern is predominant and accounts for more than 80 per cent of the boats in the village, particularly during the fishing season. Further, we have observed that the pattern of ownership changes from first to second type during the lean season for fishing. In addition, it was also observed that the fishing boats used to be leased out to a group of crew members during the lean season for fishing. It was also observed that the boat owner who leased out the boat in general was also a member of the group of the crew member leasing in the boat for operation during the lean season for fishing. The leasing out of the fishing craft by boat owners is predominant during November to June. It is, however, not to suggest that the leasing out of the fishing craft does not exist during the peak fishing season from July to October, but it is relatively low in terms of the number of boats leased out. From our discussions with the fishermen in the village we found that the ownership pattern of fishing craft and gear has not changed much.

The fish landings in the village take place on the banks of river Narmada. In view of the fact that there are only non-mechanized boats in the village the need for any modern landing facilities has not been felt. Therefore, the shift in the location of fish landing centres did not take place. However, the shift in the location of fish landing centres has been influenced by the growth of fish landings in the village to attract more fish merchants and to reduce the direct landings in the nearby urban location.

Output and income and distribution of gains

The quarterwise fish production for the past three years has been indicated in Table 7.12. The data for 1981-82 production is not complete. The comparison of fish landings during 1979-80 with the production during 1980-81 indicates that there has been over 23 per cent increase in the catches during 1980-81. Turning to the seasonality of fish production we observe that unlike in other villages in Gujarat more than 50 per cent production of the village is during the July-September quarter. The fish landings of the village during the October-December quarter are the lowest (3 per cent) of the total landing while the same quarter accounts for about 50 per cent of the fish production in other villages in Gujarat. In 1980-81 the second highest landings were observed during the January-March quarter. The contrasting seasonable variations in the landings of the village as against the pattern in the Veraval region may be because of the dependence of the village landings on estuarine resources. The total fish production in the village during 1981-82 has been estimated[5] at 486 tonnes. The single important species of fish caught in the village was Hilsa which accounted for 20 per cent of the total catch. This was followed by clupeides, mullets, and Bombay duck. Most of these have fetched a good price in the market. It was observed in this village that there were hardly any landings of pomfrets. Despite the fact that there were hardly any mechanized boats, the landings of shrimps and prawns during 1981-82 accounted for about 13.9 per cent of the landings (Table 7.11).

Value of output: The value of output in the village is based on the price information obtained by us during the survey period and the estimates of output. Since there were sharp fluctuations in the prices of various species of fish, we have taken the average prices for the major varieties in estimating the value of output. The specieswise estimated fish landings and their annual gross value of output is given in Table 7.12. The economy of the village is based on the four major varieties. These are hilsa, clupeides, jew fish, shrimps and prawns.

TABLE 7.11

Quarterwise fish production in Bhadbhut (1979 to 1981)

(*in tonnes*)

Quarter	Fish landings during		
	1979-80	1980-81	1981-82
July-September	164.75 (47.06)	248.21 (51.12)	18.11
October-December	45.21 (12.91)	15.67 (3.23)	120.53
January-March	11.15 (3.19)	142.92 (29.44)	31.79
April-June	128.99 (36.84)	78.72 (16.21)	N.A.
Total	350.10 (100.0)	485.52 (100.0)	N.A.

Note: 1. Figures in parentheses are percentages to column total.
2. N.A. indicates not available.

Source: Compiled on the basis of the data obtained from the office of the Assistant Director of Fisheries, Bharuch.

The total annual gross value of output in the village was estimated to be Rs. 30,96,750 during 1981-82.

Measurement of household incomes from fishing: The household income from fishing can be defined as the net return to the fishing assets owned by the households, and to family labour expended in operating the fishing equipment. For working out the returns on the capital invested on fishing equipment and on labour, it is necessary to work out the economics of the fishing craft and gear.

Table 7.13 gives the quarterwise gross value of output per boat. It can be seen from the table that about 60 per cent of the total value of annual output was realized during the peak season, i.e. July to October for NMBs of length up to 25 feet while it was 62.08 per cent in the case of NMB of length 25 feet and above.

TABLE 7.12

Specieswise estimated marine fish landings and average prices and annual gross value of output, Bhadbhut (1981-82)

Species	Fish landings of stated* variety (in tonnes)	Price per kg. (Rs.)	Annual gross value of output ('000 Rs.)
1. Bombay duck	54.93(10.2)	2.25	123.59(4.0)
2. Jew fish	52.78(9.8)	8.50	448.63(14.5)
3. Hilsa	108.26(20.1)	7.25	784.89(25.3)
4. Clupeids	94.79(17.6)	4.75	450.25(14.5)
5. Shark	9.69(1.8)	3.00	29.07(0.9)
6. Mullet	57.09(10.6)	6.50	371.09(12.0)
7. Catfish	52.24(9.7)	3.00	156.72(5.1)
8. Shrimps	47.93(8.9)	5.50	263.62(8.5)
9. Prawns (medium)	26.95(5.0)	14.25	384.04(12.4)
10. Others	33.94(6.3)	2.50	84.85(2.8)
Total	538.60(100.0)	—	3096.75(100.0)

Note: 1. *Excluding the household consumption in the village.
2. Figures in parentheses are percentages to column total.
3. (—) indicates nil.

It was also observed that fishing during the lean season was done on the basis of sharing. Each of the crew members in the group owned a net and the catch of that particular net belonged to the owner of the net. During this season the boat owner was paid a fixed rent collected equally from all the crew members. The seasonwise differences were similar for both types of boats—up to 25 feet and above.

The itemwise average variable cost for boats up to 25 feet was Rs. 34.85 and for boats above 25 feet Rs. 51.6 per day. The items of variable costs are given in Table 7.14. Since the boats are non-mechanized, the food expenditure of the crew is the largest single item of the variable cost, followed by the cost of net twine, ice and water and fuel for lighting devices during the fishing trip.

TABLE 7.13

Seasonwise gross value of output per boat of different lengths, Bhadbhut (1981-82)

(*in Rupees*)

Season	Gross value of output in stated quarter of NM boat of length			
	Up to 25 ft.	% share in total	25 ft. and above	% share in total
1. Peak Season				
July and August	4691	22.68	7857	26.23
September and October	7651	36.99	10734	35.84
Sub-total	12341	59.67	18591	62.08
2. Lean Season*				
November to June	8340	40.33	11358	37.92
Total	20681	100.00	29949	100.00

Note: *The fishing during the lean season is done on the basis of sharing system. Each of the crew members in the group owns a net and the catch of that particular net belongs to the owner of the net. During this season the boat owner is paid a fixed rent collected equally from all the crew members.

The annual fixed costs incurred for the operation of boats of different length groups is shown in Table 7.15. It can be seen from this table that salary to crew members is the most important single item among the annual fixed costs. There are many variations in the mode of operations of boats and the employment of crew. One is as follows. The boat owner employs crew members on a salary basis during the first four months of the peak season and during the remaining period the owner hires out the boat to a group of crew members in which the owner himself is a member. The other important items of annual fixed cost per boat are depreciation, dry docking and oil painting, repairs and maintenance of the boat and others. The total annual fixed cost for operating a boat of less than 25 feet works out to be Rs. 13,830 and in the case of a boat of 25 feet and above it comes to Rs. 18,843.50.

TABLE 7.14

Itemwise variable cost incurred per boat per day for different types of boats, Bhadbhut (1981-82)

(in Rupees)

Items of expenditure	Expenditure on stated items for NM boat	
	Length up to 25 ft.	Length between 25 ft. and above
1. Fuel*	3.65	3.75
2. Wages to daily labourers	—	—
3. Ice and water	2.50	5.25
4. Food expenditure of crew	15.70	23.50
5. Cost of net twine	8.50	12.80
6. Others	4.50	6.30
Total	34.85	51.60

Note: 1. (—) indicates nil.
2. *indicates the expenditure incurred for lighting devices during the fishing trip.

The annual gross and net returns of both types of non-mechanized boats are presented in Table 7.16. The net returns of different sizes of boats show a similar pattern as that of gross returns. The net returns are higher for boats of 25 feet and above (Rs. 6,827.50). The net returns of boats up to 25 feet in length work out to be only Rs. 3,813. The net returns also include the lean season rent of Rs. 800 in the case of boats of less than 25 feet in length and Rs. 1,000 in the case of boats of 25 feet and above. The rate of return on investment works out to 18.52 per cent in the case of boats up to 25 feet in length and 23.14 per cent in the case of boats of length of 25 feet and above.

Distribution of income: The majority of households in Bhadbhut derive their major portion of income from occupations within the fisheries sector. We have computed the incomes accruing to each household taking the occupation of every person gainfully employed within each household into

TABLE 7.15

Itemwise annual fixed expenditure for operating the NM boats of different length groups, Bhadbhut (1981-82)

(*in Rupees*)

Items	Expenditure incurred on stated items by NM boat of	
	Less than 25 ft.	25 ft. and above
1. Salaries to Crew Members*	10890.00 (3600.00)	14908.00 (4800.00)
2. Repairs and Maintenance of boat	280.00	360.50
3. Dry docking and Dil Painting	300.00	347.50
4. Insurance	—	—
5. Depreciation**	2100.00	2867.00
6. Others	260.00	325.50
Total	13830.00 (6540.00)	18843.50 (8735.50)

Note: *There are many variations in the mode of operation of boats and the pattern of employment of crew. The predominant type of mode of operation is as follows: the boot owner employs crew members on a salary basis during the remaining period, the owner hires out the boat to a group of crew members in which the owner himself is a member. The figures in parentheses in these columns indicate the salary during four months for the total crew employed.

**For working out depreciation the economic life of boat and gear has been taken as 15 and 5 years respectively and the investments are taken at 1979 prices.

account. The distribution of income by occupation and source is shown in Table 7.17. The income generated from the occupations other than fisheries by the villagers account for about 4 per cent of the total income of the village. As expected, the boat-owning households derive about 90 per cent of the total income generated in the village. The 10 per cent of the remaining income goes to the 46 (31 per cent) non-boat owning households. This is reflected in the member household income

TABLE 7.16

Gross and net returns of non-mechanized boats, Bhadbhut (1981-82)

(in Rupees)

Particulars	Return of NM boats	
	Less than 25 ft.	25 ft. and above
1. Gross returns*	12341.00	18591.00
2. Expenditure		
(a) Variable cost*	2788.00	4128.00
(b) Fixed cost	6540.00	8735.50
Sub-total	9328.00	12863.50
3. Net returns	3813.00**	6827.50***
4. Rate of return on investment (%)	18.52	23.14

Note: *The data relates to the peak season only, since during the lean season the boat owners get rent. The variable cost during the season has been estimated by multiplying the average daily expenditure and number of fishing days (80 in this case).

**Includes the lean season rent of Rs. 800.

***Includes the lean season rent of Rs. 1,000.

as well as the per capita income in the village. While the non-mechanized boat-owning households derive Rs. 16,362 as the household income, the crew member households get only Rs. 3,866 as the household income. The per capita income of the non-mechanized boat-owning households comes to about Rs. 2,392. The per capita income of crew member households is only Rs. 797. Therefore the crew member households were much poorer than the boat-owning households in this village. There was hardly any difference between the various castes in the village because most of the members of the fishermen community (both boat owners and crew members) belonged to the Machhi community.

We have used Gini ratios as a summary measure of the income inequality. Estimated Gini ratios and the Lorenz curve for the distribution of productive assets and incomes are

TABLE 7.17

Distribution of income according to occupation, Bhadbhut (1981-82)

(in Rupees)

Occupation	Income			Per household income	Per capita income
	Fishery	Non-fishery	Total		
1. NMB	1690688.00 (87.15)	60100.00 (3.10)	1750788.00 (90.25)	16362.50	2391.79
2. CRM	169713.00 (8.75)	12000.00 (0.62)	181713.00 (9.37)	3866.20	796.99
3. Others	—	7500.00	7500.00 (0.38)	7500.00 (0.38)	3750.00
Total	1860401.00 (95.90)	79600.00 (4.10)	1940001.00 (100.00)	12516.14	2016.64

Note: 1. Figures in parentheses are percentages to column total.
2. (—) indicates nil.

shown in Figure 7.2. The Gini ratio of inequality of income in the village is 0.3345. In this case the incomes are slightly more unequal than the assets in the village. This is mainly because of a large gap between the per capita earnings of boat-owning households and the crew member households. But the Gini ratios for both incomes and assets are much lower as compared to the other villages in Gujarat. In this sense we can say that incomes in this village are more equally distributed than in other villages with more mechanized boats.

Disposal of fish landings

The disposal of fish landings is conditioned by the species composition and the availability of infrastructure facilities for processing of fish. In this village the landings are mainly used for fresh consumption and sun-drying or salt-curing. Our observation with regard to the utilization of catches is summarized in Table 7.18. The share of fresh fish has been about 71 per cent in 1981-82. The share of sun-drying and

TABLE 7.18

Changes in utilization of fish production in Bhabhut (1960-82)

Utilized for	Share of the stated form in total during	
	1960-61	1981-82
1. Fresh consumption	65.2	71.2
2. Sun-drying and salt-curing	32.3	18.4
3. Fishmeal extraction	2.5	5.6
4. Exports (Freezing/canning)	—	4.8
Total	100.00	100.00

Note: (—) indicates negligible.

salt-curing has been 18.4 per cent, followed by fishmeal extraction with 5.6 per cent and exports with 4.8 per cent.

MARKETS IN THE VILLAGE

In this section, we shall now examine the markets for inputs, labour, credit and output in the village with a view to gauging the changes in these markets over time.

Market for inputs

The various inputs which are considered for study in this section include supply of boats and gear and service facilities for boats. The distribution of sample boats according to the place of construction/purchase is presented in Table 7.19. All the new boats constructed were from the boat-building yards within the state; and about 70 per cent of the boats were constructed within the district itself. The transaction of boats within the fishermen of the village is relatively unknown in the village. Of the total 40 sample boats only 5 (12.5 per cent) were acquired through such transactions while 35 have been obtained from boat-building yards and were new. Further, of the five used boats, four were obtained from fishermen of the other village within the district and one within the village.

TABLE 7.19

Distribution of boats owned by sample respondents according to place of purchase/construction, Bhadbhut (1981-82)

Location of the source of purchase	NMB Flat Bottom New	NMB Flat Bottom Old	Total
1. Within the village	—	1(20.0)	1(2.5)
2. Outside the village but within the district	25(71.4)	4(80.0)	29(72.5)
3. Outside the district but within the state	10(28.6)	—	10(25.0)
4. Outside the state	—	—	—
Total	35(100.0)	5(100.0)	40(100.0)

Note: 1. (—) indicates nil.
2. Figures in parentheses are percentages to column total.

The repairs of boats are attended to by the two carpenters of the village and an equal number of carpenters from other neighbouring villages. The village being a predominantly non-mechanized village no other inputs are required other than facilities for building and repairing of boats, and mending and repairing of nets. The readily mended nets or material for net mending (such as nylon and synthetic twine) are available from the stores in the nearby town and also through the fishermen co-operative society in the village.

Market for labour

As already seen in the last section, the productive assets are owned by about 75 per cent of the households while the rest of the households derive an overwhelming share of their income by selling labour time for actual fishing. In this section we will examine the selling of labour time by the households.

There are various types of labour contracts prevailing in the village. The first type is a wage paid labour contract. The second is share contract. Further, a labourer is employed on a wage paid basis during the peak season for fishing and on a sharing basis during the lean period. The wage paid system is quite simple. In this each labourer gets a fixed monetary wage during the period of employment. In the second system of labour contract there are two alternative forms. In the first, during the lean season for fishing, the boat owner himself may be a crew member. The group of crew operates a set of nets individually owned. All the crew members work together for putting the net into the sea and hauling the net into the boat after fishing. Every crew member has the right on the fish caught in proportion to his contribution to the whole operation. In the second, the boat owner also owns the net and the crew are paid a fixed share in the total catch which is shared equally by all the crew members. The first form is more prevalent. The second form is restricted to fishing boats which operate at Okha and is known as *dalede* fishing.

Supply of and demand for labour in the village: To have a better grasp of the employment and unemployment, we have attempted to estimate the surplus labourers in the village labour market.

Table 7.20 gives the estimates of surplus labourers. There is a deficit of 184 labourers which accounts for about 40 per cent of the total number of members required for operating all the boats and gear in the village. In an apparently labour short economic situation, the boat owners tend to employ all the members of the family to the maximum extent and then only accommodate hired labourers from other villages. The deficit of labourers was of the order of 1.19 persons per household.

The estimated labour participation in terms of family and hired labourers in the operation of the fishing craft of the village is presented in Table 7.21. It can be seen from the table that 182 persons have been estimated to be involved in fishing from the boat-owning households while they have a potential for supply of only 176 persons. The excessive rate of involvement of boat-owning households could be either due to a sampling error or because of the part-time involvement of students from boat-owning households in operating the fishing craft. In any case it indicates that the work allocation is based on the optimal allocation pattern. Thus, we find the

TABLE 7.20

Estimate of surplus labourers according to occupation, Bhadbhut (1981-82)

Particulars	No. of households of			Total
	NMB owners	Crew	Others	
1. Number of households	107	47	1	155
2. Number of able-bodied adult male members of family	203	80	1	284
3. Number of adult male members with occupation other than fishing	11	2	1	14
4. Number of adult male members who have not yet entered the working force (students)	16	—	—	16
5. Number of members actively engaged or at best having no other occupation	176	78	—	254
6. Number of members required for operating the fishing equipment in peak season	438	—	—	438
7. Surplus labourers in the fishing workforce	—262	78	—	—184
8. Surplus labourers in the fishing households	—2.45	1.66	—	—1.19

Note: 1. (—) indicates nil.
2. Negative surpluses indicate the deficits.

scarcity of labourers in the village is overcome by hiring labourers from other villages.

Labour and occupational mobility: All the 10 sample crew members had a low labour mobility ratio. Thus, the labourers are relatively immobile in the village. The reason for change of employer by the crew during their immediate past change is presented in Table 7.22. It is found that the crew changed employer for various reasons. Dispute with the boat owner and hope of getting higher returns are the important reasons for change of employer by crew members.

TABLE 7.21

Estimated labourers' participation pattern, family and hired, for operating boats, Bhadbhut (1981-82)

Type of boat	Total No. of boats	Estimated avg. crew size required per boat	Total crew required	Estimated source of crew		
				Family	Hired	
					Sharing	Salary
NMB (flat bottomed)						
(a) Up to 25 ft.	10	3.7	37	13(35.14)	—	24(64.86)
(b) 25 ft. +	109	3.68	401	169(42.14)	—	232(57.86)
Total	119		438	182	—	256

Note: Estimated on the basis of the information from sample respondents.

TABLE 7.22

Reasons for change of employer by the crew members during their immediate past change, Bhadbhut (1981-82)

Reason for change of employer	No. of crew who indicated the stated reason	% share in total
1. Dispute with the boat owner	3	18.75
2. Hope of getting higher returns due to efficient working of the craft	3	18.75
3. Hope of having good company in other owner's boat	2	12.50
4. No special reason	2	12.50
5. Others (no change)	6	37.50
Total	16	100.00

The interlocking of labour and credit, though very weak in the village, takes place in the form of lending money to the crew by the boat owners. Size distribution of sample crew members according to the amount borrowed at the time of joining the employer and outstanding debt as on 31 December, 1981, is presented in Table 7.23. Four of the 10 sample crew members did not borrow any money at the time of joining, and three borrowed money up to Rs. 500 only. The maximum amount borrowed was less than Rs. 2,000. The outstanding debt as on 31 December, 1981, indicates the tendency of crew to repay the loan as soon as possible.

TABLE 7.23

Size distribution of sample crew members according to the amount borrowed at the time of joining from and outstanding debt to the employer/owner as on December 31, 1981, Bhadbhut

Frequency interval (Rs.)	Number of crew with stated range of borrowings	% share in total	Number of crew with outstanding debt in the stated range	% share in total
No borrowing/ outstanding debt	4	40.00	9	90.00
1—500	3	30.00	1	10.00
501—1000	3	20.00	—	—
1001—2000	1	10.00	—	—
Total	10	100.00	10	100.00

Note: (—) indicates nil.

The distribution of working population in the sample households, according to the pace of graduation to current position, is presented in Table 7.24. For all the boat owners but for one the pace of graduation was slow and took 6 to 15 years. For about 21 per cent of the sample crew the pace of graduation was quite high and was within less than two years, while on the other hand for about 73 per cent it took from 6 to 15 years.

TABLE 7.24

Distribution of working population in sample households according to pace of graduation to current position, Bhadbhut (1981-82)

Pace of graduation	No. of individuals with stated pace in			Total
	NMB owners	Crew in NMB	Other	
1. High	—	8(21.62)	—	8(10.39)
2. Medium	1(2.56)	2(5.41)	—	3(3.90)
3. Low	38(97.44)	27(72.97)	1(100.00)	66(85.71)
Total	39(100.00)	37(100.00)	1(100.00)	77(100.00)

Note: 1. (–) indicates nil.
2. Figures in parentheses are percentages to column total.

Market for credit

We shall now present the sources of credit to the fishermen, and their terms and conditions. Various individuals are involved in the credit market. Occasionally both the roles are played by a single agency at a time. For example, boat owners borrow from various sources and also lend to crew simultaneously. Generally, the lenders are of the same village, and from the fishermen community itself. The main credit sources for the fishermen consist of commercial banks, informal sources like friends/relatives, moneylenders, fish merchants, etc. It was found that a majority of them borrow from multiple sources, say, two to four sources at a time, for single purpose. The main source was observed to be fish merchants/boat owners. It was interesting to note that no fisherman of the village has borrowed from the co-operative society. The only formal lending agency is the commercial banks. The terms and conditions of loan advances by various agencies are similar to those explained in the profile of Chorwad (see page 168).

The outstanding debt of NMB owner households accounts for over 86 per cent of the total outstanding debt. The total outstanding debt of the fishermen households has been estimated at Rs. 5,29,690 as on 31 December, 1981, with an average outstanding of Rs. 3,866 per household. Fish merchants account for about 2.9 per cent of the total outstanding debt. Multiple sources account for over 67 per cent of the total outstanding debt. The average outstanding debt is higher for boat owner households as compared to crew households. Of the total 155 households 138 were borrowing households (Table 7.25). It can be seen from Table 7.26 that fishermen have borrowed money for replacement of gear, purchase of craft/gear and household expenses. Of the 138 borrower households almost 58 per cent have borrowed for the replacement of gear. Thirty NMB households have purchased their craft and gear on credit and 25 households have borrowed to meet their household expenses. It is also observed that 13 NMB owners have borrowed to run their households and two of the crew households have borrowed for social functions also.

Market for product

The changes in the number of various market intermediaries to market the fish output of the villagers, the structure of the fish market and channels of distribution are discussed in this section.

Changes in the number of different market intermediaries from 1960 to 1982 is presented in Table 7.27. It can be seen from the table that during 1960-61 only fresh fish wholesalers were working in the fish market of Bhadbhut. No other channel members were involved in fish marketing. In 1981-82 the number of intermediaries increased. In addition to fresh fish wholesalers, one commission agent, one retailer and one semi-wholesaler are working in the market. It is interesting to note that about 40 per cent of the channel members are from non-fishermen community. In addition to these, the fishermen sometimes land their catch directly in the nearby consuming centre, i.e. Bharuch.

The direct retailing or vending of fish by fishermen themselves is negligible in the village. The one retailer who has a retailing business is from the non-fishermen community. It was observed that one fisherman is working as a commission agent.

Channel members and structure of fish market: The marketing channel comprises: wholesalers, semi-wholesalers, dry fish

TABLE 7.25

Distribution of households according to the source of borrowing and occupations and their outstanding debt as on December 31, 1981, Bhadbhut

(*in Rupees*)

Source of borrowing	No. of households having outstanding debt					
	NMB owners		CRM		Total	
	No.	Outstanding debt	No.	Outstanding debt	No.	Outstanding debt
I. Formal Lending Agencies:						
(a) Commercial banks	6	12300 (2050)	3	4800 (1600)	9	17100 (1900)
(b) Co-op. Societies/Bank	—	—	—	—	—	—
Sub-total	6	12300	3	4800	9	17100
II. Private or Informal Source:						
(a) Friends and Relatives	2	5000 (2500)	1	2000 (2000)	3	7000 (2333)
(b) Money-lenders	—	—	2	4000 (2000)	2	4000 (2000)
(c) Fish merchants/Boat owners	30	121500	21	43800 (2386)	51	165300 (3241)
Sub-total	32	126500	24	49800	56	176300
III. From multiple sources	63	316935 (5031)	10*	19350 (135)	73	336285
Total	101	455735 (4512)	37	73950	138	529685

Note: 1. (—) indicates nil.
2. Figures in parentheses indicate the per household outstanding debt.
3. *Includes one other household.

TABLE 7.26

Distribution of households according to the purpose of borrowing of the outstanding debt and occupations, Bhadbhut (1981-82)

Reasons for borrowing the outstanding debt	Number of households for stated reason of borrowing of			Total
	NMB owners	Crew	Others	
1. No. outstanding debt	6(5.60)	11(23.40)	—	17(10.97)
2. Replacement of gear	58(54.21)	21(44.68)	—	79(50.97)
3. Purchase of craft and gear	30(28.04)	—	—	30(19.35)
4. To meet household expenditure	13(12.15)	22(25.53)	—	25(16.13)
5. To meet the expenditure for social functions	—	2(4.26)	1(100.0)	3(1.94)
6. Others	—	1(2.13)	—	1(0.64)
Total	107(100.0)	47(100.0)	1(100.0)	155(100.0)

Note: 1. (—) indicates nil.
2. Figures in parentheses are percentages to column total.

merchants, and retailers/vendors. The functions of these intermediaries are similar to those explained in the Chorwad village profile (see page 175). For understanding the structure of the fish market in the village, we have attempted to compute the share of each market intermediary in the landings of the village. The four fresh fish wholesalers in the village accounted for over 75 per cent of the total landings while the commission agent, semi-wholesaler and the retailer accounted for the rest. Of the four wholesalers two accounted for over 60 per cent of the total turnover of four fresh-fish wholesalers. The number of boat owners having a credit and marketing linkage with each of the

TABLE 7.27

Changes in the number of different marketing intermediaries, Bhadbhut (1960-82)

Marketing intermediaries	No. of stated persons/organizations during					
	1960-61			1981-82		
	Fishermen community	Non-fishermen community	Total	Fishermen community	Non-fishermen community	Total
1. Retailers/Vendors	—	—	—	—	—	—
2. Wholesalers						
(a) Fresh Fish	2	1	3	3	1	4
b) Dry Fish	—	—	—	—	—	—
(c) Fishmeal	—	—	—	—	—	—
3. Commission Agents	—	—	—	1	—	1
4. Semi-wholesaler	—	—	—	—	1	1
5. Processable variety suppliers	—	—	—	—	—	—
6. Fishmeal varieties	—	—	—	—	—	—

Note: (—) indicates nil.

wholesalers was more or less in proportion to their annual turnover. The channels of distribution for fish output in the village are presented in Figure 7.3.

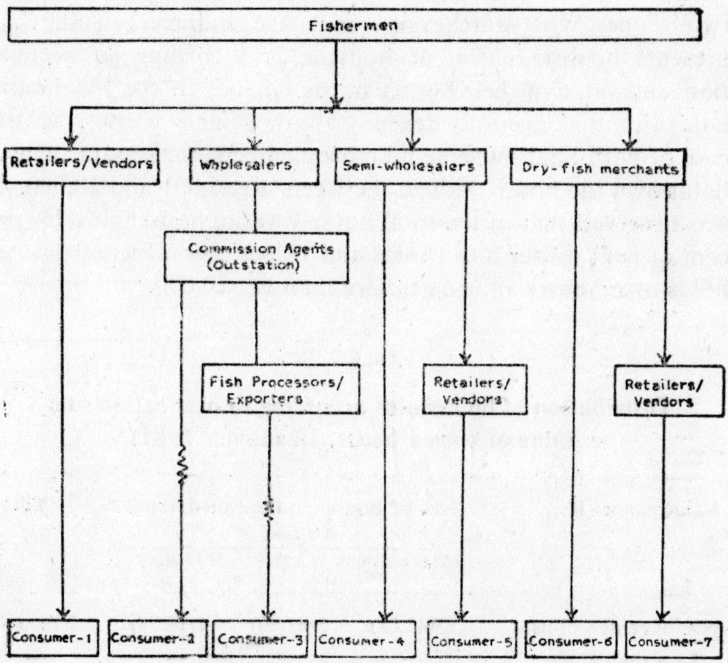

Note: 1. ~~~ indicates the existence of other channel members for which no information is available.

FIG. 7.3: *Channels of distribution for fish output, Bhadbhut (1981-82)*

THE VILLAGE ECONOMY

The village production and marketing systems have been described earlier. In this section an attempt is made to describe the assets structure and expenditure of the fishermen.

Assets structure of fishermen

Owned house is the single most form of non-fishery assets of the villagers, in view of their lower savings to invest in other items. The houses owned by the fishermen of the village are either thatched or tiled depending upon their economic position. It is, however, not to suggest that the fishermen of the village do not own any other assets. In fact, some of the households own gold, jewellery, entertainment articles like radio and two-in-ones, wrist-watches or some office equipment. Table 7.28 presents the distribution of households according to occupation and value of their houses in the village. Of the 155 households in the village only seven stay in rented houses. In the case of both boat owners and crew members, maximum households own the house valued between Rs. 5,001 and 10,000. It was observed that of the total house-owning households 25 per cent of boat owner households and 18 per cent of crew households own houses valued at more than Rs. 10,000.

TABLE 7.28

Distribution of households according to occupation and value of owned house, Bhadbhut (1981)

Value range (Rs.)	No. of houses in the stated range of value of			Total
	NMB owners	Crew	Others	
No. of rented houses	3(42.88)	3(42.86)	1(14.28)	7(100.00)
Less than 1000	—	—	—	—
1001-3000	7(58.33)	5(41.67)	—	12(100.00)
3001-5000	17(53.13)	15(46.87)	—	32(100.00)
5001-10000	54(77.14)	16(22.86)	—	70(100.00)
10001+	26(76.47)	8(23.53)	—	34(100.00)
Sub-total of owned houses	104(70.27)	44(29.73)	—	148(100.00)
Total	107(69.03)	47(30.32)	1(0.65)	155(100.00)

Note: 1. (—) indicates nil.
2. Figures in parentheses are percentages to row total.

Ownership of different household items according to occupation is presented in Table 7.29. Boat owners own more than 80 per cent of the different items of households in

TABLE 7.29

Ownership of different household items according to occupation, Bhadbhut (1981-82)

Items	No. of households owning the stated items						Total	
	NMB owners		Crew members		Others			
	No. of items	HH	NI	HH	NI	HH	NI	HH
1	2	3	4	5	6	7	8	9
I. Transport Vehicles:								
Cycle	3	3	—	—	—	—	3	3
II. Communication/Ent.:								
Radio/Transistor	38	38	3	3	1	1	42	42
TV/2 or three-in-one	8	1	1	1	2	1	11	9
III. Office Equipment;								
Chairs	18	11	1	1	1	1	20	13
Tables	15	12	1	1	—	—	16	13
Wooden Almirah	35	35	7	4	1	1	43	40
Steel Almirah	4	4	—	—	—	—	4	4
Sewing Machine	2	2	—	—	—	—	2	2

TABLE 7.29 (*Contd.*)

1	2	3	4	5	6	7	8	9
IV. Time Indicators:								
Wrist-watch	59	51	10	10	—	—	69	61
Clock	4	4	—	—	1	1	5	5
V. Cooking Apparatus								
Non-kerosene Stove	162	107	77	46	1	1	240	154
Kerosene Stove	24	24	2	2	1	1	27	27
VI. Kitchenware:								
Earthen	341	105	165	47	3	1	509	153
Aluminium	768	104	365	47	5	1	1138	152
Steel	371	79	85	26	5	1	461	106
Others	850	99	338	43	9	1	1197	153

Note: 1. (—) indicates nil.
2. HH: Households.
NI: No. of Items.

the village, particularly modern items. All the transport vehicles available in the village, i.e. cycle and majority (more than 95 per cent) of office equipment are owned by boat owners. Non-kerosene stove is the predominant cooking apparatus in the village. TV as well as two- or three-in-one are also owned by the boat owners of the village. Kitchenware from earthen to modern metal one are available with each of the category of households, with a concentration in the households of boat owners.

Consumption and expenditure pattern of fishermen households

The fishermen of Bhadbhut have an entirely different pattern of expenditure compared to other villages. At an aggregate of about Rs. 10,62,890 of the total expenditure of Rs. 14,52,810 was spent on food items while the rest was on non-food items. Of the total expenditure in the village the boat owner households account for 78 per cent, while they account for 69 per cent of the households.

The expenditure on food-items is mainly on foodgrains, edible oils and fish which all together account for 69 per cent of the total expenditure on food items in the village. As indicated above, the expenditure on non-food items is higher in the village. Clothes alone account for 59 per cent of the total expenditure on non-food items. The expenses on medicines are also quite high (26 per cent) which shows that hygienic condition of the village is not so good. The boat owner households spend a good amount on their children's education also (6 per cent). It is quite interesting to note that the expenditure on food, fuel and light is only one per cent in all the categories of households (Table 7.30).

The itemwise per capita and per household consumer expenditure by various occupations is presented in Table 7.31. In the case of boat owner households and crew households the per capita consumer expenditure is almost similar.

Table 7.32 shows distribution of the households according to the value of the household articles. Of the total 155 households 40 per cent own articles valued at below Rs. 500. In the case of boat owners this size class accounts for only 26 per cent and in the case of CRM households it accounts for over 72 per cent. The households owning household articles valued at more than

TABLE 7.30

Itemwise annual consumption expenditure by occupation, Bhadbhut (1981-82)

(in '000 Rupees)

Item	Expenditure on stated item by			
	NMB households	Crew	Others	Total
I. *Food Items*:				
(a) Foodgrains	237.17(77.29)	68.12(22.20)	1.56(0.51)	306.85(100)
(b) Milk and Milk Products	39.47(76.43)	11.96(23.16)	0.21(0.41)	51.64(100)
(c) Edible Oils	140.61(78.44)	38.22(21.32)	0.42(0.24)	179.25(100)
(d) Meat and Chicken	4.94(87.90)	0.68(12.10)	—	5.62(100)
(e) Fish	166.45(73.95)	58.34(25.91)	0.36(0.16)	225.15(100)
(f) Vegetables	36.04(74.83)	11.39(23.65)	0.73(1.52)	48.16(100)
(g) Fruits and Nuts	21.22(90.45)	2.24(9.55)	—	23.46(100)
(h) Sugar, Gur and Khandsari	74.57(75.87)	23.40(23.81)	0.31(0.32)	98.28(100)
(i) Salt and Spices	59.90(74.61)	20.23(25.20)	0.15(0.19)	80.28(100)
(j) Beverages	1.56(100.0)	—	—	1.56(100)
(k) Pan, Tobacco and Supari	34.42(80.72)	8.22(19.28)	—	42.64(100)
Sub-total	816.35(76.81)	242.80(22.84)	3.74(0.35)	1062.89(100)

II. *Non-food Items*:				
(a) Entertainment	3.82(88.23)	0.41 (9.47)	0.10(2.30)	4.33(100)
(b) Education	11.16(93.70)	0.75 (6.30)	–	11.91(100)
(c) Medicines	49.60(76.57)	14.68(22.66)	0.50(0.77)	64.78(100)
(d) Domestic Utensils	6.55(66.97)	3.23(33.03)	—	9.28(100)
(e) Clothes	113.70(77.93)	31.20(21.38)	1.00(0.69)	145.90(100)
(f) Footwear	7.36(79.57)	1.79(19.35)	0.10(1.08)	9.25(100)
(g) Fuel and Light	101.09(77.54)	28.55(21.90)	0.73(0.56)	130.37(100)
(h) Travel and Transport	9.52(70.00)	4.08(30.00)	Neg.	13.60(100)
Sub-total	302.80(77.65)	84.89(21.72)	2.43(0.63)	389.92(100)
Total	1119.15(77.03)	327.49(22.54)	6.17(0.43)	1452.81(100)

Note: 1. (—) indicates nil.
2. Figures in parentheses are percentages to row total.
3. Neg.=Negligible.

TABLE 7.31

Itemwise per capita and per household consumer expenditure by occupation, Bhadbhut

Item	NMB households	Crew	Others	Total
I. *Food Items*:				
(a) Foodgrains	124(2217)	229(1449)	780(1566)	319(1980)
(b) Milk and Milk Products	54(369)	53(254)	104(208)	54(333)
(c) Edible Oils	192(1314)	167(813)	208(416)	183(1156)
(d) Meat and Chicken	7(46)	3(15)	—	6(36)
(e) Fish	227(1556)	256(1741)	182(364)	234(1453)
(f) Vegetables	49(337)	50(242)	364(729)	50(31)
(g) Fruits and Nuts	29(198)	10(47)	—	24(151)
(h) Sugar, Gur and Khandsari	102(697)	102(498)	156(312)	102(634)
(i) Salt and Spices	82(568)	89(431)	78(156)	83(518)
(j) Beverages	2(15)	—	—	2(10)
(k) Pan, Tobacco and Supari	47(322)	36(175)	—	44(275)
Sub-total	1115(7631)	1065(5165)	1872(3750)	1105(6857)
II. *Non-food Items*:				
(a) Entertainment	5.22(36)	1.78(9)	49.50(99)	4.50(28)
(b) Education	15.25(104)	3.29(16)	—	12.38(77)

(c) Medicines	67.76(463)	64.36(312)	250(500)	67.33(418)
(d) Domestic Utensils	8.95(61)	14.14(69)	—	10.16(63)
(e) Clothes	155.33(1062)	136.84(664)	500(1000)	151.66(941)
(f) Footwear	10.05(72)	7.83(38)	50(100)	9.61(60)
(g) Fuel and Light	138.00(945)	125.00(607)	364	136.00(841)
(h) Travel and Transport	13.01(89)	17.90(87)	Neg.	14.00(88)
Sub-total	413.57(2832)	371.14(1802)	1213.5(2427)	405.64(2516)
Total	1528.57(10463)	1436.14(6967)	3085.50(6177)	1510.67(9373)

Notes : 1. (—) indicates nil.
2. Figures in parentheses indicate expenditure per household.
3. Neg.=Negligible.

TABLE 7.32

Size distribution of households according to the value of the household articles, Bhadbhut (1981-82)

Frequency interval (Rs.)	NMB	CRM	Others	Total
Below 500	29(27.10)	34(72.34)	—	63(40.64)
501-1000	26(34.30)	8(17.02)	—	34(21.93)
1001-1500	15(14.02)	1(2.13)	—	16(10.32)
1501-2000	12(11.21)	1(2.13)	—	13(8.38)
2001-2500	8(7.48)	2(2.25)	—	10(6.45)
2501-3000	4(3.74)	—	—	4(2.58)
3001-3500	4(3.74)	—	—	4(2.58)
3501-4000	—	—	—	—
4001-4500	2(1.88)	—	—	2(1.29)
4501-5000	—	—	—	—
5001-5500	1(0.93)	—	—	1(0.65)
5501-6000	1(0.93)	1(2.13)	—	2(1.29)
6001-6500	1(0.93)	—	—	1(0.65)
6501-7000	1(0.93)	—	—	1(0.65)
7001-7500	2(1.88)	—	—	2(1.29)
7501-8000	—	—	—	—
8001-8500	—	—	—	—
8501-9000	—	—	—	—
9001-9500	—	—	—	—
9501-10000	—	—	1(100)	1(065)
10001 and above	1(0.93)	—	—	1(065)
Total	107(100.0)	47(100.0)	1(100.0)	155(100.0)

Note: 1. (—) indicates nil.
2. Figures in parentheses represent percentages to column total.

Rs. 1,000 account for 37 per cent in the village. Only one household in the other category owns articles valued at between Rs. 9,501 and 10,000 and one boat owner owns costly articles valued at more than Rs. 10,000.

Incomes and savings of fishermen households

The total income of the villagers during 1981-82 is estimated at Rs. 19,40,000 of which 90 per cent is accounted by boat owners only. It is quite surprising to note that more than 25 per cent of the income is estimated to be the savings in the village (Rs. 5,40,450). In the case of boat owner households it is 38 per cent while crew households and others made a dissaving of Rs. 1,16,450 and Rs. 1,780 respectively (Table 7.33).

TABLE 7.33

Occupationwise income: Expenditure and savings of fishermen in Bhadbhut

(in '000 Rupees)

Occupation	Income	Expenditure	Savings
1. NMB	1759.79	1092.11	658.68
2. CRM	181.71	298.16	—116.45
3. Others	7.50	9.28	—1.78
Total	1940.00	1399.55	540.45

It seems that the CRM households make these dissavings because of their overexpenditure on unnecessary items as well as some of them may be working on a share basis where they get fish towards their wages and not money. Hence their incomes may be underestimated and overall incomes of CRM households may be higher.

REFERENCES

1. The 1971 census figure for Bhadbhut village was 2,346 for both fishermen and non-fishermen. Separate population data for fishermen alone were not available. Therefore, the population data from livestock census and our census could not be compared with the 1971 census data to gauge the growth of the fishermen population in the village.
2. Bhadbhut is a large village. Only a small part of it is inhabited by the fishermen and the rest is inhabited by other castes and communities which are either involved in agriculture or village service

industries. In this chapter, unless otherwise stated, Bhadbhut refers to the fishing village.

3. The bag nets, otherwise known as dol nets, are predominant in estuarine fishing. As the name indicates, the net is of bag shape with varying mesh sizes.
4. Some of the boat-owning households may have fishing labourers. It should be noted that such households also have been classified as NMB owning households.
5. The estimate of total landings during 1981-82 is based on the sample information collected during the stay of the team in the village. On the basis of the information collected from boat owners, the total landing per boat has been estimated. The landing of fish per boat per annum so estimated is multiplied by the number of boats to obtain the total landings.

8

Kadekar-Padukare Village, Dakshin Kannada District, Karnataka

KADEKAR-PADUKARE[1], a coastal village, is situated in Dakshin Kannada District of Karnataka State. The fishing village has taken shape on the sand belt lying between river Udyavar and the Arabian Sea. The fishing village is part of the Kadekar main or the revenue village and is separated by river Udyavar from the main village. The main village of Kadekar alongwith the fishing village covers four blocks of the Nidamboor Gram Panchayat and the fishing village covers one block (Number 10). The two neighbouring villages which are again fishing villages along the coastline are Kuthpadi and Kidiyar (Fig. 8.1). The district headquarters (Mangalore) and the taluk headquarters (Udipi) are located at a distance of 50 km. and 6 km. respectively.

According to the 1971 census, the average number of rainy days was maximum in the month of July and the normal rainfall during this month is as high as 244.37 cm. The seasonal fluctuations in the temperature of the village recorded at Mangalore indicated small changes. Usually the highest temperature around 93.3°F is recorded in the month of February. The average highest temperature during the summer is about 92.2°F, and the average lowest temperature during the winter is about 66.2°F.

The location of the fishing village usually known as Padukare region was initially a sandy beach without any inhabitants. About 90 years ago, fishermen belonging to the Mogaveera

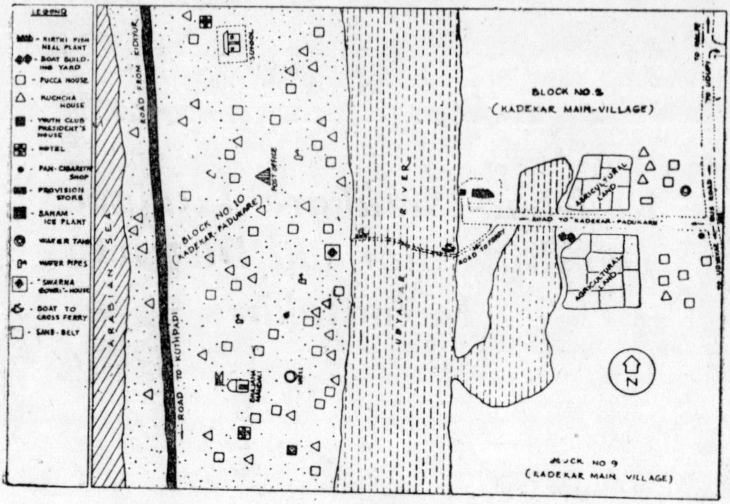

FIG. 8.1: *Map showing Kadekar-Padukare*

community came to the sandy beach and built thatched houses. The introduction of rampani mode of fishing had played an important role in the settlement of the fishermen in the village. Rampani fishing being a group and community activity, has attracted a large number of fishermen to choose this village to pursue their occupations. It was only in 1968 that the mechanization made inroads into the village with a trawler.

Kannada and Tulu are the principal languages spoken in the village, though Tulu[2] continues to be the most important spoken language of the fishermen community. However, after the introduction of educational facilities, some of the fishermen have started learning spoken and written Kannada. There are a few individuals, who are capable of communicating in Hindi and English also.

Population and caste

The population of Kadekar, according to the 1971 census, was 710 and the number of households 90. When this study was carried out in 1981, the population was 810 and the number of households 103. The population of the village has increased by 12.34 per cent and the households by 12.27 per cent during the decade 1971-1981. The average family size of the fishermen households was 7.88 persons per household in 1971 and remained almost the same in 1981 with 7.86 persons.

Mogaveera and Billava are the main fishermen communities in the village and both are Hindus. The people of the Mogaveera community were spread all over the district. Mogaveera is derived from the word *Mogera* which means a warrior who after the demolition of the kingdom continued to live on river belts and coastal belts and pursue their traditional occupation of fishing.[3] The Mogaveeras who have taken up fishing as their profession are called Marakalas. Some of them have taken up agriculture and others have become artisans. The Mogaveera was notified as a backward class by the Government of Karnataka. The community assumes a dominating role by virtue of its strong caste structure all over the district. They have caste associations at three levels: Gramasabha at the village level, Samyuktha Patna at the regional level and Mahajan Sabha at the district level. They have separate organizations to promote social, religious, recreational, cultural and welfare activities for the benefit of the community.

The traditional occupation of the Billavas used to be the extraction of toddy and agriculture. The Mogaveeras and Billavas were said to be the generations of two sisters who took up separate organizations. Both Mogaveeras and Billavas, it is learnt, have the same kind of clans based on Aliyasanthana or Aliyakattu. Hence all practices and rituals are found to be similar in the Mogaveera and Billava communities. However, the Billavas have their own separate caste associations called Seva Samithis.

Aliyasanthana or Aliyakattu is a system of inheritance through which the family descent is traced through the female line. The system entitles the women to assume important positions and equality with men in their family. The children use their mother's surname and the maternal uncle acts as the head of the family.[4]

The distribution of population and households, on the basis of our census taken in 1981, according to castes indicates that the Mogaveera caste, with 89 households and a population of 699, is the single most important caste in the village. Of the remaining 14 households, 13 belonged to the Billavas. The population of the Billavas was 101 members.

Village amenities, industries and infrastructure

The infrastructure can broadly be classified into: general and fishery related.

General infrastructure: No transport is available to the fishermen within the village. The main village is connected with the nearest town Udipi, 6 km. away, by bus and autorickshaw. In order to facilitate the fishermen to reach the village of Kadeker, a boat is operated between 6 and 9 p.m. The separate road along the coastal line called Padukare region, about 6 km. in length, is available for transport of stone or any other construction materials by lorries, tractors and such other vehicles. The nearest railway station is Mangalore. Boat service is regularly used by fishermen to reach the main village. Fish catches are being transported by the fishermen themselves as the quantities are not large. Catches of mechanized boats are landed at the Malpe fishing harbour.

Drinking water was supplied through 8 pipes since 1975. The facilities are, however, for only two hours in the morning. The village is electrified and 35 houses were so far given electricity connections. Malaria is very common in the village. Spraying of D.D.T. as a preventive measure has not yet been carried out in the village.

Most fishermen go outside the village for their basic needs, such as flour mill, sheller, pottery, cloth, medicines, vegetables, etc. Some 25 years ago the first provision store was started in the village and continues to operate.

Educational facilities were provided in 1923 with the setting up of a primary school, later upgraded to middle school, to cater to the fishermen children of not only this village but also from other villages on the coastline. The Government Primary School, located in a pucca building, presently has a strength of seven teachers, and 342 students.

The post office was established in the village in 1955 and provides most of the postal facilities. A telephone is available in the main village. More than 50 per cent of the saving bank accounts and 75 per cent of the recurring deposit accounts in the area are maintained by the fishermen of the village. The part-time post master is a permanent resident of the village.

A branch office of the Syndicate Bank is located in the main village to cater to the banking needs of the fishermen. The bank extends all banking facilities including lending to the fishermen. However, the bank has stopped lending for boats and gear since the past 3 to 4 years.

A Primary Health Centre was set up in 1964 at Hiriadka about 18 km. from the village. But the fishermen usually visit the nearest town of Udipi for medical aid as it has a number of public and private health centres. The main village has a rural maternity health centre run by K.M.C. Hospital, Manipal, and provides pre- and post-natal assistance. The centre also organizes a camp once a week in the village.

The Youth Club and the Mahila Mandali were established in 1957, the Bhajan Mandali came into existence during 1948 and the caste associations of the Mogaveera and Billava communities in the village have been functioning for the past 20 years. The caste associations in the village function as religious organizations and do not get involved in any political activities. The objectives and functions of other associations are limited to social activities.

The village is under the Gram Panchayat of Nidamboor and is represented by two members from the village. The political awareness among the fishermen of the village was found to be reasonably high.

Fishery-related infrastructure: Most of the fishery-related infrastructure does not exist in the village. Facilities like ice plants, cold storages and boat-building yards are available either at the main village or at Malpe. A few households have curing yards and normally sun-drying of fish is practised. The village has four fish merchants and a number of fish vendors. Fishermen were normally involved in marketing of fresh and dried fish in the nearby market.

The fisheries officials including the Fisheries Assistant had to be contacted either at Malpe or at Udipi. The fishermen had to go to Malpe to get even minor repairs done to their boats and engines. Most of the fishermen were enrolled as members of the fishermen co-operative society at Udyavara. The fishery-related infrastructure is relatively underdeveloped in the village as compared to other facilities and is perhaps due to the landing and berthing of mechanized boats of the village at Malpe. In fact we find that the situation has deteriorated with the shift in the place of landing as a consequence of mechanization.

Production equipment and occupation

The main occupation of the villagers is fishing, with 95 out of 103 households involved mainly in fishing and related activities. The major portion of the income came from fisheries.

Occupationwise distribution of the population is presented in Table 8.1. The gainfully employed 258 persons of the village in both fishery and non-fishery activities account for over 31.78 per cent of the population. Out of the 258 gainfully employed the fisheries sector accounts for about 90.70 per cent with 234 persons. The persons employed in fisheries activities have been classified into 11 categories. Crew with gear accounts for the maximum of the total population employed in fishery activities with 76 and is followed by NMB owner full-time fishing with individual ownership, MB owner full-time fishing with joint ownership and a few without gear with 45, 39 and 32 respectively. The number of individuals engaged in marketing fish in retail account for over 3 per cent of the total population with 25. Of the 234 employed in fishery-related activities the individuals belonging to the Mogaveera community accounted for the maximum with 220 persons. The involvement of the Billava community in fishery-related activities is observed to be relatively lower as compared to Mogaveeras in the village. Most of the crew required for operating both mechanized and non-mechanized boats in the village is supplied by the Mogaveera community.

The total working population of 234 in fisheries came from 95 households. There were a few households which are represented in multiple occupations of fisheries. For a systematic analysis[5] the households were divided into four categories: (i) Owners or partners of mechanized boats, (ii) Non-mechanized boat owners, (iii) Crew members, and (iv) others.

Of the total 103 households 23 owned or had a partnership in mechanized boats, 30 owned non-mechanized boats, 42 only supplied crew required for operating boats and 8 households

TABLE 8.1

Occupationwise distribution of population according to caste, Kadekar

Occupation	No. of persons from the			Total
	Mogaveera	Billava	Others	
I. *Economic Activities: Fishery*				
(a) MB—full-time fishing with own boats	4(0.57)	—	—	4(0.49)
(b) MB—full-time fishing with joint owners	35(5.01)	4(3.96)	—	39(4.81)
(c) NMB—full-time fishing with own boats	45(6.44)	—	—	45(5.55)
(d) NMB—full-time fishing with joint boats	1(0.014)	—	—	1(0.12)
(e) Crew with gear	76(10.87)	—	—	76(9.38)
(f) Crew without gear	27(3.86)	5(4.95)	—	32(3.95)
(g) Net mending/ repairing	2(0.29)	—	—	2(0.25)
(h) Rampani	3(0.43)	—	—	3(0.37)
(i) Marketing of fish—retail	21(3.00)	4(3.96)	—	25(3.09)
(j) Shell collection	5(0.72)	1(0.99)	—	6(0.74)
(k) Marketing of fish—wholesale	1(0.14)	—	—	1(0.12)
Sub-total	220(31.47)	14(13.86)	—	234(28.81)
II. *Economic Activities: Non-fishery*				
(a) Business	1(0.14)	1(0.99)	—	2(0.25)
(b) Service	11(1.57)	5(4.95)	—	16(1.97)
(c) Agricultural labour	2(0.29)	4(3.96)	2(20.00)	6(0.74)
Sub-total	14(2.00)	10(9.90)	2(20.00)	24(2.96)
III. *Non-Economic Activities:*				
(a) Dependants/Retired/ Not working	150(21.46)	18(17.82)	4(40.00)	172(21.24)
(b) Student	130(18.60)	27(26.73)	—	157(19.38)
(c) Housewife/House-work	185(26.47)	27(26.74)	4(40.00)	216(26.67)
(d) Others	—	5(4.95)	—	7(0.86)
Sub-total	465(66.53)	77(76.24)	8(80.00)	552(68.15)
Grand Total	699(100.00)	101(100.00)	10(100.00)	810(100.00)

Note : 1. (—) indicates nil.
2. Figures in parentheses are percentages to column total.

were mainly involved in activities other than fishing. Occupationwise distribution of fishermen households, according to caste, is presented in Table 8.2. Of the total 23 households

TABLE 8.2

Distribution of households and population according to the occupational pattern and caste, Kadekar (1981)

Occupational pattern	Caste				Total No. of persons
	Mogaveera	Billava	Others	Total	
1. MB	20 (22.47)	3 (23.08)	—	23 (22.30)	200 (24.70)
2. NMB	30 (33.71)	—	—	30 (29.10)	264 (32.60)
3. Crew	37 (41.57)	5 (38.46)	—	42 (40.80)	282 (34.80)
4. Others	2 (2.25)	5 (38.46)	1 (100.0)	8 (7.80)	64 (7.90)
Total	89 (100)	13 (100)	1 (100)	103 (100)	810 (100)

Note: 1. Figures in parentheses are percentages to column total.
2. (—) indicates nil.

owning/having partnership in mechanized boats, 20 were from the Mogaveera community and the rest from the Billavas. Of the total 13 households belonging to the Billava, three were MB owning or having partnership in MB boats, five were crew households and five were other households. The households belonging to others, whose main occupation is other than fishing, is over-represented by the Billavas with five (38.46 per cent) of the total 13 households while the other households account for only 7.80 per cent of the total households in the village with eight.

SOCIO-ETHNOGRAPHIC PROFILE OF THE FISHERMEN

In this section the social characteristics of the fishermen in the village are analysed. These characteristics include the family size and structure, level of education, age groupwise distribution, migration pattern and social participation of the fishermen and their households.

Family size and structure of households

The size of the fishermen households varies considerably. As indicated earlier the variation in the size of the households may be due to the tendency of some castes and fishing equipment owners[6] to live in extended households. The distribution of households, according to the family size and occupation, is presented in Table 8.3. It is observed that the equipment owning households (mechanized boat and non-mechanized boat

TABLE 8.3

Occupationwise distribution of households according to family size, Kadekar

Family size (members)	Number of households of				Total
	MB	NMB	Crew	Others	
1	—	—	—	—	—
2	—	—	2(4.8)	—	2(1.9)
3	—	—	3(7.1)	—	3(2.9)
4	—	—	3(7.1)	—	3(3.9)
5	1(4.4)	—	3(7.1)	1(12.5)	5(4.9)
6	5(21.7)	4(13.3)	4(9.5)	2(25.0)	15(14.6)
7	1(4.4)	3(10.0)	12(28.6)	—	16(15.6)
8	1(17.4)	5(16.7)	8(19.1)	—	17(16.5)
9	3(13.0)	7(23.4)	4(9.5)	3(37.5)	17(16.5)
10	3(13.0)	6(20.0)	1(2.4)	2(25.0)	12(11.7)
11	4(17.3)	4(13.3)	1(2.4)	—	9(8.7)
12	1(4.4)	1(3.3)	—	—	2(1.9)
13	1(4.4)	—	1(2.4)	—	2(1.9)
Total	23(100)	30(100)	(42(100)	8(100)	103(100)

Note : 1. (—) indicates nil.
2. Figures in parentheses represent percentages to column total.

owners) had larger families than the crew member households. The maximum family size was 13 and above members and several of these families had brothers and their families living together and fishing jointly. The average family size of households in the villages was 7.86 per cent. Over 86.4 per cent of households had 6 or more persons and only 4.9 per cent households had 1 to 3 persons. It is interesting to note that there were no fishery equipment owning households which had the household size of less than 5 members. The modal value of family sizes for MB owners, NMB owners, crew member and other households were 8 and 9 respectively.

The family structure consists of only 2 categories—nuclear and joint families. It was observed that while MBO and crew member households were approximately equally divided between those having nuclear families and those having joint families, the NMB owning households had a marked predominance of joint family system (Table 8.4).

TABLE 8.4

Distribution of households by occupational pattern and type of family, Kadekar

Occupational pattern	No. of households of		Total
	Nuclear	Joint	
1. MB	11 (23.91)	12 (21.05)	23 (22.33)
2. NMB	10 (21.74)	20 (35.09)	20 (29.13)
3. CRM	22 (47.83)	20 (35.09)	42 (40.78)
4. Others	3 (6.52)	5 (8.77)	8 (7.76)
Total	46 (100)	57 (100)	103 (100)

Note: Figures in parentheses represent percentages to column total.

Agewise distribution and educational level of the fishermen

The agewise distribution is shown in Table 8.5. It was observed that there are more males than females in the population among all occupational groups. At an aggregate level there were 433 males and 377 females. In terms of age groups it was observed that the ratio of males to females is substantially more in the case of population groups between 13—20, 21—30 and 31—45 years. The maximum number of male members belonged to MB owner households. Similarly the maximum number of male members in the case of NMB owner households, crew and other households were in the age groups of 21—30, 1—12 and 13—20 years respectively. The least number of males in general were in the age group above 46 for all the occupational groups. At the village as a whole the age group of less than 12 years accounts for maximum of the population with 225 and is followed by the age group of 21-30 years with a population of 179.

The frequency distribution of age gaps between the surviving children of same parents, according to the occupational pattern, is presented in Table 8.6. It was observed that in the case of NMB owning households, crew members and others, the age gap between the surviving children was lower than in the case of MB owning houses. In the case of MB owner households the age gap less than three years accounted for 85 per cent of the surviving children while in the case of NMB owner households and crew member households it was over 58 per cent.

The data on the educational level are analysed as per the higher level of education in a household. The highest qualification attained by any single member of the family is treated as the qualification attained by the household irrespective of the educational qualifications of other members of the family.

The distribution of households according to the occupational pattern and highest level of education in the household is presented in Table 8.7. Of the total 103 households 11 were not having any literates in their households. The highest number of households (34) had the higher secondary as the highest level of education and these households accounted for about 33 per cent of the total households in the village.

TABLE 8.5

Age and sex distribution of village population according to occupational pattern, Kadekar

Occupational age	01-12		13-20		21-30		31-45		46-55		56 and above		Total	
	M	F	M	F	M	F	M	F	M	F	M	F	M	F
1. MB	26 (23.00)	26 (23.21)	21 (22.11)	24 (33.80)	30 (30.00)	19 (24.05)	13 (19.12)	14 (22.95)	11 (36.67)	10 (28.57)	1 (3.70)	5 (26.32)	102 (23.56)	98 (25 99)
2. NMB	33 (29.20)	38 (33.93)	30 (31.58)	26 (36.62)	37 (37.00)	23 (29.11)	22 (32.35)	18 (29.51)	9 (30.00)	10 (28.57)	15 (55.56)	3 (15.79)	146 (33.72)	118 (31.30)
3. CRM	48 (42.48)	40 (35.71)	35 (36.84)	16 (22.54)	27 (27.00)	30 (37.97)	26 (38.24)	23 (37.71)	6 (20.00)	13 (37.14)	9 (33.33)	9 (47.37)	151 (34.87)	131 (34.75)
4. Others	6 (53.32)	8 (7.15)	9 (9.47)	5 (7.04)	6 (6.00)	7 (8.87)	7 (10.29)	6 (9.83)	4 (13.33)	2 (5.72)	2 (7.41)	2 (10.52)	34 (7.85)	30 (7.96)
Total	113 (100)	112 (100)	95 (100)	71 (100)	100 (100)	79 (100)	68 (100)	61 (100)	30 (100)	35 (100)	27 (100)	19 (100)	433 (100)	377 (100)

Note: Figures in parentheses represent percentages to column total.

TABLE 8.6

Frequency distribution of age gaps between surviving children for same parents according to occupational pattern, Kadekar

Age group interval	No. of instances in which the age gap falls in the stated interval for				Total
	MB	NMB	Crew	Others	
1.0-1.9	2 (5.00)	6 (16.22)	7 (13.46)	4 (44.45)	19 (13.78)
2.0-2.9	20 (50.00)	16 (43.24)	25 (48.08)	1 (11.11)	62 (44.93)
3.0-3.9	10 (25.00)	13 (35.14)	6 (11.54)	—	29 (21.01)
4.0-4.9	5 (12.50)	1 (2.70)	9 (17.31)	1 (11.11)	16 (11.59)
5.0-5.9	2 (5.00)	1 (2.70)	4 (7.69)	2 (22.72)	9 (6.52)
6.0 and above	1 (2.50)	—	1 (1.92)	1 (11.11)	3 (2.17)
Total	40 (100)	37 (100)	52 (100)	9 (100)	138 (100)

Note: 1. (—) indicates nil.
2. Figures in parentheses represent percentages to column total.

Further, there were about 11 households which had at least one graduate in their households. Of the 11 households with the highest level of education as graduation, four were from others, three were MB owner/partner households and two each of NMB and crew households. Further, all the 23 MBO households had at least one person with at least primary education. Households belonging to MBO are relatively highly educated as compared to NMB and crew households.

Migration and typology of migrants

Table 8.8 shows the distribution of households by occupational patterns and birthplace location of the head of the households. Most of the households belonged to the same village, about 5

TABLE 8.7

Distribution of households according to occupational pattern and highest level of education in the household, Kadekar

Level of education	Number of households of				Total
	MB	NMB	CRM	Others	
1. Illiterate	—	5 (16.7)	5 (11.9)	1 (12.5)	11 (10.7)
2. Primary	2 (8.7)	5 (16.7)	17 (40.5)	2 (25.0)	26 (25.2)
3. Middle	5 (21.7)	7 (23.3)	9 (21.4)	— (12.5)	21 (33.0)
4. Higher Secondary	13 (56.5)	11 (36.7)	9 (21.4)	1 (12.5)	34 (33.0)
5. Graduate and above	3 (13.1)	2 (6.6)	2 (4.8)	4 (50.0)	11 (10.7)
Total	23 (100)	30 100)	42 (100)	8 (100)	103 (100)

Notes: 1. (—) indicates nil.
2. Figures in parentheses represent percentages to column total.

TABLE 8.8

Distribution of households by occupational pattern and birthplace location of the household head, Kadekar

Location of birthplace	Number of households which had their heads' birthplace indicated for				Total
	MB	NMB	CRM	others	
1. Same village	21 (91.3)	29 (9.67)	41 (67.9)	7 (87.5)	98 (95.1)
2. Outside the village	2 (8.7)	—	1 (2.4)	1 (12.5)	4 (3.9)
3. Outside the district	—	1 (3.3)	—	—	1 (1.0)

Note: 1. (—) indicates nil.
2. Figures in parentheses represent percentages to column total.

per cent of the households had migrated to the village from other places.

During the census we took in 1981 we found no locked households. However, this may not suggest the non-existence of short-term outmigration. The migration is in the form of migration of boat alongwith crew without distributing the household establishment in the village. The duration of migration is less than 40 days spread over two or three absences from the normal place of operation. About 55 per cent of the mechanized boats outmigrated from the village.

Social participation of fishermen

The occupationwise distribution of members and households having at least one member in various organizations is presented in Table 8.15.

Fishermen co-operative society: In the village 67.17 per cent households were members of the fishermen co-operative societies. In terms of their occupational groups 76.7 per cent of NMBO households had membership in the fishermen co-operative society, followed by MBO households with 69.7 per cent. Among the members in the society at the village 54.7 per cent of the households enrolled themselves as members during the past 6 to 15 years. Fifty per cent of the MBO households, 52.2 per cent of the NMBO households and 58.3 of the crew member households had been members for the past 6 to 15 years.

Youth club: At the village level 31 per cent of the households had membership of the Youth Club but the representation of these households in the activities of the Youth Club was very dismal. It was observed that the representation of MBO households was very high in the activities of the Youth Club. Among the members of the Youth Club 37.5 per cent of them were continuing as members for the past 6 to 15 years. Of the MBO households 33.3 per cent had joined the Youth Club about 16 to 25 years back. As against this only 16.7 per cent NMBO households had enrolled themselves as members of the Youth Club, about 16 to 25 years back. About 33.3 per cent of the NMBO households has joined the Youth Club in recent years (1 to 5 years). Of the crew member households 44.5

per cent had the membership of the Youth Club for the past 6 to 15 years.

Membership of caste associations: The Mogaveera and Billava communities have their own caste associations. The associations which have been in existence for the past 26 years, are affiliated to their caste associations at the district and regional levels. At the village level, 76.7 per cent of the households were members of the caste associations. About 95.7 per cent of the MBO households, 73.3 per cent of the NMBO households and 69 per cent of the crew member households have had their membership of the caste association for the past 6 to 15 years.

Others: The Gram Panchayat, Nidumboor, has two members from the villages and both are MBs. Besides the above cited organizations/associations, the village has Bhajan Mandals and Mahila Mandalis which can be categorized under other associations. At the village level 60.2 per cent of the households were members of these associations and 78.3 per cent of the MBO households had their membership. Further, about 50 per cent of them had enrolled themselves as members about 6 to 15 years back.

MECHANIZATION: ITS IMPACT ON PRODUCTION SYSTEM

In this section we shall try to present the technology of production, ownership of productive assets, production patterns, output, incomes and distribution of gain, and disposal of fish landings.

Technology of production

We find in the village small dugout canoes in the traditional sector and trawlers and purse-seiners in the modern sector.

Traditional sector: The level and type of technology in the traditional sector of marine fishing in the village was never the same over the time horizon of last 15 to 20 years. It has been changing because of the rapid changes in the modern sector. The traditional sector of marine fishing in the village presently uses only one type of fishing craft, i.e. canoes. The canoes can be further subdivided into two categories: dugout canoes and plank built canoes.[7] However, most of the canoes in the

TABLE 8.9

Occupationwise distribution of households and members in various social organizations, Kadekar (1981-82)

Occupation	Fishermen Co-op. Society		Youth club		Caste association	
	No. of members	No. of households representing	No. of members	No. of households representing	No. of members	No. of households representing
1. MBO	35 (28.0)	16 (30.0)	18 (42.9)	12 (37.5)	53 (32.9)	22 (27.8)
2. NMBO	50 (40.0)	23 (35.9)	8 (9.0)	6 (18.0)	50 (31.1)	22 (27.8)
3. Crew	39 (31.2)	24 (37.5)	9 (21.4)	9 (28.1)	45 (27.9)	29 (36.8)
4. Others	1 (0.8)	1 (1.6)	7 (16.7)	5 (15.6)	13 (8.1)	6 (7.6)
Total	125 (100.0)	64 (100.0)	42 (100.0)	32 (100.0)	161 (100.0)	79 (100.0)

Note: Figures in parentheses are percentages to column total.

village are dugout canoes. They are generally less than 25 feet in length, and use either gill nets or cast nets for fishing. Rampani fishing, otherwise known as shore-seine fishing, is almost fully absent in the state. To understand the reasons for the sweeping away of rampani fishing with the introduction of purse-seine fishing in the state, we need to understand the operating characteristics of rampani and purse-seine fishing.

The rampani fishing unit consists of a very long fishing net (usually owned by 75 to 100 individuals in small pieces), two smaller plank built canoes of a length less than 35 feet and a bigger canoe of a length over 55 feet. The fishing with rampani consists of locating the fish shoals first. After the locating of a fish shoal near the shore it is encircled by the net from the shore with the help of a large rampani boat and the fish is caught with the help of other nets in the encircled portion. It requires a crew ranging from 50 to 100 depending upon the size of the net.[8]

Mechanized sector: The mechanized sector consists of trawlers and purse-seiners. The operating characteristics of a trawlers are similar to those explained in the Chorwad village profile earlier (see page 141). The resource bases of trawlers were different to those of non-mechanized boats using different types of gear. However, the location of the resource bases of both traditional sector and trawlers is more or less the same.

The operation of a purse-seine nets is almost the same to that of rampani. However, purse-seine using a mechanized boat is operated on the high seas while rampani is operated from the shore. The resource bases in terms of the species of rampani and purse-seine are the same. This similarity of the resource base has resulted in the conflicting of interests and extinction of rampani fishing. The extinction of rampani fishing has taken place mainly because of the catching of fish on the high seas before they reach the regions within the reach of the rampani nets. The effective catching of the pelagic fish—the mainstay of rampani nets—on the high seas by purse-seines is facilitated by the mechanization of the fishing craft.

The mechanization of the fishing craft in the village was initiated[9] with the introduction of two trawlers in 1975. The impetus for mechanization of fishing craft in the village has been derived from the demonstration effects of the trawlers in other parts of the state with good economic returns and a high rate of capital subsidy to the extent of 25 per cent of the total cost. The purse-seiners were introduced in the village subsequently in 1977. This was soon after the intensive operations of purse-seine boats on an experimental basis by the research organizations in the year 1974 in the state. In the initial stages of the introduction of purse-seiners the state government extended a capital subsidy to the extent of 33.33 per cent of the total cost of the net and 25 per cent of the cost of the boat to promote fishing with purse-seiners.

The village represents a case of very high degree of mechanization with ownership or partnership of villagers in 11 trawlers and 13 purse-seiners in 1981. Further, in 1981 the villagers owned about 40 non-mechanized boats. The effective number of mechanized boats in the village was less than the figures mentioned above since a few of them were jointly owned by the fishermen of the village and the neighbouring villages. After discounting for the share of the joint owners from other villages in the boats shared by the villagers we found that there were 9.1 trawlers and 7.2 purse-seiners[10] in the village in 1981.

When we looked at the historical background of the boat-and-gear mix in the village, we found that during the pre-mechanization period till 1970 there were about six rampani units effectively operating in the village. The number of non-mechanized boats was as high as it was in 1981, say, around 40 boats. With the introduction of mechanized boats in the village and in other places the number of rampani units and their intensity of operations have decreased. The number of rampani units in the village decreased from six in 1970 to zero in 1980.

The distribution of mechanized and non-mechanized boats, according to the year of purchase, is presented in Table 8.10. The first set of two trawlers was purchased by the villagers in 1975 and a majority (4 out of 11) of trawlers were purchased in the year 1980. In the case of purse-seiners 5 out of a total of 13 boats were acquired by the villagers in 1978, a year after the introduction of purse-seines to the mechanization scene of fishing craft in the village with a modest two craft. The distribution of non-mechanized craft according to the year of purchase indicated an even distribution over the period—from 1969 to 1979.

The fishing gear used by the fishermen in the village consisted of gill nets, cast nets, on-trawl nets and purse-seine nets. While the first two types of nets are usually associated with the non-mechanized boats, the latter two are associated with the mechanized boats. The mesh size of gill nets varied from ½ to 4 inch. The distribution of gill nets owned by different types of households according to the mesh size in the village is presented in Table 8.11. An overwhelming percentage (50 per cent) of the gill nets in the village was having a mesh size between 1 and 2 inch. Usually, these nets are used for catching small-size pelagic fish such as sardines, cluepeids, mackerel, etc. Of the total 24 gill nets five were owned by mechanized boat

TABLE 8.10

Distribution of different types of boats according to the year of purchase, Kadekar

Year of acquiring*	Mechanized boat		NMB (Dugout canoe) below 25 ft.
	Trawler	Purse-seiner	
Up to 1969	—	—	8
1970	—	—	4
1971	—	—	—
1972	—	—	1
1973	—	—	3
1974	—	—	—
1975	2	—	3
1976	—	—	2
1977	2	2	5
1978	2	5	4
1979	—	1	—
1980	4	1	7
1981	1	4	3
Total	11	13	40

Note: 1. (—) indicates nil.
2. *Indicates the year of purchase of boat but not the year of motorization.

TABLE 8.11

Distribution of gill nets owned by different households according to the mesh size, Kadekar (1981)

Mesh size (in inch)	Gill nets owned by the households			Total
	MBO	NMBO	CRM	
0-1.0	1(20.00)	3(30.00)	1(11.11)	5(20.83)
1.1-2.0	2(40.00)	3(30.00)	7(77.78)	12(50.00)
2.1-3.0	2(40.00)	3(30.00)	1(11.11)	6(25.00)
3.1-4.0	—	1(10.00)	—	1(4.17)
Total	5(100.00)	10(100.00)	9(100.00)	24(100.00)

Note: 1. (—) indicates nil.
2. Figures in parentheses are percentages to column total.

owner households[11], 10 by NMBO households and 9 by crew member households.

The total number of cast nets in the village was estimated to be 30 as per our census taken in 1981. Of the total 30 caste nets 21 were owned by NMBO households and the rest by crew member households. The mesh size of the cast nets was uniform with ½ inch for almost all nets. Further it was observed that few of the cast nets were operated in combination with gill nets in different seasons while there were a few (16) exclusive cast net units which have operated only cast nets during the entire fishing season.

The number of trawl nets and purse-seine nets owned by the villagers were 26 and 14 respectively. The mesh size of the trawl nets, as indicated earlier, varies from mouth to code end. The mesh sizes of purse-seine nets were in the mesh range of 1 to 2 inch. It should, however, be noticed that the variations in the mesh sizes of trawl nets and purse-seine nets in the village were relatively less as compared to gill nets in the village. The length of purse-seine nets in the village was from 2,000 to 2,300 metres while all the trawl nets were less than 24 metres. All the gill nets in the village were less than 500 feet in length.

Ownership of productive assets

As indicated earlier, the fishing craft in the village are owned by the fishermen either individually or jointly.[12] Individual ownership has been observed to be predominant with regard to non-mechanized boats while collective ownership is an important aspect of the mechanized boats. All the 40 non-mechanized boats in the village were observed to be individually owned. Of the total 11 trawlers and 13 purse-seiners in the village only three trawlers and four purse-seiners are individually owned and the rest are collectively owned.

Of the six possible ownership patterns[13] only four patterns were observed in the village. They are: (i) Individual owner, owner worker and non-owner partner; (ii) Individual owner, owner non-worker and non-owner partner; (iii) Collective owner, owner worker and non-worker partner; and (iv) Collective owner, owner non-worker and non-owner partner.

The first is the most predominant in the case of non-mechanized boats and accounts for more than 90 per cent of these boats. The remainder of the 10 per cent boats have a ownership pattern of the second type. All the mechanized boats having individual ownership can again be classified as of pattern two. All the boats but for one with collective ownership[14] were having a ownership pattern of the third type. There was only one trawler which was collectively owned but operated by all the employed crew on a sharing basis.

The other aspect of the ownership of productive assets in fishing can be to compare the equipment-owning households and non-owning households. In Kadekar 54 of the 103 households, among themselves, owned the boats in the village. Distribution of fishery assets owning households, according to ownership of or partnership in different types of boats and castes, is presented in Table 8.12. There were 31 households owing non-mechanized boats alone and all of them belonged

TABLE 8.12

Distribution of fishery assets owning households according to ownership/partnership in different types of boats and castes, Kadekar (1981)

Ownership/Partnership in type of boats	Caste		Total
	Mogaveera	Billava	
1. Purse-seine+Trawler +NMB	1(100.00)	—	1(100.00)
2. Purse-seine+Trawler	2(100.00)	—	2(100.00)
3. Purse-seine+NMB	4(100.00)	—	4(100.00)
4. Purse-seine	8(100.00)	—	8(100.00)
5. Trawler+NMB	4(100.00)	—	4(100.00)
6. Trawler	1(25.00)	3(75.00)	4(100.00)
7. NMB	31(100.00)	—	31(100.00)
Total	51(94.44)	3(5.56)	54(100.00)

Note: 1. (—) indicates nil.
2. Figures in parentheses are percentages to row totals.

to the Mogaveera caste. On the other extreme there was one household again belonging to the Mogaveera caste, which had a partnership or ownership of trawler, purse-seiner and non-mechanized boats. All the three Billava households collectively or individually owned trawlers only.

The above analysis, however, does not indicate the inequality of the ownership of productive assets particularly in view of the collective ownership in varying levels of mechanized boats. Therefore, to assess the inequality of ownership of productive assets, the Gini ratio for distribution of the productive assets in value[15] terms has been computed. The estimated value of the Gini coefficient for the distribution of the value of productive assets over the households in the village has been found to be 0.8288. The estimated value of Gini coefficient indicates a highly inequitable distribution of fishing assets in the village. Figure 8.2 shows the Lorenz curve of the distribution of fishery assets in the village. Despite the collective ownership of boats after the mechanization of fishing craft, the distribution of fishing assets in terms of value has been highly biased towards a few well-to-do households. The highly inequitable distribution of fishing assets over the households notwithstanding the collective ownership of mechanized boats has been mainly because of the capital-intensive technology of fish production with purse-seiners, and till partnership of members of a few well-to-do households in the ownership of mechanized boats. Another qualitative change that has taken place in the fishing activities of the village relates to the collective participation of the households from different villages for fish production using a single unit of production.

Production pattern of fish: Present and past

The specieswise estimates of marine fish landings and value of landings during pre-mechanization (1968-69) and current (1981-82) periods in the village is presented in Table 8.13. The total landings in the village increased from 2,162 tonnes during 1968-69 to 3,096 tonnes during 1981-82. Further, the value of the total landings at current prices was Rs. 11,65,300 during 1968-69 and Rs. 53,30,900 during 1981-82. The increase in the value of the landings has increased over 78.14 per cent between 1968-69 and 1981-82 while the landings have increased by only

TABLE 8.13

Specieswise estimates of marine fish landings and value of landings during pre-mechanization (1968-69) and current (1981-82) periods, Kadekar

(*Qty. in tonnes*)
(*Value in '000 Rupees*)

Species	Pre-mechanization period (1968-69)			Landings and value of landings during current (1981-82) period by							
				Mechanized boats*				Non-mechanized boats			
	Qty.	Price** per tonne	Value	Qty.	Price**	Value	Qty.	Price**	Value	Qty.	Value
1. Oil Sardines	908	175	158.9	1204	580	698.4	53	580	30.7	1257	729.1
2. Indian Mackerel	576	1029	592.7	550	3740	2057.0	78	3740	291.7	628	2346.7
3. Pomfret	8	960	7.7	62	6230	386.3	13	6230	81.0	75	467.3
4. Seer fish	46	1445	66.5	25	5500	137.5	32	5500	176.0	57	313.5
5. Catfish	188	628	118.1	328	1200	393.6	22	1200	26.4	350	420.0
6. Prawns	8	4165	33.3	35	13850	484.8	2	13850	27.7	37	512.5
7. Others	418	450	188.1	679	780	529.6	13	780	10.1	692	539.8
Total	2162	—	1165.3	2883	—	4687.2	213	—	643.6	3096	5330.9

Note: * The landings of the mechanized boats in the village are not taking place in village in view of the lack of availability of landing facilities. Further the villagers have partnership in 13 purse-seiners and 11 trawlers but the total share of the villagers is equivalent to about 7 purse-seiners and 9 trawlers.

**The information on prices has been compiled on the basis of the data on landings and value of landings obtained from the Assistant Director of Fisheries, Malpe. However, the price data have been changed whenever the data appeared to be unrealistic.

30.17 per cent during the same period. Further, the species composition of the total landings did not change much with the introduction of mechanized craft in the village. In quantity terms oil sardines, mackerel, and catfish accounted for more than 70 per cent of the total landings both during pre- and post-mechanized periods. During both pre- and post-mechanized periods mackerel accounted for the maximum of the total value of landings.

Another qualitative change which has taken place after the mechanization of the fishing craft in regard to the pattern of landings relates to the shift in the location of fish landings. The landings of mechanized craft normally take place in the nearby fishing harbour, viz. Malpe, in view of the lack of availability of landing facilities while the total landings during the pre-mechanization period used to take place in the village only.

Household income and distribution of gains

For estimating the household income from fishing for each of the households it is necessary to estimate the return to capital invested in fishing equipment and to the family labour employed on the boat. In addition, the salary or share earned by a household member in the other boats needs to be added to the above. The details of the measurement of household income from various sources and its distribution over castes and occupations is presented below:

Measurement of household income: The majority of the households in the village derived their income from fishing alone while others derived from both fishing and other activities. The income from other activities is estimated on the basis of the information obtained from the enumeration of the households. The income from fishing is obtained on the basis of the detailed economics of different types of boats and returns to labour.

Table 8.14 gives the quarterwise estimated gross value of output per boat of different types of boats in the village. The total value of output per boat in the case of dugout canoes was only Rs. 17.86,000 while in the case of trawlers and purse-seiners it was Rs. 1,32,320, and Rs. 5,45,850 respectively. The distribution of the total value of landings over the four

TABLE 8.14

Quarterwise gross value of output per boat of different types, Kadekar (1981-82)

(in Rupees)

Quarter	Gross value of output in stated quarter for Trawlers	Purse-seiners	Output canoes* of length between 15 and 25 ft.
July-September	20450 (15.45)	60390 (11.06)	2680 (15.00)
October-December	60675 (45.85)	230630 (42.26)	8590 (48.10)
January-March	35985 (27.20)	160450 (29.39)	4320 (24.19)
April-June	15210 (11.50)	94380 (17.29)	2270 (12.71)
Total	132320 (100.00)	545850 (100.00)	17860 (100.00)

Note: 1. Figures in parentheses represent percentages to column total.
2. *The information relates to the boats operated throughout all seasons. Some of the boats are operated only during the off-season in riverine estuarine waters, and these are not considered.

quarters was more or less similar for all the types of boats. The October-December quarter accounted for the maximum of the total value of output for all types of boats and the share of the quarter in the total was in the range of 48.1 per cent for dugout canoes to 42.26 per cent for purse-seiners. The itemwise average variable cost per day for different types of boats is presented in Table 8.15. It can be seen from the table that the variable cost per day for purse-seiners is Rs. 690 as against only Rs. 229.85 for trawlers and Rs. 17.40 for non-mechanized boats. In the case of purse-seiners the major items of variable costs are fuel, oil, food expenditure for the crew members, lubricants, cost of non-mending yarn, and ice and water. This pattern by and large was observed for the trawlers also except

TABLE 8.15

Itemwise variable cost per day for different types of boats Kadekar (1981-82)

(*in Rupees*)

Items	Expenditure on stated items for		
	Trawlers	Purse-seiners	Dugout canoes of length between 15 and 25 ft.
1. Fuel Oil	173.50	488.50	—
2. Mobile Oil and other Lubricants	18.00	35.00	—
3. Wages (daily) to labourers	5.50	—	2.60
4. Ice and Water	5.65	28.50	—
5. Food Expenditure for Crew	8.40	85.50	3.80
6. Cost of net-mending yarn	3.50	35.50	8.25
7. Others	15.30	17.00	2.75
Total	229.85	690.00	17.40

that the food expenditure for the crew was relatively small. In the case of the dugout canoes about 50 per cent of the variable cost per day was on the cost of yarn for repairing the net.

The itemwise annual fixed costs for different types of boats in the village are given in Table 8.16. In the case of purse-seiners the annual expenditure by way of fixed cost worked out to be as high as Rs. 3,16,725. In the case of trawlers this expenditure was about Rs. 72,356. As against this in the case of dugout cases the cost was only Rs. 12,022. The estimates of gross and net returns of different types of boats are presented in Table 8.17. It can be seen from the table that the net incomes are the highest in the case of purse-seiners (Rs. 94,575) followed by trawlers (Rs. 15,143.25) and non-mechanized boats (Rs. 2,358). In terms of the rates of return we find that it is 20.74 per cent on investment in purse-seiners, 15.93 per cent in the case of non-mechanized boats and only 10.43 per cent in the case of trawlers.

TABLE 8.16

Itemwise annual fixed costs for different type of boats, Kadekar (1981-82)

(in Rupees)

Item	Annual expenditure on stated items for		
	Trawler	Purse-seiners	Dugout canoes of length between 15 and 25 ft.
1. Salary to Crew[1]	39696.00	163755.00	8930.00
2. Repairs and Maintenance	4050.00	15390.00	572.00
3. Dry Docking and Oil Painting	1560.00	3560.00	590.00
4. Insurance	2370.00	8550.00	—
5. Interest on borrowed capital[2]	10380.00	37620.00	—
6. Depreciation[3]	12450.00	66300.00	1480.00
7. Others	1850.00	21550.00*	450.00
Total	72356.00	316725.00	12022.00

Note: 1. The salaries of crew members include salaries of total crew required, i.e. the salary of the owner-operator is estimated at market rates and added to the paid-out wages. In all the cases the wages to the crew are paid in the form of the share from the total gross returns. The share of crew in the case of trawlers and purse-seiners is 30 per cent of the gross returns and in the case of non-mechanized boats it is 50 per cent.

2. For working out the interest on borrowed capital it has been assumed that about 75 per cent of the total investment is borrowed from banks or any other formal lending sources at the rate of 11 per cent in the case of trawlers and purse-seiners, and in the case of non-mechanized boats no formal loan is available.

3. For estimating the depreciation the life of hull and engine is taken as 15 and 12 years respectively. In the case of gear the life is taken to be four years in case of purse-seine nets, one year in the case of trawl nets and three years in the case of gill nets.

4. *includes the hiring charges of carrier boats.

TABLE 8.17

Gross and net earnings per unit of different type of fishing craft per annum, Kadekar (1981-82)

Particulars	Trawlers	Purse-seiners	Dugout canoes of length between 15 and 25 ft.
1. Gross Earnings	132320.00	545850.00	17860.00
2. (a) Expenditure of variable costs per annum	44820.75	134550.00	3480.00
(b) Annual Fixed Costs*	72356.00	316725.00	12022.00
Sub-total	117176.75	451275.00	15502.00
3. Net Income**	15143.25 (5843.25)	94575.00 (80875.00)	2358.00 (3838.00)
4. Rate of Return on Investment	10.43%	20.74%	15.93%

Note: 1. *Estimated by multiplying the number of fishing days by the average daily expenditure. The number of fishing days for trawlers, purse-seiners and dugout canoes were estimated to be 195, 195, 200 respectively.

2. **Excluding the loan repayment instalments. Figures in parentheses of net income column indicate the income after allowing for loan repayment but after adding back the depreciation.

After working out the economics of different types of boats, the incomc accruing to all the households from fishing has been estimated taking the partnership/ownership of fishing craft by each household and the returns to labour into account. As indicated earlier, the income from other than fishing activities has been estimated for each of the households on the basis of the household enumeration. Thus, for working out the total income according to each household, the income from fishing and other activities has been added. Further, while working out the total income of a household, the occupation of every person gainfully employed has been taken into account.

The distribution of income: The distribution of income according to occupations and sources in the village is presented in Table 8.18. The mechanized boat owning households

TABLE 8.18

Distribution of income according to occupation, Kadekar (1981-82)

Occupation	Income			Per house-hold	Per capita
	Fishery	Non-fishery	Total		
1. MB	1113266 (53.34)	17400 (15.06)	1130666 (51.33)	49159.39	5653.33
2. NMB	536252 (25.69)	16800 (14.54)	553052 (25.11)	184305.07	2094.89
3. Crew	433573 (20.77)	20740 (17.95)	454313 (20.63)	10816.98	1611.04
4. Others	4000 (0.20)	60620 (52.45)	64620 (2.93)	8077.50	1009.69
Total	2087091 (100)	115560 (100)	2202651 (100)	21384.96	2719.32

Note: Figures in parentheses represent percentages to column total.

accounted for over 51 per cent of the total income of all the households while they accounted for less than 23 per cent of the total households. The per capita and per household incomes were highest for MB owner households with Rs. 5,633 and Rs. 49,153 respectively. The per capita income was in the range of Rs. 1,009 for others to Rs. 5,653 for MB owner households. The MB households were having the economic dominance in view of their higher income and ownership of assets.

As a summary measure of income inequality, the Gini ratio for the income distribution has been computed. The Gini ratio of income inequality was 0.5048 while it was over 0.8288 for assets inequality. This indicates that the returns to labour

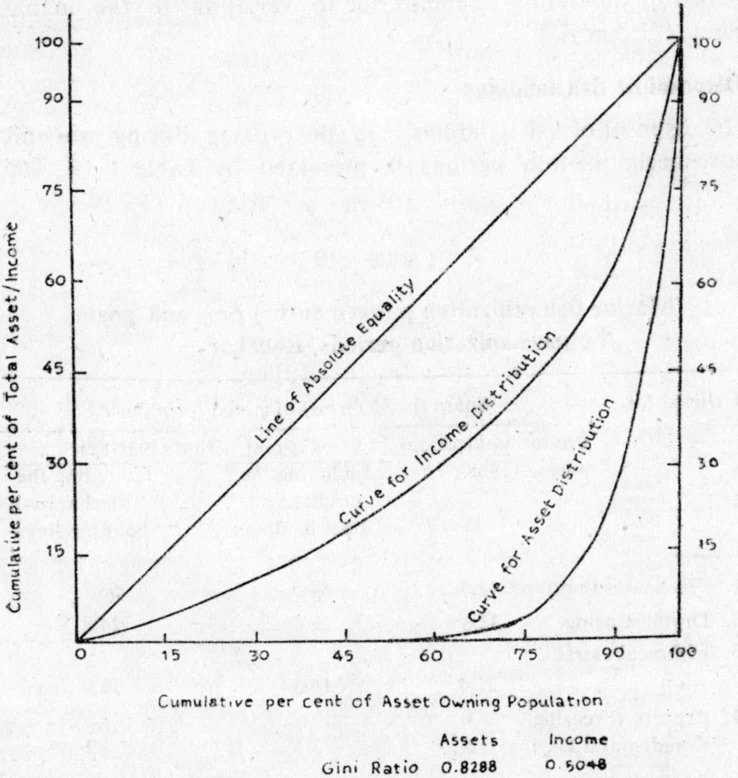

FIG. 8.2: *Lorenz Curve for assets and income distribution, Kadekar (1981-82)*

were comparatively higher as compared to other villages. However, the income inequality in the village was higher as compared to the income inequality in the highly mechanized village in Gujarat, i.e. Chorwad. Here it should also be emphasized that inequality of income on the basis of household income may be higher as compared to income inequality on the basis of personal income because the larger households have a higher income. Further, the income inequality on the basis of the economics worked out for each boat in the village would have been higher as compared to the one computed on the basis of averages. This variation may be mainly because of the variations in gross and net returns of similar types of boats owned by different households due to variations in the managerial efficiency.

Disposal of fish landings

The disposal of fish landings[16] in the village during pre- and post-mechanization periods is presented in Table 8.19. The

TABLE 8.19

Marine fish utilization pattern during pre- and post-mechanization periods, Kadekar

Utilized for	Share (in % terms) of stated form during		
	Pre-mechanization period (1968-69	Current period (1981-82)	
		Including the mechanized boat landings	Excluding the mechanized boat landings
1. Fresh consumption	42.5	54.5	58.2
2. Drying/Curing	32.8	25.6	24.8
3. Fishmeal extraction	23.4	16.3	15.9
4. Exports (Freezing/Canning and Drying)	1.3	3.6	1.1
Total	100.00	100.00	100.00

fresh consumption accounts for maximum of the total landing with 42.5 per cent during the pre-mechanization period and 54.5 per cent during the post-mechanization period. Further, the utilization pattern after the introduction of mechanized boats in the village has undergone many changes. For example, utilization in the fresh form has increased from 42.5 per cent during the pre-mechanization period to 54.5 per cent during the post-mechanization period. The share of dry fish and fish for meal extraction has gone down by about 7.2 per cent and 7.1 per cent respectively during the same period. The changes in the utilization pattern of marine fish landings in the village to a large extent were due to the improved infrastructure for the fish landings during the post-mechanized period in Kadekar and the nearby harbour. The changes in the utilization pattern due to variations in the species composition after the mechanization of fishing craft only relate to the increased share of exports.

MARKETS IN THE VILLAGE

In this section, we shall now examine the markets for inputs, labour, credit and output in the village with a view to understanding the changes in these markets after the introduction of mechanized craft in the village.

Market for inputs

The various inputs considered for analysis in this section relate to the supply of craft and gear, fuel oil and lubricants, ice and facilities for landing and berthing of boats. At the outset it should be noted that almost all the above inputs are required for the operation of mechanized craft only while the supply of boats and gear relate to both mechanized and non-mechanized sectors.

Boats are bought from boat-building yards or from fishermen of either the same village or other villages. The latter type of transactions may not add to the stock of the boats in the state. Karnataka, in general, and South Kanara district, in particular, is a pioneer supplier of non-mechanized boats to almost all the maritime states in the country.

Of the 43 boats for which we have data, 13 were purse-seiners, 11 trawlers, and the remainder dugout canoes. There were 39 new and four old boats. Of the four old boats, three were trawlers and one dugout canoe. The old trawlers were in general used as carrier boats for purse-seiners. All the boats have been acquired from within the district. Further, the majority of the non-mechanized craft were purchased/constructed within the village while the majority of mechanized craft were purchased/constructed by boat builders outside the village but within the district. Thus, it clearly indicates the shift in market location for boats after the introduction of mechanized craft. The size and structure of boat-building yards[17] in the district indicate that the boat builders in the district are in theory operating in a fairly competitive market and, therefore, one might expect them to charge lower prices for boats. However, because of the rising timber prices the prices of boats have increased three to fourfold during the post-mechanization period. There are many companies which supply marine diesel engines but Ashok Leyland and Kirloskar account for over 80 per cent of the diesel engines installed in purse-seiners and trawlers of the district and village. The engines are directly acquired by boat builders for installation in boats supplied by them to fishermen. The market for marine diesel engines in the district and the village is a new development in the post-mechanization period.

Two important changes in the market for net mending and repairing yarn in the district as well as the village during the post-mechanization period relate to the improved technology of production of yarn and the market concentration for nets and yarn.[18] Though the developments in the market for nets and gear appear to be independent it may be argued that the developments in this sector may be mainly because of the need for improved gear for fishing with mechanized craft.

There are two principal sources for supply of yarn for mending and repairing of nets in the village. They are the co-operative society and private traders. In addition, fishermen also buy yarn from Udipi and Malpe. However, the co-operatives supply the bulk of the yarn for repairing nets while private traders dominate in the supply of yarn for mending nets or readily mended nets. Both nylon and synthetic twine are used for mending and repairing.

High-speed diesel is used for operating both types of mechanized craft in the village. The principal sources of diesel are the private diesel pumps in the landing centre. In addition, the fishermen co-operative federation of South Kanara also supplies diesel. The supplies by the federation were found to be predominant during periods of short supply.

Landing and berthing facilities for mechanized boats in the village are available at the Malpe fishing harbour. However, these facilities were found to be inadequate at Malpe. The service facilities for boats and gear are available once again in Malpe. The boat owners of the village felt that the service charges were higher particularly during the peak season as compared to other service centres at other assembling centres mainly because of the short supply of facilities.

Market for labour

As already said, the productive assets in the village are owned by only 51.46 per cent of the households while the rest derive income by selling labour. In this section we will examine the selling of labour time by the households with particular reference to fishing labourers in the village.

The share contract is the prominent pattern in hiring labourers in the case of both mechanized and non-mechanized boats. The system of paying to crew members is standard for the state and is worth describing. The fishing labourers, as in other fishing villages of the district, go fishing with the gear owned by the craft owner. In the case of purse-seiners which employ a crew of 25 labourers for fishing, the labourers get 30 per cent of the gross value of the landings. Similarly, the crew of trawlers get 30 per cent of the gross value of the landings towards remuneration, and there are in general six crew for operating the boat. Generally the dugout canoes using gill nets carry a crew of three members. The crew in the case of dugout canoes get about 60 per cent of the gross value of the output. The crew share is equally distributed. Further, the crew share is paid in cash after the realization of the sale proceeds of the entire catch by the boat owners. Payment to the crew is made once in a week or two. There are certain variations in the pattern of operation of the craft. One or more family members of the equipment owner household may also be fishing. In such cases the equipment owner or boat owner gets a proportionate share in the returns of the fishing labourers in addition to the share of boat and gear. In all the above cases the operating cost of the boat is borne by the boat owner. During the normal fishing trips the crew in the case of either mechanized or non-mechanized craft are provided with food by the employer. However, the food for the full crew is supplied by the boat owner during the long trips particularly in the case of mechanized craft. On the basis of the above analysis we find that the system of payment to the labourers did not change with the introduction of mechanized craft in the village.

Supply of demand for labourers in the village

As indicated earlier, the supply of labourers in the village was more or less constant throughout the year, while the requirement of the labourers or demand for fishing fluctuates widely over the season. However, the demand for labourers is estimated to be the highest during the fishing season immediately after the off-season for fishing. The supply-demand situation for labourers in the following paragraphs relates to the peak fishing season, during which all the boats and gear in the village are used for fishing.

The estimates of labour supply and demand are presented in Table 8.20. Labourers required for operating the fishing equipment in the village have been estimated to be 326 while those at best having no other occupation to be only 220, leaving a deficit of 106 members. The deficit was the highest in the case of MB owner households with 194 and for NMB owner households it was 40. As against the total deficit of 234 crew members, the crew households and other households have potential for supply of 129 members. The aggregate deficit is about 1.03 persons per household. Many able-bodied adult male members in the village are involved in occupation other than fishing. The share of members in occupations other than fishing in total able-bodied adult male members is maximum for other households with 72.41 per cent and minimum for NMB owner households with 3.33 per cent.

The estimated labour participation in terms of family and hired in the operation of different types of craft is presented in Table 8.21. Only 31 members of the MB owner households are involved in fishing while they have potential for supply of at least 42 members. On the other hand about 52 persons have been estimated to be involved in fishing while they have potential for 49 persons in the case of non-mechanized boat owner households. In other words, all the able-bodied adult male members of the NMB households are involved in fishing and the hiring of the crew is only after allocating work to all possible persons in the households. Thus, there is a clear evidence that the fishermen tend to withdraw family labour from active fishing as the level of fishing technology and income increases. The share of hired crew in the total crew

TABLE 8.20

Estimates of surplus labourers according to occupation, Kadekar (1981-82)

Particulars	No. of members in households of				
	MB owners	NMB owners	Crew members	Others	Total
1. Number of households	23	30	42	8	103
2. Number of able-bodied adult male members of family	67	60	137	29	293
3. Number of adult male members with occupation other than fishing	10	2	9	21	42
4. Number of adult male members who have not yet entered the working force (students)	15	9	2	5	31
5. Number of members actively engaged or at best having no other occupation	42	49	126	3	220
6. Number of members required for operating the fishing equipment	236	90	—	—	326
7. Surplus labourers in the 194 fishing workforce	—194	—40	126	3	—106
8. Surplus labourers per houschold	—8.43	—1.37	3.00	0.38	—1.03

Note : 1. (—) indicates nil.
2. Negative surpluses indicate deficits.

required is maximum in the case of purse-seiners with 88.89 per cent and minimum in the case of NMBs with 42.22 per cent.

TABLE 8.21

Estimated[1] labour participation pattern, family and hired for operating different type of boats, Kadekar (1981-82)

Type of boat	Total No. of boats	Estimated average crew size required per boat	Total crew required	Estimated source of crew hired		
				Family	Sharing	Salary
1. Purse-seiner	7	27	189	21 (11.11)	168 (88.89)	— —
2. Trawler	9	5.2	47	10 (21.28)	37 (78.73)	— —
3. NMB	40	2.25	90	52 (52.78)	38 (48.22)	—
Total	56	—	326	93 (28.53)	233 (71.47)	

Note : 1. Estimated on the basis of information from the sample respondents.
2. Figures in parentheses indicate the share of family hired labourers in total crew required.
3. (—) indicates nil.

The structure of the labour force has not changed with the introduction of mechanized craft in the village. Almost all the labourers for fishing are employed on a permanent basis. Casual labourer is a relatively unknown phenomenon.

Impact of mechanization of fishing craft on demand for labourers

The net displacement of labour is measured in terms of thousand mandays per tonne of output on the basis of unit economies of different types of boats. The capital-labour ratios are also calculated for different types of boats to understand the changes in capital requirements with the mechanization of fishing craft. The estimated capital-labour and output-labour ratios for different type of fishing craft/techniques are presented in Table 8.22. The capital requirement for generating the thousand mandays of employment was the highest for trawlers with Rs. 1,46,830 followed by purse-seiners, dugout canoes, and rampani units with Rs. 1,25,250, Rs. 35,060 and Rs. 19,620 respectively. The comparable fishing techniques in terms of resource base (rampani units in the traditional sector) and purse-seiners in the mechanized sector were having a wide gap of over Rs. 1,05,630 between the capital requirement for generation of the employment of thousand mandays. Thus, the capital requirement for fishing with mechanized craft particularly with purse-seiners has increased substantially. The output per thousand mandays of employment was in the range of 13.09 tonnes for dugout canoes to 77.08 tonnes for purse-seiners. Once again the comparable techniques of fishing had the output-labour ratio of 53.33 tonnes for rampanis and 77.05 tonnes for purse-seiners. The high output-labour ratios for mechanized craft indicates that the labour has got displaced because of the mechanization of fishing craft for a constant level of output. In order to absorb the labour displaced because of mechanization of fishing craft particularly because of purse-seiners, the mechanization of fishing craft consequently the output in the mechanized sector should increase at a rate of over 30 per cent per annum till all the rampanis are replaced by the purse-seiners. Otherwise the unemployment in fishing villages affected by the mechanization of fishing craft goes on increasing and the labourers in fishing may turn to other sectors for employment.

Now turning to the situation in the village, it should be expected that the village has a labour abundant situation with a high level of mechanization of fishing craft. However, the actual situation indicated that the village was in a labour shortage situation. This suggests one of the following two employment patterns in the village:

(1) The village was in a labour shortage situation even in the pre-mechanization period and this situation in fact motivated the fishermen to mechanize their fishing craft.

(2) The fishermen of the village have acquired more number of mechanized craft than the labour in the village because

TABLE 8.22

Estimated capital-labour and output-labour ratios for different types of boats, Kadekar (1981)

Type of boat	Investment per unit* ('000 Rs.)	Crew required for operation of boat	Active No. of fishing days	Total employment ('000 man-days)	Output (tonnes)	Capital (in '000 Rs.) per '000 mandays of employment	Output (in tonnes) per '000 man-days of employment
1. Purse-seiner	625.63	27	185	4.955	385	125.25	77.08
2. Trawler	146.83	5	200	1.000	46	146.83	46.00
3. Rampani unit**	176.58	100	90	9.000	480	19.62	53.33
4. Dugout canoe	21.56	3	205	0.615	8	35.06	13.09

Note : 1. *including the investment on gear.

2. **Rampani unit consists of one rampani boat, three dugout canoes of size over 25 ft. and the gear or shore-seine net.

of their progressive nature and easy access to financing agencies. The employment displacement of mechanized craft also spills over to non-mechanized sectors of other villages. The supply of labourers from other affected villages has contributed to the rapid growth of mechanized craft beyond the capability of the labour in the village.

Our study indicates that the more probable reason for the labour shortage situation in the village was the second.

Labour mobility: Let us now consider the labour mobility situation in the village. Distribution of sample crew members in purse-seiners and trawlers according to the labour-mobility ratio is presented in Table 8.23. Of the sample crew (22) in purse-seiners over 81 per cent (18) has been found to be either totally immobile or with a low mobility. The corresponding immobile crew or crew with low mobility in the case of trawlers account for about 70 per cent. Each crew member worked with an employer at least for a year before they changed. Further, no change of employer takes place during the fishing season.

TABLE 8.23

Distribution of sample crew members according to the labour-mobility ratio, Kadekar (1981-82)

Labour mobility	Number of crew with stated mobility		Total
	of Purse-seiner	of Trawler	
1. High	—	—	—
2. Medium	4(18.18)	3(30.00)	7(21.87)
3. Low	18(81.82)	7(70.00)	25(78.13)
Total	22(100.00)	10(100.00)	32(100 00)

Note: 1. (—) indicates nil.
2. Figures in parentheses are percentages to column total.

The crew changed their employer in search of better income or better relations with the employer. Ten mobile crew in purse-seiners indicated 34 reasons and four mobile crew in trawlers indicated 18 reasons for change of employer. Almost all the crew members in the case of both purse-seiners and trawlers changed the employer mainly because of labourer-employer relations. In the majority of cases the hope to get better income also motivated the crew to change the employer (Table 8.24).

TABLE 8.24

Reasons for change of employer by the crew members during their immediate past change, Kadekar (1981-82)

Reason for change of Employer	No. of crew purse-seiner	% share in total	No. of crew trawler	% share in total
1. Dispute with the boat owner	10	29.41	4	22.22
2. Fishing in that boat is not profitable	8	23.53	4	22 22
3. Others	16	47.06	10	55.56
Total	34	100.00	18	100.00

The interlocking of credit and labour, though weak, takes the form of lending money to the crew by the boat owner. The lending of money by the boat owner to the crew is mainly towards wage advance. The size distribution of sample crew according to the amount borrowed at the time of joining and the outstanding debt as on December 31, 1981, in Table 8.25 indicates that 28 of the total 34 crew borrowed money from the employer and in all the cases it was less than Rs. 200. As on December 31, 1981, about 21 of the crew repaid the advance and only six were having an outstanding debt of less than Rs. 100.

Occupational mobility: Taking the economic and social status into account, the four fishing occupations in the village in descending order are: (a) MB owners (both purse-seiner

TABLE 8.25

Size distribution of sample crew members according to the amount borrowed at the time of joining from and outstanding debt to the employer owner as on December 31, 1981, Kadekar

Frequency interval (Rs.)	Number of crew with stated range of borrowings	% share in total	No. of crew with outstanding debt in stated range	% share in total
No borrowing/ outstanding debt	7	20.59	28	82.35
1—100	23	67.65	6	17.65
100—200	4	11.76	—	—
Total	34	100.00	34	100.00

Note: (—) indicates nil.

and trawler); (b) NMB owner; (c) crew in mechanized boats; and (d) crew in non-mechanized boats. It is also true that individuals at the lower rung of the occupational ladder are always ambitious to reach the higher rung and to take less demanding occupations such as service or business. The ambitions of the fishermen are the contributing causes for the occupational changes.

Distribution of the working population in the sample households, according to the pace of graduation to the current occupation in Kadekar, is presented in Table 8.26. It can be seen from the table that the pace is quite fast in the case of MB owners as compared to the other occupations. The distribution of crew in MB is even across different levels of pace while it is skewed towards lower pace for NMB owners.

Market for credit

The important sources of credit in the village are commercial banks and co-operative banks in the formal sector and friends and relatives in the informal sector. In the village, the fishermen

TABLE 8.26

Distribution of working population in sample households according to the pace of graduation to current position, Kadekar (1981-82)

Name of graduation	Number of individuals with stated pace in					Total
	MB owners	NMB owners	Crew in MB	Crew in NMB	Others	
1. High	4 (19.05)	1 (9.09)	3 (12.00)	1 (100.00)	8 (47.00)	17 (22.67)
2. Medium	1 (4.76)	—	1 (4.00)	—	—	2 (2.67)
3. Low	16 (76.19)	10 (90.91)	21 (84.00)	—	9 (52.94)	56 (74.67)
Total	21 (100.00)	11 (100.00)	25 (100.00)	1 (100.00)	17 (100.00)	75 (100.00)

Note: 1. (—) indicates nil.
2. Figures in parentheses are percentages to column total.

were also observed to borrow from multiple sources. Further, commercial banks play a dominant role.

Co-operatives and commercial banks lent mainly for buying fishing equipment and charged an interest rate of about 13 per cent. The repayment schedules for these loans are fixed on the basis of the estimated economies of the fishing craft and gear. Loans from friends and relatives carry an interest ranging from 12 to 36 per cent, and generally is not purpose-oriented. The interlocking of credit and marketing and of credit and labour are not at all observed in the village.

The distribution of households according to the sources of borrowing and the amount outstanding as on December 31, 1981, is presented in Table 8.27. It can be noticed from the table that 44 (42.72 per cent) households were having an outstanding debt of Rs. 8,11,900 million or a debt of

TABLE 8.27

Distribution of households according to the source of borrowing and occupation and their outstanding debt as on December 31, 1981, Kadekar

(*in Rupees*)

Source of borrowing	Number of households having outstanding debts to the									
	MB owner		NMB owner		Crew		Others		Total	
	No.	Debt	No.	Debt	No.	Debt	No.	Debt	No.	Debt
I. *Formal Lending Agencies*:										
(a) Commercial Banks	22	708500 (32204)	14	32250 (2304)	3	3500 (1168)	1	2000 (2000)	40	746250 (18656)
(b) Co-op. Banks	—	—	—	—	—	—	1	50000 (50000)	1	50000
Sub-total	22	708500	14	32250	3	3500	2	52000	41	796250
II. *Informal Sources*:										
Friends and Relatives	—	—	—	—	2	5250 (2625)	—	—	2	5250 (2625)
Sub-total	—	—	—	—	2	5250	—	—	2	5250
III. *Multiple Source*	—	—	—	—	1	1700	1	8700	2	10400
Total	22	708500 (32204)	14	32250 (2304)	6	10450 (1742)	3	60700 (20233)	45	811900 (18402)

Note: 1. (—) indicates nil.
2. Figures in parentheses indicate the per household outstanding debt.

Rs. 18,400 per borrower household. Interestingly, an overwhelming share (98.07 per cent) of the total outstanding debt was from the commercial banks. The average outstanding debt of MB owners was very high with Rs. 32,200 and the total outstanding debt of MB owner households was only to commercial banks.

Though the available data did not permit us an exact assessment of supply-demand conditions in the credit market of the village, the less fragmentation of loans for the same purpose indicates relatively easy availability of credit and credit abundance in the village. This is also supported by the absence of moneylenders charging a high rate of interest in the village. The borrower tends to go to the moneylender only when he cannot get loan from any other source where the rate of interest is low.

The distribution of households according to the purpose of borrowing (Table 8.28) indicates that most of the boat owners have borrowed for replacement of boats and gear. Borrowing for meeting household expenditure was completely absent in the case of MB owner households and was relatively high in the case of NMB owner and other households. The share of households with no outstanding debt was the highest for crew households with 85.72 per cent and lowest for MB owner households with 4.35 per cent.

The size distribution of households according to the total oustanding debt and occupation in the village is presented in Table 8.29. There are seven MB owner households with an outstanding debt of over Rs. 35,000. Only one household of some other category had an outstanding debt of over Rs. 35,000.

Some important changes which have taken place in the credit market after the introduction of mechanized craft are:

(a) There was shift in the sources of credit—from informal to formal.

(b) The average loan amount borrowed has increased considerably.

(c) The credit-marketing interlinkages have disappeared.

(d) The purpose of borrowing has shifted from meeting household expenditure to investment on boats and gear.

TABLE 8.28

Distribution of households according to the purpose of borrowing of the outstanding debt and occupation, Kadekar (1981)

Reasons for borrowing the outstanding debt	Number of households for stated reason of borrowing of				Total
	MB owners	NMB owners	Crew	Others	
1. No outstanding debt	1 (4.35)	16 (53.33)	36 (85.72)	5 (62.50)	58 (56.31)
2. Replacement of boats/gear	15 (65.22)	5 (16.67)	1 (2.38)	—	21 (20.39)
3. Purchase of fishing craft and gear	7 (30.43)	5 (16.67)	3 (7.14)	—	15 (14.56)
4. To meet household expenditure	—	4 (13.33)	2 (4.76)	2 (25.00)	8 (7.77)
5. Others	—	—	—	1 (12.50)	1 (0.97)
Total	23 (100.00)	30 (100.00)	42 (100.00)	8 (100.00)	103 (100.00)

Note: 1. (—) indicates nil.
2. Figures in parentheses are percentages to column total.

TABLE 8.29

Size distribution of households according to the occupation and the total outstanding debts, Kadekar, 1981

Range of outstanding debt (Rs.)	Number of households with outstanding debt in stated range of				Total
	MB owner	NMB owner	Crew	Others	
Zero outstanding	1 (4.35)	16 (53.34)	36 (85.72)	5 (62.50)	58 (56.31)
Up to 1000	—	4 (13.33)	3 (7.14)	—	7 (6.80)
1001-3000	1 (4.35)	6 (20.00)	2 (7.14)	1 (12.50)	10 (9.71)
3001-6000	3 (13.04)	2 (6.67)	1 (2.38)	—	6 (5.82)
6001-10000	1 (4.35)	1 (3.33)	—	1 (12.50)	3 (2.91)
10001-15000	5 (21.74)	1 (3.33)	—	—	6 (5.83)
15001-25000	4 (17.39)	—	—	—	4 (3.88)

25001-35000	1 (4.35)	—	—	—	1 (0.97)
35001+	7 (30.43)	—	—	1 (12.50)	8 (7 77)
Total	23 (100.00)	30 (100.00)	42 (100.00)	8 (100 00)	103 (100.00)

Note: 1. (—) indicates nil.
2. Figures in parentheses are percentages to column total.

Market for product

Having analysed the market for inputs, labour and credit, we shall now embark on the analysis of market for output.

Historical analysis of fish marketing

During 1910s there were no fish traders in the village nor any trader used to visit Kadekar to buy fish. Therefore, the fishermen used to carry fish on their heads to other places outside the village. Transportation of fish by any other means was not possible because the village was surrounded by sea and river on all four sides. It was only in late 1950s that the traders from other villages started visiting the village for purchasing fish from the fishermen of the village. Our inquiry with the fishermen of the village indicated that the visiting of fish traders from other villages coincided with the construction of an approach road along the coastline of the village. In the beginning there were only two commission agents and three fresh fish wholesalers. In addition, there were less than 10 retailers/vendors to buy fish from the fishermen of the village. The interlocking of credit and marketing started in the village sometime in early 1950s with advancing of short-term interest-free loans ranging from Rs. 200 to Rs. 500 by the fresh fish wholesalers in order to direct access to fish landings.

The number of various marketing intermediaries is presented in Table 8.30. The number of market intermediaries has decreased after the introduction of mechanized craft in the village mainly because of the shift in the landing centre and the extinction of rampani fishing. It has been estimated that currently there are 12 retailers/vendors, two commission agents, one wholesaler, one agent of processors and three agents of fishmeal and oil plant owners for marketing the fish landings in the village. An overwhelming number of the fish marketing intermediaries in the village was from the fishermen community. In addition, there are many fish marketing intermediaries at Malpe who market the landings of the mechanized boats.[19] Shells collected by the fisherwomen of the village are marketed through a different channel. They are usually sold directly to the wholesalers or retailers in consuming centres by the fisherwomen of the village. Further, it was observed that

TABLE 8.30

Changes in the number of marketing intermediaries of different types after mechanization of fishing craft, Kadekar

Type of intermediaries*	Number of persons/organizations of stated type during					
	Pre-mechanization period (1968-69)			Currently** (1981-82)		
	Fishermen community	Non-fishermen community	Total	Fishermen community	Non-fishermen community	Total
1. Retailers/Vendors Fresh Fish	21	7	28	10	3	13
2. Wholesalers						
(a) Fresh Fish	6	—	6	—	—	—
(b) Dry Fish	4	—	4	—	—	—
3. Commission agents	12	3	15	1	2	3
4. Wholesaler-cum-commission agents	—	—	—	1	—	1
5. Sun-drying/salt-curing agents	—	—	—	—	—	—
6. Processing variety suppliers	—	—	—	—	—	—
7. Agents of processors	2	—	2	—	1	1
8. Agents of fishmeal and oil plant owners	4	—	4	3	—	3

Note: 1. *The location of the selling or reselling of these intermediaries is not necessarily in the village. However, the major sources of purchase for these intermediaries are the landing centres in the village.

2. **Relates to the number of individuals involved in marketing the landings in the village. The individuals involved in marketing the landings of the mechanized boats in other locations could not be identified in view of the large number of intermediaries in the assembling centres, where the boats of the village landed their catch.

3. (—) indicates nil.

the quantum of business of the existing marketing intermediaries has decreased as compared to the pre-mechanization period.

Channel members and structure of fish market

As indicated earlier, the channel of fish marketing in the village consists of commission agents, wholesaler-cum-commission agents, retailers/vendors, agents of processors and agents of fish meal and oil plant owners. The functions of various marketing intermediaries are similar to the pattern explained in the profile of Chorwad (see page 175). However, some specific characteristics are given here.

The commission agents in the village play a central role. Their functions include the arranging of the auction of fish landings and receiving and payment of sale proceeds to the fishermen for which the agents get a commission of 5 per cent on the sale proceeds. The handling charges are borne by the commission agents only.

The typical market intermediaries in the marketing channels of the village are the agents of fishmeal/oil plant owners. These agents are authorised to buy fish for fishmeal/oil extraction by oil plant owners in the open auction. These agents get a fixed salary for their services. The fish purchases of these agents are transported to the meal/oil plant immediately by the agents.

The channels of distribution as observed in the village at the time of our survey are presented in Fig. 8.3. The structure of the fish market with a large number of retailers and vendors and a few wholesalers/commission agents was found to be fairly competitive. Further, it was observed that the scale of operations of various market intermediaries has decreased because of a decrease in the landings within the village.

Mechanization of fishing craft and changes in output marketing

The mechanization of fishing craft has brought about three important changes in the output market of the village. These changes relate to the extinction of fresh fish and dry fish wholesalers, and increase in the loan advanced for having the

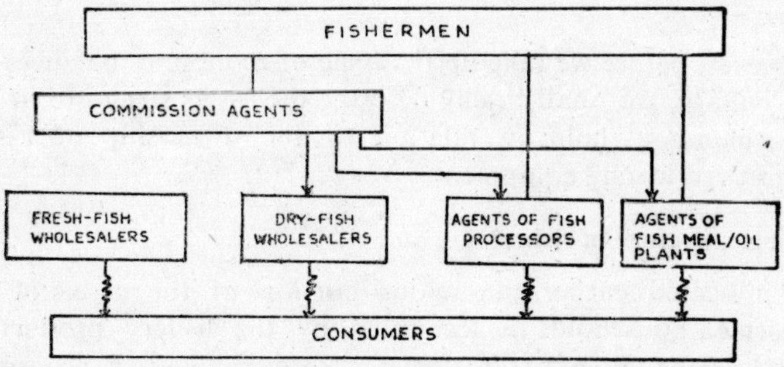

Note: ~~~ indicates existence of other channel members for which details are not available.

FIG. 8.3: *Channels of distribution for fish, Kadekar (1981-82)*

interlocking of marketing and credit. In addition, the pattern of selling in the case of most varieties has shifted from count to weight.

After mechanization competition in the product market within the village has decreased and the output is marketed through different channels in the assembling centres. The market channels in the assembling centres are more competitive and are at the same time lengthier than the corresponding channels in the village. With the decreased landings in the village the wholesalers of dry fish and fresh fish have stopped their business and only commission agents are observed to handle the landings of the fishermen of the village.

The change regarding the increase in the loan amount for having the interlocking of marketing and credit mainly relates to the product market in the assembling centres. Though no sample respondent from the village was observed to have the interlocking of credit and marketing, it was observed to be high in the assembling centres with an average borrowing per fisherman to be over Rs. 10,000 while it was less than Rs. 1,000 during the pre-mechanization period in the village.

During the pre-mechanization period the selling of fish was predominantly by count while currently almost all varieties are sold by weight. However, the bulk landings have been transporated in truck or tempoloads.

THE VILLAGE ECONOMY

However, before we take up the issue of economic balances in the village, we shall briefly describe the assets structure of the fishermen households in relation to the ownership of assets other than fishing equipment.

Assets structure of fisheries

As indicated earlier, the major portion of the assets of the fishermen households is accounted by the fishery productive assets in the village. Nevertheless, there are few rich fishermen who have invested large amounts of money in various household goods and some immovable properties such as houses and land. However, there was no household which has invested in arable land. The investments were usually in non-agricultural lands. In addition to the fishing equipment, house and cattle, the fishermen of the village also own tape-recorders, two-in-one, stereo-systems and transport vehicles. The distribution of households, according to the ownership of various assets and consumer durables, is presented below.

Distribution of households according to the value of owned house and occupation is presented in Table 8.31. Of the six households without any owned house, one was NMB owner household and five were crew households. There is a large concentration of MB households with the value of the house over Rs. 10,000 in MB owners with 12 out of 23 in the category. In the case of NMB owners the concentration was in the range of Rs. 5,001—10,000, while in the case of crew it was the size class up to Rs. 1,000 which accounted for the maximum.

As already indicated earlier, the fishermen of the village own both agricultural and non-agricultural land. The size distribution of the households according to the value of agricultural and non-agricultural land, and occupation in the village is presented in Table 8.32. At an aggregate level 100 households do not have any agricultural land and 49 non-agricultural land. On the other hand, three households own agricultural land valued at between Rs. 16,000 and Rs. 21,000 and nine households own non-agricultural land in the same range of value. The incidence of ownership of non-agricultural land is more

TABLE 8.31

Distribution of households according to occupation and value of owned house, Kadekar (1981)

Value range (Rs.)	Number of houses on the stated range of value of				Total
	MB owners	NMB owners	Crew	Others	
No owned houses	—	1 (16.67)	5 (83.33)	—	6 (100.00)
Less than 1000	3 (9.09)	9 (27.27)	17 (51.52)	4 (12.12)	33 (100.00)
1001-3000	1 (10.00)	1 (10.00)	8 (80.00)	—	10 (100.00)
3001-5000	2 (18.18)	5 (45.46)	4 (36.36)	—	11 (100.00)
5001-10000	5 (20 83)	10 (41.67)	6 (25.00)	3 (12.50)	24 (100.00)
10001+	12 (63.16)	4 (21.05)	2 (10.53)	1 (5.26)	19 (100.00)
Sub-total of owned houses	23 (23.71)	29 (29.90)	37 (38.14)	2 (8.25)	97 (100 00)
Total households	23 (23.33)	30 (29.13)	42 (40.77)	8 (7.77)	103 (100.00)

Note: 1. (—) indicates nil.
2. Figures in parentheses are percentages to row total.

as compared to the ownership of arable land and a majority own land valued at less than Rs. 8,000. Further, the ownership of non-agricultural land is highly predominant for occupations in fisheries while the ownership of agricultural land is predominant in the case of other households. Three of the total eight other households own all the agricultural land in the village. The number of non-agricultural land owners was 17 in MB owners while it was only 15 in the case of NMB owners and 16 in the case of crew households.

TABLE 8.32

Size distribution of households according to the value of land, both agricultural and non-agricultural, owned and occupation, Kadekar (1981-82)

Interval (Rs.)	Number of households with value of land owned in stated range of								Total	
	MB owners/partners		NMB owners		Crew		Others			
	Agri.	Non-Agri.	Agri.	Non-Agri.	Agri.	Non-Agri.	Agri.	Non-Agri.	Agri.	Non-Agri.
No land	23 (100.0)	6 (26.1)	30 (100.0)	15 (50.0)	42 (100.0)	26 (61.9)	5 (62.5)	2 (25.0)	100 (97.1)	49 (47.6)
Up to 2000	—	1 (4.4)	—	1 (3.33)	—	6 (14.3)	—	—	—	8 (7.8)
2001-4000	—	1 (4.4)	—	4 (13.3)	—	4 (9.5)	—	—	—	9 (8.7)
4001-6000	—	5 (21.7)	—	3 (10.3)	—	5 (11.9)	—	2 (25.0)	—	8 (14.6)
6001-8000	—	—	—	1 (3.3)	—	—	—	1 (12.5)	—	2 (1.9)
8C01-10000	—	5 (21.7)	—	—	—	—	—	—	—	5 (4.9)

10001-16000	—	3 (13.0)	—	2 (6.67)	—	1 (2.4)	—	—	—	6 (5.8)
16001-22000	—	2 (8.7)	—	4 (13.3)	—	—	3 (37.5)	3 (37.5)	3 (2.9)	0 (8.7)
Total	23 (100.0)	23 (100.0)	30 (100.0)	30 (100.0)	42 (100.0)	42 (100.0)	8 (100.0)	8 (100.0)	103 (100.0)	103 (100.0)

Note: 1. (—) indicates nil.
2. Figures in parentheses are percentages to column total.

The frequency distribution of households, according to the value of household articles and occupations as shown in Table 8.33, indicates that over 50 per cent of the households own articles valued at less than Rs. 500, while about 7 per cent of households own articles valued at between Rs. 4,000 and

TABLE 8.33

Frequency distribution of households according to the value of household articles and occupation, Kadekar (1981-82)

Interval (Rs.)	Number of households with value of household articles in stated range of				Total
	MB owners/ partners	NMB owners	Crew	Others	
Below 500	8 (34.78)	15 (50.00)	32 (76.19)	4 (50.00)	56 (50.48)
501-1000	1 (4.35)	9 (30.00)	2 (4.76)	—	12 (11.65)
1001-1500	2 (8.70)	3 (10 00)	2 (4.76)	—	7 (6.80)
1501-2000	1 (4.35)	2 (6.67)	4 (9.53)	—	7 (6.80)
2001-2500	3 (13.04)	1 (3.33)	—	—	4 (3.88)
2501-3000	1 (4.35)	—	1 (2.38)	—	2 (1.94)
3001-3500	1 (4.35)	—	—	2 (25.00)	3 (2.91)
3501-4000	1 (4.35)	—	1 (2.38)	—	2 (1.94)
4001-10000	5 (21.73)	—	—	2 (25.00)	7 (6.80)
Total	23 (100.00)	32 (100.00)	42 (100.00)	8 (100.00)	103 (100.0[illegible]

Note: 1. (—) indicates nil.

2. Figures in parentheses are percentages to column total.

Rs. 10,000. Of the total nine households with household articles valued at between Rs. 4,000 and Rs. 10,000 five were MB owner households and two other households. In the case of crew the value of household articles was less than Rs. 500. These account for over 76 per cent of the total households with 32. The distribution also indicates that in general MB owner and other households ranked much higher as compared to NMB owner and crew households.

The ownership of poultry birds is not observed in the case of 32 households.

The ownership of different household articles in the village is given in Table 8.34. It can be seen from the table that most of the modern items/equipment are owned by MB owner households. This is particularly true in the case of transport vehicles, radios and watches. On an average one out of four households owns a radio in the village while in the case of MB owners it was one out of two. The MB owner households account for over 45 per cent of the modern household items in the village while they account for only 24 per cent of the total households.

Consumption and expenditure pattern of fishermen

The pattern of consumption of various items and the corresponding expenditure pattern is likely to be effected by the habits and social customs, income and other household characteristics such as size, education, etc. Therefore, we shall discuss itemwise the expenditure pattern for households of different occupations below.

For analysing the consumption pattern of fishermen households, the items of consumption have been grouped into food items and non-food items. The itemwise annual consumer expenditure by occupation is presented in Table 8.35. An overwhelming percentage (77.49 per cent) of the total consumer expenditure is accounted by food items. Of the total consumer expenditure of Rs. 8,69,110 on food items, expenditure on foodgrains, edible oils and fish alone accounts for about Rs. 5,59,960. The MB owner households account for about 27.44 per cent of the total consumer expenditure while they account for about 26.88 per cent of the total expenditure on food items. The consumer expenditure of different occupational households was in proportion to their households in total.

TABLE 8.34

Ownership of different household items according to occupation, Kadekar (1981-82)

Items	No. of households owning the stated items									
	MB owner		NMB owner		Crew		Others		Total	
	NI	HH	NI	HH	NI	HH	NI	HH	NI	HH
I. *Transport Vehicles*:										
Cycle	—	—	—	—	—	—	1	1	1	1
Scooter/Motorcycle	1	1	—	—	—	—	—	—	1	1
II. *Communication/Ent.*:										
Radio/Transistor	14	14	8	8	3	3	3	3	28	28
III. *Office Equipment*:										
Chairs	46	14	19	12	17	8	10	4	92	38
Tables	18	9	7	5	5	4	8	4	38	22
Wooden Almirah	1	1	—	—	—	—	1	1	2	2
Steel Almirah	1	1	—	—	—	—	—	—	1	1
Electric Fan	3	3	—	—	2	2	2	2	7	7
Sewing Machines	1	1	2	2	1	1	1	1	5	5

IV. *Time Indicators*:										
Wrist-watches	24	14	19	14	9	5	8	4	60	37
Clock	6	5	3	2	—	—	—	—	9	7
V. *Cooking Apparatus*:										
Non-kerosene Stove	18	18	29	29	39	39	5	4	91	90
Kerosene Stove	5	5	1	1	3	3	4	4	13	13
VI. *Kitchenware*:										
Earthen	113	20	153	25	240	38	54	8	560	91
Aluminium	186	22	223	30	273	42	58	8	740	102
Steel	153	20	134	26	63	16	40	6	390	68
Others	—	—	12	12	19	19	8	8	39	39

Note: (—) indicates nil.

TABLE 8.35

Itemwise annual consumption expenditure by occupation, Kadekar (1981-82)

(in '000 Rupees)

Item	Expenditure on the stated item by				
	MB households	NMB households	Crew	Others	Total
I. *Food Items*:					
(a) Foodgrains	80.81(23.32)	116.43(33.60)	112.67(35.40)	26.62(7.68)	346.53(100.00)
(b) Milk and Milk Products	9.31(31.58)	7.75(26.29)	9.25(31.38)	3.17(10.75)	29.48(100.00)
(c) Edible Oils	14.42(29.35)	18.62(36.88)	13.36(26.46)	3.69 (7.31)	50.49(100.00)
(d) Fish	40.87(28.19)	45.50(31.39)	51.74(35.69)	6.86 (4.73)	144.97(100.00)
(e) Vegetables	11.13(30.28)	7.96(21.56)	14.82(40.14)	2.96 (8.02)	36.92(100.00)
(f) Fruits and Nuts	11.49(36.78)	7.12(22.79)	10.76(34.44)	1.87 (5.99)	31.24(100.00)
(g) Sugar, Gur and Khandsari	4.37(26.03)	5.46(32.52)	5.56(33.11)	1.40 (8.34)	16.79(100.00)
(h) Salt and Spices	11.75(27.23)	12.79(29.63)	16.12(37.35)	2.50 (5.79)	43.16(100.00)
(i) Beverages	35.10(28.99)	35.78(29.56)	42.17(34.83)	8.01 (6.62)	121.06(100.00)
(j) Pan, Tobacco and Supari	13.94(28.76)	12.69(26.18)	18.25(37.65)	3.59 (7.41)	48.47(100.00)
Sub-total	233.64(26.88)	278.00(31.98)	304.70(35.06)	60.67 (6.98)	869.11(100.00)

II. *Non-food Items*:					
(a) Entertainment	1.57(33.19)	1.52(32.13)	1.22(25.79)	0.42 (8.89)	4.73(100.00)
(b) Travel and Transport	2.43(24.67)	3.21(32.59)	3.43(34.82)	0.78 (7.92)	9.85(100.00)
(c) Education	7.83(48.58)	3.21(19.91)	3.06(18.98)	2.02(12.53)	16.12(100.00)
(d) Medicines	5.22(30.98)	5.67(33.65)	4.96(29.44)	1.00 (5.93)	16.85(100.00)
(e) Ornaments	2.53(39.97)	1.69(26.70)	1.66(26.22)	0.45 (7.11)	6.33(100.00)
(f) Domestic Utensils	3.05(39.51)	2.11(27.33)	1.94(25.13)	0.62 (8.03)	7.72(100.00)
(g) Clothes	14.00(33.43)	12.40(29.62)	12.12(28.95)	3.35 (8.00)	41.87(100.00)
(h) Footwear	2.19(40.33)	1.69(31.12)	1.13(20.81)	0.42 (7.74)	5.43(100.00)
(i) Fuel and Light	35.36(24.62)	35.46(24.69)	62.09(43.23)	10.71 (7.46)	143.62(100.00)
(j) Others	—	—	—	—	— (100.00)
Sub-total	74.18(29.38)	66.96(26.51)	91.61(36.28)	19.77 (7.83)	252.59(100.00)
Total	307.82(27.44)	344.96(58.20)	396.31(35.33)	80.44 (7.17)	1121.63(100.00)

Note: 1. (—) indicates nil.
2. Figures in parentheses are percentages to row totals.

TABLE 8.36

Itemwise annual consumption expenditure by occupation for per capita and per household, Kadekar (1981-82)

Item	MB owner	NMB owner	Crew	Others	Average of the total households
I. *Food Items*:					
(a) Foodgrains	440(3514)	441(3881)	435(2921)	416(33.28)	427.96(3364.40)
(b) Milk and Milk Products	46(4.05)	29(258)	33(220)	49(397)	36.40(286.00)
(c) Edible Oils	74(644)	71(620)	47(318)	58(462)	62.40(490.36)
(d) Fish	204(1777)	172(1517)	184(1232)	107(854)	178.88(1407.64)
(e) Vegetables	56(486)	30(265)	53(353)	46(371)	45.76(358.28)
(f) Fruits and Nuts	58(500)	27(238)	38(256)	29(234)	38.48(303.16)
(g) Sugar, Gur and Khandsari	22(190)	21(182)	20(133)	22(176)	20.80(163.28)
(h) Salt and Spices	59(511)	48(426)	57(384)	39(312)	53.04(419.12)
(i) Beverages	176(1526)	136(1192)	150(1004)	125(1001)	149.24(1175.20)
(j) Pan, Tobacco and Supari	70(606)	48(423)	64(435)	56(449)	56.80(470.60)
Sub-total	1169(10159)	1023(9002)	1081(7256)	947(7588)	1072 76(8438.04)

II. *Non-food Items*:					
(a) Entertainment	7.84(68.17)	5.75(50.57)	4.34(29.14)	6.50(52.00)	5.83(45.87)
(b) Travel and Transport	12.16(105.76)	12.16(107.02)	12.16(81.55)	12.16(99.31)	12.16(95.63)
(c) Education	39.16(340.52)	12.16(107.00)	10.87(72.98)	31.64(253.13)	19.92(156.62)
(d) Medicines	26.13(227.17)	21.50(189.17)	17.59(118.10)	15.62(125.00)	20.81(163.69)
(e) Ornaments	12.68(110.22)	6.40(56.33)	5.89(39.52)	7.03(56.28)	7.82(61.50)
(f) Domestic Utensils	15.27(132.83)	7.99(70.33)	6.88(46.19)	9.69(77.50)	9.54(75.00)
(g) Clothes	70.00(608.70)	46.97(413.33)	42.98(288.57)	52.34(418.75)	51.64(406.50)
(h) Footwear	10.95(95.22)	6.40(56.33)	4.02(26.02)	6.64(53.12)	6.72(52.82)
(i) Fuel and Light	177(1537)	134(1182)	220(1478)	167(1334)	177.32(1394.64)
(j) Others	—	0.04(0.33)	0.39(262)	—	0.15(1.17)
Sub-total	371.19(3225.59)	253.37(2232.41)	325.12(2183.79)	308.62(2472.06)	311.91(2453.44)
Total	1540.19(13384.59)	1276.37(12234.41)	1406.12(9439.79)	1255.62(10060.60)	1384.67(10891.48)

Note: 1. (—) indicates nil.
2. Figures in parenthesis are the expenditure incurred per household.

The itemwise per capita and per household consumer expenditure by occupation is presented in Table 8.36. The per capita consumer expenditure was marginally higher for MB owner households as compared to the overall per capita expenditure. The per capita annual consumer expenditure for MB owner households was Rs. 1,540 while it was only Rs. 1,384.67 for all the households.

Incomes and savings of fishermen households

The distribution of annual incomes and consumer expenditure by occupation is presented in Table 8.37. The total income of

TABLE 8.37

Occupationwise income, expenditure and savings of fishermen, Kadekar (1981-82)

(in '000 Rupees)

Occupation	Income	Expenditure*	Savings
1. MB	1130.67	266.95	863.72
2. NMB	553.05	299.46	253.59
3. Crew	454.31	344.57	109.74
4. Others	64.62	77.09	—12.57
Total	2202.65	988.07	1214.58

Note: 1. Negative sign of the savings indicates dissavings.
2. *The excluding expenditure is of the expenditure on fish since most of the households were observed to consume fish from their own output. However, in the case of other households only 50 per cent of the fish consumption was from gifts from boat owners.

the village has been estimated to be Rs. 22,82,650, while the consumer expenditure Rs. 9,88,070 leaving a net saving of Rs. 12,41,580 (over 55 per cent). However, the net saving was only Rs. 6,12,380 when the debt service of institutional loans is taken into account and the income from other occupations is not considered.

Further, all the households in fishing occupations had savings while other households had a dissaving of the order of Rs. 12,470. The savings of the MB owner households were Rs. 8,63,720 and those of the crew were only Rs. 1,09,740. The savings per household after allowing for debt service was in the range of Rs. 12,560 for MB owner households and Rs. 2,610 for crew households.

The above estimates of savings should be viewed with caution in view of the periodical fish famine years and decreasing economies of return of purse-seine boats.[20] Nevertheless, the aggregate savings in the village are expected to be positive. The hypothesis is strengthened by the observed pattern of owning of household articles and the ownership of other assets.

REFERENCES

1. Hereafter referred to as Kadekar.
2. Tulu is written in the Kannada script. It has borrowed a number of words from languages like Tamil, Kannada and Malayalam, and sounds like Malayalam.
3. For further historical background, see Madhava Hejimody, *A Study of Social Structure of Mogaveera Community in D.K.*, unpublished dissertation (Mangalore: School of Social Work, Rohini Nilaya, 1979).
4. A legend ascribes the origin of this system of inheritance to a ruler called Bhutalpandya. The ruler wanted to offer one of his sons as a sacrifice to the gods, but was thwarted by the maternal affection of his wife and had to resort to the sacrifice of his nephew. As an acknowledgement of this gesture the ruler Bhutalpandya decreed that all sons of this lineage should forfeit their right in favour of sisters' sons.
5. Each household was a class by itself. In view of the difficulty of studying each household separately, we have divided them into four homogeneous categories.
6. The tendency of fishing equipment owners to live in extended households mainly arises in a labour short economy, where getting labourers to work on boats is very difficult.
7. For a detailed description of these craft and methods of construction, see Gupta, V.K., *et al*, *Marine Fish Marketing in India*, Vol. II, and *Current Situation: Production and Marketing* (Ahmedabad: Indian Institute of Management, 1983) and Kurien, J., *Towards an Understanding of the Fish Economy of Kerala*, op. cit., pp. 19-22, 1978.
8. For a detailed analysis of the operations of rampani, see Gupta, V.K., *et al*, *Marine Fish Marketing in India*, Volume II (Ahmedabad: Indian Institute of Management, 1983).

9. Mechanized boats came to the village long after the introduction of mechanized trawlers in the State in 1956. Further, the mechanization of fishing craft in the State started with the introduction of IBE trawlers while in Gujarat it started with motorization of the traditional fishing craft. This was mainly because the then existing traditional craft in the State were found to be unsuitable for motorization.
10. For working out the effective number of mechanized boats in the village we have taken the census of the total number of partners in each boat unit and their place of residence. From the list of owners of or partners in mechanized boats we have segregated the owner/partners from the village and their respective share. The effective number of mechanized boats in the village has been worked out by adding the shares of the villagers. Therefore, we find the effective number of mechanized boats in the village to be in fractions.
11. The gill nets owned by mechanized boat owner households were used for fishing from non-mechanized boats owned by MBO households.
12. The individual ownership implies that only one person owns the craft/gear and in joint ownership more than one person from different households collectively own the boat/gear.
13. These ownership patterns can be identified on the basis of the status of owner of and non-owner worker on the boat. For further details see the profile of Chorwad village in Gujarat.
14. If at least one partner of the boat is an active worker, the boat has been classified into category three of the ownership pattern.
15. Though the boats and gear owned by different households were acquired in different years from 1960 to 1981, we have taken the value of assets owned by the households at 1979 prices. This has been mainly to neutralize the increase in the prices of boats and gear over time.
16. The estimates of utilization pattern of fish landings are based on our discussions with the fishermen in relation to various end uses of different species during both pre- and post-mechanization periods. To that extent the estimates are only rough approximations.
17. For details about the structure of the market for boat building in the district, see Gupta, V.K., *et al*, *Marine Fish Marketing in India*, Volume II (Ahmedabad: Indian Institute of Management, 1983).
18. For details in this regard please see the profile of Chorwad village in Gujarat.
19. For details about the number of market intermediaries at Malpe, see Gupta, V.K., *et al*, *Marine Fish Marketing in India*, Vol. II (Ahmedabad: Indian Institute of Management, 1983).
20. For further details see Heywood, K.H., and Curr, C.T.W., "Economic Evaluation of Purse-seine Industry", *FAO Fisheries Circular*, 151, pp. 3-5.

9

Bokkapatna Bengre Village, Dakshina Kannada District, Karnataka

BOKKAPATNA BENGRE is situated in Mangalore taluk of Dakshina Kannada district. This calm fishing hamlet is situated on the sand belt lying between river Gurapur and the Arabian Sea. The hamlet is bounded by the new Mangalore Port towards the north and Kudroli Bengre towards the south, the Arabian Sea towards the west, and river Gurapur towards the east. Bokkapatna and Kudroli villages are on the other bank of the river. Mangalore, the district and taluka headquarters, is about 2 km. to the east of Bokkapatna Bengre (Fig. 9.1).

Fishermen in the nearby villages of Mangalore identified the sand belt between the sea and the river and quickly migrated to the village to pursue fishing activities. This was said to have taken place about 50 years ago. Later the Mangalore Port authorities took over the entire sand belt which runs between Bokkapatna Bengre village and Thannerbavi village. Since this place is very close to Bokkapatna village, it is identified as Bokkapatna Bengre. The villagers may have to vacate the place as soon as the port authorities ask them to do so, since they are occupying it unauthorizedly.

Kannada and Tulu are the principal languages spoken by the fishermen of the hamlet. Tulu is spoken by all, while Kannada is spoken by mostly the elite and well-to-do communities, a few know Hindi and English also.

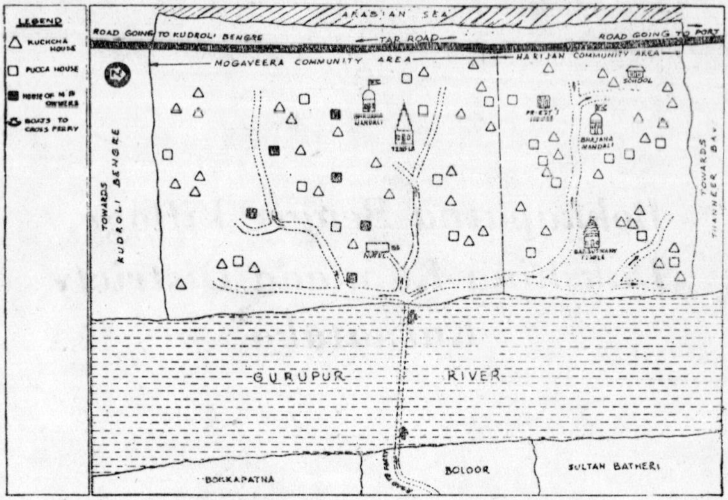

FIG. 9.1: *Map showing Bokkapatna Bengre*

Population and castes

As Bokkapatna Bengre was neither considered as part on the Municipal Corporation nor the Gram Panchayat, no organized census of the hamlet has been undertaken. The enumeration of the households in the village for this study during 1981 indicated the total population to be 493 members in 79 households. The fishermen community of Bokkapatna Bengre consists only of Hindus. There are two major sub-castes of Hindu fishermen in the village. They are Mogaveera and Harijan. Of the total 79 households, 44 were from the Mogaveera community and 35 were Harijans.

Village amenities, industries and infrastructure

Village amenities, industries and infrastructure in the village are listed under two broad categories: general village infrastructure and fishery-related infrastructure.

General village infrastructure: No transport is available within the village. Bokkapatna is connected with Mangalore, the nearest city, by bus, taxi and autorickshaw. In order to facilitate the fishermen to reach Bokkapatna, a boat service is operated randomly from 5 a.m. to 9 p.m. There is another road towards the west of the village which runs parallel to the sea. This is normally used for transportation of stone and other heavy material. About 100 to 150 fishermen daily visit Mangalore for various purposes. About 50 to 60 children attend school at Mangalore and Bokkapatna. Fishermen visit the nearby places for marketing of fresh and dry fish at the fresh fish market.

The source of drinking water is dug wells. Almost each and every house had a drinking water well. The village is not electrified. Lavatory facilities are available only in a few houses.

Village industry and trade are practically non-existent in the village. With the exception of a refreshment stall and a pan shop, a carpenter and a mason, all other facilities relating to trade and industry are available only in the nearby villages or at Mangalore.

The educational facilities were provided in the village in 1967 with the setting up of a primary school. The school had a strength of 30 children and a lady teacher responsible for all four classes. The children normally go to Mangalore to pursue further studies.

The facilities such as post office, bank and the Primary Health Centre are available at Mangalore. Further, the police station is located at Bhudev which is 3 km. from the village.

The village has caste associations, and Bhajan Mandal for social, cultural, recreational and religious activities. Some of the fishermen are members of the Youth Club of Bokkapatna, which is active since 1948. The caste associations and Bhajan Mandal have been operating in the village for the past 30 years.

Fishery-related infrastructure: The information of the major fishery-related infrastructure facilities is available in the village. Icc plants are located at Bollur and Bhudev. A boat-building yard is located at Hoige Bazaar which is on the other side of the river. A fishmeal plant was also established there in 1970. No fish-drying facilities are available in the village and generally the fishermen dry the fish on the sandy beaches. All the other fishery-related infrastructure facilities are available at Mangalore. A sardine oil extraction unit was established in the village about 50 years ago and the owner belonged to

Bolur village. The crushing for meal and oil extraction is usually done during the peak months of September-November when the sardine catches are large and the prices are relatively low. Usually about 20 to 25 tonnes of fish is crushed and the yield is around 50 to 70 tins of oil.

Two organizations have been set up at Mangalore for the development of fishermen. They are the Hadinavapatna Meemvir Market Veyavastha Samithi, and the Fish Market Arrangement Establishment. This was set up basically to avoid middlemen while auctioning fish catches. The Karnataka purse-seiners' Meenugura Samithi was set up at Mangalore in 1977 to help fishermen secure government facilities and bank loans. In addition, some of the fishermen have enrolled themselves as members of the Fishermen Co-operative Society at Bokkapatna.

Production equipment and occupations

Most of the economic activities in Bengre centre around marine fishing. The village population consists of boat owners (both mechanized and non-mechanized), labourers in the fishing activity, fish marketers and others. The number of persons actively involved in economic activities from each household varies considerably and the activities such as operation/ownership of boats, crew, retailers, etc., represented by households also varies from one to as many as four. Taking the occupational pattern of various members of a household they have been divided into four main categories: owner/partner of mechanized boat (MBO), owner of non-mechanized boat, crew and others.

The distribution of households according to main occupation and caste is presented in Table 9.1. In 1981 there were six MB owner households with a population of 38 and all the six households were Mogaveera households. The NMB owner households consisted of 22 Harijan households and 17 Mogaveera households. The MB owners and crew households were over-represented by Mogaveera households while NMB owner and other households were predominated by the Harijans.

The above analysis of households, according to occupation, however, does not give the information about the number of persons in the various occupations. Therefore, we have tabulated

TABLE 9.1

Distribution of households according to caste and occupational patterns, Bengre

Occupational pattern	Caste		Total	Total No. of persons
	Mogaveera	Harijan		
1. MB	6 (13.64)	—	6 (7.59)	38 (7.71)
2. NMB	17 (38.63)	22 (62.86)	39 (49.37)	260 (52.74)
3. Crew	15 (34.09)	3 (8.57)	18 (22.78)	109 (22.11)
4. Others	6 (13.64)	10 (28.57)	16 (20.25)	86 (17.44)
Total	44 (100)	35 (100)	79 (100)	493 (100)

Note: Figures in parentheses are percentages to column total.

the occupationwise distribution of population according to caste in Table 9.2. About 23 per cent of the total population in the village was employed in economic activities related to fishery. These included fishing with mechanized boats, non-mechanized boats, crew member with gear and without gear and other activities like shell collection and fish retailing. About 6 per cent of the total population was engaged in economic activities not related to fishery. This included preliminary services and agricultural labourers. About 71 per cent of the population was not involved in any economic activity in the village. These included the dependants/non-working, students, housewives and others. In terms of the caste distribution about 26 per cent of the Mogaveera community members were involved in fishery-related economic activities as against only 20 per cent of the Harijan population. Percentagewise more families of Harijan households were involved in service and as agricultural labourers than the Mogaveera households.

TABLE 9.2

Occupationwise distribution of population according to caste, Bengre

Occupation	No. of persons from the		Total
	Mogaveera	Harijan	
I. *Economic Activities: Fishery*			
(1) Fishing with MB (joint)	7(2.45)	—	7(1.42)
(2) Fishing with NMB (own)	21(7 37)	21(10.10)	42(8.52)
(3) Crew with gear	23(8.07)	8(0.96)	25(5.07)
(4) Crew without gear	8(2.81)	3(1.44)	11(2.23)
(5) Shell collection	1(0.35)	6(2.88)	7(1.42)
(6) Fish retailing	14(4.91)	9(4.33)	23(4.66)
Sub-total	74(25.96)	41(19.71)	115(23.32)
II. *Economic Activities: Non-fishery*			
(1) Business	2(0.70)	—	2(0.41)
(2) Service	8(2.81)	11(5.29)	19(3.85)
(3) Agricultural labour	—	9(4.33)	9(1.83)
Sub-total	10(3.51)	20(9.62)	30(6.09)
III. *Non-economic Activities*:			
(1) Dependants/Not working	81(28.42)	48(23.08)	129(26.17)
(2) Students	52(18.25)	52(25.00)	104(21.09)
(3) Housewife	65(22.81)	27(12.98)	92(18.66)
(4) Others	3(1.05)	20(9.61)	23(4.67)
Sub-total	201(70.53)	147(70.67)	348(70.59)
Total	285(100.00)	208(100.00)	493(100.00)

Note: 1. (—) indicates nil.
2. Figures in parentheses are percentages to column total.

SOCIO-ETHNOGRAPHIC PROFILE OF FISHERMEN

The social characteristics analysed in this section relate to the family size and structure, level of education, age distribution of fishermen population, migration pattern and social participation of the fishermen and their households.

Size and structure of households

The average family size of fishermen households in the village, as per the census taken during 1981, was 6.2 persons per household. The occupationwise distribution of households, according to family size, in Bokkapatna Bengre is presented in Table 9.3.

TABLE 9.3

Occupationwise distribution of households according to family size, Bengre

Family size (members)	Number of households of				Total
	MB	NMB	Crew	Others	
1	—	—	—	—	—
2	—	2(5.13)	—	1(6.25)	3(3.80)
3	—	2(5.13)	1(5.55)	3(18.75)	6(7.60)
4	2(33.33)	4(10.26)	3(16.68)	3(18.75)	12(15.19)
5	1(16.67)	6(15.38)	3(16.68)	2(12.50)	12(15.19)
6	—	5(12.82)	5(27.76)	1(6.25)	11(13.92)
7	—	3(7.69)	3(16.68)	3(18.75)	9(11.40)
8	2(33.33)	7(17.96)	1(5.55)	1(6.25)	11(13.92)
9	1(16.67)	6(15.38)	1(5.55)	2(12.50)	10(12.66)
10	—	1(2.56)	—	—	1(1.26)
11	—	3(7.69)	1(5.55)	—	4(5.06)
Total	6(100.00))	39(100.00)	18(100.00)	16(100.00)	79(100.00)

Note: 1. (—) indicates nil.
2. Figures in parentheses are percentages to column total.

Over 58 per cent of the total households in the village had a family size of six and above. Of the total 46 households with six or more members, 25 households belonged to non-mechanized boat owner households. The non-mechanized boat owner households in general had a tendency to have large sized households, with 64.1 per cent households having six or more persons per household. Further, the crew member households also had larger family sizes. Half of the total six mechanized boat owner households had a family size of less than six persons and the rest had a family size of over seven persons.

In terms of the family structure 58 per cent of the fishermen households in the village had nuclear families and the rest had joint families. The nuclear and joint family structures have been equally represented in the case of mechanized boat owner households and other households, while in the case of non-mechanized boat owner and crew households the nuclear structure was predominant (Table 9.4).

TABLE 9.4

Distribution of households by occupational pattern and type of family, Bengre

Occupation	No. of households with family structure		Total
	Nuclear	Joint	
1. MB	3(6.52)	3(9.09)	6(7.60)
2. NMB	23(50.00)	16(48.48)	39(49.37)
3. Crew	12(26.09)	6(18.18)	18(22.78)
4. Others	8(17.39)	8(24.24)	16(20.25)
Total	46(100.00)	33(100.00)	79(100 00)

Note: Figures in parentheses are percentages to column total.

Age distribution of fishermen and their level of education

The age distribution of the village population, according to occupational pattern, is presented in Table 9.5. The total population of the village consisted of 241 males and 252 females. At an aggregate level the female population is more than male population in age groups 1-12, 13-20, and 56 and above years while it is less in other age groups. Further, about 36 per cent of the total population of the village was less than 13 years old. In the case of MBO households the age group of 21-30 years accounted for maximum of the total population while in other cases it was the age group of 1-12 years. The population of males in the age groups of 21-30, 31-45 and

TABLE 9.5

Age and sex distribution of villagers according to occupational pattern, Bengre

Occupation	01-12		13-20		21-30		31-45		46-55		56 and above		Total	
	M	F	M	F	M	F	M	F	M	F	M	F	M	F
1. MB	2 (2.44)	1 (1.06)	2 (6.25)	3 (6.82)	8 (16.32)	5 (12.20)	3 (6.67)	2 (5.41)	3 (17.65)	2 (11.76)	3 (18.75)	4 (21.05)	21 (8.71)	17 (6.75)
2. NMB	42 (51.22)	54 (57.45)	20 (62.45)	21 (47.73)	24 (48.99)	21 (51.22)	23 (51.11)	22 (59.46)	10 (58.82)	9 (52.94)	8 (50.00)	6 (31.58)	127 (52.70)	133 (52.78)
3. CRM	26 (31.71)	29 (30.85)	4 (12.50)	5 (11.36)	11 (12.45)	9 (21.95)	9 (20.00)	6 (16.22)	3 (17.65)	3 (17.65)	1 (6.25)	3 (15.79)	54 (22.41)	55 (21.83)
4. Others	12 (14.63)	10 (10.64)	6 (18.75)	15 (34.09)	6 (12.24)	6 (14.63)	10 (22.22)	7 (18.91)	1 (5.88)	3 (17.65)	4 (25.00)	6 (31.58)	39 (16.18)	47 (18.65)
Total	82 (100)	94 (100)	32 (100)	44 (100)	49 (100)	41 (100)	45 (100)	37 (100)	17 (100)	17 (100)	16 (100)	19 (100)	241 (100)	252 (100)

Note: Figures in parentheses represent percentages to column total.

46-55 years was more than females for most of the occupational categories.

We calculated for each family the age gaps between the surviving children to analyse the age gap and its impact on the growth of the village population. The frequency distribution of age gaps between the surviving children of same parents, according to occupation in the village, is presented in Table 9.6. In the case of crew the age gap between the surviving children was much less for a majority. Further, there were no surviving children of same parents with an age gap of more than five years in the case of crew.

TABLE 9.6

Frequency distribution of age gaps between surviving children of same parents according to occupation pattern, Bengre

Age gap interval	No. of instances in which the age gap falls in the stated interval for				Total
	MB	NMB	Crew	Others	
1-1.9	—	14(23.73)	9(23.69)	4(28.57)	27(24.11)
2-2.9	—	26(44.07)	20(52.63)	4(28.57)	50(44.64)
3-3.9	1(100.00)	10(16.95)	6(15.79)	4(28.57)	21(18.75)
4-4.9	—	8(13.56)	3(7.89)	—	11(9.82)
5-5.9	—	1(1.69)	—	2(14.29)	3(2.68)
6 and above	—	—	—	—	—
Total	1(100.00)	59(100.00)	38(100.00)	14(100.00)	112(100.00)

Note: 1. (—) indicates nil.
2. Figures in parentheses are percentages to column total.

The distribution of households according to the occupational pattern and highest level of education attained by household members in the village is presented in Table 9.7. There were six households which did not have any educated person in their households. The households with higher secondary as the highest level of education attained accounted for the

TABLE 9.7

Distribution of households according to occupational pattern and highest level of education in the household, Bengre

Level of education	Number of households of				Total
	MB	NMB	Crew	Others	
1. Illiterate	—	4(10.26)	—	2(12.50)	6(7.60)
2. Read-write	—	(2.56)	—	—	1(1.26)
3. Primary	1(16.67)	12(30.77)	11(61.11)	4(25.00)	28(35.44)
4. Middle	2(33.33)	6(15.38)	4(22.22)	1(6.25)	13(16.46)
5. Higher Secondary	2(33.33)	16(41.03)	3(16.67)	8(50.00)	29(36.71)
6. Graduate (B.A.)	1(16.67)	—	—	1(6.25)	2(2.53)
Total	6(100.00)	39(100.00)	18(100.00)	16(100.00)	79(100.00)

Note: 1. (—) indicates nil.
2. Figures in parentheses are percentages to column total.

maximum (39.72 per cent) of the total households, followed by primary, middle and graduation with 28, 13 and 2 households respectively. Further, one of the two households with graduation as the highest level of education attained was from the mechanized boat owner households. A comparison of the occupational patterns with regard to the highest level of education attained in a household indicates that the other households are better endowed with education as compared to boat owner and crew households. The average number of educated persons per household was 3.41 persons. Of the six households with all illiterates four were non-mechanized boat owner households. A comparison of the educational level of the fishermen of Bokkapatna Bengre with that of other villages indicates that the education level of Bokkapatna Bengre fishermen is high even as compared to the education level of Chorwad (a highly mechanized village in Gujarat) fishermen.

Migration and typology of migrants

The migration of the fishermen in the village has been analysed in terms of long-term and short-term migration. To analyse the long-term migration we have elicited information about the place of birth of the head of the households.

Table 9.8 gives the distribution of hodseholds by occupation and location of the birthplace of the household head. Of the total 79 households, 45 (56.96 per cent) had the birthplace of the household head outside the village but within the district. Thus, about 57 per cent of the households in the village were immigrant households. Of the total 45 immigrant households maximum (21) were the NMB households, followed by crew, others, and MB households with 4, 7 and 6 households respectively. The number of immigrant households was high in the case of Bokkapatna Bengre as compared to other fishing villages selected for the study.

TABLE 9.8

Distribution of households by occupational pattern and birthplace location of the household head, Bengre

Location of birth-place	Number of households which had their head's birth place indicated for				Total
	MB	NMB	Crew	Others	
1. Same village	—	18(46.15)	7(38.89)	9(56.25)	34(43.04)
2. Outside the village	6(100.00)	21(53.85)	11(61.11)	7(43.75)	45(56.96)
Total	6(100.00)	39(100.00)	18(100.00)	16(100.00)	79(100.00)

Note: 1. (—) indicates nil.
2. Figures in parentheses are percentages to column total.

Unlike long-term migration short-term migration is out-migration from the village. Short migrations from the village are seasonal and are mainly due to seasonal variations in the availability of fish. On the basis of the information obtained during the census taken in 1981 we found that short-term migration is restricted to two or three mechanized boat owner households only.

Social participation of fishermen

The social participation of the fishermen is analysed in terms of their membership of various organization such as the fishermen co-operative society, caste association and Gram Panchayat. In addition, their membership in each organization and multiple organizations is also analysed.

There is one fishermen's co-operative society in the village established in 1956. Our census taken in 1981 indicated the total members of the co-operative society to be 26. Of this 11 were from "others", seven each from MB and NMB owners, and one from crew. The 26 members of the co-operative society represented 12 households of the village.

The Youth Club of the village had 16 members drawn from seven households. The Club has a larger representation of NMB owner households with four and is followed by MB owner and crew with two and one households respectively.

The caste associations had the highest membership as compared to any other social organization with 99 members drawn from 22 households. Once again the NMB owner households accounted for the maximum of the members in caste associations with 49 members and are followed by others, crew and MB households with 22, 20 and 8 members respectively.

In addition to the above organizations, one MB owner household of the village had membership in the recreation club with two members.

An analysis of the participation of households according to their membership in various organizations indicated that about 17 households of the village were not having membership in any organization while two households had membership in as many as four organizations. Further, 36 households had membership in one of the above organizations, 15 in two organizations, and 9 in three organizations. The two households with membership in four organizations were from MB and NMB owner households.

MECHANIZATION: ITS IMPACT ON PRODUCTION SYSTEM

The study of the mechanization of fishing craft and its impact in terms of organizations, output, income distribution of gains from technological development, etc., on the production system will be the subject matter of this section.

Technology of production

Both traditional and modern technologies of production exist in the village. The craft technology consists of both mechanized and non-mechanized craft (dugout canoes). The dugout canoes' length ranged from 15 to 40 feet in length. The mechanized craft consisted of trawlers and purse-seiners. Before the introduction of mechanized craft in the village in 1968 the fishing activity was undertaken with the help of dugout canoes and rampani. There were three rampani units in operation till 1973 in the village. With the widespread introduction of purse-seiners in the village and other parts of the district, rampani units in the village as well as other parts of the district have disappeared.

The first mechanized boat acquired by the villagers in 1968 was a trawler. In 1981 there were 3 purse-seiners, 6 trawlers and 49 dugout canoes. The distribution of these boats according to the year of purchase is presented in Table 9.9. All the three purse-seiners which are owned jointly by the villagers and few fishermen outside the village were purchased in 1978. The six trawlers have been acquired by the villagers over a long period from 1968 to 1978. No mechanized boat in the village has been acquired after 1978, while over 56 per cent of the non-mechanized boats invariably dugout canoes of less than 25 feet in length were acquired between 1978 and 1981. Of the total 49 dugout canoes in the village only one canoe was of a length of over 25 feet and the rest were of below 25 feet. Mechanization of the fishing craft in the village started in 1968 with the introduction of only one trawler, but picked up greatly after 1975.

The gear technology of the village consisted of four main types of fishing nets. They are purse-seine nets, trawler nets, gill nets and cast nets. The first two type of nets are associated

TABLE 9.9

Distribution of different type of boats according to the year of purchase, Bengre (1981)

Year of acquiring	MB		NMB (Dugout)	
	Purse-seiner	Trawler	Below 25 ft.	Above 25 ft.
Up to 1965	—	—	—	—
1966	—	—	6	—
1967	—	—	2	—
1968	—	1	1	—
1969	—	—	—	—
1970	—	—	1	—
1971	—	1	—	—
1972	—	—	5	—
1973	—	—	1	—
1974	—	1	—	—
1975	—	2	3	—
1976	—	—	1	—
1977	—	—	1	1
1978	3	1	2	—
1979	—	—	1	—
1980	—	—	5	—
1981	—	—	19	—
Total	3	6	48	1

Nate: (—) indicates nil.

with mechanized craft and the other two with non-mechanized craft.

In 1981 there were three purse-seine nets and 10 trawl nets in the village. There was not much variation in the length and mesh size of these nets. The total number of gill nets in the village was 17 of which one was owned by household owning MB and NMB, 11 were by NMB owner households, and 5 by crew households. The mesh size of these nets was between ½ and 2 inch. These are usually used for catching small pelagic fish such as sardines and mackerel. The length of all these nets was less than 500 feet. The number of cast nets in the village in 1981 was 36. There were more cast net units (31) as compared to gill net units (17) in the non-mechanized sector of the village. The yarn used for mending all the above type of nets consisted of both nylon and monofilament. The nets made out of nylon yarn account for 100 per cent in the case of purse-seine nets.

Ownership of productive assets

In the village there were 3 purse-seiners, 6 trawlers and 49 dugout canoes owned by 55 households indicating more than one owner/partner of boat in a household in some cases. Usually, mechanized boats were jointly or collectively owned and non-mechanized boats were owned individually. The distribution of households, according to caste and partnership/ownership of boats in the village, is presented in Table 9.10. There was

TABLE 9.10

Distribution of households according to caste and partnership/ownership of the boat, Bengre (1981)

Partnership/ownership of type of boat	No. of boats owned by the stated caste		Total
	Mogaveera	Harijan	
1. Purse-seiner+Trawler+Dugout	1(100.00)	—	1(100.00)
2. Purse-seiner	2(100 00)	—	2(100.00)
3. Trawler+Dugout	1(100.00)	—	1(100.00)
4. Trawler	4(100.00)	—	4(100.00)
5. Dugout	18(38.30)	29(61.70)	47(100.00)

Note: 1. (—) indicates nil.
2. Figures in parentheses are percentages to row total.

one household which had partnership in both purse-seiner and trawler and owned a dugout canoe. There was another household with partnership in trawler and ownership of a dugout canoe. There are 47 households owning 47 dugout canoes. Of these 47 households 29 were of the Harijan community and the rest were of the Mogaveera community. All the partners in the mechanized boats of the village were from the Mogaveera community. Thus, the Mogaveera community as a whole is better endowed with the mechanized and non-mechanized boats. However, 29 (82.86 per cent) of the 35 Harijan households owned some or the other form of productive assets while in the case of Mogaveera only 26 (59.1 per cent) of the 44 households owned the productive assets. Thus, the distribution of boats and gear is more equitable in the case of Harijans as compared to the Mogaveeras. All the partnerships in the mechanized boats by the fishermen of the village add up to one purse-seiner and three trawlers.

The above analysis, however, does not indicate the extent of inequitability of the distribution of productive fishery assets over households. Therefore, we have computed the Gini coefficient for the distribution of value[1] of productive assets over the households. The estimated Gini coefficient for the distribution of productive assets with its value of 0.8122 indicates a highly inequitable distribution of assets. Figure 9.2 gives the Lorenz curve of the distribution of fishery assets in terms of value.

Of the six possible combinations of ownership and status of owner and worker on the boat, we found the following three to be predominant in the village:

(a) Individual owner, owner worker and non-owner partner (IO, OW and NOP),
(b) Collective owner, owner worker and non-owner partner (CO, OW and NOP), and
(c) Collective owner, owner non-worker and non-owner partner (CO, ONW, and NOP).

The first pattern accounts for almost all the non-mechanized boat in the village. Further, a large portion of the mechanized boats follow a pattern as indicated in (b) above while a few are operated in the pattern indicated in (c).

Fish production and distribution of income: Present and past

The aspects of fish production covered in this section relate to the location of the landing place and quantity of landing during the pre- and post-mechanization periods.

While all the non-mechanized boats in the village landed their catches on the open sandy beach of the village, trawlers and purse-seiners landed their catches at Mangalore for want of landing, berthing and marketing facilities. Before the mechanized boats were introduced in the village in 1968, the rampani owners also used to land their catches in the village landing centre. In this sense the introduction of mechanized craft in the village brought about a shift in the location of the landing centre.

The specieswise production and value of production during the pre- and post-mechanization periods in the village are presented in Table 9.11. The total marine fish production and its value at current prices during the pre-mechanization period (1967-68) has been estimated to be 1,092 tonnes and Rs. 4,87,120 respectively. During 1967-68, sardines accounted for maximum of the total landing in terms of both quantity and value with 506 tonnes and the corresponding value of Rs. 1,18,910. Sardines, mackerel, catfish and sharks between themselves accounted for over 72 per cent of the total landings in terms of quantity and about 75 per cent in terms of value. The comparison of the landings during the pre- and post-mechanization periods indicated that the total landings by the boats owned by the fishermen of the village decreased from 1,092 tonnes during 1967-68 to 975 tonnes during 1981-82. Further, the landing centre for the mechanized boats has shifted to the nearby larger assembly centre. Thus, the actual landings in the village amounted to only 417 tonnes. However, the value of landings has increased from Rs. 4,87,120 to Rs. 13,77,830 after the mechanization of fishing craft. A clear understanding of the increasing trend in the value of landings indicated that the major portion of the increase in the value of landings is largely because of the increased prices of fish and to a smaller extent because of the changing species composition in favour of high priced species. With the introduction of mechanized craft, the share of non-mechanized craft in the total landings has gone down to 57.23 per cent in terms of quantity and 38.72 per cent in terms of value while during the pre-mechanization period the total landings were by non-mechanized

TABLE 9.11

Specieswise marine fish landings and gross value of output during pre- and post-mechanization periods, Bengre

(*Qty.: in tonnes*)
(*Value: in '000 Rupees*)

	Landings and value of landings during									
	Pre-mechanization period (1967-68)			Post-mechanization period						
	Price* per tonne	Landings	Value of landings	Price* per tonne	Landings by NMB	Value of landings	Landings by MB†	Value of landings	Total landings	Total value of landings
1	2	3	4	5	6	7	8	9	10	11
1. Sardines	0.235	506	118.91	0.517	140	72.38	205	105.99	345	178 37
2. Mackerel	0.916	124	113.58	2.612	69	180.23	42	109.70	111	289.23
3. Catfish	0.613	103	63.14	0.876	36	31.54	79	69.20	115	100.74
4. Sharks	0.824	87	71.69	3.651	0	29.21	16	58.42	24	87.62
5. Carangids	0.934	54	50.44	3.152	10	31.52	15	47.28	25	78.80
6. Pomfret	1.132	2	2.26	6.391	1	6.39	6	38.35	7	44.74

TABLE 9.11 (*Contd.*)

1	2	3	4	5	6	7	8	9	10	11
7. Seer fish	1.292	4	5.17	3.659	3	10.98	9	32.93	12	43.91
8. Silver Belly	0.320	3	0.96	1.035	Neg.	Neg.	61	63.14	61	63.14
9. Prawns and Lobsters	2.094	3	6.26	12.713	1	12.71	16	203.36	17	216.07
10. Others	0.2656	206	54.71	1.064	149	59.54	109	115.98	258	274.51
Total	—	1092	487.12	—	417	533.50	558	844.35	975	1377.83

Note: Neg. indicates negligible.

*The information about the prices is obtained mainly from the office of the Assistant Director of Fisheries, Bangalore.

†The landings of the mechanized boats are not in the village. Further the landings relate to the number of boats owned fully by the villagers. The villagers' share in the total boats works out to one purse-seiner and three trawlers.

craft. Our observation about the decrease in the total landings of the village is also found to be true on the basis of the landing centrewise data from the Department of Fisheries, Government of Karnataka. The data indicated that the total landings in the village had decreased from 1,483.81 tonnes during 1971-72 to 698.44 tonnes during 1980-81.

Measurement of household income: In this section we shall attempt to estimate the income from both fishery and non-fishery activities for each of the households. The income from fishery sources mainly consisted of the returns on the investment in fishing equipment and family labour expended for fishing, and returns from fish marketing. For working out the returns on the capital invested in fishing equipment and labour, it is necessary to estimate the economics of the fishing craft and gear. The details of the economics of different type of fishing craft are presented below.

The quarterwise gross value of output per unit of different type of boats in the village at 1981-82 prices is shown in Table 9.12. While in the case of purse-seiners and trawlers 43 to 50 per cent of the gross value of output is gained in the October-December quarter, the value of output from the non-mechanized boats in the same quarter ranges between 17 and 41 per cent of the total value of catches. The second important quarter is January-March in all cases excepting dugout canoes operating the cast net units.

As expected, the annual gross value of output per unit is the highest in the case of purse-seiners (Rs. 5,29,895) and is followed by trawlers (Rs. 1,38,370), dugout canoes with gill nets (Rs. 12,487) and dugout canoes with cast nets (Rs. 2,946).

Itemwise variable costs for operating different type of boats in the village are given in Table 9.13. The total variable cost will be observed to be Rs. 684.15 for purse-seiners, Rs. 221.50 for trawlers, Rs. 8.25 for dugout canoes with gill nets and only Rs. 1.50 for dugout canoes with cast nets. In the case of both purse-seiners and trawlers, the bulk of the variable cost was accounted for buying the fuel and lubricants.

It was observed that crew salaries were mainly paid in terms of the share in the gross returns. In the case of trawlers and purse-seiners, the share of the crew was 30 per cent and in the case of dugout canoes, it was 60 per cent of the gross

TABLE 9.12

Quarterwise gross value of output of different type of boats, Bengre (1981-82)

(in Rupees)

Quarter	Gross value of output in stated quarter for			
	Trawler	Purse-seiner	Cast net unit (dugout canoes)	Gill net unit* (dug-out canoes)
July-September	18349 (13.26)	78452 (14.81)	1159 (39.34)	2315 (18.54)
October-December	69360 (50.13)	226395 (42.72)	512 (17.38)	5160 (41.32)
January-March	30985 (22.39)	156450 (29.52)	360 (12.22)	3019 (24.18)
April-June	19676 (14.22)	68598 (12.95)	915 (31.06)	1993 (15.96)
Total	138370 (100)	529895 (100)	2946 (100)	12487 (100)

Note: 1. Figures in parentheses represent percentages to column total.
2. *All the sample units are mackerel gill net units.

returns. Further, the crew share was equally distributed for all crew members. In our computations of the annual fixed cost for operating different type of boats we have taken crew salaries as part of fixed cost. The itemwise annual fixed cost for operating different type of boats in the village were estimated. The total fixed costs were as follows: purse-seine Rs. 3,16,363, trawler Rs. 80,021, dugout canoe with gill nets Rs. 9,885 and dugout canoes with cast nets Rs. 590 (Table 9.14).

The annual gross and net returns of different type of boats are presented in Table 9.15. It is observed that the net returns per unit for purse-seiners were Rs. 78,754. In the case of trawlers, the net returns were Rs. 14,271. In the case of dugout canoes with cast nets, the net returns were Rs. 2,018. Surprisingly the returns from dugout canoes with gill nets were lower than the returns from the dugout canoes with cast nets. The net returns from the dugout canoes with gill nets were only Rs. 1,034.

TABLE 9.13

Itemwise variable cost for operating different type of boats, Bengre (1981-82)

(in Rupees)

Items of expenditure	Expenditure on stated item for			
	Trawler	Purse-seiner	Dugout canoe cast net unit	Dugout canoe gill net unit
1. Fuel	186.50	506.35	—	—
2. Mobile oil and other lubricants	10.40	29.50	—	—
3. Wages to daily labourers	4.60	—	—	—
4. Ice and Water	3.50	25.40	—	—
5. Food expenditure for crew	2.75	75.00	—	2.25
6. Cost of net twine	4.25	29.40	1.50	4.75
7. Others	9.50	18.50	—	1.25
Total	221.50	684 15	1.50	8.25

Note: (—) indicates nil.

On the basis of the economics of different type of boats, and the household ownership of fishing assets and employment patterns, we have estimated the income accruing for each household from fishing. The data on income accruing for fishing are supplemented by the data on income from fish marketing and other non-fishery-related activities, to estimate the total annual income of each of the households. The basis for the income from fish marketing particularly retailing and non-fishery sources was the recall data collected during the census of the households. The total income generated by all the households from all economic activities in the village has been estimated to be Rs. 8,77,630 of which Rs. 6,99,910 was from fishery-related activities and the rest Rs. 1,77,720 was from non-fishing activities.

Distribution of income: The distribution of income by occupation and sources is given in Table 9.16. It can be observed

TABLE 9.14

Itemwise annual fixed costs for operating different type of boats, Bengre (1981-82)

(*in Rupees*)

Items of expenditure	Expenditure on stated items for			
	Trawler	Purse-seiner	Dugout canoe cast net unit	Dugout canoe gill net unit
1. Salaries of crew*	41511(6)	158968(28)	NA†	8325(2)
2. Repairs and Maintenance	5680	13685	—	550
3. Dry docking and Oil painting	1730	3950	150	370
4. Insurance	2680	10560	—	—
5. Interest on borrowed capital**	12470	39280	—	—
6. Depreciation***	14560	64490	350	760
7. Others	1390	25430	90	250
Total	80021	316363	590	9885

Note: *The crew salaries usually are paid in terms of share in gross returns. In the case of trawlers and purse-seiners, the share of crew was 30 per cent and in the case of dugout canoes, it was 60 per cent of the gross returns. The crew share was distributed equally among the total crew required.

**About 75 per cent of the total investment on the equipment is assumed to be the borrowed capital and the interest is calculated at the rate of 10 per cent.

***For working out the depreciation, we have used a variety of assumptions regarding the life of various components. For details, see the profile of Kadekar.

†NA indicates Not Available.

that non-mechanized boat owners accounted for about 60 per cent of the total income arising out of the fishery-related activities. The share of mechanized boat owners was about 17 per cent and crew member households got about 18 per cent of the income. The remaining income went to "other" categories. In the case of incomes from non-fishery-related activities, the

TABLE 9.15

Gross and net return of different type of boats, Bengre (1981-82)

Particulars	Trawler	Purse-seiner	Dugout canoe cast net unit	Dugout canoe gill net unit
1. Gross returns	138370	529895	2946	12487
2. Expenditure:				
(a) Annual variable costs*	44078(199)	134778(197)	338(225)	1568(190)
(b) Fixed costs	80021	316363	590	9885
Sub-total	124099	451141	928	11453
3. Net returns	14271	78754	2018	1034

Note: *Estimated by multiplying the average daily expenditure by the number of fishing days. The estimated number of fishing days for different type of boats are indicated in parentheses of the row.

TABLE 9.16

Distribution of income according to occupation, Bengre (1981-82)

Occupation	Income			Per household	Per capita
	Fishery	Non-fishery	Total		
1. MB	117487 (16.79)	2000 (1.13)	119487 (13.61)	19914.50	3144.39
2. NMB	416671 (59.53)	68040 (38.28)	484711 (55.23)	12428.48	1864.27
3. CRM	125718 (17.96)	4400 (2.48)	130118 (14.83)	7228.78	1193.74
4. Others	40036 (5.72)	103280 (58.11)	143316 (16.33)	8957.25	1666.47
Total	699912 (100)	177720 (100)	877632 (100)	11109.27	1780.19

Note: Figures in parentheses represent percentages to column total.

"other" categories got 58 per cent of the total income followed by the non-mechanized boat owners with 38 per cent and a very small proportion of this income was earned by mechanized boat owners. As expected, the per household and per capita incomes were the highest in the case of mechanized boat owners. The mechanized boat owners earned Rs. 19,914.50 per household income and Rs. 3,144.39 per capita income. This was followed by the non-mechanized boat owners with Rs. 12,428.48 per household income and Rs. 1,864.27 as per capita income. The crew member households earned Rs. 7,288.78 per household income and Rs. 1,193.74 as per capita income. The households in the category of others were slightly better off than the crew members. They earn an income of Rs. 8,957.25 per household and Rs. 1,666.47 per capita.

The computed value of the Gini ratio was 0.3136 and indicated a more even distribution of income as compared to the distribution of assets. However, the computed Gini ratio for income distribution was higher than the corresponding ratio for a highly mechanized fishing village, viz. Chorwad in Gujarat. The large variation of Gini ratios for assets and income distribution in the village was mainly because of the large number of non-mechanized boats, with their favourable factor shares to labour in the village. The Lorenz curve for income distribution in the village is presented in Figure 9.2.

Disposal of fish

The estimated utilization pattern of the fish landings in the village is presented in Table 9.17. Although the species composition of the marine fish landings did not undergo any major changes in the village, the utilization pattern of marine fish in the village has changed in favour of sun-drying, fishmeal/oil extraction and exports.

The shares of sun-drying, fishmeal/oil extraction and exports has increased from 20.76 per cent, 18.63 per cent and 0.02 per cent to 21.00 per cent, 23.76 per cent and 2.26 per cent respectively. The share of fresh consumption has decreased from 60.59 per cent to 52.98 per cent during the period under consideration. The major contributing factor for the observed shift in the utilization pattern of fish landings in the village can be attributed to the introduction of trawlers in the fishing

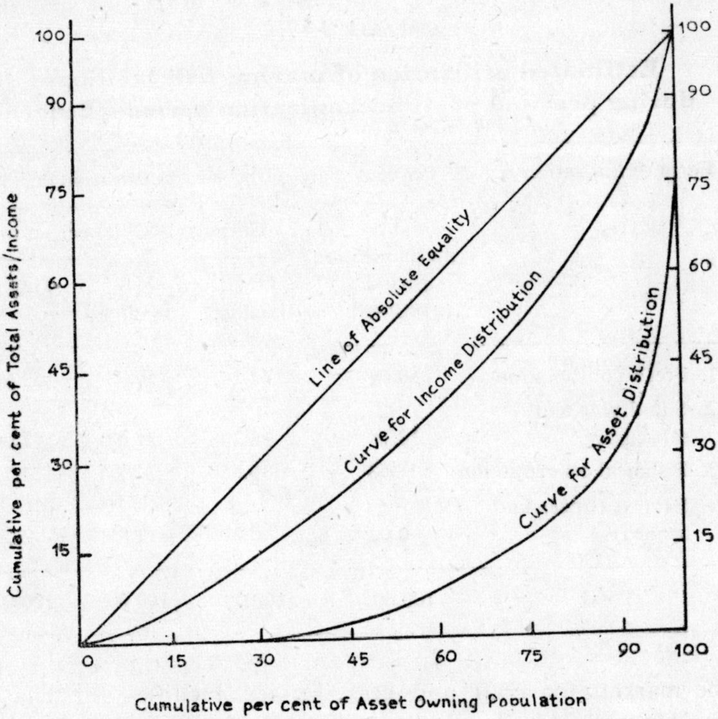

	Assets	Income
Gini Ratio	0.8122	0.3136

FIG. 9.2: *Lorenz Curve for assets and income distribution, Bengre (1981-82)*

activity of the village and the rapid development of the processing industry.

MARKETS IN THE VILLAGE

In this section we shall examine the markets for inputs, labour credit and output in the village with a view to understanding the changes in these markets with the mechanization of fishing craft.

Market for inputs

The various input markets considered in this section relate to

TABLE 9.17

Estimated utilization of marine fish landings during pre- and post-mechanization periods, Bengre

Form of utilization	Per cent share of the stated utilization during			
	Pre-mechanization period (1967-68)	Current (1982-83) period in		
		NMB landings	MB landings	Total
1. Fresh consumption	60.59	62.14	50.78	52.98
2. Sun-drying and salt-curing	20.76	18.20	21.67	21.00
3. Fishmeal/oil extraction	18.63	19.65	24.75	23.76
4. Exports (frozen and canned)	0.02	0.01	2.80	2.26
Total	100.00	100.00	100.00	100.00

the markets for craft and gear, service facilities for boats/engines, and fuel oil and lubricants. All the inputs except for craft and gear indicated above were unknown to the traditional fishermen. Even in the market for craft and gear also there are some structural changes with the growth of mechanized craft in the village. The changes in these markets are presented below.

The distribution of boats owned by sample respondents according to the place of purchase/construction indicated that all the boats owned by villagers were purchased/constructed outside the village but within the district. Further, of the total 43 boats for which we have information nine were new boats acquired from boat builders while 34 were old boats acquired from fishermen. This shows that the transaction of boats among fishermen in the village is very common. Generally, acquiring of old boats was predominant in the case of non-mechanized boats, which accounted for 30 of the total 34 old boats.

The service facilities for boats are available to the fishermen of the village only in the nearby large assembling centre. However, the repairs of smaller non-mechanized boats is undertaken by the carpenter who visits the village periodically from the nearby larger fishing centre. Further, as the mechanized boats of the village operate from the nearby assembling centre, facilities for supply of fuel oils and lubricants are not available nor are required in the village. The market for these inputs in the nearby assembling centre was fairly well developed and competitive. The sources for fuel oil and lubricants in the assembling centre consist of both private entrepreneur and co-operatives. The supply from co-operative sources was predominant especially during scarcity conditions. At such times the co-operatives supply fuels and lubricants in limited quantities which are found to be insufficient for normal fishing trips. Therefore, fishermen buy fuel oil and lubricants at a premium. And the frequency of short supply of fuel oils in the recent period of the village fishing scene was found to be gradually increasing and was said to be around 15 to 20 days in a fishing season. Gear and yarn for net mending for the fishermen of the village were supplied by various stores in the nearby assembling centre.

Market for labour

As indicated earlier, only 45 of the total 79 households own the fishing equipment while the remaining derive their major income by selling labour time. Of the total 34 households which derive their income by selling labour time about 53 per cent are involved in selling labour time for fishing. Thus, hiring of labour to undertake fishing is a predominant activity. The different labour contracts, demand-supply situation of labour, labour mobility and effects of mechanization on the labour market in the village are discussed below.

The labour contract in the village is completely share contract in the case of mechanized and non-mechanized boats. The detailed sharing pattern of crew in the village is similar to the pattern explained in the profile of Kadekar. The sharing of fish produce is usually in terms of money, that is, the craft owner markets the total landings of the boat and the share of the crew is paid after the realization of sale proceeds. The crew in either mechanized craft or non-mechanized craft is not provided with free meal by the employer during the normal fishing trips. However, during the longer trips the entire food expenditure of crew is borne by the craft owners and the long trips in general are limited to mechanized boats.

Demand for and supply of labourers in the village: In order to understand the employment situation in the village, we have estimated the surplus labourers in the village. Table 9.18 gives the estimates of surplus labourers according to occupation in the village during 1981. It can be seen from the table that at an aggregate level there was a deficit of 37 labourers in the village as compared to the total requirement of the craft owned by the village fishermen. The total requirement of crew for operating the fishing craft owned by the fishermen was 134 consisting of 44 for mechanized and 90 for non-mechanized boats, while the supply of labourers from crew and boat owner households was only 73 and 22 respectively. In addition, two labourers were estimated to be available from other households for fishing. It is interesting to note that about 12 members are involved in occupations other than fishing while a short supply of labourers for fishing was found in the village. The involvement of the fishermen household members owning fishing craft was again found to be mainly because of the tendency of well-to-do fishermen to turn to occupations other than fishing. Of the total 12 members in occupations other than fishing, at least 6 were found to be in better rewarding occupations as compared to fishing.

The estimated labour participation pattern in terms of family and hired labourers for operating different type of boats in the village during 1981-82 is presented in Table 9.19. The tendency of affluent fishermen to withdraw the family members from drudgerous and risky fishing operations is also strengthened by the data on labour participation pattern in Table 9.19. The involvement of family labourers accounts for about 6.9 per cent in the case of purse-seiner partners, 33.33 per cent in the case of trawler owners and 62.22 per cent in the case of dugout canoe owners. At an aggregate level about 47 per cent of the total crew required is drawn from the equipment owner households and the remaining are hired.

Labour mobility: To understand the labour mobility in the context of fishing activity in the village, we have computed the labour mobility ratio for the sample crew. About 94 per cent

TABLE 9.18

Estimates of surplus labourers according to occupation, Bengre (1981)

Particulars	No. of members in households of				Total
	MB owners	NMB owners	Crew	Others	
1. Number of households	6	39	18	16	79
2. Number of able-bodied male members of family	20	73	28	25	146
3. Number of adult male members with occupation other than fishing	3	9	4	20	36
4. Number of adult male members who have not yet entered the working force (students)	—	8	2	2	12
5. Number of members actively engaged or at best having no other occupation	17	56	22	2	97
6. Number of members required for operating the fishing equipment	44	90	—	—	134
7. Surplus labourers in the fishing workforce	—27	—34	22	2	—37
8. Surplus labourers in fishing per household	—4.5	—0.87	1.22	0.13	—0.47

Note: 1. (—) indicates nil.
2. Negative surplus indicates deficits.

TABLE 9.19

Estimated* labour participation pattern, family and hired, for operating different types of boats, Bengre (1981-82)

Type of boat	Total No. of boats**	Estimatad average crew size required per boat	Total crew required	Estimated source of crew		
				Family	Hired	
					Sharing	Salary
1. Purse-seiners	1	28.6	29	2 (6.90)	27 (93.10)	—
2. Trawlers	3	5	15	5 (33.33)	10 (66.67)	—
3. Dugout canoes	35	2.57	90	56 (62.22)	34 (37.78)	—
Total	39	—	134	63 (47.01)	71 (52.99)	—

Note: 1. Figures in parentheses indicate the share of family and labourers in total crew required.
2. (—) indicates nil.

*Estimated on the basis of information from sample respondents.

**Relate to the number of boats fully owned by the fishermen of the village.

of the crew in the case of purse-seiners and 75 per cent in the case of trawlers of the village were found to be immobile, i.e. they did not change their employer any time ever since they started fishing as crew. For the remainder also the labour mobility ratio was very low. It is quite puzzling to find that an overwhelming portion of the sample crew was found to be immobile in a labour shortage situation in the village. This, however, may be because of the relatively better economic returns of the crew in mechanized boats. This also suggests that labour mobility may be very high in the case of the crew in non-mechanized boats. An analysis of reasons for change of employer for crew with non-zero labour mobility indicated that the dispute with the boat owner was the main reason for the change of employer and it was found that the crew identified the new employer after breaking relations with the current employer. Interlocking of labour and credit was observed to be practically non-existing in the case of crew in mechanized boats. All the sample crew were neither having any outstanding debt as on the date of survey nor did they borrow from the boat owner at the time of joining the owner.

Occupation mobility: The size distribution of working population in the sample households, according to the pace of graduation to current position in the village, is presented in Table 9.20. The pace of graduation of majority of the boat owners and crew was found to be very low. However, the higher pace of graduation accounted for over 28.57 per cent in the case of MB owners while it was less than 14.29 per cent for all others.

Market for credit

Though credit is not an input, it plays an important role in fisheries particularly in the mechanized sector to acquire various inputs such as boats, gear, fuel oil, ice, etc., and other household articles. The main source of credit observed in the village were commercial banks, co-operative societies/banks, village funds, and friends and relatives. The first three sources are known as formal lending agencies while the last is an informal source. It was observed that few of the fishermen have borrowed from both sources. It was also observed that no interlinking of

TABLE 9.20

Distribution of working population in sample househoulds according to the pace of graduation to current position, Bengre (1981-82)

Pace of graduation	No. of individuals with stated pace of graduation					Total
	MB owners	NMB owners	Crew in MB	Crew in NMB	Others	
1. High	2 (28.57)	1 (4.35)	2 (11.11)	1 (14.29)	—	6 (9.23)
2. Medium	1 (14.29)	1 (4.35)	1 (5.56)	—	—	3 (4.62)
3. Low	4 (57.14)	21 (91.30)	15 (83.33)	6 (85.71)	10 (100.00)	56 (86.15)
Total	7 (100.00)	23 (100.00)	18 (100.00)	7 (100.00)	10 (100.00)	65 (100.00)

Note: 1. (—) indicates nil.
2. Figures in parentheses indicate percentages to column total.

marketing and credit exists in the product market of the village.

The distribution of households, according to the source of borrowings and occupations, and their outstanding debt as on December 31, 1981 in the village, is presented in Table 9.21. The total outstanding debt of the fishermen has been estimated to be over Rs. 2,03,950 of which MB owner households accounted for less than 12.66 per cent with outstanding debt of Rs. 25,800. Other households accounted for maximum of the total outstanding debt with Rs. 87,100 and is followed by NMB owners with Rs. 77,550. Average outstanding debt per household was in the range of Rs. 1,687 for crew to Rs. 10,887 for other households and the average for all households was Rs. 4,078 per household. The formal sources of credit account for maximum of the total outstanding debt in the village with Rs. 1,40,750. Of the total outstanding debt from formal lending agencies, the commercial banks alone account for about 96.80 per cent with Rs. 1,36,250. Thus, the commercial banks are the single most important source of credit for the fishermen of the village. The amount outstanding with multiple sources and the number of accounts in the category indicated that the borrowing by the fishermen from many sources for the same purpose was relatively low. This in turn indicates the easy availability of credit for acquiring boats and gear, and for maintenance of boats. The distribution of households according to the purpose of borrowing of the outstanding debt and occupations in the village is presented in Table 9.22. About 36.71 per cent of households did not have any outstanding debt. Of the total 50 households having an outstanding debt as on December 31, 1981, about 30 borrowed for purchase of fishing craft and gear, 9 borrowed to meet fishing and personal expenditure and the remaining 11 borrowed to meet the household expenditure. All the MB owners with an outstanding debt have borrowed for the purchase of craft and gear. To meet the household expenditure is the major reason for borrowing in the case of other households. However, there were three households accounting for 18.75 per cent of the total who have borrowed for purchasing the craft and gear in the case of other households.

The size distribution of households, according to the

TABLE 9.21

Distribution of households according to the source of borrowing and occupation and their outstanding debt as on December 31, 1981, Bengre

(in Rupees)

Source of borrowing	No. of households having outstanding debts to the								Total	
	MB		NMB		Crew		Others			
	No.	Debt	No.	Debt	No.	Debt	No.	Debt	No.	Outstanding debt
I. *Formal Lending Agencies*:										
Commercial Banks	4	25200 (6300)	17	31050 (1826.47)	—	—	4	80000 (20000)	25	136250 (5450)
Co-operative Societies/ Banks	1	600 (600)	1	1500 (1500)	—	—	—	—	2	2100 (1050)
Village Funds	—	—	1	1000	1	300 (300)	2	1100 (550)	4	2400 (600)
Sub-total	5	25800	19	33550	1	300	6	81100	31	140750
II. *Informal Source*:										
Friends and Relatives	—	—	6	17200 (2866.67)	2	3000 (1500)	2	6000 (3000)	10	26200
III. *Multiple Source*	—	—	4	26800 (6700)	5	10200 (2040)	—	—	9	37000
Total	5	25800 (5160)	29	77550 (2674.14)	8	13500 (1687.50)	8	87100 (10887.50)	50	203950 (4079)

Note: 1. (—) indicates nil.
2. Figures in parentheses represent per household outstanding debt.

TABLE 9.22

Distribution of households according to the purpose of borrowings of the outstanding debt and occupation, Bengre (1981)

Reason for borrowing the outstanding debt	Number of households for stated reason of borrowing of				Total
	MB owners	NMB owners	Crew	Others	
1. No outstanding debt	1 (16.67)	9 (23.08)	12 (66.67)	7 (43.75)	29 (36.71)
2. Purchase of fishing craft and gear	5 (83.33)	21 (53.84)	3 (5.56)	3 (18.75)	30 (37.97)
3. To meet fishing and personal expenditure	—	7 (17.95)	1 (5.55)	1 (6.25)	9 (11.39)
4. To meet household expenditure	—	2 (5.13)	4 (22.22)	5 (31.25)	11 (13.92)
Total	6 (100.00)	39 (100.00)	18 (100.00)	16 (100.00)	79 (100.00)

Note: 1. (—) indicates nil.
2. Figures in parentheses represent percentages to column total.

occupation and total outstanding debt in the village at the time of survey (Table 9.23), indicates that majority have outstanding debt between Rs. 1,000 and Rs. 3,000 and one household in others had an outstanding debt of over Rs. 35,000. The modal value of the outstanding debt was in the range of Rs. 3,001 to Rs. 6,000 for MB owners, Rs. 1001 to Rs. 3,000 for NMB owners, less than Rs. 1,000 for crew and other households.

Further, the field observations during the data collection for study in the village reveals the following two major changes

TABLE 9.23

Size distribution of households according to occupation and total outstanding debt, Bengre, 1981

Range of outstanding debt (Rs.)	Number of households with outstanding debt in stated range or				Total
	MB owners	NMB owners	Crew	Others	
Zero outstanding	1 (16.67)	9 (23.08)	12 (66.67)	7 (43.75)	29 (36.70)
Up to 1000	—	7 (17.95)	5 (27.78)	4 (25.00)	16 (20.25)
1001-3000	1 (16.66)	16 (41.03)	1 (5.55)	3 (18.75)	21 (26.58)
3001-6000	—	4 (10.26)	—	1 (6.25)	5 (6.33)
6001-10000	4 (66.67)	1 (2.56)	—	—	5 (6.33)
10001-15000	—	1 (2.56)	—	—	1 (1.27)
15001-25000	—	1 (2.56)	—	—	1 (1.27)
25001-35000	—	—	—	—	—
35001 and above	—	—	—	1 (6.25)	1 (1.27)
Total	6 (100)	39 (100)	18 (100)	16 (100)	79 (100)

Note: 1. (—) indicates nil.
2. Figures in parentheses represent percentages to column total.

which have taken place in the credit market of the village. First, the average amount of borrowings by the fishermen has increased manifold, mainly because of the large capital requirement of mechanized boat owners. At the time of the survey the average outstanding debt of MB owner households was over

Rs. 5,000 while it was less than Rs. 2,700 for NMB households. Second, the share of formal lending agencies in the total credit extended to the fishermen of the village increased considerably. The increased share of the formal agencies in the credit market of the village was mainly because of the developmental policy of the government to promote mechanized fishing through a liberal credit facility.

Market for product

The discussion in this section is going to be around the historical evolution of fish market in the village and its structure, and the changes which have been brought about by the mechanization of fishing craft.

The fish marketing activity gained significant importance in the village only after the introduction of rampani fishing in the village. During the early period of rampani fishing the marketing activity in the village was not well developed and there were no wholesalers for marketing of fish landing in the village till 1930. However, fish marketing activity in the village picked up with the establishment of a fish meal and oil extraction unit and the starting of business by a wholesaler in the village in 1930. Subsequently, the number of market intermediaries increased considerably. During the immediate preceding period for mechanization of fishing craft in the village there were over 100 retailers, 50 vendors, 5 wholesalers of dry fish, 5 drying agents and 2 fish meal/oil unit owners to buy fish from the village fishermen. Being very close to Mangalore, the entire fish marketing activity of fresh fish was undertaken by mainly retailers and vendors. Therefore, there was a considerable reduction in the quantity of fish landings in the village because of the replacement of rampani by purse-seiner and the subsequent shift in the place of landing of mechanized boats. As a result of decreased landings in the village, the number of market intermediaries to buy the fish landings of the villagers decreased. At the time of survey it was found that only 20 retailers, 15 vendors, 2 dry fish wholesalers, 2 drying agents and 2 fish meal/oil plant owners were dependent on the fish landings at the village landing centre. Further, it was also found that the scale of operation of the existing market intermediates has decreased because of the decreased landings in the village. For example, the sardine oil extraction unit in the village used to crush about 15 tonnes of sardines per day for about 40 days in a year for extracting oil and fish meal during the pre-mechanization period while the same unit crushed only 350 tonnes of sardines during 1981-82. All the fish marketing intermediaries both during pre- and post-mechanization periods were from the fishermen community only. The functions of various marketing intermediaries have been explained in the last section.

With the existence of a large number of retailers/vendors the market conditions for output in the village appear to be fairly competitive. The landings of mechanized craft take place in the nearby city of Mangalore. The output market in Mangalore also was found to be fairly competitive.[2]

Two qualitative changes which have taken place in the product market of the village after the introdution of mechanized craft in the village are indicated below.

First, the predominant pattern for sale of fish in the village has changed from count to weight after the introduction of mechanized boats in the village. This is, however, not to suggest that the sale of fish during the current period by count does not exist in the village, but only that the predominant pattern is by weight. Further, only one variety of fish is sold by both weight and count during the current period in the village. A major change has taken place in the case of prawns—its selling pattern during the pre-mechanization period was by count but is by weight during the current period. Some low-priced varieties such as sardines were sold in terms of standard baskets during both periods, but the share of total landings sold in terms of baskets has decreased after mechanization.

Second, the interlinkage of marketing and credit has reduced after the introduction of mechanized craft in the village. However, the amount of loans advanced by fish traders has increased three or fourfold during the same period. The incidence of marketing and credit linkage in the case of prawn agents and fish processors was relatively high as compared to other marketing intermediaries during the current period while no marketing intermediaries of the above nature existed during the pre-mechanization period.

THE VILLAGE ECONOMY

In this section, we shall attempt to describe the assets of fishermen, consumer expenditure and savings and dissavings.

Assets structure of fishermen

The assets in addition to fishing equipment of the fishermen of the village were in the form of land as well as domestic livestock, house as well as household items. The majority of them (over 70 per cent) do not invest in such assets as the earnings of these fishermen are quite low and just sufficient to maintain their households. The possible smaller savings in general are invested for the development of fishing equipment. Thus, the production equipment constitutes the major part of their owned assets. Very few have invested in house, household items or any other such items.

Occupationwise distribution of the same is presented in Table 9.24. All the six MB households are without their own house and stay in rented houses. NMB owner households are the households with the highest number of owned houses with 13 followed by other households with 10 owned houses. Majority of the houses are valued at less than Rs. 5,000 while only two houses owned by other households are valued at more than Rs. 10,000.

Household items like transport vehicles, entertainment items, time indicators or kitchenware are owned by NMB owners in the village. One cycle is available in the village and it is owned by an NMB household. Of the total 79 households in the village, 19 own radios and 29 have some or the other kind of time indicators. In total six wrist-watches and five clocks are owned by MB households. Stove is used by 75 out of a total of 79 households in the village (Table 9.25).

The distribution of households according to the value of household articles is given in Table 9.26. More than 80 per cent of them own articles valued at less than Rs. 1,000 and 67 per cent less than Rs. 500. Only five households own articles valued at more than Rs. 2,500. It is observed that two MB owner households own household articles valued at more than Rs. 8,000 and it shows their tendency to invest in the items other than a house. The tendency of investment in articles

TABLE 9.24

Distribution of households according to occupation and value of owned houses, Bengre (1981)

Value range (Rs.)	No. of houses in the stated range of value of				Total
	MB owners	NMB owners	Crew	Others	
No own houses	6 (11.32)	26 (49.06)	15 (28.30)	6 (11.32)	53 (100)
Less than 1000	—	7 (58.33)	2 (16.67)	3 (25.00)	12 (100)
1001-3000	—	4 (66.66)	1 (16.67)	1 (16.67)	6 (100)
3001-5000	—	2 (50.00)	—	2 (50.00)	4 (100)
5001-10000	—	—	—	2 (100.00)	2 (100)
10001-10000	—	—	—	2 (100.00)	2 (100)
Sub-total of owned house	—	13 (50.00)	3 (11.54)	10 (38.46)	27 (100)
Total	6 (7.60)	39 (49.37)	18 (22.78)	16 (20.25)	79 (100)

Note: 1. (—) indicates nil.
2. Figures in parentheses represent percentages to row total.

other than a house in the village is mainly because of the lack of ownership right of the house plots in the villages.

The domestic livestock mainly in the form of poultry birds is owned by only 27 per cent households. Of the total 21 households owning some of the other form of livestock, 17 have the livestock valued at less than Rs. 50, three households have livestock valued at between Rs. 51 and Rs. 100, and one has livestock valued at over Rs. 150. Thus, not much investment is made on livestock in the village (Table 9.27).

TABLE 9.25

Ownership of different household items according to occupation, Bengre (1981-82)

Items	No. of households owning the stated items								Total	
	MB		NMB		Crew		Others		NI	HH
	NI	HH	NI	HH	NI	HH	NI	HH		
I. Transport Vehicles										
Cycle	—	—	1	1	—	—	—	—	1	1
II. Communication/ Entertainment										
Radio/Transistor	3	3	7	7	2	2	7	7	19	19
III. Office Equipment										
Chairs	13	4	25	10	5	3	26	8	69	25
Tables	2	2	2	2	4	2	8	5	16	11
Sewing Machines	1	1	—	—	—	—	—	—	1	1
Wooden Almirah	—	—	—	—	1	1	1	1	2	1
Steel Almirah	—	—	—	—	—	—	1	1	1	2
IV. Time Indicators										
Wrist-watches	6	4	8	5	2	2	9	7	25	18
Clocks	5	4	2	2	1	1	4	4	12	11
V. Cooking Apparatus										
Non-kerosene Stove	4	4	39	39	18	18	14	14	75	75
Kerosene Stove	2	2	—	—	—	—	2	2	4	4
VI. Kitchenware										
Earthen	46	6	246	37	100	18	83	14	485	75
Aluminium	48	6	232	37	95	16	78	14	453	73
Steel	14	2	83	16	12	3	52	8	161	29
Others	9	1	—	—	14	2	—	—	23	3

Note: 1. NI=number of items.
2. HH=Households.
3. (—) indicates nil.

TABLE 9.26

Size distribution of households according to the value of household articles and occupation, Bengre (1981-82)

Frequency interval (Rs.)	Number of households with the value of household articles in stated range of				Total
	MB	NMB owners	Crew	Others	
Up to 500	2 (33.3)	32 (82.1)	12 (66.7)	7 (43.8)	83 (67.1)
501-1000	2 (33.3)	2 (5.1)	2 (11.1)	5 (31.2)	11 (13.9)
1001-1500	—	3 (7.7)	3 (16.7)	1 (6.2)	7 (8.9)
1501-2000	—	2 (5.1)	1 (5.5)	—	3 (3.8)
2001-2500	—	—	—	—	—
2501 and above	2* (33.4)	—	—	3** (18.8)	5 (6.3)
Total	6 (100)	39 (100)	18 (100)	16 (100)	79 (100)

Note: 1. (—) indicates nil.

2. Figures in parentheses represent percentages to column total.

*indicates one household whose value of household articles is over Rs. 8,000.

**The value of household articles owned by each of the householders is less than Rs. 5,000.

A few of the households (24 per cent) invested in land used mainly for non-agricultural purposes. Four out of six MB households own land valued at less than Rs. 4,000. Of the total five households owning land valued at more than Rs. 8,000, one NMB owner owns land valued up to Rs. 20,000 (Table 9.28). Thus, a considerable amount has been invested in land by the fishermen of the village.

TABLE 9.27

Distribution of households according to the value of livestock owned and occupation, Bengre (1981-82)

Frequency interval	Number of households with the value of livestock in stated range of				Total
	MB owners	NMB owners	Crew	Others	
No livestock	1 (16.67)	30 (76.92)	14 (77.78)	13 (51.25)	58 (73.42)
1-50	3 (50.00)	8 (20.51)	4 (22.22)	2 (12.50)	17 (21.52)
51-100	2 (33.33)	1 (2.57)	—	—	— (3.80)
101-150	—	—	—	—	—
151 and above	—	—	—	1* (6.25)	1 (1.26)
Total	6 (100)	39 (100)	18 (100)	16 (100)	79 (100)

Note: 1. (—) indicates nil.
2. Figures in parentheses represent percentages to column total.
*the value of livestock owned by the households was about Rs. 550.

Consumption and expenditure pattern of fishermen households

The consumption items are classified into food items and non-food items.

Itemwise annual expenditure by occupation is presented in Table 9.29. Of the total Rs. 8,86,910, 11.54 per cent is accounted by MB households while they account for only 7.59 per cent of the households. The consumer expenditure of NMB owner and crew households was in proportion to their households in total, while it was lower for other households. About 77 per cent of the consumer expenditure was on food items. Foodgrains and fish are the major food items which account for 35 per cent of the expenditure on food items. It is noted that beverages account for 12 per cent of the food expenditure.

TABLE 9.28

Distribution of households according to the value of land owned (for non-agricultural purposes) and occupation, Bengre (1981-82)

Frequency	Number of households with the value of non-agricultural land* in stated range of				Total
	MB owners	NMB owners	Crew	Others	
No land	2 (33.3)	32 (82.0)	16 (88.9)	60 (62.5)	60 (75.9)
Up to 2000	2 (33.3)	1 (2.6)	—	2 (12.5)	5 (6.3)
2001-4000	2 (33.4)	1 (2.6)	2 (11.1)	2 (12.5)	7 (8.9)
4001-6000	—	1 (2.6)	—	1 (6.3)	2 (2.5)
6001-8000	—	—	—	—	—
8001 and above	—	4** (10.2)	—	1*** (6.2)	5 (6.4)
Total	6 (100)	39 (100)	10 (100)	16 (100)	79 (100)

Note: 1. (—) indicates nil.
2. Figures in parentheses represent percentages to column total.
*None of the households own agricultural land.
**includes one household for which the land is over Rs. 20,000.
***The value of land owned was in the range of Rs. 10,420 to Rs. 20,000.

In non-food items, fuel and light are the major heads of expenditure. Of the total expenditure of Rs. 2,01,440 on non-food items, more than 40 per cent is spent on clothes. The expenditure on clothes is followed by the expenditure on fuel and light, medicines, education, travel and transport, and domestic utensils with Rs. 79,550, Rs. 13,350, Rs. 7,160, Rs. 6,500 and Rs. 4,550 respectively.

TABLE 9.29

Itemwise annual consumption expenditure by occupation, Bengre (1981-82)

(in '000 Rupees)

Item	Expenditure on stated item of households by				
	MB	NMB	Crew	Others	Total
1	2	3	4	5	6
I. *Food Items*:					
(a) Foodgrains	24.96 (10.75)	129.32 (55.70)	43.84 (18.88)	34.06 (14.67)	232.18 (100)
(b) Milk and Milk Products	4.47 (14.19)	13.47 (42.75)	6.97 (22.12)	6.60 (20.94)	31.51 (100)
(c) Edible Oil	3.59 (7.28)	19.86 (40.29)	14.82 (30.07)	11.02 (22.36)	49.29 (100)
(d) Fish	18.20 (12.37)	72.70 (49.42)	34.63 (23.54)	21.58 (14.67)	147.11 (100)
(e) Vegetables	1.14 (5.28)	11.49 (53.27)	2.70 (12.52)	6.24 (28.93)	21.57 (100)
(f) Fruits and Nuts	2.81 (19.80)	5.98 (42.14)	2.96 (20.86)	2.44 (17.20)	14.19 (100)
(g) Sugar, Gur and Khandsari	1.25 (7.96)	7.90 (50.32)	3.17 (20.19)	3.38 (21.53)	15.70 (100)
(h) Salt and Spices	6.03 (13.37)	22.57 (50.06)	11.26 (26.30)	4.63 (10.27)	45.09 (100)
(i) Beverages	10.92 (12.84)	39.62 (46.61)	17.99 (21.16)	16.48 (19.39)	85.01 (100)
(j) Pan, Tobacco and Supari	5.61 (12.80)	22.25 (50.78)	9.72 (22.18)	6.24 (14.24)	43.82 (100)
Sub-total	78.98 (11.52)	345.16 (50.35)	148.66 (21.69)	112.67 (16.44)	685.47 (100)
II. *Non-food Items*:					
(a) Entertainment	0.39 (19.31)	0.92 (45.54)	0.30 (14.85)	0.41 (20.30)	2.02 (100)
(b) Travel and Transport	0.50 (7.69)	3.43 (52.77)	1.44 (22.15)	1.13 (17.39)	6.50 (100)

TABLE 9.25 (*Contd.*)

1	2	3	4	5	6
(c) Education	0.25 (3.49)	4.71 (65.78)	1.08 (15.08)	1.12 (15.65)	7.16 (100)
(d) Medicines	1.75 (13.11)	6.40 (47.94)	2.48 (18.58)	2.72 (20.37)	13.35 (100)
(e) Domestic utensils	0.95 (20.88)	2.20 (48.35)	0.90 (19.78)	0.50 (10.99)	4.55 (100)
(f) Clothes	8.60 (10.54)	38.92 (47.71)	15.95 (19.55)	18.10 (22.19)	81.57 (100)
(g) Ornaments	0.60 (45.11)	0.11 (8.27)	0.30 (22.56)	0.32 (24.06)	1.33 (100)
(h) Footwear	1.00 (25.25)	1.24 (31.31)	0.50 (12.63)	1.22 (30.81)	3.96 (100)
(i) Fuel and Light	9.31 (11.70)	37.77 (47.48)	17.30 (21.75)	15.17 (19.07)	79.55 (100)
(j) Others	—	1.20 (82.76)	0.10 (6.90)	0.15 (10.34)	1.45 (100)
Sub-total	23.35 (11.59)	96.40 (48.10)	40.35 (20.03)	40.84 (20.28)	201.44 (100)
Total	102.33 (11.54)	442.06 (49.48)	189.01 (21.31)	153.51 (17.31)	886.91 (100)

Note: 1. (—) indicates nil.
2. Figures in parentheses represent percentages to row total.

The per capita expenditure in the village in 1981-82 is about Rs. 1,787.89 of which Rs. 1,393 is spent on food and the rest on non-food items. Except for the MB households, the per capita expenditure is less than the average in all the categories of households. It is interesting to know that the per capita expenditure in MB households is almost 50 per cent more than that of the average in the village. In the case of NMB households it is reported to be the lowest in all categories (Table 9.30).

Incomes and savings of fishermen households

The distribution of annual income and consumer expenditure according to occupation is presented in Table 9.31. The

TABLE 9.30

Itemwise annual per household per capita consumption expenditure by occupation, Bengre (1981-82)

(*in Rupees*)

Item	Expenditure on stated item of household by				Average of the total house-holds
	MB	NMB	Crew	Others	
1	2	3	4	5	6
I. *Food Items*:					
(a) Foodgrains	669 (4160)	498 (3316)	402 (2435)	396 (2129)	471 (2939)
(b) Milk and Milk Products	118 (743)	52 (343)	64 (387)	77 (413)	64 (399)
(c) Edible Oil	95 (598)	76 (509)	136 (923)	128 (689)	100 (624)
(d) Fish	479 (3033)	280 (1864)	318 (1924)	251 (1349)	299 (1863)
(e) Vegetables	30 (191)	44 (295)	25 (150)	73 (390)	44 (272)
(f) Fruits and Nuts	74 (468)	23 (153)	27 (165)	29 (153)	29 (180)
(g) Sugar, Gur and Khandsari	33 (208)	30 (203)	29 (176)	40 (211)	32 (199)
(h) Salt and Spices	159 (1005)	87 (579)	109 (659)	54 (289)	92 (571)
(i) Beverages	288 (1820)	152 (1016)	165 (999)	192 (1030)	173 (1077)
(j) Pan, Tobacco and Supari	148 (936)	86 (570)	89 (540)	73 (390)	89 (555)
Sub-total	2079 (13164)	1328 (8851)	1364 (8259)	1314 (7062)	1393 (8680)
II. *Non-food Items*:					
(a) Entertainment	10.32 (65.33)	3.54 (23.59)	2.74 (16.61)	4.80 (25.81)	4.11 (25.62)
(b) Travel and Transport	13.18 (83.47)	13.18 (87.87)	13.18 (79.81)	13.18 (70.84)	13.18 (82.27)

TABLE 9.30 (*Contd.*)

1	2	3	4	5	6
(c) Education	6.58 (41.67)	18.12 (120.77)	9.95 (60.28)	13.02 (70.00)	14.53 (90.70)
(d) Medicines	46.05 (291.67)	24.63 (164.23)	22.71 (137.50)	31.69 (170.31)	27.09 (169.05)
(e) Domestic Utensils	25.00 (158.33)	8.48 (56.64)	8.26 (50.00)	5.81 (31.25)	9.24 (57.66)
(f) Clothes	121.05 (766.67)	72.79 (485.26)	54.59 (330.56)	94.19 (506.25)	76.22 (475.63)
(g) Ornaments	15.79 (100.00)	0.42 (2.82)	2.75 (16.67)	3.78 (20.31)	2.71 (16.90)
(h) Footwear	26.32 (166.67)	4.79 (31.92)	4.59 (27.38)	14.24 (76.56)	8.05 (50.25)
(i) Fuel and Light	350.00 (2219)	222.00 (1418)	251.00 (1517)	293.00 (1573)	250.00 (1564)
(j) Others	—	4.62 (30.77)	0.92 (5.56)	1.74 (9.37)	2.94 (18.35)
Sub-total	601.11 (3809.33)	359.38 (2333.90)	357.50 (2161.94)	462.28 (2482.88)	394.89 (2468.16)
Total	2680.11 (16973.33)	1687.38 (11184.90)	1721.50 (10420.94)	1776.28 (9544.88)	1787.89 (11148.16)

Note: 1. (—) indicates nil.
2. Figures in parentheses represent per household expenditure.

total income of the villagers is estimated to be Rs. 8,77,640 while the consumer expenditure in terms of cash is estimated to be Rs. 7,50,590 leaving a net saving of Rs. 12,7,050. All the households except for crew households had savings in the range of Rs. 600 for other households to Rs. 1,15,350 for NMB owner households. The amount of dissavings in the case of crew households was Rs. 24,260 or Rs. 1,340 per household per annum. The extent of the dissavings of crew households may be little lower than the estimated amount or equal to zero when the food given by the boat owners to the crew members is taken into account. Thus, the crew households may be in an equilibrium situation with regard to income and expenditure.

TABLE 9.31

Occupationwise income expenditure and savings of fishermen households, Bengre (1981-82)

(in '000 Rupee

Occupation	Income	Expenditure	Savings
1. MB owners	119.49	84.13	35.36
2. NMB owners	484.71	369.36	115.35
3. Crew	130.12	154.38	—24.26
4. Others	143.32	142.72	0.60
Total	877.64	750.59	127.05

Note: 1. Negative value in the savings column indicates dissavings.
2. The expenditure does not include expenditure on fish consumption since the boat owners and crew eat fish from their own catches for which there is no income or expenditure. In the case of other households, it is assumed that 50 per cent of the fish consumption is from gifts.

The level of actual savings may be very normal when we consider the periodical fish famines, and the income relates to the normal fishing year. The nominal positive savings hypothesis in the village is supported by the observed slow growth of mechanized craft and the tendency of fishermen to own household articles of a lower value.

REFERENCES

1. The value of productive assets has been estimated at the constant prices of 1978 for all the households.
2. For details about the market conditions and the channel flows in Mangalore, see Gupta, V.K., *et. al., Marine Fish Marketing in India*, Volume II (Current Situation: Production and Marketing), Indian Institute of Management, Ahmedabad, 1983.

10

Idya Village, Dakshin Kannada District, Karnataka

IDYA (also known as Guddakopla) is situated in Mangalore taluk of Dakshin Kannada district. It is bounded by Mangalore city towards the south and Mulki towards the north. It is bounded by the Arabian Sea towards the west and Suratkal towards the east. The fishermen village, for all administrative purposes, has been merged with the Suratkal Municipality (Fig. 10.1).

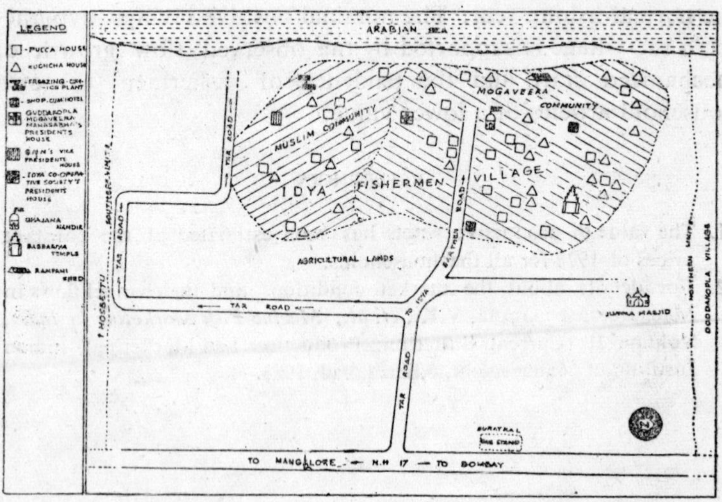

FIG. 10.1: *Map showing the Idya Fishermen Hamlet*

Kannada, Tulu and Malayalam are the major languages spoken in the village. Tulu is the local language of the fishermen. Most of the young people now speak Kannada. Muslims, in general, speak Malayalam only. Some villagers can communicate in Hindi and English as well.

Population and castes

The enumeration carried out for the purpose of this study (1982) indicated the total population of the fishermen village as 721 and the number of households as 99 of the total households in the village. The castewise distribution of households was: Mogaveeras 71, Billivas 16, Muslims 9 and others 3. Mogaveeras and Billivas are the two main fishermen communities in the village.

Village amenities, industries and infrastructure

General village infrastructure: Under the general village infrastructure we have analysed six sub-categories of facilities, viz. transport facilities, civic amenities, trading facilities, and social, cultural and religious organizations. The availability of these facilities and the extent of access to these facilities is given below:

The village is well provided with various means of transportation. Buses, taxis and autorickshaws are available at a distance of a quarter of a kilometre from the village during all seasons. The nearest railway station is Mangalore. The new Mangalore Airport is about 10 km. away from the village. The fishermen village has an all-weather approach road connecting it to the highway. Thus, the transportation network of the village is highly developed even as compared to the intensively mechanized fishing village of Kadekar.

Draw wells are the main source of drinking water in the village. About 46 per cent of the households have their own drinking water wells. The village has been electrified and there were 67 households which had availed for the facility.

Village industry and trade have not developed in the village. The fishermen visit the nearby town of Suratkal for their basic necessities. There is a weekly market at Suratkal every Wednesday. At the village only the facilities like barber, tailor, pan, cigarette and tea/coffee stalls are available for the past 12 years. Proximity to a large town did not offer any incentive for the growth of village industry and trade within the village.

No private or governnent agencies were operating in the village. School, post office, bank and hospitals were located at Suratkal.

The social, cultural and religious organizations of the village consisted of caste associations, Bhajan Mandali and a Mahila Mandali. The members of the caste associations were considered as members of the Bhajan Mandali. Hence there was no separate registration for the Bhajan Mandali. There were three caste associations: (1) Guddakoppala (Idiya) Mogaveera Mahajan Sabha (1956), (2) Idya Billiva Samaja Seva Sangam (1962) and (3) Jamat Adalab Mandali. The Mahila Mandali was established in 1960. The village was under the jurisdiction of Suratkal Municipality.

Fishery-related infrastrcture: Except a freezing-cum-ice plant, no other fishery-related infrastructure is available in the village. Other facilities like drying yards, curing, boat-building yards and even fish merchants were available either at Suratkal or Mangalore. About 15 fishermen from the village were engaged in fish retailing/vending. There is one co-operative society, viz. Idya Fishermen Cooperative Society, in the village. It was established in 1918 and it had 138 members on June 30, 1981.

Production equipment and occupations

All economic activities in Idya centre around marine fishing. The fishing village population consisted of the owner/partners of fishing equipment, labourers in fishing, fish marketers and village functionaries. In addition, a small portion of the population is also involved in activities other than fishery related.

The boat owners consisted of both mechanized boats (MB) and non-mechanized boats (NMB) The fishing labourers also consisted of crew in mechanized boats and non-mechanized boats. On the basis of major occupations,[1] the households in the village can be classified into four categories: mechanized boat owners or partners, non-mechanized boat owners, crew, and others.

The distribution of households according to occupation and caste and their population is presented in Table 10.1. About 56-57 per cent of the households in the village did not own any

TABLE 10.1

Distribution of households and population according to occupational pattern and caste, Idya

Occupation	Caste					Total No. of persons
	Mogaveera	Billivas	Muslims	Others	Total	
1. MB	33 (46.48)	—	—	—	33 (33.33)	249 (34.5)
2. NMB	9 (12.68)	1 (6.25)	—	—	10 (10.10)	71 (9.8)
3. CRM	7 (9.86)	— —	1 (11.11)	1 (33.33)	9 (9.10)	74 (10.3)
4. Others	22 (30.98)	15 (93.75)	8 (88.89)	2 (66.67)	47 (47.47)	327 (45.4)
Total	71 (100)	16 (100)	9 (100)	3 (100)	99 (100)	721 (100)

Note: 1. (—) indicates nil.
2. Figures in parentheses are percentages to column total.

fishing assets. The population of these households without any fishing assets accounts for about 55.7 per cent of the village population. Of the households without any fishing assets, over 83.9 per cent derive their major income from occupations other than fishing-related activities. The potential source of fishery labour force in Idya was just nine households and accounted for 9.1 per cent of the households in the village.

The above analysis, however, does not indicate the extent of employment in various activities relating to fishing and non-fishing. In order to identify the extent of employment in these activities we have tabulated the occupationwise distribution of the total population in the village according to castes in Table 10.2. About 84 per cent of the total population in the village is

TABLE 10.2

Occupationwise distribution of population according to caste, Idya (1981)

Occupation	No. of persons from the				Total
	Mogaveera	Billivas	Muslims	Others	
I. *Economy Activities: Fishery*					
(i) MB full-time fishing with joint owners	46 (9.37)	—	—	—	46 (6.38)
(ii) NMB full-time fishing with owners on boats	7 (1.43)	—	—	—	7 (0.97)
(iii) Crew with gear	6 (1.22)	—	—	—	6 (0.83)
(iv) Crew without gear	4 (0.81)	—	1 (1.09)	—	5 (0.69)
(v) Rampani/Purse-seiner	30 (6.11)	1 (0.85)	1 (1.09)	1 (4.76)	33 (4.58)
(vi) Marketing of fish, retail	21 (4.28)	—	2 (2.17)	—	23 (3.19)
Sub-total	114 (23.22)	1 (0.85)	4 (4.35)	1 (4.76)	120 (16.64)

TABLE 10.2 (*Contd.*)

II. *Economic Activities: Non-fishery*					
(i) Busines	—	—	1 (1.09)	—	1 (0.14)
(ii) Service	8 (1.62)	11 (9.40)	—	—	19 (2.64)
(iii) Agriculture	—	4 (3.42)	—	—	4 (0.55)
(iv) Agricultural Labour	7 (1.42)	8 (6.84)	5 (5.43)	—	20 (2.77)
(v) Others	—	—	—	3 (14.28)	3 (0.42)
Sub-total	15 (3.04)	23 (19.66)	6 (6.52)	3 (14 28)	47 (6.52)
III. *Non-economic Activities:*					
(i) Dependants/Retired/ Non-working	65 (13.24)	29 (24.79)	16 (17.39)	—	110 (15.26)
(ii) Student	116 (23.63)	28 (23.93)	20 (21.74)	5 (23.81)	169 (23.44)
(iii) Housewife/House work	119 (24.24)	16 (13.68)	26 (28.26)	8 (38.10)	169 (23.44)
(iv) Others	62 (12.63)	20 (17.09)	20 (21.74)	4 (19.05)	106 (14.70)
Sub-total	362 (73.72)	93 (79.49)	82 (89.13)	17 (80.95)	554 (70.89)
Total	491 (100.00)	117 (100.00)	92 (100.00)	21 (100.00)	721 (100.00)

Note: 1. (—) indicates nil.

2. Figures in parentheses are percentages to column total.

not involved in any economic activities. This category of population consisted of dependants/retired and non-working, students, housewives and others. The share of this category of population was over 89 per cent for Muslims and 81 per cent for others. The population involved in economic activities relating to fishery accounted for 16.64 per cent of the population. Of 120 in fishing activities, 114 were from the Mogaveera community. Further, the population involved in non-fishery economic activities accounted for 6.52 per cent. This category of population was over-represented by the Billiva community. Agricultural labourers and service population accounted for about 82.98 per cent of the population in this category. Of the total 120 persons involved in fishery-related activities, the population of MB partner fishing on a full-time basis accounted for maximum with 46 and is followed by rampani operators, fish retailers, NMB owner workers and crew with gear with 33, 23, 7 and 6 respectively.

SOCIO-ETHNOGRAPHIC PROFILE OF FISHERMEN

The social characteristics analysed in this section include family size and structure, level of education, age distribution, migration pattern and social participation of the fishermen and their households.

Size and structure of households

The average family size of the fishermen households was 7.29 persons. About 65 per cent of the households had six or more persons and only 35 per cent households had less than six persons. Among MBO families, about 64 per cent households had six or more persons. A similar pattern was observed in the case of crew member households. In the case of NMBO families, 80 per cent households had six or more members. The maximum family size in MBO households was 13. followed by 12° in crew member households and 10 in NMBO households; other households also had maximum family size of 13 (Table 10.3).

The data on the family structure of the household were analysed according to their occupational pattern. Of the total households in the village, 49.5 per cent had joint families, 48.5 per cent maintained nuclear families, and the others were single persons. Among the MBO households, 52 per cent consisted of nuclear families. In all the cases, except other households, the nuclear family structure was predominant. However, in the case of other households the joint family structure accounted for more than 53 per cent of the households (Table 10.4).

Age distribution and education level of fishermen

The population of the village has been divided into six different

TABLE 10.3

Occupationwise distribution of households according to family size, Idya (1981)

Family size (members)	Number of households of				Total
	MB	NMB	CM	Others	
1	—	—	—	2 (4.26)	2 (2.02)
2	1 (3.03)	—	—	2 (4.26)	3 (3.03)
3	4 (12.12)	—	—	3 (6.38)	7 (7.07)
4	4 (12.12)	1 (10.10)	—	6 (12.76)	11 (11.11)
5	3 (9.09)	1 (10.00)	1 (11.11)	7 (14.89)	12 (12.12)
6	3 (9.09)	2 (20.00)	2 (22.22)	6 (12.76)	13 (13.14)
7	2 (6.06)	2 (20.00)	1 (11.11)	4 (8.51)	9 (9.09)
8	3 (9.09)	1 (10.00)	—	7 (14.89)	11 (11.11)
9	1 (3.03)	2 (20.00)	3 (33.33)	2 (4.26)	8 (8.08)
10	5 (15.16)	1 (10.00)	—	2 (4.26)	8 (8.08)
11	1 (3.03)	—	1 (11.11)	3 (6.38)	5 (5.05)
12	3 (9.09)	—	1 (11.11)	1 (2.13)	5 (5.05)
13	3 (9.09)	—	—	2 (4.26)	5 (5.05)
Total	33 (100.00)	10 (100.00)	9 (100.00)	47 (100.00)	99 (100.00)

Note: 1. (—) indicates nil.

2. Figures in parentheses are percentages to column total.

TABLE 10.4

Distribution of households by occupational pattern and type of family, Idya (1981)

Occupation	Number of households with family structure			Total
	Single	Nuclear	Joint	
1. MB	—	17 (35.42)	16 (32.66)	33 (33.33)
2. NMB	—	6 (12.50)	4 (8.16)	10 (10.10)
3. CM	—	5 (10.42)	4 (8.16)	9 (9.09)
4. Others	2 (100.00)	20 (41.66)	25 (51.02)	47 (47.48)
Total	2 (100.00)	48 (100.00)	49 (100.00)	99 (100.00)

Note: 1. (—) indicates nil.
2. Figures in parentheses are percentages to column total.

age groups for analysing the age distribution of the fishermen population. The age distribution of the village population according to occupational pattern and sex is presented in Table 10.5. At aggregate level the female population is more than the male population as per our census taken in 1981. The age groups with more females as compared to males were 01-12, 13-20, 31-45, 46-55 and 56 and above. Only in the case of the age group 21-30 years the male population was more than the female population. The converse situation in the age group 21-30 years may mainly be because of the early marriage of female children and the tendency of boat owners to have more male children. In the village, the maximum number of persons were in the age group up to 12 years. A similar trend was observed in the case of MB, NMB and other households. However, in the case of crew households the age group 13-20 years accounted for the maximum of the population in crew households.

TABLE 10.5

Age and sex distribution of village population according to occupational pattern, Idya (1981)

Occupation	10-12		13-20		21-30		31-45		46-55		56 and above		Total	
	M	F	M	F	M	F	M	F	M	F	M	F	M	F
1. MB	28 (37.84)	42 (44.21)	21 (28.37	27 (35.06)	27 (32.53)	29 (43.28)	24 (36.92)	19 (24.68)	5 (21.74)	7 (24.14)	8 (34.78)	12 (34.29)	113 (33.14)	136 (35.79)
2. NMB	9 (12.16)	8 (8.41)	7 (9.59)	10 (12.99)	9 (10.84)	2 (2.99)	5 (7.69)	10 (12.99)	5 (21.74)	1 (3.45)	3 (13.04)	2 (5.71)	38 (11.14)	33 (8.68)
3. CRM	6 (8.11)	7 (7.37)	8 (10.96)	9 (11.69)	10 (12.03)	5 (7.46)	5 (15.58)	12 (13.04)	3 (13.04)	4 (13.79)	2 (8.70)	3 (8.57)	34 (9.97)	40 (10.53)
4. Others	31 (41.89)	38 (40.00)	37 (50.68)	31 (40.26)	37 (44.58)	31 (46.27)	31 (47.70)	36 (46.75)	10 (43.48)	17 (58.62)	10 (43.47)	18 (51.43)	156 (45.75)	171 (45.00)
Total	74 (100.0)	95 (100.0)	73 (100.0)	77 (100.0)	83 (100.0)	67 (100.0)	65 (100.0)	77 (100.0)	23 (100.0)	29 (100.0)	23 (100.0)	35 (100.0)	341 (100.0)	380 (100.0)

Note: Figures in parentheses are percentages to column total.

Further, it was observed that in about 44 per cent of the cases the age gap between two surviving children was less than three years. The data in Table 10.6 indicate that the spacing of

TABLE 10.6

Frequency distribution of age gaps between children of same parents according to occupational pattern, Idya (1981)

Age gap interval	Number of instances in which the age gap falls in the stated interval for				Total
	MB	NMB	CM	Others	
1-1.9	8 (26.67)	2 (18.18)	2 (40.00)	7 (21.88)	19 (24.36)
2-2.9	7 (23.33)	1 (9.09)	—	7 (21.88)	15 (19.23)
3-3.9	6 (20.00)	4 (36.37)	1 (20.00)	9 (28.13)	20 (25.64)
4-4.9	3 (10.00)	3 (27.27)	—	3 (9.37)	9 (11.54)
5-5.9	4 (13.33)	—	1 (20.00)	3 (9.37)	8 (10.26)
6 and above	2 (6.67)	1 (9.09)	1 (20.00)	3 (9.07)	7 (8.97)
Total	30 (100.00)	11 (100.00)	5 (100.00)	32 (100.00)	78 (100.00)

Note: 1. (—) indicates nil.
2. Figures in parentheses are percentages to column total.

children was same for all the occupational patterns but for crew. In the case of crew about 40 per cent of the surviving children had an age gap of less than two years. The corresponding figures for MB, NMB and other households were 26.27 per cent, 18.18 per cent and 21.88 per cent respectively.

The distribution of households in the village, according to occupational pattern and highest level of education in the household, is presented in Table 10.7. There were only four households with all illiterates and these households accounted for about 4.04 per cent of the total 99 households in the village. Of these four households three were from others and one household was of MB owner. Higher secondary as the highest level of education attained by a household accounted for maximum 52.33 per cent of the total households in the village with 52 and is followed by middle education, primary education and graduation with 17 (17.17 per cent), 15 (15.15 per cent) and 11 (11.11 per cent) respectively.

TABLE 10.7

Distribution of households according to occupational pattern and highest level of education in the household, Idya (1981)

Level of education	Number of households of				Total
	MB owner	NMB ower	CM	Others	
1. Illiterate	1 (3.03)	—	—	3 (6.38)	4 (4.04)
2. Primary	5 (15.15)	2 (20.00)	—	8 (17.02)	15 (15.15)
3. Middle	7 (21.21)	1 (10.00)	3 (33.33)	6 (12.77)	17 (17.17)
4. Higher Secondary	20 (60.61)	6 (60.00)	6 (66.67)	20 (42.55)	52 (52.53)
5. Graduate (B.A.)	—	1 (10.00)	—	10 (21.28)	11 (11.11)
Total	33 (100.00)	10 (100.00)	9 (100.00)	47 (100.00)	99 (100.00)

Note: 1. (—) indicates nil.
2. Figures in parentheses are percentages to column total.

Migration pattern

The migration pattern analysed in this section included both long and short-term migrations. To analyse the long-term migration we have elicited the information, as in most census and surveys, about the place of birth of the head of the family. On the basis of the information so collected we found that all the household heads had their birthplaces in the village except four. All the four households belonged to the occupational category of others and had moved into the village about 20 years ago from other villages in the same district. The major reason for the migration of the households was to find a better employment. Further, these four households had their family members involved both in fishery and non-fishery-related activities. However, they have derived their major income from activities other than fishing and fishery-related activities such as agriculture, agricultural labourer, beedi-making, etc. Of the four immigrated households three belonged to the Mogaveera community. The other aspect of the migration pattern relating to the village is migration of fishermen households to other urban centres in search of employment. The data collected during our census of the village in 1981 also support the existence of such migration. Besides, our discussions with the knowledgeables of the village confirmed this. At least four or five households have migrated to other urban locations during the past six to seven years. The major reasons identified on the basis of the discussions for the migration from the village were their displacement from fishing with the introduction of mechanized boats particularly purse-seiners and the decreasing levels of returns from non-mechanized fishing.

We hardly find any short migration from the village or to the village, though it is very typical in fisheries, particularly with the existence of the mechanized craft in the village. The reason for the short-term migration of fishermen with boats from the village may be mainly because of the collective ownership of the mechanized boats, the major type which migrate often, with owners from different villages and a smaller number of mechanized boats in the village.

Social participation of fishermen households

The social participation of the fishermen households was analysed in terms of the membership of the fishermen co-operative society, caste associations and Mahila Mandalis.

Caste association: The Mogaveera, Billiva and Muslim communities of the village had their own caste associations and they were associated to other district and regional level associations. For the purpose of analysis, all the three associations were clubbed together and were analysed according to their occupational category and caste. Of the total households in the village, 43 per cent had enrolled themselves as members of the associations. About 64 per cent of the MBO households and all the NMBO households were members of the associations. The castewise analysis indicated that less than 50 per cent of the households were members of the respective caste associations. It was observed that all the households actually participated in the activities of their respective associations. Their formal membership was not a handicap.

Mahila Mandali: Forty-six per cent of all the households enrolled as members of the Mahila Mandali. The representation of MBO households was 58 per cent followed by other occupational category. Castewise analysis indicated that 59 per cent of the Mogaveera households had enrolled themselves as members of the Mandali. There was no representation of the Billivas and "other" caste groups. About 50 per cent of Muslim households had enrolled themselves as members of the Mahila Mandali.

Of all the members of the Mandali, 21 per cent of the households had their membership of the Mandali for the past 16-25 years and the remaining households had enrolled themselves as members during the past five years. About 79 per cent of the members from MBO households have joined the Mandali only during the past five years.

Fishermen co-operative society: At the village 90 per cent of the households were members of the fishermen co-operative society. Of the total membership 40.74 per cent and 33.33 per cent belonged to NMBO and MBO households respectively. Among the members in the Society the maximum (37.04 per cent) households enrolled themselves as members during the past 6-15 years.

MECHANIZATION OF FISHING CRAFT: ITS IMPACT ON PRODUCTION SYSTEM

The study of the mechanization of fishing craft and its impact, in terms of organization, output, income, distribution of gains from technological developments, etc., on the system are going to be the subject matter of this section. The contents of the section include technology of production, ownership of productive assets, production pattern, output and income distribution and disposal of fish landings.

Technology of production

The technology of fish production in the village is characterized by the existence of traditional and modern technologies. The equipment for catching fish from the waters off the village consisted of non-mechanized (mostly dugout canoes) and mechanized craft. The non-mechanized boats operated gill nets and cast nets. In addition, there is one rampani unit with necessary fishing craft. The mechanized craft of the village operated either trawl nets or purse-seine nets.

In 1982, there were two purse-seiners, one trawler, one rampani unit and nine dugout canoes in the village. The distribution of these craft according to their year of purchase is presented in Table 10.8. All the mechanized boats—two purse-

TABLE 10.8

Distribution of different type of boats according to the year of purchase, Idya

Year of acquiring	Mechanized boats		Non-mechanized boats		
	Purse-seine	Trawler	Rampani units	Dugout below 25 ft.	Canoe above 25 ft.
Up to 1971	—	—	1	2	1
1972	—	—	—	1	—
1979	2	1	—	1	—
1981	—	—	—	3	—
1982	—	—	—	1	—
Total	2	1	1	8	1

Note: (—) indicates nil.

seiners and a trawler—which are owned by the fishermen of the village were purchased in 1979. The single rampani unit[3] in the village has been operating from 1972. More than half of the dugout canoes in the village have been acquired after 1979. Of the total nine dugout canoes in the village one was over 25 feet low and the remaining were less than 25 feet.

The total number of nets owned by the fishermen of the village consisted of two purse-seine nets, three trawl nets, nine gill nets and four cast nets. In addition, the villagers owned the pieces of rampani net. The number of parts which make the total net was 70 of which 60 parts were owned by the fishermen of the village. The length and mesh size of the purse-seine nets, trawl nets, cast nets and rampani net pieces were not amenable to any tabulation in view of their shape and varying mesh sizes.

Of the nine gill nets six had their mesh sizes less than or equal to one inch, two had the mesh sizes between 1.1 and 2 inch and one had the mesh size in the range of 4.1 to 5 inch. The first category of nets are used for catching small pelagic fish like sardines. The second type with a mesh size between 1.1 and 2 inch is used for catching fishes like mackerel while others with mesh sizes in the range of 4.1 to 5 inch are used for catching catfish, seer fish and pomfret. Of the total nine nets three were owned by MB owners, four by NMB owners and two by crew members. The lengthwise distribution of the nets indicated that all the nine nets were of a length less than 1,000 feet; one was in the length range of 501—1000 feet and the rest were of a length up to 500 feet.

Gill nets, cast nets and purse-seine nets were mended with nylon yarn. However, all the trawl nets in the village were mended with hemp twine. No cotton nets were observed in operation while they had predominated the fishing scene of the village during the late fifties.

Ownership of productive assets

In Idya there were 34 partners in purse-seine boats, 14 partners in trawlers, 14 rampani partners and 7 dugout canoe owners, from 46 households. This indicates the multiple ownership/partnership for a few of the households. The distribution of the households according to their caste and level of ownership of fishing assets is presented in Table 10.9. Of the 46 households 5 were having partnership in purse-seiner, trawler and rampani and they were from the Mogaveera caste. Further, all the boat owners are partners but for two—one each from Billivas and others. No fishing assets were owned by any Muslim household in the village. Of the total 71 Mogaveera households 44 owned almost all the fishing assets in the village. Thus, the Mogaveera community had a monopoly over the ownership of fishery-related productive assets. About 55 per

TABLE 10.9

Distribution of different type of boats (ownership/partnership) according to caste, Idya (1981)

Type of boat owned individually or collectively	Caste			Total
	Mogaveera	Billivas	Others	
1. Purse-seine+Trawler+Rampani	5 (100.00)	—	—	5 (100.00)
2. Purse-seine+Trawler	1 (100.00)	—	—	1 (100.00)
3. Purse-seine+Trawler	8 (100.00)	—	—	8 (100.00)
4. Purse-seine+Rampani	1 (100.00)	—	—	1 (100.00)
5. Purse-seine	19 (100.00)	—	—	19 (100.00)
6. Rampani+Dugout	2 (100.00)	—	—	2 (100.00)
7. Rampani	4 (66.66)	1 (16.67)	1 (16.67)	6 (100.00)
8. Dugout	4 (100.00)	—	—	4 (100.00)
Total	44 (96.65)	1 (2.17)	1 (2.18)	46 (100.00)

Note: 1. (—) indicates nil.
2. Figures in parentheses are percentages to row total.

cent of the housholds in the village did not own any sort of fishing assets. The inequality of ownership of fishing assets is measured by the help of the Gini coefficient. The value of the Gini coefficient for the distribution of value of productive assets over the households was 0.6151. The Lorenz curve for the distribution of productive assets is presented in Figure 10.2. The Gini coefficient for distribution of productive assets indicates a highly inequitable distribution of assets.

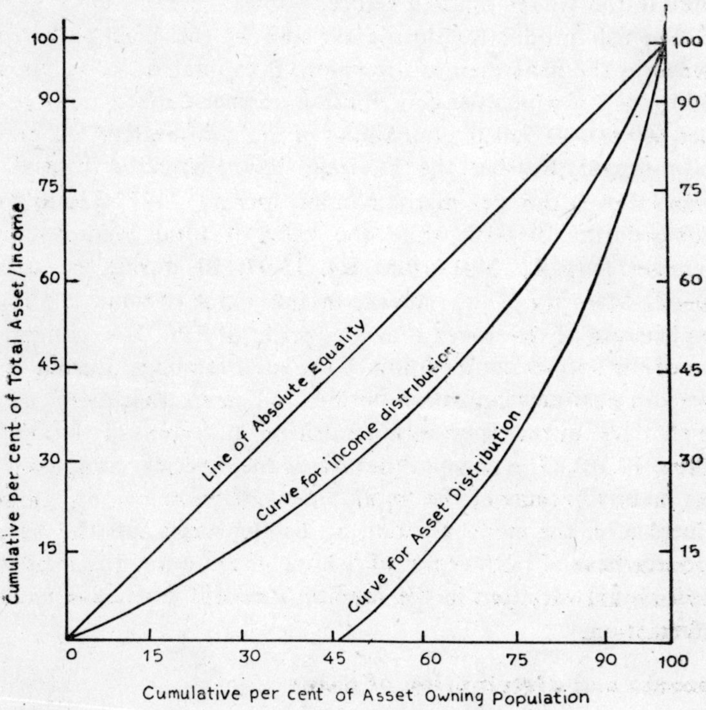

	Assets	Income
Gini Ratio	0.6151	0.3135

FIG. 10.2: *Lorenz Curve for assets and income distribution, Idya (1981-82)*

The predominant form of ownership pattern for mechanized boats in the village was collective ownership, owner worker and non-owner partner and in the case of non-mechanized boats it was individual owner, owner worker and non-owner partner (IO, OW, NOP). The ownership and operation of rampani was collective.

Production of marine fish: Present and past

Fish landings take place on the open sandy beach. After the introduction of mechanized boats the landing place was shifted from the village to the nearby fishing harbour in Mangalore. However, the non-mechanized boats in the village land their catch in the village landing centre.

The fish production during 1981-82 by the craft and gear owned by the fishermen of the village is estimated to be about 767 tonnes of which the contribution of mechanized craft was over 669 tonnes and the remaining of the non-mechanized craft and rampani. Further, the landings have increased from 628 tonnes during the pre-mechanization period (1972-73) to 767 tonnes during 1981-82, while the value of total landings has increased from Rs. 2,40,010 to Rs. 13,97,120 during the same period. Majority of the increase in the value of total landings was because of the increase in the price of fish. The comparison of the species composition of the total landings during the pre- and post-mechanization periods indicated that there were no changes in the species composition of the total landings (Table 10.10). The constant nature of the species composition was mainly because of the replacement of rampanis by purse-seiners after the mechanization of fishing craft and the same resource base of both types of fishing techniques. In terms of the seasonal variation in the landings, we did not have much information.

Income and distribution of gains

In this section we shall attempt to estimate the income from fishing for each household and to find the extent of equitable distribution of gains due to mechanization of fishing craft. The income to a household consisted either of the returns from fishing or other activities or both. The method adopted for measuring the income from fisheries is explained below, while the income from other sources has been obtained by recall from the household head.

For working out the returns on the capital invested in fishing equipment and in labour, it is necessary to estimate

TABLE 10.10

Specieswise landings and gross value of output during pre- and post-mechanization periods, Idya

(*Qty.*: *in tonnes*)
(*Value*: *in '000 Rupees*)

Species	Landings and value of landings during									
	Pre-mechanization period (1972-73)						Current (1981-82) period			
	Price per tonne*	Landings	Value of landings	Price per tonne**	Landings by NMBs	Value of landings	Landings* by MBs	Value of landings	Total landings	Value of landings
1. Oil sardine	0.1558	242	37.70	0.5678	32	18.17	263	149.33	295	167.50
2. Mackerel	0.4063	129	52.41	3.7126	28	103.95	135	501.20	163	605.15
3. Catfish	0.7072	59	41.72	0.8765	7	6.14	88	77.13	95	83.27
4. Sole fish	0.2811	42	11.81	1.4251	4	5.70	72	102.61	76	108.31
5. Pomfret	0.5064	1	0.51	10.3910	Neg.	—	4	41.56	4	41.56
6. Seer fish	1.0339	2	2.07	3.8591	3	11.58	9	34.73	12	46.31
7. Sharks	0.9189	27	24.81	4.0000	6	24.00	12	48.00	18	72.00
8. Sciaenids and Silver Belly	0.4015	21	8.43	1.5349	7	10.74	32	49.12	39	59.86
9. Prawns and Lobster	1.8984	Neg.	0.00	15.0000	Neg.	—	7	105.00	7	105.00
10. Others	0.2338	105	25.55	1.8649	11	20.51	47	87.65	58	108.16
Total	—	628	240.01	—	98	200.79	669	1196.33	767	1397.12

Note: Neg. indicates negligible.
*Landings are by the boats owned by the villagers and usually the place of landing is not in the village but in Mangalore. The villagers own trawlers and 1.3 share in two purse-seiners.
**The prices for different varieties of fish have been obtained from the office of the Assistant Director of Fisheries, Malpe.

the economics of the fishing craft. It would have been ideal to calculate the economics of each of the boat in the village for working out an accurate measure of income distribution. However, in view of the limitation of time and resource to collect the necessary information from all the boat owners, we have worked out the income of each household on the basis of the model economics based on the information from sample respondents. The details of economics of different type of boats are presented below.

Quarterwise average gross returns per boat of different type of boats in the village is presented in Table 10.11. The

TABLE 10.11

Quarterwise average gross returns per boat of different type, Idya (1981-82)

Quarter	Gross returns in stated quarter for		
	Trawler	Purse-seiner	Dugout canoes of 2 lengths 15 ft.—25 ft.
July-September	21330(18.93)	60250(11.70)	4196(13.69)
October-December	51890(46.05)	241460(46.90)	12738(41.53)
January-March	24850(22.05)	113980(22.14)	8569(27.94)
April-June	14610(12.97)	99160(19.26)	5168(16.84)
Total	112680 (100.00)	514850(100.00)	30671(100.00)

Note: 1. (—) Figures in parentheses are percentages to column total.
2. All the sample units are mackerel gill net units.

gross returns from the purse-seiners were the highest—about Rs. 5,15,850. This was followed by the gross returns from trawlers and non-mechanized boats with Rs. 1,12,680 and Rs. 30,670 respectively. The quarter October-December was the most important in the case of all type of boats and its contribution ranged between 42 and 47 per cent of the value of annual landings.

The itemwise average variable cost per day for different type of boats in the village is presented in Table 10.12. As in

TABLE 10.12

Average variable cost per day for different type of boats, Idya (1981-82)

(*in Rupees*)

Item	Expenditure on stated items for		
	Trawler	Purse-seiners	Dugout canoes of length 15 ft.— 25 ft.
1. Fuel	182.00	473.50	2.60
2. Mobile oil and other lubricants	9.50	29.00	—
3. Wages to casual labourers	3.50	2.50	1.75
4. Ice and Water	2.50	15.60	—
5. Food expenditure for crew	5.25	78.00	1.50
6. Cost of net twine	2.75	30.25	12.50
7. Others	10.30	17.80	6.40
Total	215.80	646.55	24.75

Note: (—) indicates nil.

the case of other villages in Karnataka the average variable cost per day per purse-seiner was the highest at Rs. 646.65. This was followed by the average variable cost per day for the trawler at Rs. 215.80. The dugout canoes in the village need only Rs. 24.75 per day to operate. In the case of both purse-seiners and trawlers the most important item of expenditure was for fuel and mobile oil and other lubricants. In the case of purse-seiner the food expenditure for the crew was very important. The cost of twine for net repair was also a significant item in the case of purse-seiners.

The annual fixed costs incurred per boat for different type of boats in the village in 1981-82 are presented in Table 10.13. The crew salaries are the most important part of the annual fixed cost for operating the trawlers and purse-seiners. The crew salaries are usually paid in the villages in terms of the share of the value of output. In the case of trawlers and purse-seiners the share of crew is 30 per cent and in the case of

TABLE 10.13

Itemwise annual fixed costs for operating different type of boats, Idya (1981-82)

(in Rupees)

Item	Expenditure on stated item for		
	Trawler	Purse-seiner	Dugout canoes of length between 15 ft. and 25 ft.
1. Salaries of crew[1]	33804(5)	154455(27)	18403(5)
2. Repairs and Maintenance	5285	16793	958
3. Dry docking and oil painting	1382	3275	785
4. Insurance	2890	9350	—
5. Interest on borrowed capital[2]	12480	34850	—
6. Depreciation	10540	63400	2650
7. Others	695	18950*	480
Total	67076	301073	23276

Notes: 1. The crew salaries usually are paid in terms of share in gross returns. In the case of trawlers and purse-seiners the share of crew is 30 per cent and in the case of dugout canoes it is 60 per cent of the gross returns. The crew share is distributed equally over all the crew members. Figures in parentheses of this row indicate the total crew required.

2. About 75 per cent of the total investment on the equipment is assumed to be borrowed capital and the interest is calculated at the rate of 10 per cent.

3. *Includes the carrier hiring charges.

dugout canoes the share is 60 per cent of the gross returns. The purse-seiners usually require a crew of about 27 per boat. The only trawler in the village was usually operated by about five persons. The dugout canoes in the village were operated by four persons. Since these dugout canoes were usually owned by a fisherman, they also needed help of hired crew members to operate them. The other major items of expenditure in the nature of fixed cost for purse-seiners and trawlers are depreciation, interest on borrowed capital and repair and maintenance. All the three mechanized boats in the village were purchased with the help of substantial borrowings from financial institutions. This aspect will be discussed further in the next section.

The annual gross and net returns of different type of boats are shown in Table 10.14. The net returns in the case of purse-seiners in the village work out to Rs. 90,267. In the case of trawlers the net returns amount to only Rs. 4,602 and in the case of dugout canoes the net returns are Rs. 2,519.

TABLE 10.14

Gross and net returns of different type of boats, Idya (1981-82)

Particulars	Trawlers	Purse-seiners	Dugout canoes of length between 15 ft. and 25 ft.
1. Gross returns	1,12650	514850	30671
2. Expenditure			
(a) Annual variable costs*	41002(190)	123510(191)	4876(197)
(b) Annual fixed costs	67076	301073	23276
Sub-total	108076	424583	28152
3. Net returns	4602	90267	2519

Note: *Estimated by multiplying the average daily expenditures by the number of fishing days. The estimated number of fishing days for different type of boats are indicated in parentheses of the row.

Distribution of income: Taking the economics of different type of boats and the employment pattern in each of the household we have worked out the income accruing to each household from fishing. This information is supplemented by the information on the income from other sources to estimate the total household income.

We have observed that the total income of the households in the village during 1981-82 amounted to Rs. 10,22,580. Of this about one-third was derived from non-fishery activities. Thus unlike other villages the contribution of non-fishery activities in this village was much larger. The average per household income in the village was Rs. 10,329 and the per capita income of the village was Rs. 1,418.

In terms of distribution of income according to occupation, it was observed that mechanized boat owners derived the highest per household income and also the per capita income (Table 10.15). It was interesting to note in this village that

TABLE 10.15

Distribution of income according to occupation, Idya (1981-82)

(in Rupees)

Occupation	Income			Per household	Per capita
	Fishery	Non-fishery	Total		
1. MB	467654 (70.75)	23600 (6.52)	491254 (48.04)	14886.48	1972.91
2. NMB	84230 (12.74)	15000 (4.15)	99230 (9.71)	9923	1397
3. CRM	55096 (8.34)	43200 (11.95)	98296 (9.61)	10921.78	1328.32
4. Others	54000 (8.17)	279800 (77.38)	333800 (32.64)	7102.13	1020.79
Total	660980 (100.00)	361600 (100.00)	1022580 (100.00)	10329.09	1418.28

Note: Figures in parentheses are the percentages to column total.

the crew member households earned a higher per household income than the non-mechanized boat owning households. This indicates that the incomes from the non-mechanized boats are very low and there is an incentive for these boat owners to become crew members partly in the mechanized boats.

The Gini ratio for the inequality in income in the village amounted to 0.3135 which indicates an extremely low level of inequality in income despite the fact that assets were distributed quite unequally. The even distribution of income has been possible because of better earnings on the part of crew members and larger size of crew required to operate the purse-seiners. The Lorenz curve for income distribution in the village is presented in Figure 10.2.

Disposal of fish landings

It was observed that the percentage of fish landings in the village going for fresh consumption increased from 42.56 per cent in the pre-mechanization period to 52.55 per cent in the current period. And this was compensated by a lower percentage going for sun-drying/salt-curing and fish meal/manure extraction. There was a very small increase in the percentage going for exports (Table 10.16). This was mainly because of the introduction of a trawler which increased the catch of prawns and lobsters. The purse-seiners do not make any difference with regard to supplies of exportable varieties.

TABLE 10.16

Changes in the utilization pattern of marine fish landing after the mechanization of fish craft, Idya (1972-82)

(*in percentages*)

Utilized for	Share of the stated utilization during		
	Pre-mechanization period (1972-73)	Currently (1981-82)	
		excluding MB landings	including MB landings
1. Fresh consumption	42.56	59.64	52.55
2. Sun-drying/salt-curing	32.87	31.16	26.35
3. Fishmeal/manure extraction	23.52	8.45	19.35
4. Exports (frozen, canned a d dried)	1.05	0.75	1.75
Total	100.00	100.00	100.00

MARKETS IN THE VILLAGE

In this section an analysis of the input markets, labour situation, credit market and output markets in the village with a view to understanding the changes due to mechanization of fishing craft is presented.

Market for inputs

The various inputs considered for analysis in this section include boat-building yards, service facilities, facilities for landing and berthing, facilities for supply of fuel oils and lubricants, and facilities for supply of nets and yarn.

It was observed that most of the mechanized and non-mechanized boats in the village were constructed in the boat-building yards in the village within the district. Two of the three new dugout canoes constructed by villagers were acquired from the boat-building yards outside the village. The acquisition of old boats by the fishermen of the village was observed to be relatively high in the village. Of the total 13 sample boats 9 were old boats acquired from the fishermen of other village. Of the total 9 old boats acquired by the fishermen of the village 5 were mechanized boats.

There are no facilities for supply of fuel oils and lubricants, for landing and berthing for mechanized craft in the village. Therefore, all the mechanized craft of the village are operated from the nearby bigger landing centre. The service facilities for non-mechanized boats are also not available in the village. However, the lone carpenter from a nearby village undertakes the repairing of the non-mechanized craft in the village. The readily mended nets and the yarn for mending and repairing of nets is available from Mangalore only. The above analysis indicates the relatively underdeveloped nature of the input markets.

Market for labour

As already seen in the last section, the productive assets are owned by less than 45 per cent of the households while the rest of the households are potential suppliers of labourers. Of the households which derive their income by selling labour time only 15 per cent are involved in fishing. Further, the supply of labour is more or less constant while the demand fluctuates between seasons or between days depending upon several factors mentioned in the earlier profiles.

Only one type of labour contract is predominant in the fishing scene of the village, i.e. share contract. Under this type of labour contract the labourer receives a share of the fish caught during his work. The contract also stipulates that the labourer is entitled to get a share in monetary terms and not only in kind. The payment to crew towards his share by the boat owner in general is after the realization of fish sale proceeds by the boat owner.

Demand for and supply of labourers in the village: An estimated surplus of labourers according to occupation is presented in Table 10.17. It has been estimated from the sample respondent that 77 crew are required to operate the existing fishing craft in the village and the number of persons actively engaged in fishing or at best having no other occupation are 116. The number of surplus labourers has been estimated as the difference of the total crew required for operating the existing fishing craft in the village and the potential supply of labourers by all the households in the village and was found to be 39. The labour supply was short of demand only in the case of NMB households while in other households there was an excess supply of labourers as compared to the demand. The surplus labourers per household were in the range of 0.85 for MB owner households to 3.22 for crew households.

Labour participation pattern in terms of family and hired labourers in the village is presented in Table 10.18. At aggregate level about 56 per cent of the crew were estimated to be from boat owner families and the remaining were hired. In the case of purse-seines and dugout canoes 84.21 per cent and 44.44 per cent of the required crew respectively were estimated to be drawn from the family and the remaining were hired on a share basis. All the five crew required for operating the trawler were hired on a share basis.

Labour mobility: The labour mobility ratios have been computed for sample crew members to understand the extent of labour mobility in the village. The distribution of crew members according to their labour mobility ratio is given in Table 10.19. It can be seen that in the case of purse-seines only one crew is

TABLE 10.17

Estimates of surplus labourers according to occupation, Idya (1981)

Particulars	Number of members in households of				
	MB owners	NMB owners	Crew members	Others	Total
1. No. of households	33	10	9	47	99
2. No. of able-bodied male members of family	69	31	33	105	238
3. No. of adult male members with occupation other than fishing	3	4	1	78	86
4. No. of adult male members who have not yet entered the working force (students)	6	8	3	19	36
5. No. of members actively engaged or at best having no other occupation	60	19	29	8	116
6. No. of members required for operating fishing equipment	32	45	—	—	77
7. Surplus labourers in the fishing workforce	?8	—26	29	8	39
8. Surplus labourers per household	+0.85	—2.60	3.22	0.17	0.39

Note: 1. (—) indicates nil.
2. Negative surpluses indicate deficits.

selected and is found totally immobile, while in the case of rampani, out of three crew, two are found immobile and the mobile one has low mobility. In the case of two crew of dugout

TABLE 10.18

Estimated* labour participation pattern, family and hired, for operating different type of boats, Idya (1981-82)

Type of boat	Total No. of boats	Estimated avg. crew size required per boat	Total crew required	Estimated source of crew		
				Family	Hired	
					Sharing	Salary
1. Purse-seiner	1+	27	27	23 (85.19)	4 (14.81)	—
2. Trawler	1	5	5	—	5 (100.0)	—
3. Dugout canoes	9	5	45	20 (44.44)	25 (55.56)	—
Total	11	37	77	43 (55.84)	34 (44.16)	—

Note: Figures in parentheses indicate the share of family hired labourers in total crew required.

*Estimated on the basis of information from sample respondents.

+Though there are 2 purse-seiner boats in the village, some partners are from outside the village, therefore, the effective number was only one.

canoes, one is immobile and the other has the medium mobility ratio. Thus, the labourers in the village are found to be highly immobile. This may be mainly because of the observed imbalance in demand for and supply of labourers. The major reason for change of employer in the case of labourers with the labour mobility ratio of over 0.10 was their low income while working for the previous owner.

In view of the weak bargaining position of labourers in the village mainly because of the structural conditions in the labour market, the interlinkage of credit and labour is unknown. Of the total six sample crew only one was observed to have

TABLE 10.19

Distribution of crew members according to the labour mobility ratio, Idya (1981-82)

Labour mobility	No. of individuals with stated mobility of			Total
	Crew in dugout canoes	Crew in rampani	Crew in purse-seiner	
1. High	—	—	—	—
5. Medium	1 (50.00)	—	—	1 (16.67)
3. Low	1 (50.00)	3 (100.00)	1 (100.00)	5 (83.33)
Total	2 (100.00)	3 (100.00)	1 (100.00)	6 (100.00)

Note: 1. (—) indicates nil.
2. Figures in parentheses are percentages to column total.

borrowed an amount of Rs. 800 at the time of joining his employer, which had been cleared subsequently. Thus, the crew member was observed to have no outstanding debt to the owner employer as on December 31, 1981.

Occupational mobility: The distribution of working population in sample households according to the pace of graduation to current position is presented in Table 10.20. It is observed that the majority of the sample respondents have a low pace of graduation. Only one out of total 51 samples have the higher pace of graduation and belonged to MB owner category.

Credit for market

The distribution of households, according to the sources of borrowing and the amount of outstanding debt per household as on December 31, 1981, is presented in Table 10.21. It is observed that about 61 per cent of the total households were borrower households, with an outstanding debt on December 31, 1981. Two major sources of borrowing for the fishermen of Idya village are commercial banks and friends and relatives.

TABLE 10.20

Distribution of working population in sample households according to pace of graduation to current position, Idya (1981-82)

Pace of graduation	No. of individuals with stated pace in					Total
	MB owners	NMB owners	Crew in MB	Crew in NMB	Others	
1. High	1 (6.25)	—	—	—	—	1 (1.96)
2. Medium	—	—	—	2 (9.52)	—	2 (3.92)
3. Low	15 (93.65)	9 (100.00)	1 (100.00)	19 (90.48)	4 (100.00)	48 (94.12)
Total	16 (100.00)	9 (100.00)	1 (100.00)	21 (100.00)	4 (100.00)	51 (100.00)

Note: 1. (—) indicates nil.
2. Figures in parentheses are percentages to column total.

The total outstanding debt of the households in the village as on December 31, 1981, is estimated to be Rs. 9,35,800 of which 88.98 per cent is borrowed by MB owners and the remaining 11.04 per cent distributed over NMB crew and other households in proportion to the number of households in total. Of Rs. 8,32,500 borrowed by MB households, about 82 per cent was from commercial banks. The commercial banks started giving loans to fishermen only after the mechanization of fishing craft. The advantages of getting loans from commercial banks are fully exploited by MB owners. The average size of a loan per household was the highest for MB owner households with Rs. 26,016 and the lowest for other households with Rs. 3,194. Further, of the 61 borrower households only four borrowed from multiple sources. The borrowers from multiple sources consisted of three MB owner households and one NMB household.

It is interesting that not a single MB owner has borrowed from friends/relatives. The total amount borrowed from this

TABLE 10.21

Distribution of households according to the source of borrowing and occupation and their outstanding debt as on December 31, 1981, Idya

(Figures in Rupees)

Source of borrowing	No. of households having outstanding debts to the									
	MB owner		NMB owners		Crew		Others		Total	
	No.	Debt	No.	Debt	No.	Debt	No.	Debt	No.	Debt
I. Formal lending agencies:										
Commercial banks	29	683000 (23552)	7	22450 (3207)	3	9250 (3083)	15	50100 (3340)	54	764800 (14162)
II. Informal sources:										
Friends and relatives	—	—	1	2500 (2500)	1	8000 (8000)	1	10000 (1000)	3	11500 (3833)
III. From multiple sources	3	149500 (49833)	1	10000 (10000)	—	—	—	—	4	159500 (39875)
Total	32	832500 (26016)	9	34950 (3883)	4	17250 (4312.50)	16	51100 (3194)	61	935800 (15340.98)

Note: 1. (—) indicates nil.
2. Figures in parentheses indicate per household outstanding debt.

source, however, was hardly one per cent of the total borrowings. The relatively low share of borrowings from multiple sources indicates the easy availability of credit from different sources.

The distribution of households, according to the purpose of borrowing, is given in Table 10.22. Over 38 per cent of the total households were non-borrowing households. It is interesting that the majority of non-borrowers (81.58 per cent) were other

TABLE 10.22

Distribution of households according to the purpose of borrowing of the outstanding debt and occupation, Idya (1981)

Reason for borrowing outstanding debt	Number of households for stated reason of borrowing of				Total
	MB owner	NMB owner	Crew	Others	
1. No outstanding debt	1 (3.03)	1 (10.00)	5 (55.56)	31 (65.96)	38 (38.38)
2. Purchase of fishing craft and gear	26 (78.79)	5 (50.00)	3 (33.33)	1 (2.13)	35 (35.36)
3. Fishing operations	5 (15.15)	—	—	—	5 (5.05)
4. To meet household expenditure	1 (3.03)	4 (40.00)	1 (11.11)	8 (17.02)	14 (14.14)
5. To meet expenditure for social functions	—	—	—	1 (2.13)	1 (1.01)
6. Others	—	—	—	6 (12.76)	6 (6.06)
Total	33 (100.00)	10 (100.00)	9 (100.00)	47 (100.00)	99 (100.00)

Note: 1. (—) indicates nil.
2. Figures in parentheses are percentages to column total.

households. At an aggregate level, over 35 per cent have borrowed to purchase fishing equipment, while in the case of MB owners about 78.79 per cent of the total borrowed was for the purchase of fishing equipment. One MB household has borrowed to meet household expenditure. Only five MB owners have borrowed for fishing operations.

The distribution of households according to outstanding debt is presented in Table 10.23. Over 38 per cent of the house-

TABLE 10.23

Size distribution of households according to occupation and total outstanding debts, Idya, 1981

Range of outstanding debt (Rs.)	Number of households with outstanding debt in stated range of				Total
	MB owner	NMB owner	Crew	Others	
Zero outstanding	1 (3.030)	1 (10.00)	5 (55.55)	32 (68.09)	38 (38.39)
Up to 1000	—	2 (20.00)	1 (11.11)	3 (6.38)	6 (6.06)
1001-5000	—	6 (60.00)	2 (22.22)	10 (21.27)	18 (18.18)
5001-10000	—	1 (10.00)	1 (11.11)	1 (2.13)	4 (4.04)
10001-15000	2 (6.06)	—	—	1 (2.13)	3 (3.03)
15001-20000	11 (33.33)	—	—	—	11 (11.11)
20001-25000	10 (30.30)	—	—	—	10 (10.10)
25001-30000	2 (6.06)	—	—	—	2 (2.02)
30001 and above	7 (21.21)	—	—	—	7 (7.07)
Total	33 (100.00)	10 (100.00)	9 (100.00)	47 (100.00)	99 (100.00)

Note: 1. (—) indicates nil.
2. Figures in parentheses are percentages to column total.

holds were having zero outstanding debt and of the borrower households the majority had an outstanding debt of less than Rs. 5,000. When we consider the persons engaged in fishing only, then we find that all the households except MB owner households, have borrowed less than Rs. 10,000 and the majority of them have borrowed less than Rs. 5,000. One each of NMB and crew households has borrowed in the range of Rs. 5,001 to 10,000. In the case of MB owners, the majority of the borrowing was more than Rs. 10,000. The highest number of MB owner households (33.33 per cent) borrowed an amount in the range of Rs. 15,001—20,000 and over 21 per cent of them crossed Rs. 30,000.

Market for product

The discussion in this section is going to be around fish marketing in the village and its structure and the predominant changes which have taken place after the mechanization of fishing craft.

Various qualitative changes have taken place in the fish market scene of the village. The quantity of fish arrivals in the product market of the village has decreased mainly due to the shift in the fish landing from the village to a nearby assembly centre after mechanization. The pattern of selling has changed from count to weight during the same period. Further, the mode of transportation of fish has also changed from headload to motor transport during the last 35 years.

During 1972-73, only three types of market intermediaries were operating in Idya. They were retailers/vendors, fresh fish wholesalers and commission agents. Almost all the business was in the hands of the fishermen community; only 15 retailers/vendors from other communities were working.

It is interesting to note that the number of market intermediaries decreased from 50 in 1972-83 to 40 in 1981-82. The number of retailers/vendors has gone down steeply from 45 (1972-73) to 22 (1981-82). Both the fresh fish wholesalers wound up their business and now the fresh fish is sold only by retailers/vendors. Only 10 fishermen are working as dry fish wholesalers on a very small scale. They purchase fish directly from the fishermen, dry themselves and sell the dried fish to the wholesalers of the large transit market. The dried fish is not sold within the village.

The persons outside the village are also involved in the fish market of Idya. They have their business in their location but come to purchase fish in Idya. This type of channel members do not purchase fish to sell fish in the usual form. They work as agents for processors or fish meal plant owners. On behalf of the processors or fish meal plant owners, they go to Idya and purchase fish to supply to the processing industry on commission basis. In other words, they work as commission agents for them. At present, in the Idya market four agents of processors and four agents of fish meal or oil plant owners are involved (Table 10.24). An analysis of the structure of the fish market in the village indicated a fairly good competitive market.

THE VILLAGE ECONOMY

In this section we shall briefly describe the assets, other than fishing equipment, structure of fishermen households and their incomes as well as savings.

Assets structure of fishermen

The most important assets which form the assets structure of fishermen in the village are fishing equipment and owned houses. Most of the fishermen were found to have invested mostly in immovable property like land, household goods and domestic animals.

The distribution of households according to occupation and value of owned house in the village is given in Table 10.25. About 88 per cent of MB households own houses valued at more than Rs. 5,000. Only two out of the 33 households own houses valued at less than Rs. 1,000. Over 70 per cent of the other households own houses valued at more than Rs. 5,000.

Ownership of household items, according to occupation, in Table 10.26 indicates that the other households own almost all the listed items. MB households possess most of the listed items as compared to NMB and crew households with the exception of one particular item, electric fan. Of the 11 electric fans in the village not even one is possessed by MB households whereas each one of the NMB and crew households possess one and

TABLE 10.24

Changes in the number of marketing intermediaries for the distribution of fish after the mechanization of fishing craft, Idya

Type of intermediaries	Number of persons/organizations of stated category during					
	Pre-mechanization period (1972-73)			Currently (1981-82)		
	Fishermen community	Non-fishermen community	Total	Fishermen community	Non-fishermen community	Total
1. Retailers/ Vendors	30	15	45	14	8	22
2. Wholesalers						
(a) Fresh fish	2	—	2	—	—	—
(b) Dry fish	—	—	—	10*	—	10
3. Commission agents	3	—	3	—	—	—
4. Processing variety agents	—	—	—	4+	—	4
5. Agents of fishmeal and oil plant owners	—	—	—	4+	—	4

Note: (—) indicates nil.

+These intermediaries are having bases in other locations but visit the village regularly.

*These are mainly involved in drying the fish brought from the fishermen and to sell it to the wholesalers in large transit markets.

two fans respectively. Of the total 1,669 items of kitchenware in the village, 30 per cent are possessed by the MB owner households.

The data revealed that the fishermen have invested more money to own a house as compared to household articles.

TABLE 10.25

Distribution of households according to occupation and value of owned houses, Idya (1981)

Value range (Rs.)	Number of houses in the stated range of value of				Total
	MB	NMB	Crew	Others	
No owned house	—	1 (14.3)	1 14.3)	5 (71.4)	7 (100.0)
Less than 1000	2 (66.7)	—	—	1 (33.3)	3 (100.0)
1001-3000	1 (33.3)	—	—	2 (66.7)	3 (100.0)
3001-5000	1 (11.1)	1 (11.1)	1 (11.1)	6 (66.7)	9 (100.0)
5001-10000	13 (34.2)	3 (7.9)	2 (5.3)	20 (52.6)	38 (100.0)
10001 and above	16 (41.0)	5 (12.8)	5 (12.8)	13 (33.4)	39 (100.0)
Sub-total of own houses	33 (35.9)	9 (9.8)	8 (8.7)	42 (47.5)	92 (100.0)
Total households	33 (33.3)	10 (10.1)	9 (9.1)	47 (47.5)	99 (100.0)

Note: 1. (—) indicates nil.
2. Figures in parentheses are percentages to row total.

Majority of the houses (34 per cent) possess articles valued at less than Rs. 500. Only six out of total 99 households possess articles valued at more than Rs. 5,000 of which three are "others" and only one is an MB owner household (Table 10.27).

Details of the livestock owned by different households are presented in Table 10.28. About 70 per cent of the households do not maintain any livestock; and of the remaining 30 per cent, 58 per cent "other" households. This analysis indicates that about 23 per cent of the total fishermen households

TABLE 10.26

Ownership of different household items according to occupation, Idya (1981-82)

Items	No. of households owning the stated items								Total	
	MB		NMB		CRM		Others			
	NI	HH	NI	HH	NI	HH	NI	HH	NI	HH
1	2	3	4	5	6	7	8	9	10	11
I. *Transport Vehicles*										
Cycle	—	—	—	—	—	—	2	2	2	2
II. *Communication/Entertainment*										
Radio/Transistor	10	10	5	5	4	4	13	13	32	32
TV/2 or 3-in-one	—	—	—	—	—	—	—	—	—	—
Electric fan	—	—	1	1	2	1	8	4	11	6
III. *Office Equipment*										
Chairs	29	13	22	7	20	6	74	31	145	57
Tables	8	8	5	5	3	2	26	22	42	37
Wooden almirah	—	—	—	—	—	—	1	1	1	1
Sewing machine	1	1	1	1	—	—	4	2	6	4

TABLE 10.26 (*Contd.*)

1	2	3	4	5	6	7	8	9	10	11
IV. *Time Indicators*										
Wrist-watches	12	11	7	5	7	4	33	17	59	37
Clock	10	10	3	3	4	4	15	15	32	32
V. *Cooking Apparatus*										
Non-kerosene stove	23	23	5	5	8	8	42	40	78	76
Kerosene stove	2	2	3	3	—	—	7	7	12	12
VI. *Kitchenware*										
Earthen	152	31	41	8	41	9	245	43	479	91
Aluminium	227	31	65	9	63	9	315	45	670	94
Steel	133	22	50	7	56	9	252	37	491	75
Others	11	4	13	2	—	—	5	1	29	7

Note: 1. (—) indicates nil.
2. NI indicates number of items.
3. HH indicates number of housholds.

TABLE 10.27

Size distribution of households according to the value of owned household articles and occupation, Idya (1981-82)

(in Rupees)

Frequency interval (Rs.)	Number of households with the value of household articles in the stated range of				Total
	MB owners	NMB owners	Crew	Others	
Up to 500	12 (36.4)	3 (30.0)	1 (11.1)	18 (38.4)	34 (34.3)
501-1000	5 (15.2)	1 (10.0)	3 (33.4)	7 (14.9)	16 (16.2)
1001-1500	1 (3.0)	—	1 (11.1)	4 (8.5)	6 (6.1)
1501-2000	3 (9.1)	1 (10.0)	1 (11.1)	4 (8.5)	9 (9.1)
2001-2500	3 (9.1)	—	2 (22.2)	1 (2.1)	6 (6.1)
2501-3000	1 (3.0)	—	—	1 (2.1)	2 (2.0)
3001-3500	1 (3.0)	1 (10.0)	—	2 (4.3)	4 (4.0)
3501-4000	4 (12.1)	1 (10.1)	1 (11.1)	4 (8.5)	10 (10.1)
4001-4500	2 (6.1)	—	—	2 (4.3)	4 (4.0)
4501-5000	—	1 (10.0)	—	1 (2.1)	2 (2.0)
5001 and above	1 (3.0)	2 (20.0)	—	3* (6.4)	6 (6.1)
Total	33 (100.0)	10 (100.0)	9 (100.0	47 (100.0)	99 (100.0)

Note: (—) indicates nil.

Figures in parentheses are percentages to column total.

*Includes one household with household articles valued at over Rs. 10,000 and in all other cases the value of household articles is less than Rs. 8,000.

TABLE 10.28

Size distribution of households according to the value of livestock owned and occupation, Idya (1981-82)

Interval (Rs.)	Number of households with the value of owned livestock in the stated range of				Total
	MB owners	NMB owners	Crew	Others	
No livestock	28 (84.35)	6 (60.0)	6 (66.67)	29 (60.70)	69 (69.70)
1-50	4 (12.12)	1 (10.0)	2 (22.22)	9 (19.15)	16 (16.16)
51-100	1 (3.03)	1 (10.0)	1 (11.11)	2 (4.26)	6 (5.05)
101-150	—	1 (10.0)	—	2 (4.26)	3 (3.03)
151-200	—	—	—	—	—
201+	—	1 (10.0)	—	5* (10.63)	6 (6.06)
Total	33 (100.0)	10 (100.0)	9 (100.0)	47 (100.0)	99 (100.0)

Note: (—) indicates nil.
Figures in parentheses are percentages to column total.
*The five households own livestock valued at over Rs. 500.

maintain livestock, mostly goat, sheep and poultry birds. Only two of them have invested more than Rs. 100 in livestock.

The distribution of households, according to their ownership of land, is presented in Table 10.29. None of the categories of the fishermen have invested in agricultural land. But more than 50 per cent of them have purchased land for non-agricultural purposes. Almost all the investors have purchased land of the value less than Rs. 10,000. Only three NMB households own land valued at more than Rs. 10,000 and one NMB and one crew household own land valued at between Rs. 14,001 and Rs. 16,000.

TABLE 10.29

Size distribution of households according to the value of owned land, both agricultural and non-agricultural purposes, and occupation, Idya (1981-82)

Frequency interval (Rs.)	Number of households with value of land in the stated range of									
	MB owners		NMB owners		Crew		Others		Total	
	Agri. land	Non-Agri.	Agri.	Non-Agri.	Agri.	Non-Agri.	Agri.	Non-Agri.	Agri.	Non-Agri.
No land	33	14	10	3	9	5	42	28	94	50
0001-2000	—	1	—	—	—	—	—	2	—	3
2001-4000	—	15	—	2	—	2	1	6	1	25
4001-6000	—	2	—	2	—	1	1	5	1	10
6001-8000	—	1	—	—	—	—	—	1	—	2
8001-10000	—	—	—	1	—	—	—	—	—	1
10001-12000	—	—	—	1	—	—	—	—	—	1
12001-14000	—	—	—	—	—	—	—	1	—	1
14001-16000	—	—	—	1	—	1	1	1	1	3
16001 +	—	—	—	—	—	—	2+	3*	2	3
Total	33	33	10	10	9	9	47	47	99	99

Note: (—) indicates nil.
*Includes two households with land value of over Rs. 20,000.
+Both households own land valued at over Rs. 20,000.

Consumption and expenditure pattern of fishermen households

The pattern of expenditure on food and non-food items mainly depends on income, social customs, habits, etc., of the fishermen households. The expenditure on food items accounts for about 70 per cent of the total expenditure of the fishermen households.

The itemwise annual consumption expenditure is presented in Table 10.30. As indicated above, the expenditure on food

TABLE 10.30

Itemwise annual consumption expenditure by occupation, Idya (1981-82)

(in '000 Rupees)

Item	Expenditure on the stated item by				Total
	MB	NMB	CRM	Others	
I. *Food Items*:					
(a) Foodgrains	105.56 (35.87)	30.99 (10.53)	30.58 (10.39)	127.14 (43.21)	294.27 (100.00)
(b) Milk and milk products	6.55 (24.65)	3.12 (11.74)	1.82 (6.85)	15.08 (56.42)	26.57 (100.00)
(c) Edible oil	7.23 (27.31)	2.34 (8.84)	2.76 (10.43)	14.14 (53.42)	26.47 (100.00)
(d) Meat and chicken	—	—	—	—	—
(e) Eggs	—	—	—	—	
(f) Fish	33.49 (35.64)	10.09 (10.74)	10.97 (11.67)	39.42 (41.95)	93 97 (100.00)
(g) Vegetables	11.08 (33.44)	3.43 (10.35)	3.33 (10.05)	15.29 (46.16)	33.13 (100.00)
(h) Fruits and nuts	5.67 (28.62)	2.54 (11.81)	2.70 (13.65)	9.10 (45.24)	19.81 (100.00)
(i) Sugar, gur and khandsari	4.11 (24.85)	1.56 (9.43)	1.56 (9.43)	9.31 (56.29)	16.54 (100.00)

(j) Salt and spices	9.98 (31.57)	2.60 (8.23)	2.03 (6.42)	17.00 (53.78)	31.61 (100.00)
(k) Beverages	14.40 (22.98)	7.28 (11.62)	6.50 (10.37)	34.48 (55.03)	62.66 (100.00)
(l) Pan, tobacco and supari	11.39 (41.88)	2.65 (9.74)	3.38 (14.43)	9.78 (35.95)	27.20 (100.00)
Sub-total	209.46 (31.95)	66.40 (13.70)	65.63 (10.01)	290.74 (44.34)	632.23 (100.00)
II. *Non-food Items*:					
(a) Entertainment	1.27 (29.60)	0.60 (13.99)	0.59 (13.75)	1.83 (42.66)	4.29 (100.00)
(b) Traval and transport	3.30 (33.33)	1.00 (10.10)	0.90 (9.09)	4.70 (47.48)	9.90 (100.00)
(c) Education	3.30 (28.13)	2.38 (20.29)	1.06 (9.04)	4.99 (42.54)	11.73 (100.00)
(d) Medicines	3.72 (29.36)	1.65 (13.02)	1.13 (8.92)	6.17 (48.70)	12.67 (100.00)
(e) Domestic utensils	0.77 (32.49)	0.39 (16.46)	0.22 (9.28)	0.99 (41.77)	2.37 (100.00)
(f) Clothes	11.93 (30.16)	5.05 (12.77)	3.32 (8.39)	19.25 (48.68)	39.55 (100.00)
(g) Footwear	2.00 (31.30)	0.95 (14.87)	0.86 (13.46)	2.58 (40.37)	6.39 (100.00)
(h) Ornaments	0.57 (22.18)	0.53 (20.62)	0.31 (12.06)	1.16 (45.14)	2.57 (100.00)
(i) Fuels and light	64.43 (35.18)	20.54 (11.21)	17.42 (9.51)	80.76 (44.10)	183.15 (100.00)
(j) Others	0.10 (12.66)	0.20 (25.32)	0.18 (22.78)	0.31 (39.94)	0.79 (100.00)
Sub-total	91.39 (33.43)	33.29 (12.18)	25.99 (9.51)	122.74 (44.89)	273.41 (100.00)
Grand Total	300.85 (33.22)	99.69 (11.01)	91.62 (10.12)	413.48 (45.66)	905.64 (100.00)

Note : 1. (—) indicates nil.
2. Figures in parentheses are percentages to row total.

items accounts for Rs. 6,32,230 (69.8 per cent) out of the total Rs. 9,05,640. The main items of expenditure are foodgrains and fish which together account for 61 per cent of the total expenditure on food items. In the case of MB owners it is reported to be 66 per cent while in NMB households it accounts for 46 per cent. About 10 per cent of the total food expenditure goes to beverages and only 5 per cent is spent on vegetables.

The main items of non-food expenditure are fuel and light which account for 67 per cent of the expenditure followed by the expenditure on clothing (15 per cent).

The per capita and per household annual consumption expenditure (Table 10.31) reveals that the per capita expenditure

TABLE 10.31

Itemwise annual consumption expenditure by occupation according to household and per capita for Idya (1981)

(in Rupees)

Item	MB	NMB	CRM	Others	Total
I. *Food Items*:					
(a) Foodgrains	423 (3199)	436 (3099)	413 (3397)	389 (2705)	408.14 (2972.40)
(b) Milk and milk products	27 (199)	44 (312)	84 (202)	46 (321)	36.85 (268.40)
(c) Edible oil	29 (219)	33 (234)	37 (306)	43 (301)	36.71 (267.35)
(d) Fish	135 (1015)	142 (1009)	148 (1219)	121 (839)	130.32 (949.13)
(e) Fruits and nuts	23 (172)	33 (234)	36 (301)	28 (193)	27.48 (212.12)
(f) Vegetables	45 (335)	48 (348)	45 (370)	47 (326)	45.94 (334.59)
(g) Sugar, gur and khandsari	17 (124)	22 (156)	21 (173)	29 (198)	22.93 (167.03)
(h) Salt and spices	40 (306)	36 (260)	28 (225)	52 (363)	43.85 (312.35)

(i) Beverages	58 (436)	102 (728)	88 (722)	106 (734)	86.91 (632.93)
(j) Pan, tobacco and supari	46 (345)	37 (365)	46 (375)	30 (208)	37.72 (274.71)
Sub-total	843 (6350)	933 (6640)	886 (7290)	891 (6187)	876.85 (6383.01)
II. *Non-food Items*:					
(a) Entertainment	5.12 (38.61)	8.46 (60.10)	8.04 (66.11)	5.59 (38.91)	5.96 (43.42)
(b) Travel and transport	13.25 (99.97)	14.08 (99.97)	12.16 (99.91)	14.37 (99.97)	13.73 (99.99)
(c) Education	13.23 (99.85)	33.45 (237.50)	14.32 (117.78)	15.27 (106.26)	16.26 (118.42)
(d) Medicines	14.94 (112.73)	23.24 (165.00)	15.20 (125.00)	18.85 (131.17)	17.56 (127.88)
(e) Domestic utensils	3.08 (23.27)	5.49 (39.00)	2.91 (23.89)	3.02 (21.00)	3.37 (23.84)
(f) Clothes	47.89 (361.36)	71.13 (505.00)	44.86 (368.89)	58.85 (409.47)	54.84 (394.39)
(g) Footwear	8.03 (60.61)	13.31 (94.50)	11.55 (95.00)	7.89 (54.89)	8.85 (64.44)
(h) Ornaments	2.27 (17.12)	7.39 (52.50)	4.12 (33.89)	3.55 (24.68)	3.54 (25.81)
(i) Fuel and Light	259.00 (1953)	289.00 (2054)	236.00 (1935)	247.00 (1718)	253.76 (1850.16)
(j) Others	0.40 (3.03)	2.82 (20.00)	2.36 (19.44)	0.93 (6.49)	1.08 (7.88)
Sub-total	376.22 (2769.55)	468.37 (3327.57)	351.54 (2884.98)	375.33 (2610.84)	378.86 (2761.24)
Total	1210.22 (9119.55)	1401.37 (9967.57)	1237.54 (10174.84)	1266.33 (8797.84)	1255.71 (9147.25)

Note: 1. (—) indicates nil.
2. Figures in parentheses indicate the expenditure per household.

of MB and crew households is less than the per capita average in the viliage. The highest per capita expenditure is observed in the case of MB households (Rs. 1,401.37) and the lowest in MB households (Rs. 1,216.22).

Income and savings of fishermen

Having analysed the income and expenditure pattern of fishermen households in the last section we shall now study the pattern of savings. The occupationwise income, expenditure and savings in the village are presented in Table 10.32. The total income of

TABLE 10.32

Occupationwise income, expenditure and savings, Idya (1981-82)

(in '000 Rupees)

Occupation	Income	Expenditure	Savings
1. MBowner	491.25	267.36	223.89
2. NMB owner	99.23	89.60	9.63
3. Crew	98.30	80.65	17.65
4. Others	333.80	393.77	—59.97
Total	1022.58	831.38	191.20

Note: 1. Negative savings indicate dissavings.
2. The consumer expenditure is excluding the expenditure on fish. The expenditure on fish is excluded from the total expenditure as the income does not include the value of captive consumption of fish by fishermen. In case of other households half of their fish consumption is assumed to be obtained from the boat owner in the form of gifts.

the villagers is estimated at Rs. 10,22,580 and the expenditure at Rs. 8,31,380 leaving a net saving of Rs. 1,91,200. The households in all the occupations relating to fisheries had savings in the range of Rs. 9,630 for NMB owner households to Rs. 2,23,870 for MB owner households. The households in the other categories had dissavings of the order of Rs. 59,970 or Rs. 1,280 per household per annum. The negative savings of other households are offset by the high savings of MB owner households. At an aggregate level the savings were of the order of Rs. 1,930 per annum per household.

REFERENCES

1. The classification of households into occupational categories is based on major occupation. The major occupation of households which consisted of family members in more than one occupation, like NMB owner and crew, has been identified on the basis of income from different occupations. The households are classified into the category from which the major portion of the annual income is derived.
2. The rampani unit consists of three non-mechanized boats of which one is large plank built canoes to carry the net and two dugout canoes. The year of purchase of the rampani unit relates to the large plank built canoe. Further the small dugout canoes were replaced about 8 to 10 years ago.

Selected Bibliography

Alexander, P., "Innovation in a Cultural Vacuum: The Mechanization of Sri Lanka Fisheries," *Human Organisation*, 34(4), pp. 333-44, 1975.

Amin, R.K., Socio-Economic Study of a Charoter Village, *Valasan*, Vallabh Vidyanagar, Sardar Vallabhbhai Vidyapeeth.

Anonymous, *A Study of the Economy of Fisherfolk in Kerala* (Trivandrum: Economic Research Council, 1959).

———, *Evaluation of the Programme of Mechanization of Fishing Boats* (New Delhi: Programme Evaluation Organisation Planning Commission, February 1971).

———, *Proceedings of the Seminar on the Role of Small-Scale Fisheries and Coastal Acquaculture in Integrated Rural Development* (Cochin: CMFRI Bulletin 30A, 1978).

———, *Present Status of Small-Scale Fisheries in India and A Few Neighbouring Countries* (Cochin: CMFRI Bulletin 30B, 1978).

———, "Impact of Mechanised Fishing on the Socio-Economic Conditions of the Fishermen of Sakthikulangara-Neendakara, Kerala," *Marine Fishing Information Service*, No. 29, July 1981).

———, *Techno-Economic Survey of Kerala* (New Delhi: National Council of Applied Economic Research).

———, *An Evaluation of Fishery Financing Scheme of the State Bank of India at Mangalore* (Bombay: Economic Research Department, State Bank of India, October 1982).

Apte, D.P., *Prospects of Development in a Backward Region: A Socio-Economic Survey of 15 Villages in Kolaba District, Maharashtra State* (Poona: Agro-Economic Research Centre, Gokhale Institute of Politics and Economics, 1975).

Barnabas, A.P., *Social Change in a North Indian Village* (New Delhi: Indian Institute of Public Administration, 1969).

Barth, F., *Models of Social Organisation* (London: Royal Anthropological Institute of Great Britain and Ireland, 1966).

Bartsch, W.G., *Employment Effects of Alternative Technologies and Techniques in Asian Crop Production: A Survey of Evidence* (Geneva: International Labour Organization, 1973).

Baum, G.A., and Maynaro, J.A., *Coron/Tagumpay: A Socio-Economic Study and Development Proposal* (Manila: South China Sea Fisheries Development and Coordinating Programme, SCS/76/WP/33, 1976).

Billings, M.H., and Singh, A., "Mechanization and Rural Employment with Some Implication for Rural Income Distribution," *Economic and Political Weekly*, 5(26), June 1970.

Binswanger, H.P., "The Measurement of Technological Biases with Many Factors of Production," *American Economic Review*, 74(4), pp. 964-76, 1974.

———, *Induced Innovation Technology: Institutions and Development* (Baltimore: John Hopkins University Press, 1978).

Blake, B.A., "Technological Change Among the Coastal Marine Fishermen of Madras State," Ph. D. Dissertation in Anthropology, University of Wisconsin, Madison, 969.

———, "Cultural Adaptation and Technological Change Among Madras Fishing Population," in *Those Who Live from the Sea*, M.E. Smith (Editor) (San Francisco: West Publishing, 1977).

Bhushan, B., "Technological Change in Fishing in Kerala: 1953-1977", M. Phil. Dissertation, Centre for Development Studies, Trivandrum, 1979.

Brochl, Wayne, G., *The Village Entrepreneur: Change Agents in Indian Rural Development* (Cambridge: Harvard University Press, 1978).

Chandra Prakash, R., *Marine Fish Industry of South Kanara* (Mysore: Institute of Development Studies, University of Mysore, April 1976).

Chattopadhyay, S.N., and Pareek, W., "Prediction of Multi-practice Adoption Behaviour from same Psychological Variables," *Rural Sociology*, 32, pp. 324-33, 1967.

Christensen, J.B., Problems Resulting from Technological

Change: The Case of the Fanti Fishermen of Ghana, speech delivered at a Symposium on Fishery Modernization, East Calorina University, 27-29 April, 1978.

Dasgupta, B., (Editor), *Village Studies in the Third World* (New Delhi: Hindustan Publishing Company, 1977).

De Silva, N.N., "The Role of Technology in Fisheries Development in Ceylon," *Bulletin of the Fisheries Research Station*, 17(2), pp. 257-65, 1964.

Devaraj, J., *Keel Handling of Traditional Fishermen: The Impact of Purse-seiner Operations on the Fish Economy of Dakshana Kanara District in Karnataka* (Trivandrum: Programme for Community Organisation, 1980).

Emmerson, D.K., *Orders of Meaning: Understanding Political Change in a Fishing Community in Indonesia*, Address delivered to the Annual Meeting of the American Political Science Association, 2-5 September, 1975.

Epple, G.M., "Technological Change in a Grenada, W.I. Fisheries—1950-70," in Smith, M.E. (Editor), *Those Who Live From the Sea* (San Francisco: West Publishing Co., 1977).

Epstein, T.S., *Economic Development and Social Change in South India* (Manchester: Manchester University Press, 1967).

Firth, Raymond, *Elements of Social Organisation* (London: Watts & Co., 1983).

———, *Malay Fishermen: Their Peasant Economy* (2nd Edition) (Hamden C.T.: Archon, 1966).

Fonseca, C., *et al.*, "The Traditional Fishermen of India Demand Appropriate Technology in the Indian Fisheries Sector," Paper presented at the workshop on Alternative Approach to the Management of Research and Technology, Indian Institute of Management, Bangalore, 1980.

Foster, S.M., *Traditional Cultures and the Impact of Technological Change* (New York: Harper, 1973).

Foster, G.M., "Peasant Society and the Image of Limited Good," *American Anthropologist*, 67, pp. 293-315, 1965.

———, *Traditional Societies and Technological Change* (2nd Edition) (Berkeley: University of California Press, 1973).

Fraser, T.M. (Jr.), *Rusembilan: A Malay Fishing Village in Southern Thailand* (Ithaca: Cornell University Press, 1980).

Fraser, T.M., *Fishermen of South Thailand* (New York: Holt, Rinehart and Winston, 1966).

Galtung, J., "Technology and Dependence: The Internal Logic of Excessive Modernisation in a Fisheries Project in Kerala," *Ceres*, September-October 1974, p. 45-50.

George, G.M., *Traditional Cultures and the Impact of Technological Change*," (New York: Harper Row, 1962).

Gerherdsen, G.M., *Strategies for Development Projects in Small-Scale Fisheries* (Rome: Food and Agriculture Organisation, 1977).

Hagen, E.G., *On the Theory of Social Change* (Homewood: Dorsey Press, 1962).

Halpern, J.M., *The Changing Village Community* (Englewood Cliffs: Prentice Hall, 1967).

Iswaran, K., *Change and Continuity in India's Villages* (New York: Columbia University Press, 1970).

Kestevan, G.L., and Williams, G.R., "Fishing Regulations: Conflicts in Exploitation of Fishing Resources," in G.L. Kestevan, *et al.*, *Essays in Fisheries Sctence* (Division of Fisheries and Oceanography Circular No. 6, Melbourne, Commonwealth Scientific and Industrial Research Organisation, Australia), pp. 77-91, 1971.

Klansen, A.M., *Kerala Fishermen and the Indo-Norwegian Pilot Project*, (Oslo: Universities for Laget, 1968).

Kurien, J., "Entry of Big Business into Fishing: Its Impact on the Fish Economy," *Economic and Political Weekly*, 13(36), pp. 1557-65, July-September, 1978.

———, "Social Factors and Economic Organisation of the Traditional Small Scale Fishermen of India," *Social Action*, 30(2), 1980.

———, and Vijayan, A.J., *Capitalist Relations in Traditional Fishing: The Case of the Goan Rampon* (Trivandrum: Fisheries Research Cell Working, WP/1, 1980).

———, and Willmann, R., *Economics of Artisanal and Mechanized Fisheries in Kerala* (Madras: Bay of Bengal Programme Development of Small Scale Fisheries, July 1982).

———, and Mathew, S., *Technological Change in Fishing: Its Impact on Fishermen* (Trivandrum: Centre for Development Studies, 1982).

Kumaran, E., "The Mechanisation of the Inshore Fisheries and Relationship to Fisheries Development in Ceylon," *Bulletin of the Fisheries Research Station,* 17 (2), pp. 298-310, 1964.

Lacis, V., *The Fishermen's Son,* Translated from Russian by T. and T. Lit Vindow (Moscow: Foreign Languages Publishing House, 1954).

Lawson, R.M., *Interim Report on Socio-Economic Aspects of the Development of Artisanal Fisheries on the East Coast of Malaysia* (Manila: South China Sea Fisheries Development and Co-ordinating Programme, SCS/75/WP/15, 1975).

Lewis, Oscar, *Village Life in Northern India* (New York: Vintage Books & Random House, 1965).

Lofgren, O., "From Peasant Fishing to Industrial Trawling; A Comparative Discussion of Modernisation Processes in some North Atlantic Regions (Speech delivered to a symposium on Fishery Modernisation, East Carolina University, 27-29 April, 1978).

Majumdar, D.N., *Cast and Communication in an Indian Village* (Bombay: Asia Publishing House, 1962).

Majumdar, M.R., *Cultural History of Gujarat: From Early Times to Pre-British Period* (Bombay: Popular Prakashan, 1965).

Marnot, Mckim (ed.), *Village India* (Bombay: Asia Publishing House, 1961).

Mathur, P.R.G., *The Mappila Fisherfolk of Kerala* (Trivandrum: Kerala Historical Society, 1978).

Mesthene, E.G., *Technological Change, Its Impact on Man Society* (Cambridge: Harvard University Press, 1970).

Mohan, K.P., "The Situation of Indian Fishing Industry and Indian Fishermen," in *Concern,* ISI Documentation Centre, Bangalore, 1980.

Murray, C.A., *A Behavioural Study of Rural Modernisation and Social and Economic Change in Thai Villages* (New York: Praeger Publishers, 1977).

Norbeck, E., *Takashima : A Japanese Fishing Village* (Salt Lake City: University of Utah Press, 1954).

Norr, K., *A South Indian Fishing Village in Comparative Perspective,* Ph. D. Dissertation, University of Michigan, 1972.

Panchardikar, K.C., and Panchardikar, R.P.S., *Determinates of Social Structure and Social Change in India and Other Papers* (Bombay: Popular Prakashan, 1970).

Patnaik, N., *Caste and Social Change* (Hyderabad: National Institute of Community Development, 1969).

Plattearu, J. Ph., *et al.*, *Credit and Indebtedness Among the Marine Fishermen of South Kerala* (New Delhi: Indian Social Institute, 1979).

———, "Interlinkage of Credit, Labour and Marketing Relations in Traditional Marine Fishing: The Case of Purakkad (Kerala)," *Social Action*, 31 (2), April-June 1981, pp. 182-212.

Pollnac, R.B., *Continuity and Change in Marine Fishing Communities*, Anthropology Working Paper No. 10 (Kingston: International Centre for Marine Resources Development, University of Rhode Island, 1976).

———, "Socio-cultural Factors Influencing Success of Intermediate Food Technology Programme," *Food Technology*, pp. 80-92, April 1978.

———, *Socio-cultural Aspects of Technological and Institutional Change Among Small Scale Fishermen*, Anthropology Working Paper No. 22 (Kingston: University of Rhode Island 1978).

———, and S.J. Littlefield, *Socio-cultural Aspects of Fisheries Management*, Anthropology Working Paper No. 40, (Kingston: University of Rhode Island, 1981).

Rao, M.S.A., *Tradition Rationality and Change : Essays in Sociology of Economic Development and Social Change* (Bombay: Popular Prakashan, 1972).

Rao, C.H.H., *Technological Change and Distribution of Gains in Indian Agriculture* (Delhi: MacMillan Company of India, 1975).

Rao, R.S., "Some Aspects of Economics of Fisheries in India," *Indian Journal of Agricultural Economics*, 23 (4), 1968.

Sachchidananda, *Profiles of Tribal Culture in Bihar* (Calcutta: Firma K.L. Mukhopadhay, 1965).

Saeger, J., "Do Trawling Bans Work in Tropical Waters," *Iclarm News Letter*, 4 (1), 1981.

Sarojono, I., "Trawlers Banned in Indonesia'.' *Iclarm News Letter*, 3 (4), 1980.

Scott, A., "The Fishery: The Objectives of Sole Ownership," *Journal of Political Economy*, 63 (1), pp. 116-24, 1955.

Sidhu, S.S., "Economies of Technological Change in Wheat

Production in the Indian Punjab," *American Journal of Agricultural Economics*, 56 (1), pp. 217-25, May 1974.

Sivasankara Pillai, T., *Chemmeen* (Translated by Narayana Menon) (New York: Harper, 1962).

Smith, M.E. (ed.), *Those who Live from the Sea*, Monograph No. 628, American Ethnological Society, 1977.

Spicer, E.H. (cd), *Human Problems in Technological Change* (New York: Russel Sage Foundation, 1952).

Srinivas, M.N., *The Remembered Village* (Delhi: Oxford University Press, 1976).

Subba Rao, N., Mechanisation and Its Effects: A Case Study of Marine Fishermen in Visakhapatnam, Ph. D. Thesis, Andhra University, Waltair, 1981.

Subramanyam, Y., and Subhashini, *Social Change in Village India, Andhra Case Study* (New Delhi: Prithvi Raj Publishers, 1975).

Thankappan Achary, T.R., *The Impact of the Indo-Norwegian Project on the Growth and Development of Indian Fisheries*, FE/IFI/69/BP/12 (Rome: Food and Agricultural Organisation, 1969).

Thomson, D.D., "Intermediate Technology and Alternative Energy Systems to Small Scale Fisheries," in *Proceedings of the 19th Session of Indo-Pacific Fisheries Council*, Kyoto, Japan, 1980.

Vattamattam, J., "Factors that Determine the Income of Fishermen: A Case Study of Pooithura Village in Trivandrum District," M. Phil. Dissertation, Centre for Development Studies, Trivandrum, 1977.

Vijayan, A.J., *Migrant Fishermen in Paradeep, Orissa*, ICSSR/FRC Study (Trivandrum: Programme for Community Organization, 1980).

Welcome, R.L., "Resource Constraints to the Development of Small-scale Fisheries," (IPFC/80/SYMP/SP/8) in *Proceedings of the 19th Session of Indo-Pacific Fisheries Council*, Kyoto, Japan, 1980.

Yap, C.L., *Trawling: Its Impact on Employment and Resource Use on the West Coast of Peninsular Malaysia*, in B. Lockwood and K. Ruddle (eds.), *Small-Scale Fisheries Development: Social Science Contribution* (Honolulu: East-West Centre, 1977).

Index